CLASSROOM
APPLICATIONS of
MICROCOMPUTERS

Second Edition

Robert V. Bullough, Sr./LaMond F. Beatty

CLASSROOM APPLICATIONS OF MICROCOMPUTERS

SECOND EDITION

Robert V. Bullough, Sr.
LaMond F. Beatty
University of Utah

Merrill, an imprint of
Macmillan Publishing Company
New York

Collier Macmillan Canada, Inc.
Toronto

Maxwell Macmillan International Publishing Group
New York   Oxford   Singapore   Sydney

Cover Art: Westlight
Editor: Linda A. Sullivan
Production Editor: Regina Sanford
Art Coordinator: Mark Garrett
Production Buyer: Janice E. Wagner
Text Designer: Connie Young
Cover Designer: Russ Maselli

This book was set in Bookman.

Macmillan Publishing Company
866 Third Avenue, New York, NY 10022

Collier Macmillan Canada, Inc.

Library of Congress Catalog Card Number: 90–61375
International Standard Book Number: 0–675–21163–8

Printing: 1 2 3 4 5 6 7 8 9   Year: 1 2 3 4

PREFACE

Many changes have taken place in educational computing since the first edition of *Classroom Applications of Microcomputers* was introduced. The role of the computer has become more clearly defined, and many more educators have embraced the idea of integrating computers into the existing curriculum.

A growing number of teachers use the computer's tool capabilities such as word processing, graphics generation, spreadsheets, and data base management to enhance instruction, and those who have discovered classroom management software find recordkeeping and testing tasks to be much less demanding than they once were.

The study of the computer as a subject has diminished somewhat except in computer science and certain math classes. In many classrooms the trend is toward using the technology to enhance the teaching of traditional subjects.

Revision Changes

Various changes have been made in the second edition to reflect these trends:

☐ A completely new chapter is devoted to integrating computers into the curriculum and using them in selected subject areas.
☐ Coverage of application programs has been expanded to include graphics software, electronic gradebooks, test generators, and other useful tools.
☐ Information regarding trends, research, and new developments in technology has been upgraded to reflect current conditions in instructional computing.

Text Organization

This book is arranged to be used sequentially, chapter by chapter; however, selected chapters can be pulled out to be used in a workshop or course tailored by the instructor. It is designed with preservice and inservice teachers in mind, but it can also be of interest to those using computers in the home or desiring an overview of the technology.

Chapter 1 provides an overview of computing from an historical perspective, with an emphasis on educational developments. Selected research studies of interest to the classroom teacher also are discussed.

In **Chapter 2** the equipment is discussed, including both the computer and the peripherals or "add-ons." A brief explanation of the way computers store and manipulate data is also included. Because maintenance is always a problem, some suggestions are offered on how to keep the system operating efficiently.

Educational software is covered extensively in **Chapter 3**, which describes various types of computer-assisted instruction (CAI) programs, including drills, simulations, and tutorials. The evaluation of instructional software is aided by a detailed, step-by-step approach to using an evaluation form.

Chapter 4 provides information on approaches to integrating computers into the curriculum, including a discussion of computer use in curriculum areas such as mathematics, language arts, and social studies. A description of typical software and suggestions for various classroom activities in each subject area completes the chapter.

BNA 1/30/91

Word processing software and activities are emphasized in **Chapter 5**. A discussion of a generic word processor is followed by an examination of several specific programs suitable for school use. Practical word processing exercises for three popular programs are included in the appendix on word processing.

The use of the computer as a tool is expanded in **Chapter 6** to include applications such as data base management, spread sheeting, and classroom management. A sample spreadsheet is provided, as is an approach to setting up a data base.

Chapter 7 discusses how to "hook your computer to the world" using a modem and the telephone lines. Also included is information on how to use local area networks, which enable several computers to communicate with each other or with common printers and mass storage devices.

Chapter 8 presents arguments for and against making programming a part of the curriculum. Two popular languages, BASIC and Logo, are introduced, with classroom activities that can be carried out with these languages. The section on authoring systems has been expanded to include several of the more capable and useful programs of this kind. Two practical exercises, one in BASIC and the other in Logo, are provided in the appendix on programming.

The important concerns in formulating and successfully implementing a school microcomputer program are addressed in **Chapter 9**, including suggestions for acquiring funding and support for this effort. Finally, **Chapter 10** examines such concerns as

computer crime, privacy in the electronic age, the impact of computers on jobs, and computer equity. Potential future trends are examined, and suggestions are presented for approaching the subject of computer ethics.

The extensive appendixes provide a glossary; lists of software publishers, including sources of free and inexpensive software, software guides, catalogs, and reviews; computer magazines and newsletters; user groups; telecommunication information; word processing exercises; and programming exercises in both BASIC and Logo.

This book, along with attendant hands-on activities, will provide educators with the skills and knowledge needed to successfully integrate computers into their instructional activities. We think that teachers who are familiar with computers, and who do not feel intimidated by them, constitute the most promising force for realizing the technology's potential.

Acknowledgements

We would like to thank the following reviewers for their contributions to the second edition: David C. Byrum, University of Oklahoma at Norman; Sherry Francis, University of Arkansas at Fayetteville; Robert G. Main, California State University at Chico; Joyce R. Miller, Heidelberg College, Tiffin, Ohio; Ralph Taylor, University of Maine at Farmington; Mary C. Ware, State University of New York at Cortland; and James H. Wiebe, California State University at Los Angeles.

CONTENTS

CHAPTER 1

An Overview

CHAPTER TOPICS
☐ Approaches to using the computer in the classroom
☐ Features of computers as teaching tools
☐ Factors influencing the adoption of computers
☐ The evolution of the technology
☐ The development of computer-based instruction
☐ Pioneering projects in computer-assisted instruction
☐ Programming and authoring languages for education
☐ The development of the microcomputer
☐ Trends in instructional computing
☐ Research on the effectiveness of computer-assisted instruction

Whether or not computers will have any significant long-term impact on teaching and learning is a subject for speculation among practitioners and laymen alike. Because the length of time this technology has been used in the classroom is so short (dating from about 1979) no one knows as yet how to maximize its use in instructional settings. Indeed, many people have all but written off computerized instruction as just one more fad that will simply fade away with the passage of time, as many other instructional innovations have done.

A certain lack of faith is reasonable given the dearth of research findings to indicate precisely the context in which the computer is most effective and how it can best be used to enhance learning. Although research efforts are increasing, they still fall short of what is needed for clearer answers to these questions. This situation is due in large part to the relatively short period of time the technology has been used for widespread instructional applications.

In effect, the movement has merely taken its first halting steps; its life span is predicted to be a very long one. Robert McClintock (1988) states that the educational influence of computers "should be measured along a duration of at least one or two centuries, if not considerably more." Unfortunately, we cannot wait this long to validate the value of the computer. We have to somehow come up with legitimate ways to use the more than two million machines already in the schools and the millions more to follow.

In the absence of an established tradition, educators are trying various approaches in an attempt to tap the unique potential claimed for computer-assisted instruction (CAI). Terms other than CAI are frequently employed to identify activities in which the computer is used for various kinds of instruction. For example, you might encounter CBI (computer-based instruction) or CAL (computer-augmented learning) in your reading. While subtle differences can be identified among these and other similar terms, we have elected to use CAI for the most part throughout this text, since it is the most descriptive term for our purpose.

The integration of computer technology into the established curriculum is gaining momentum. The computer is used when it can provide experiences of an uncommon nature in the context of established subject areas. It is not central to what takes place in the classroom but is merely another tool to be used at the teacher's discretion (Figure 1.1).

Most teachers find this approach more palatable than others that have been tried. The idea that the computer should be studied as a subject has had relatively little appeal for the majority of teachers, and they have tended to resist it. Using the technology as the primary delivery system for content is seen as overkill by most teachers, who see themselves thus giving up that which they enjoy most about their jobs: working directly with their students. Using computers for content delivery has been difficult to put into practice for a more fundamental reason than lack of teacher enthusiasm: there has never been sufficient money available to purchase the expensive systems required. Where funds have been available, the integrated learning system (ILS) has proved to be an effective way to distribute a large part of the curriculum to students, and can in fact assist teachers with their integration efforts.

Curriculum integration appears to hold promise for greater teacher support, more widescale use of the technology, and perhaps some degree of validation of the claims made for the teaching potential of the computer. What of these claims? Just what are they?

Unlike other mediums such as radio, instructional television, and motion pictures, whose impact on education has been rather modest, the computer offers

FIGURE 1.1 Computers Can Enhance Learning

(Courtesy of Commodore Electronics Limited)

the potential for radically changing the way students are taught and how they learn. Alfred Bork (1984) goes so far as to say that "the computer is the most powerful new learning device since the invention of the printing press and textbook."

McClintock (1988), in his discussion of culture, points out that the computer and related technology represent a vastly different system for storing knowledge from any we have known before. For the first time we have the capability of storing "all components of our culture," be these in print, pictorial, photographic, or other formats, in the binary code of the computer. Thus all knowledge will be retrievable to those who have access to and knowledge of the technology.

However, the packaging and retrieval of the full range of recorded knowledge is but one aspect of computer uniqueness. If this represented the total of what could be accomplished, computers as instructional devices would not be quite so revolutionary after all. The unique element is the potential for students to assume command of their own learning—they need not be tied to the age-old routine of retrieving a canned body of knowledge along with its related "right" answers.

Adeline Naiman (1985) maintains that the computer can "enable us to design and carry out our own real-time experiments. It can show us the processes and thinking of great minds, not just the conclusions. It is, finally, the tool that for the first time gives each of us—not just the experts—a handle on the complex universe we were born curious about. It has no limits but those we set."

In addition to these broad capabilities, there are others more directly related to actual classroom applications. For instance, computers have the capability to present information in a variety of formats. Traditionally, instruction has been primarily text-based, although the printed word is frequently not the most effective way of representing certain kinds of objects and events. With computers, the most effective representational mode can be selected—teachers are not locked into textual materials simply because there are no suitable alternatives (Figure 1.2).

Taylor and Cunniff (1988) emphasize the importance of this characteristic in their discussion of individual learning styles. Because different learners have differing capabilities for processing, understanding, and remembering material, no single mode of presenting concepts works equally well for everybody. With the computer, the best of an array of approaches can be chosen to convey the lesson—text is used only when it is seen to be the best of several alternatives. Additionally, varying experiences can be tailored to fit different learning styles once they are identified.

A highly desirable feature is the self-paced characteristic that computers provide. Students can truly progress at their own speeds—a feat that even the most accomplished human teacher has great difficulty achieving under prevailing conditions. Also, students are given immediate feedback regarding their performance so they can move on to the next set of activities without undue delay.

A related attribute is the ability to bring more interactive learning into the crowded classroom. Due to the large numbers of students with which a teacher must deal, she gets few opportunities to actually interact with them on a one-to-

FIGURE 1.2 Computers Provide a Variety of Instructional Formats
(Courtesy of International Business Machines Corporation)

one basis. Interaction with a machine might appear to be less desirable than that with a human being, but it is infinitely better than virtually none at all. There is also an increased potential for the teacher to do more one-on-one instruction where it is most needed if the computer takes over some of the responsibility for many of the other instructional chores (Figure 1.3).

Another attribute claimed for computer-based instruction is the ability to encourage students to try new things without the fear of making mistakes. Making mistakes is a natural occurrence in the learning process, but traditional classrooms are set up in such a manner that an illogical response or incorrect answer may bring with it consequences that can be out of all proportion to the magnitude of the mistake. Many contemporary instructional microcomputer programs are highly tolerant of incorrect responses. Experimentation is actually encouraged as students explore different approaches to the solution of a problem until they discover the best one. In programs of this type, the exercise of logic and the use of problem-solving techniques are emphasized over the simple memorization of spelled-out facts.

The computer also has powerful socializing effects on students and can change attitudes in positive ways. Students tend to be more cooperative and more social when working with computers. They exhibit greater independence and require less frequent assistance from teachers. They also tend to work together to solve problems, and they tend to share knowledge and information more freely. Students eagerly look forward to classes in which computers are used effectively and, rather than attempting to miss sessions, often spend more time in class than is required (Figure 1.4).

FIGURE 1.3 Computers Permit Teachers to Do More One-on-One Instruction Where It Is Needed Most

(Courtesy of International Business Machines Corporation)

Computers can also monitor a student's progress in great detail and with precision. A human teacher can do this too, but various constraints generally prevent such an effort from being fully carried out. Diagnosis and prescription are integral and essential parts of the on-going monitoring process; these activities are tedious and time-consuming for the teacher, but not for the computer. On the basis of the student's performance, a good computer-based program will spot problem areas and supply the appropriate remedial activities with great efficiency.

With so many positive claims being made for computer-based learning, it would seem that all teachers should be clamoring to get their students busily working with it.

This is not generally the case however. The truth is, the acquisition of computers has slowed somewhat, and even in schools where they are readily available they frequently sit idle. Many teachers tend to feel threatened by computers and display anxiety over learning how to use them. In addition, many teachers continue to perceive computers as potentially destructive, not only to their established instructional routines but also to their status in the classroom. And administrators resist spending scarce dollars on what many of them see as an unproved and expensive innovation.

Although lean budgets are often cited as the main reason more computers are not acquired, there are other reasons of a more complex nature, the most pervasive of which is teacher resistance. But this resistance decreases as familiarity with the equipment and a sense of mission increase. Few involved in using a word processor in their writing activities fail to see the value of this tool, and resist any move back to typewriters or ball point pens. Those in the social studies are enthusiastic about data base management programs, finding them to be excellent for storing and organizing ethnographic data collected by students.

FIGURE 1.4 The Computer Has Powerful Socializing Effects on Students
(Courtesy of International Business Machines Corporation)

In an effort to overcome teacher resistance, many states now mandate that every student in teacher education take one or more courses in the instructional uses of microcomputers. Universities have designed courses specifically to meet such mandates and, in many colleges of education, these have become the most popular offerings in the curriculum. In addition, inservice workshops are offered in many districts.

These moves are positive, but may not be enough in light of such findings as those contained in the 1988 Office of Technology Assessment (OTA) Report. Researchers found that only half of the teachers in American schools have ever used a computer, and only a small percentage uses them consistently. In addition, a mere 30 percent of teachers have received as much as ten hours of instruction on computers, and most of this emphasized how to operate the equipment, with little time devoted to using it for instructional purposes.

On the other hand, some teacher training institutions are taking the imaginative step of incorporating computer applications into methods courses, providing students with opportunities to use computers as instructional tools in their particular subject matter areas. Once students become familiar with ways to use computers for instructional purposes, many are likely to continue to use them to help resolve problems they will encounter later, in their own classrooms.

Both teachers and students are likely to find that some familiarity with computers and related technology will prove useful in the long term. Although relatively unobtrusive, the impact of digital technology on society as a whole has been nothing less than revolutionary. All signs point to an accelerated reliance on digital systems in all institutions, including schools. It seems extremely naive to believe that the educational establishment alone can remain untouched by computer technology while the revolution races on everywhere else.

This statement could not have been made until recently, since the early technology was, for the most part, unsuitable for widescale educational applications. Now, however, extremely capable, small, and inexpensive microcomputers, together with the software to run them, are widely available from any number of suppliers. This equipment has made possible the implementation of computer-assisted instruction, which seems to have appeared out of nowhere—a case of spontaneous generation, so to speak. As with other innovations, however, computer-based instructional systems developed over time; they have a history.

It would be nice if we could say that this development was the result of a carefully executed strategy, a sort of "technological five-year plan," but this was not the case. Indeed, the manufacturers of large computers showed little interest in the early microcomputers, and with good reason. They were used to thinking in terms of very powerful machines that processed vast amounts of data at extremely high speeds. What good was a miniature computer with a tiny memory that did its work in relative slow motion? It would make an interesting toy perhaps, but little else—or so they thought.

The common perception that CAI simply evolved as a consequence of the widespread availability of the microcomputer is also a misconception. CAI was practiced in a limited fashion long before the innovations that made the microcomputer possible were invented.

Although this text is about modern microcomputers and contemporary computer-related educational practice, we would be remiss if some mention weren't made of those creative pioneers and their innovative projects that contributed so much to the current state of the art. By presenting a short survey of the history of CAI we hope to establish a point of departure for subsequent discussion.

In addition, information on trends in the acquisition and use of microcomputers will be presented in this chapter. A recent trend is the subtle shift away from an emphasis on programming (writing the instructions that run the computer) and toward the use of applications or "tool" programs such as word processors, data base management programs, and spreadsheets. This trend prompted us to decrease the amount of information on programming in the text and to include two entire chapters on tool applications. Yet another trend, discussed in this chapter and chapters to follow, is the effort to integrate computers into the traditional curriculum.

Several research studies are included. The fact that many studies point up the effectiveness of CAI should lend support to efforts aimed at broadening its use and should give encouragement to those teachers who are using the technology in their classes. While it is true that more studies are needed before a universal stamp of approval can be given to the CAI concept, the growing research efforts currently under way will most certainly clarify many of the questions being asked about this controversial movement.

THE DEVELOPMENT OF COMPUTER-BASED INSTRUCTION

Today more than ever before people involved both directly and indirectly with the educational enterprise are caught up in efforts to introduce and integrate computers into the curricula of the nation's schools. The concept involved, that of using computers for instruction, is referred to as novel, innovative, and new, but what is not generally known is that instructional computing has been around for quite awhile. Table 1.1 traces come of the notable events that contributed to the development of computer-based instruction.

Early efforts dating back to the late 1950s and early 1960s were hampered by a number of factors, one of which was a lack of suitable hardware (the computers and electronics that support them). The first computers were large, expensive, and used primarily for large-scale mathematical calculation ("number crunching"). Thousands of vacuum tubes organized into clusters produced the on-off code that the computer used (Figure 1.5). Because of the costs involved in building and maintaining such machines, only well-endowed organizations, such as departments of government, could afford to purchase them. The prototype of these "first generation" computers operated until 1955, but not even the most

TABLE 1.1   Notable Developments: From Vacuum Tubes to Computer Literacy

1946	First generation computers, based on vacuum tubes, introduced
1959	Second generation all-transistorized computer introduced by IBM
1960	The PLATO project begins at Illinois
1963	The Stanford Project begins
1964	Third generation computers, based on integrated circuits, appear; BASIC developed at Dartmouth
1965	Digital Equipment Corporation markets the inexpensive PDP-8 minicomputer; teaching of classes at the University of Illinois using PLATO
1967	The New York plan; expanded use of computer-assisted instruction in the public schools
1968	Logo introduced
1969	The first microprocessor chip developed by Intel
1972	Fourth generation begins with the introduction of expanded microchip by Intel
1975	First widescale marketing of a microcomputer (Altair 8800)
1977	Commodore Pet, Apple II, and TRS 80 microcomputers introduced
Early 1980s	Widescale adoption of microcomputers by the schools; computer literacy movement
	Advances in technology such as CD-ROM, speech-based software, interactive videodiscs
Late 1980s	Experiments in the integration of computers into the established curriculum; research in intelligent computer-assisted instruction (ICAI)

FIGURE 1.5 A Bank of Vacuum Tubes

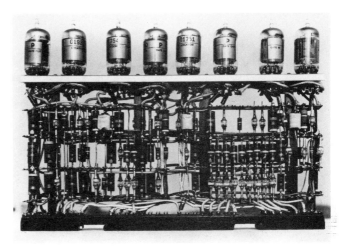

(Courtesy of International Business Machines Corporation)

far-seeing visionaries recognized in the machines anything but a rather restricted potential for educational applications.

With the advent of the "second generation" computers, which used transistors rather than vacuum tubes for creating the coded signals, reliability was improved and the size and cost of computers came down dramatically. Among the companies addressing the problems of cost and size was Digital Equipment Corporation, which introduced its first computer, the PDP-1, in 1957 (Figure 1.6). This machine was used in several of the early pioneering CAI projects. An increasing number of institutions began to purchase or rent computer systems, and although commercial data processing remained the major application, it wasn't long before the idea of developing computer science courses in departments of engineering was implemented. But this was a far cry from the universal utilization of computers as teaching devices, a futuristic scenario envisioned by a mere handful of professors in a few universities.

The Advent of the Chip

In 1959 both Texas Instruments and Fairchild Semiconductor devised ways to place electronic components, such as miniaturized transistors, on a single, thin piece of silicon. These integrated circuits (ICS) on a chip would ultimately make possible the widescale manufacture of inexpensive and reliable microcomputers of the kind that schools could afford to buy.

These diminutive marvels, known as chips, have no soldered junctions that might break. They generate little heat, use minuscule amounts of power, and are extremely reliable. They can be produced in great numbers at low cost from materials that are readily available. Figure 1.7 shows a chip (the tiny speck on the right) in comparison with a transistor and a vacuum tube. Computers built

FIGURE 1.6   The PDP-1

(Courtesy of Digital Equipment Corporation)

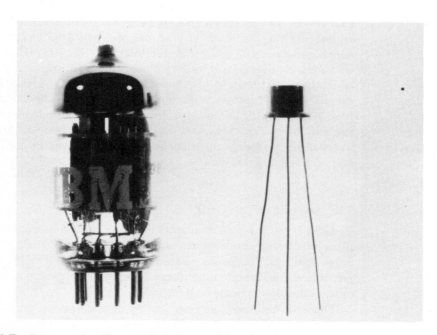

FIGURE 1.7   Comparative Sizes of the Vacuum Tube, Transistor, and Chip
(Courtesy of International Business Machines Corporation)

around collections of various kinds of chips were referred to as "third generation" computers.

The third generation of computers was ushered in with the introduction in 1964 of IBM's System 360 family (see Figure 1.8). These powerful machines used IC chips exclusively. The new generation of machines caught the public's fancy, and those who were able to purchased or rented them in increasing numbers.

In an effort to provide a range of choices to those who wanted the technology but couldn't afford it, Digital Equipment Corporation, in 1965, marketed a smaller, cheaper machine that came to be known as the minicomputer. The introduction of this innovative system made possible the purchase of computers by small companies and educational institutions that never dreamed they might afford such an apparent luxury. While the larger systems commonly sold for prices that ranged into the millions, the PDP-8 minicomputer (Figure 1.9) sold for the unheard-of low price of twenty thousand dollars.

The PLATO Project

A notable CAI project, implemented in the early 1960s at the University of Illinois, was PLATO—Programmed Logic for Automatic Teaching Operations. The first prototype system of 1960 consisted of the computer and a single student learning station. An expanded system followed, which consisted of the central computer and a network of twenty individual terminals equipped with video displays and keyboards.

The typical configuration of a CAI system was a number of stations consisting of a monitor (or cathode ray tube) and a teletype hooked to a central computer

FIGURE 1.8 An IBM System 360 Computer
(Courtesy of International Business Machines Corporation)

FIGURE 1.9   The PDP-8
Minicomputer

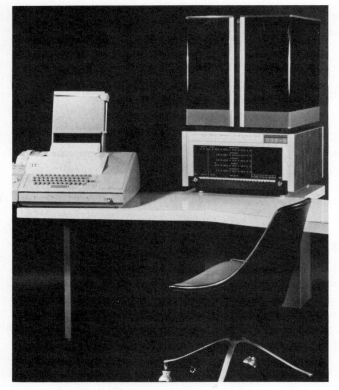

(Courtesy of Digital Equipment Corporation)

where all of the processing took place. This was referred to as a "time-sharing system" (Figure 1.10).

The development of time-sharing was one of the most important factors in the early evolution of CAI because it permitted large numbers of students to participate concurrently in individualized learning activities. Time-sharing refers to the ability of a single central computer to handle almost simultaneously the demands of a host of users. The processor operates at such a high rate of speed that the waiting time experienced by users is virtually imperceptible. Once such systems had been perfected, the economics of CAI were much less prohibitive than was formerly the case. Obviously, one student at a single work station interacting with one computer was an unacceptable arrangement for anything but an experimental session.

The PLATO system was highly interactive, providing an environment in which student and computer often engaged in an on-going dialogue of a tutorial nature. The system was quite sophisticated for its time, utilizing such innovations as touch screens in place of the traditional teletypes as the primary terminal device for communicating with the main computer ("inputting"). A touch screen is a monitor (similar in concept to a television receiver) that permits the user to input infor-

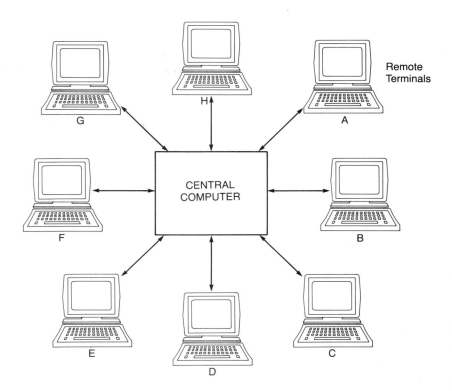

FIGURE 1.10 A Time-Sharing System

mation by touching the screen at various selected points. For example, rather than having to type in the answer to a multiple choice question, the student need only touch the answer of his choice on the screen; the display then changes in response to the action.

PLATO continued to expand with support from the National Science Foundation until, by 1965, the programs and other materials had been refined to the point that the teaching of regular university courses was undertaken at Illinois. Because a powerful central computer was used (there were no microcomputers), the programs could be sophisticated, extensive, and complex. Also, the larger computer permitted the creation of excellent graphic displays and even animation. But all of this had a price—PLATO was very expensive.

The inexpensive microcomputer gave educators an affordable alternative to networked time-sharing systems like PLATO. Although microcomputers weren't able to do many of the things the more powerful systems were capable of, they were at least obtainable. Whereas few educators were aware of the truly remarkable strides that had taken place in the development of computer-assisted instruction using large computers, the ubiquitous quality of the microcomputer stimulated an interest in this aspect of education. At first it seemed that the vast effort to create and field-test programs for the PLATO system was to be wasted, since these programs could not be used with the newer, smaller machines. But this was not the case; the effort was to pay off in a much broader fashion than was anticipated. Under the direction of Control Data Corporation, the current owners of PLATO, these excellent materials have been modified to operate on personal computers. Conversions have been made of programs in a number of areas, including foreign languages, physics, math, and computer literacy. Educators find the new versions of the PLATO programs and the print materials that go with them (collectively called "courseware") to be among the best available (Figure 1.11).

Many institutions use PLATO in various configurations. For example, seven campuses in the University of Maine system use PLATO programs sent to their microcomputers via satellite transmission from the University of Illinois.

The Stanford Project

The Stanford Project was another pioneering computer-oriented instructional project of the 1960s. The Carnegie Foundation provided the initial monetary support, but it was a grant from the U.S. Office of Education that made long-term development possible. Providing federal grants was a common practice during this period of time, one of the most used vehicles for funding being the Elementary and Secondary Education Act (ESEA) of 1965.

The Stanford Project, which began in 1963, was implemented by Patrick Suppes and Richard Atkinson of Stanford University. The project was directed toward the development of mathematics and reading programs. Suppes was involved with the former discipline and Atkinson with the latter. Suppes saw in CAI the potential for realizing the age-old dream of teaching students in a one-on-one tutorial approach. His goal was to individualize instruction for every student; however, the magnitude of the task caused him to redirect his resources and energies toward the teaching of selected groups of students, such as those who were working below grade level.

The Stanford program was based on three levels of interaction. At the first level was drill-and-practice. The exercises could be varied according to a five-

FIGURE 1.11 PLATO
Courseware for the Microcomputer

tiered hierarchy of difficulty that reflected varying levels of competence. The second level was the tutorial system, in which the emphasis was placed on concept attainment. The lessons progressed from the initial introductory segment through progressively more complex interactive activities until the concept was mastered. The tutorials were self-paced and included what was known as a "teacher-call." If the student, after having worked through the program, was unable to meet the performance requirements, a teacher would be called to assist in whatever ways were deemed necessary.

The third system was referred to as the dialogue system. This was an attempt to involve the student in a less structured and more open-ended computer-based activity. In this system the student would ask a question of the computer, just as would be the case if human teachers were involved. The problem in the sixties, as now, was programming the computer to understand the question completely. Suppes recognized that although a computer might be capable of understanding a question posed in standard English, it might not respond to the same question if a dialect were involved or if the speaker didn't enunciate the words clearly. The problems of using the spoken word for input were not sufficiently resolved to make this a viable option. Indeed, the dialogue system remained largely undeveloped, and the drill-and-practice and tutorial approaches predominated. Though speech recognition has progressed markedly over the intervening years, problems encountered in the early days of the Stanford Project remain even today.

The system employed over five hundred pages of prepared information that could be selectively displayed on a screen where the student had access to it via a light pen (a small device used to point to a portion of a screen display). Information could also be entered using a keyboard; a standard cathode ray tube (CRT), similar in concept to a TV monitor, was the display medium. This system was widely tested using remote CRTs located in the schools. The approach was mainly involved with the drill-and-practice component of the program. During these early experimental and developmental days, much wider use was made of supplemental noncomputerized equipment than is currently the case. Today the CRT is the standard output device and the keyboard represents the primary input device (along with certain less-used devices, such as the mouse and joystick). But during the 1960s it was not uncommon for a CAI system to employ not only a rear projection screen and voice output but also such specially designed equipment as slide projectors, tape recorders, "electronic blackboards," and filmstrip projectors. A common procedure during this period was to display visual materials via a projection medium (such as a filmstrip) while using the computer to respond to the material in the projected images.

PLATO received a large infusion of federal dollars in the late seventies, which enabled development to continue at an expanded pace. A similar grant was awarded to a second project, under the direction of the Mitre Corporation, called TICCIT (Time-shared, Interactive, Computer Controlled Information Television). The hardware developed for the Stanford Project was modified and expanded for use with TICCIT. A considerable quantity of courseware was created for the system, which yielded quite positive results.

The hardware components functioned well together and constituted one of the more successful attempts to develop a true computer-based instructional system. The courseware was innovative and effective, and, perhaps most important of all, students learning with TICCIT showed significant gains in achievement. Again, despite all the positive features of the system, TICCIT, like PLATO, was a very expensive approach to CAI.

Although PLATO and some other systems based on the original networked concept are still in place and operating in several locations in the United States and foreign countries, the popular microcomputer has all but monopolized instructional computing. Nevertheless, the contributions of such pioneering efforts as those undertaken by the originators of the PLATO, Stanford, and TICCIT projects—and others not mentioned here—have had much to do with the current state of the art in instructional computing, and educators continue to enjoy the fruits of these early labors.

Programming and Authoring Languages for Education

The development of a number of new computer languages was another accomplishment of those working during this exciting pioneering period of the sixties. Two kinds of languages will be mentioned in this chapter: programming languages and authoring languages. A programming language consists of a finite set of words and symbols that are used in various combinations to instruct a computer to perform a wide range of tasks. An authoring language provides the user with a matrix or template that serves as the common format for lessons. The instructions for authoring languages are much less flexible than are those used for programming. On the whole, authoring languages are easy to use, but they have less versatility than those used for writing programs.

One of the new programming languages that was to have an influence when the microcomputer become available was the Beginners All-purpose Symbolic Instruction Code, or BASIC. This language was developed at Dartmouth to meet a specific instructional need. When the Dartmouth staff made a commitment to computer training for all students, they found that a new approach was needed. John Kemeny and Thomas Kurtz directed efforts to find a way to provide computer training to the large numbers of students from diverse disciplines who would be involved. They conceived the idea of using a time-sharing approach that would permit students to interact with the computer in a one-on-one fashion. This necessitated networking a large number of terminals to the central processor, which would communicate extremely rapidly and in a specific order with each terminal. This format required the development of a new language that would be interactive; that is, the student would receive feedback as he or she typed in the program. The various programming languages that had been developed didn't lend themselves to the interactive learning of programming. The standard approach to data processing before the advent of interactive languages was to compile all the data to be processed and feed them into the computer. Punched cards were commonly used as the input medium. The results (or output) were typically printed out on sheets of fanfold paper. BASIC, on the other hand, provided immediate results on the computer screen.

The new language, which was introduced in 1964, worked very well, and it wasn't long before BASIC was adopted as the language of choice by many institutions engaged in activities similar to those being carried out at Dartmouth. But the use of BASIC was to extend beyond the time-sharing instructional systems: when microcomputers became generally available, it was selected as the language to be used with them.

Most educators have heard of Logo. The tendency is to consider this a recent innovation; however, Logo was another product of the sixties. Logo was created in 1968 by the firm of Bolt, Beranek, and Newman, Inc., under the sponsorship of the National Science Foundation. Seymour Papert and researchers at M.I.T. tested the languages in a number of different settings and continued with its development. Today, Logo operates on most microcomputers and is considered by many educators potentially to be one of the most useful of instructional programs.

The development of numerous computerized instructional systems stimulated the creation of several versions of the authoring language. One of the earliest versions was known as TUTOR, which was created for use on the PLATO system. TUTOR was complex and required considerable effort to learn. The present concept of an authoring language, however, is generally to provide a teacher with a framework into which particular questions and answers can be fitted. One purpose of the simpler authoring languages is to provide educators who are not professional programmers with the necessary tools to create their own computer-based lessons.

Several of these early authoring languages survive to this day, some of them in a form that is rather close to the original versions. PILOT and the updated SuperPILOT are examples of programs developed in the 1960s that have been modified to work with microcomputers.

Refer to Chapter 8 if you are interested in more information on programming and authoring.

The Public Schools Get Involved

Through the second half of the 1960s and into the early 1970s new technological advances, infusions of money, and a growing staff of competent people generated considerable interest, particularly in the United States, in the potential of computer-assisted instruction. Indeed, as the decade of the sixties neared its close, CAI had become a fact of life for thousands of students throughout America. The first city whose school system adopted CAI as an integral part of its overall instructional program was Philadelphia, but New York City wasn't far behind. The New York plan, which was initiated in 1967, was an ambitious one. Funded by money provided by Title III of the ESEA, the program had as its focus the study of math, spelling, and reading in the second through the sixth grades. The materials from the Stanford Project served as the core of the curriculum. Sixteen schools containing 192 student stations were connected to a central computer in a time-sharing arrangement. The system was tested extensively, and a considerable amount of useful information was collected. The experiment proved to be effective in varying degrees, with some educators favoring the approach and others showing less enthusiasm.

Other implementations might be cited, but it is sufficient to point out that CAI had come out of the laboratory and had become a reality in certain of the nation's schools. Though not all-inclusive, the examples of work accomplished during the early days of CAI should give the reader some sense of the innovative thinking that was taking place at that time. The varied accomplishments of the sixties were ultimately to come together in a blending of ideas and technology that would erupt a decade later in the form of the microcomputer revolution.

The Microcomputer Takes Over

As the 1970s dawned, advocates confidently predicted that CAI would become an indispensable element in the American classroom. But, optimistic as some were, others did not share this utopian point of view. These individuals cited the high costs and long implementation time involved in this approach and suggested that, rather than being a viable tool, CAI was merely an expensive frill. Interest and support had dropped to a low level by the mid-1970s, but an event occurred that was to stimulate a wave of renewed interest: the microcomputer was introduced. The compact, inexpensive, handsome little machine was to bring about a renaissance in instructional computing.

The small electronic calculators that were gaining notice in the late sixties suddenly became widely popular in the early seventies. Demand for these machines, which were based on the integrated circuit chip, provided manufacturers with the incentive to expand production and refine the technology. The calculators were made increasingly more capable, cheaper, and ever smaller through the use of chips in various combinations. The ongoing competitive efforts to refine the calculators ultimately led to the creation of the microprocessor, or the "computer on a chip." Before the advent of the microprocessor, specialized chips were combined in various ways to serve as the processing unit of the computer. When, through a process known as large-scale integration, the various functions that a processor performs were all integrated on a single silicon chip, the fourth-generation computer was born. In 1975 the first microcomputer in kit form was offered for sale, and things were never to be the same again.

The development of the microcomputer was phenomenal not so much for the technology, which was already there for the most part, but for the manner in which the actual fabrication took place. The first microcomputers were created by hobbyists, who obtained components from any available source, figured out their own circuit designs, and finally soldered everything together to form a unique and complex device that only they (and a few other like-minded individuals) could operate. They programmed the early machines in tedious ways, often using a bank of switches that permitted the 0s and 1s of binary machine language to be fed into the computer by flipping the switch one way for a 0 and the other way for a 1.

Some of the handcrafted microcomputers were considerably better than others, and soon a demand for these particular machines began to develop; a modest industry was born. Several technical periodicals evolved, dedicated to those who wished to build and program their own computers.

The first microcomputer to appear in the schools in any numbers was the Commodore Pet, introduced in the late seventies (Figure 1.12). Then came the Apples, Ataris, Radio Shacks, TIs, and others that caught the fancy of many educators who set out to acquire one or two for their schools using any funding method available. Fund-raising ventures such as PTA cookie sales were commonplace during this period of time.

Much of the incentive to acquire microcomputers and put them into operation came from the idea that students had to be "computer literate" in order to fit into the technological society of the future. Parents were frantic in their efforts to make certain that their sons and daughters did not miss out on this seemingly essential part of their education. Computer literacy was defined in different ways by different people. The most common approach was to establish classes, or at least units within a regular class, in which students learned about computers. The philosophy behind the "computer as subject" approach is explained by Olson and Eaton (1987) as follows: many "teachers considered 'computers' as a new school subject in its own right because of the social, cultural, and intellectual value they attributed to being able to use the technology." In order to become computer literate, students wrote programs, studied binary arithmetic and logic, examined circuits, played at being a computer by imitating the functions of the components and, in general, approached the technology much as a computer scientist might.

In the mid-1980s the infatuation began to diminish as educators started to question many of the ideas that had come to prevail. They began to chart new approaches to the random manner in which computer-related decisions were be-

FIGURE 1.12 The Commodore Pet

(Courtesy of Commodore Electronics Limited)

ing made. Many schools began acquiring and integrating computers into the curriculum in a more orderly and coordinated manner; attempts at standardizing equipment and defining uses for the technology also became more common. Meanwhile, the computer itself had become more sophisticated and capable (Figure 1.13). The new machines have larger memories than ever before. Screen resolution is much enhanced, and printers and other peripherals are not only greatly improved over older models; they are also less expensive. Now that the technology is able to perform the tasks educators would demand of it, there is hope that these capabilities will be realized in the classroom. Trends indicate that, with certain reservations, there is reason to be optimistic.

A LOOK AT TRENDS

What is the state of microcomputer education today, and what, most likely, will be the situation tomorrow? Considerable information is available that, when viewed collectively, gives a fairly good picture of the present state of affairs. A bit of interpolation is necessary in order to come up with a profile of future ap-

FIGURE 1.13 A Modern Microcomputer
(Courtesy of International Business Machines Corporation)

plications and implications; the resulting scenarios can only be classified as hypotheses, however, because the field is in such a state of flux that solid trends are difficult to identify with any kind of precision. There are those who believe that the microcomputer will, among other things, make our traditional textbooks obsolete—but this prediction is nothing new. The same pronouncement was made over sixty years ago by none other than Thomas Edison, but he was referring to the impact of another marvelous invention—his motion picture projector—and not, obviously, to the latest technological marvel, the microcomputer.

The trend toward using computers as aids to instruction in the various curriculum areas has been mentioned. Software producers, recognizing the reality of this movement, have begun to correlate their products with textbooks and other materials used in the classroom. Educators should see greater attention to this approach in the future.

A second trend seen throughout the schools and reflected in the literature is the recognition of the value of computers as tools. An expanding application is word processing—using the microcomputer as a writing tool. Other uses include creating graphics, using the great memory capacity of the modern microcomputer for storage of information in data bases, and maintaining records electronically through the use of spreadsheets. These various applications have been combined into packages referred to as "integrated software," which permit data from one application to be moved easily to a second one for additional processing.

Networks are becoming increasingly popular, both at the school and the district levels. These permit computers to be hooked together and to common peripherals to form a communication system of considerable utility. Networking is a way to provide instructional and tool applications from a central repository without the need for a library of disk-based programs that must be checked in and out and physically handled, an arrangement that subjects the software to the danger of damage or theft. Because networks provide information and activities when needed and with great speed and convenience, they support the concept of curriculum integration and encourage its adoption.

Increasing numbers of students are becoming familiar with computers; the figures are quite impressive. Approximately 75 percent of third graders, 89 percent of seventh graders, and 87 percent of eleventh graders have used a computer, according to a report from the National Assessment of Educational Progress (NAEP) group. However, much of their experience comes from playing games, with as many as 80 percent involved in this activity. Sadly, as many as 87 percent of students had not used the computer in the study of traditional subjects in school.

The number of school computers has risen steadily over the years. According to surveys by Market Data Retrieval, there were approximately 630,000 microcomputers in U.S. schools in 1984; today, according to the New York–based firm Talmis, there are well over 2 million. Nearly 100 percent of schools now have at least one microcomputer. The ratio of students to computers is still too high, with the average for all grades being about 30 students for each machine, but conditions continue to improve. According to a 1984 survey by Market Data Retrieval, the average number of students for each computer was 112 in the elementary schools, 92 in the junior high schools, and 77 in the senior highs. A 1987 report issued by the same organization showed that the ratios had been reduced to 43.7 percent in the elementary schools, 32.9 for the junior high schools, and 31.1 percent in the senior high schools.

The purchase of instructional software has continued to increase also. Estimates suggest that the market is worth over $200 million a year. As large as this seems, the figure is dwarfed by that for business software, which is calculated to be worth approximately $2 billion annually.

The trend in software is for teachers to want more programs that teach problem solving and higher-order thinking skills and fewer of the traditional drill-and-practice variety. Software producers are responding with integrated tool software, tutorials using features of artificial intelligence to make them more responsive to student needs, and challenging simulations for use in science and social studies. Also appearing in increasing numbers are word processors with built-in story starters and other features designed expressly for use in language arts classes. The microcomputer-based laboratory (MBL) for science applications provides probeware for students to use in conducting real-time experiments, while discovery-oriented programs challenge the reasoning ability of students in math and other areas of the curriculum.

This approach to software design is in keeping with an emerging process approach to learning; in this philosophy the stress is on the process, or the "how," of learning rather than on the product, or the "what," of learning.

The figures and estimates given here reflect a growth trend that will in all probability continue. One thing seems evident: the microcomputer revolution appears to be real, and educators will find themselves affected by it to one degree or another.

RESEARCH

Most computer-using educators, when asked if they feel that computers make a difference where learning is concerned, will answer with an unqualified yes. Such an answer cannot be totally unbiased, for a teacher who uses a computer must have some degree of conviction that there is value in its use. Also, such an answer is typically subjective, because little research is available that addresses the question of computer effectiveness. Much that is reported in educational journals on this subject is based upon intuitive beliefs.

Both children and adults easily get caught up in the fascination of running the computer if the experience is so structured that it is positive and nonthreatening. It is natural for the instructor to assume that the expression of enjoyment indicates that learning is taking place. However, liking and learning are not necessarily correlates. Some evidence indicates that many individuals learn the most from methods they like the least. Most people seem to enjoy computers—does this mean that entertainment is taking precedence over learning? The studies that are available, while modest in number, indicate that this is not the case. Students not only enjoy using computers; they learn from them as well.

Mention should be made, however, that the advantages for CAI tend to be present when it is used in conjunction with other instructional methods; more needs to be known about the effectiveness of the computer as the major or sole instructional medium. There is not as yet enough information to help classroom teachers determine what sort of application might best be coupled with what type of student under what circumstances to achieve the best results. A few solid studies are available that provide a foundation upon which additional research is being built. Some of these are mentioned on the following pages.

James Kulik and a group of his colleagues at the University of Michigan selected and analyzed fifty-one studies (1983). Although many were fairly current, some dated back to the early days of CAI, when the only available computers were of the large, powerful (mainframe) type. For the most part, Kulik and his staff found that students who were involved in computer-aided learning scored higher on objective tests than did those who were involved in other types of learning activities. Additionally, the studies showed that students learned the materials more rapidly and retained the information for longer periods of time when CAI was the mode of instruction.

A number of studies have been designed to examine the effects of computer-assisted instruction on mathematics achievement. Based on a meta-analysis of several studies, Burns and Bozeman (1981) determined that using CAI in mathematics instruction significantly enhances student achievement. They concluded that mathematics instruction supplemented with drill-and-practice or tutorial CAI was significantly more effective than traditional instructional methods in improving student performance. They also found that performance improved at both the elementary and secondary levels when CAI was used. This was true for high achievers, disadvantaged students, and those whose ability levels had not been differentiated. However, the performance of average students was not significantly improved by drill-and-practice CAI.

In a second study, Ragosta et al. (1981) found that students who used CAI to study mathematics showed greater gains than did a control group who studied language arts using CAI. The researchers concluded that for computer learning to be effective, sufficient time on task is required. A learning effect was noted when students used the computer for as little as ten minutes each day. Learning doubled when the time was doubled. Based on the findings from this study, it appears that as little as twenty minutes each day for four or five days each week using math-related drill-and-practice CAI affords significant gains in learning.

Enochs et al. (1986) conducted research designed to determine the extent to which the performance of two groups of students who were taught a common lesson using two approaches (traditional and computer-assisted) was related to learning style as well as other variables, including reading vocabulary and comprehension scores and aptitude for learning. It was found that CAI tends to enhance achievement to a greater extent for students with learning styles that favor individual study. Students who showed the most gain from the traditional approach were those with a more social-oriented learning style. Studies of this kind represent a step in the right direction; they begin to provide information that can assist educators to determine the kinds of students who can best benefit from computer-assisted instruction.

In another study designed to explore the relationship between preschool children's cognitive and behavioral styles and their interest in computers, Johnson (1985) identified two factors influencing high interest. Children who displayed a high interest in computers tended to engage in less concrete play than those who had low interest; high interest students also showed a tendency to play with one toy at a time in an ordered fashion. The author concluded that the child must possess a degree of representational ability before computer use is beneficial. He also noted that play style among those attracted to computers tends to be "single-minded, sequential and abstract."

The importance of the design of software in motivating students to learn has been recognized by many researchers. Smith and Keep (1986) conducted an investigation in which they examined the criteria children use to evaluate software. They found that the young students involved in the project relied on perceptions derived from the popular media rather than from education-related experiences. The students tended to apply standards developed from interacting with media such as commercial television when viewing and evaluating instructional software. Much of the instructional software reviewed received low ratings as a consequence of being compared with the more sophisticated commercial offerings.

Because schools will never be able to compete with these kinds of media, the researchers stress the importance of giving particular attention to when and how the computer is used in the classroom. They also suggest that software designers begin to pay more attention to the way their products are designed, with psychological considerations having high priority. They further admonish educators to pay more attention to pupils' evaluations, since the evidence suggests that, rather than merely being naive remarks, these evaluations are valid statements regarding students' feelings and perceptions of a product.

The fact that computers can and do influence behavior was mentioned previously. According to Becker's study at Johns Hopkins, the predominant role of microcomputers in schools may very well turn out to be social rather than academic. Kulik also found that teachers tend to perceive the social role of the computer in the classroom as being more important than its academic role (Figure 1.14).

In a study of the effect of cooperative computer use conducted by Johnson et al. (1985) eighth grade students were assigned to three treatment groups that included (1) the cooperative group, in which success at an assigned task depended on how well members worked together; (2) the competitive group, wherein success was determined by comparing performance against that of others in the group, and (3) the individualistic group, in which success was dependent upon individual performance.

FIGURE 1.14 Computers Encourage Cooperative Learning

(Courtesy of Apple Computer, Inc.)

The performance of the cooperative groups on both established measures (daily worksheets and final exam) was better than that of either of the other groups, while students in the competitive group did least well. Various indices of achievement were used in the study, including quantity and quality of daily production, success in problem solving, accuracy of recognition of factual material studied, and the ability to apply facts in questions requiring higher level reasoning and problem solving. Students in the computer-assisted cooperative learning group performed better on all indices than those in the other two groups.

In another study of computer sharing, Mevarech, Stern, and Levita (1987) involved two groups of students in the study of language using CAI. Students in the first group studied alone; those in the other studied in pairs. The activity lasted for approximately two months and was self-paced. While students who worked in pairs scored higher on tests on the content covered, the difference was not significant. However, when responses to questions relating to social attitudes were analyzed, it was found that paired students showed "improved prosocial orientation" over those who used CAI as individuals.

The study of affect nearly always leads to a consideration of the much-maligned computerized game. It is unfortunate that more research hasn't been conducted in this area, because games represent an approach to learning that holds great promise. The positive aspects are often overlooked—games continue to be the subject of much controversy and are frequently condemned.

Unfortunately, a large number of computer games tend to encourage aggressiveness over other more desirable kinds of expression. This is particularly true of arcade-type games, which often serve as models for their educational counterparts. Although research on violence in computer games is virtually nonexistent, such is not the case with other mediums, such as television. Among the significant studies is one by Stein et al. (1981) that was based on child behavior as it relates to the viewing of violence-laden television programs. The conclusion was that "high action" and "high violence" in TV programs may indeed produce aggressive behaviors in children. This combination—high action and high violence—is employed in many computer games of both the arcade type and the instructional variety. To win the typical game, a player must be both ruthless and aggressive.

In light of the simplistic game rules involved (destroy the enemy as rapidly as you are able), it is claimed by some that such worthwhile traditional instructional activities as problem solving, concept attainment, and even social skills attainment have lost out. In place of being rewarded for achievement in such areas, the player is rewarded for behaviors of an antisocial nature.

Things are not as bad as they might seem to be, however. The new generation of games is much improved. Not only has much of the violence been eliminated, but in the process the games have been made to appeal to female players, who have, in the past, been turned away by the male-oriented "shoot-'em-ups." Field tests and further studies will provide educators with the information needed to determine just how effective the new games are; first impressions tend to indicate that they are highly so.

From the modest beginnings outlined above, educators will see an explosion of useful research studies developing over the next several years. From these will come answers to questions that are raised throughout this and succeeding chapters.

SUMMARY

The early computers were not suited to educational applications because of high cost, large size, and a certain degree of unreliability. The absence of appropriate programs was another critical factor. Despite these shortcomings, a few educators saw in these complex systems the potential for improving instruction by using the power of the computer to provide individualized activities. Smaller, cheaper minicomputers, an infusion of federal funds, and the refinement of programmed sequences by a growing corps of experts led to the implementation of several notable projects, including PLATO and the Stanford Project. Both monetary and institutional support diminished in the early seventies, and a period of malaise prevailed. With the invention and implementation of the chip, a completely new generation of computers emerged. Placing thousands of miniature electronic components on a single piece of silicon to form a programmable microprocessor, or "computer on a chip," made microcomputers possible. The first such machines were the products of enthusiasts who tailor-made them in private workshops. When the microcomputer was finally introduced to the public in the mid-seventies, the response was overwhelming.

Statistics indicate that schools and homes are acquiring computers at an ever-increasing rate, with acquisition being correlated to socioeconomic status. Research indicates that the primary beneficial effects may well be in the area of affect rather than in cognitive areas. For instance, children working with computers tend to socialize in positive ways; for example, they help one another, offer suggestions, and collaborate to solve a problem. However, learning is also enhanced under some conditions and with certain groups when computer-assisted instruction is used. CAI appears to be most effective with the high- and low-achievement groups and least effective with average students.

Although research on the use of the computer in education continues to expand, much more information is needed before a clear picture of its place in the curriculum and the extent of its effectiveness is obtained.

SELF-TEST

1. List several characteristics that make the computer unique as a teaching tool.
2. List three factors that keep computers from being more widely used in education.
3. Computers work with a binary code consisting of 0s and 1s. What device did first generation computers use to generate the code? What component was used by second generation machines? What by third generation computers?
4. Summarize the reasons early computers were not suited to instructional applications.
5. Describe the PLATO and Stanford projects.
6. Why did CAI fall from favor in the mid-1970s?
7. Identify and discuss several emerging trends in instructional computing.
8. The following True or False questions are related to CAI research:
   a. Gains in learning are noted when a student spends as little as ten minutes each day with CAI.
   b. Studies show that CAI is especially effective in mathematics instruction.
   c. Student evaluations of educational software are biased because they use mass-media standards for comparison.
   d. Studies show that students learn best when working alone at the computer.
   e. Use of CAI fosters the development of positive social attitudes.

REFERENCES

Becker, H. *The Impact of Computer Use on Children's Learning: What the Research Has Shown and What It Has Not.* Baltimore: Center for Research on Elementary and Middle Schools, John Hopkins University, 1988.

Bork, A. "Computer Futures in Education." *Creative Computing* (November 1984): 178–80.

Bracey, G. "Computers in Class: Some Social and Psychological Consequences." *Electronic Learning* (May/June 1988): 28.

Bracey, G. "Still Anxiety Among Educators Over Computers." *Electronic Learning* (March 1988): 20.

Brawer, J. "A+ Teachers' Toolbox." *A+ Magazine* (October 1988): 88–93.

Bruder, I. "Electronic Learning's Eighth Annual Survey of the States, 1988." *Electronic Learning* (October 1988): 38–49.

Burns, P., and W. Bozeman. "Computer-Assisted Instruction and Mathematics Achievement: Is There a Relationship?" *Educational Technology* (October 1981): 32–39.

Enochs, J., H. Handley, and J. Wallenberg. "Relating Learning Style, Reading Vocabulary, Reading Comprehension, and Aptitude for Learning to Achievement in Self-paced and Computer-Assisted Instructional Modes." *Journal of Experimental Education* (Spring 1986): 135–39.

Hirschbuhl, J., ed. *Computers in Education.* 3d ed. Guilford, Conn.: Dushkin Publishing Group, Inc., 1988.

Johnson, J. "Characteristics of Preschoolers Interested in Computers." *Journal of Educational Research* 78 (May/June 1985): 299–305.

Johnson, R., D. Johnson, and M. Stanne. "Effects of Cooperative, Competitive and Individualistic Goal Structures on Computer-Assisted Instruction." *Journal of Educational Psychology* (December 1985): 668–77.

Kulik, J., R. Bangert, and G. Williams. "Effects of Computer Based Teaching on Secondary School Students." *Journal of Educational Psychology* 75 (1983): 19–26.

Kulik, J., C. Kulik, R. Bangert-Drowns. "Effectiveness of Computer-Based Education in Elementary Schools." *Computers in Human Behavior* 1 (1985): 59–74.

McCarthy, R. "Making the Future Work—The Road to Curriculum Integration." *Electronic Learning* (September 1988): 42–46.

McClintock, R. "Marking the Second Frontier." *Teachers College Record* (Spring 1988): 345–51.

Market Data Retrieval. *Microcomputers in Schools, 1984–1985.* Westport, Conn. Market Data Retrieval, 1985.

Mevarech, Z., D. Stern, and I. Levita. "To Cooperate or Not To Cooperate in CAI: That Is the Question." *Journal of Educational Research* (January/February 1987): 164–167.

Naiman, A. "Serving Inquiring Minds." *Personal Computing* (May 1985): 35.

Niemac, R., and H. Walberg. "Computers and Achievement in the Elementary Schools." *Journal of Educational Computing Research* 14 (1985): 435–43.

OTA. *Power On! New Tools for Teaching and Learning.* Washington, DC: Office of Technology Assessment, 1988.

Olson, J., and S. Eaton. In James Calderhead, ed. *Exploring Teachers' Thinking.* London: Cassell Educational Limited, 1987.

Pogrow, S. "How to Use Computers to Truly Enhance Learning." *Electronic Learning* (May/ June 1988): 6–7.

Pournelli, J. "The Literacy Game." *Popular Computing* (May 1985): 45–49.

Ragosta, M., P. Holland, and D. Jameson. *Computer-Assisted Instruction and Compensatory Education: The ETS/LAUSD Study.* Princeton: Educational Testing Service, 1981.

Roberts, N., R. Carter, S. Friel, and M. Miller. *Integrating Computers into the Elementary and Middle School.* Englewood Cliffs, N.J.: Prentice Hall, 1987.

Smith, D., and R. Keep. "Children's Opinions of Educational Software." *Educational Research* (June 1986): 83–88.

Stein, A., A. Huston-Stein, S. Fox, D. Green, B. Watkins, and J. Whitaker. "The Effects of TV Action and Violence on Children's Social Behavior." *The Journal of Genetic Psychology* (June 1981): 138, 183–91.

Taylor, R., ed. *The Computer in the School: Tutor, Tool, Tutee.* New York: Teachers College Press, 1980.

Taylor, R., and N. Cunniff. "Moving Computing and Education beyond Rhetoric." *Teachers College Record* (Spring 1988): 164–167.

Thornburg, D. "Learning Curve." *A+ Magazine* (October 1988): 87–88.

CHAPTER 2

The Microcomputer System

CHAPTER TOPICS
☐ The three types of computers
☐ Components of microcomputer systems
☐ Peripheral devices for the microcomputer system
☐ Peripheral storage devices
☐ Components used as display devices
☐ Devices used to produce hard copy
☐ Various alternative input devices
☐ Techniques used in preventive and hands-on maintenance

To many people the word *computer* conjures up an image of huge, intimidating machines banked in climate controlled rooms hidden away in large corporate buildings. The people who use computers are thought to be an elite group, different from ordinary people, hunched over their glowing cathode ray tubes and whirring disk drives like sorcerers gathered around a bubbling cauldron of unknown substances.

Nothing could be further from the truth. Although the manner in which a computer is constructed is highly technical, and the precise way that data and instructions are managed is complex, modern microcomputers are so designed that with a modest amount of effort and study, anyone can learn to use them effectively.

When you sit down at the microcomputer system, several aspects of its physical presence are immediately apparent. The keyboard is there, with an arrangement of keys that reveals its typewriter heritage. There is a monitor, looking much like a television set but lacking a tuner and certain other controls. One or two disk drives are off to the side. Sometimes the drives are built in, as with units such as the IBM and the Apple Macintosh. Some machines incorporate the keyboard and perhaps the monitor in a modularized system; others provide a keyboard that is movable and can be positioned either on a desk or across your lap, if this is the most comfortable way to work. A printer might also be a part of the system, and other devices are often included. These add-ons are called peripherals. The one part of the system that isn't very obvious is the actual computer. It is tucked away in a case that often looks very much like a plastic or metal box. The computer, or *microprocessor* (that part of the computer that actually does the computing, a processor on a single chip), is very small, as you shall see; all of the devices mentioned above are simply there to permit you to get at the computer, use it, and store the results of its work. The keyboard of an Apple or Commodore is an extension of the case in which the computer is housed. The IBM and many others have a separate case to which the keyboard is attached with a cord. Opening the cases on those machines that permit access by the user reveals the microprocessor (a long ceramic or plastic integrated circuit with numerous pins that are engaged in matching sockets) and the various memory units, input/output circuits, power supply, and other components necessary to support the microprocessor.

Having seen the complex contents of the case, many people simply put the cover back on and begin to type on the keyboard or run a program. Indeed, it really isn't necessary to know how a computer is constructed and how it does its work to use one effectively. The overused analogy of the car and driver is frequently offered in support of this argument: you don't have to know how an internal combustion engine works in order to operate your automobile. As a general rule, this is a compelling argument; however, teachers are in a rather unique position when compared to computer users in general. There is a very real possibility that a teacher will be called upon to explain some of the intricacies of the computer to her students as well as to colleagues who are just learning about the technology. In addition, knowing something about the mechanics and the manner in which the work is done can be most useful in dispelling the mystery surrounding computers. Teachers who understand how computers operate, even at a basic level, will not be intimidated or frightened by them. They will come to know the machines for what they are—electronic devices that slavishly and logically follow the instructions of their human masters.

Just what is a computer? A computer is a tool for accomplishing the data processing functions of input, processing, output, and storage. The computer has proliferated because it processes data and delivers information in large volumes, efficiently, and at relatively low costs. Further, the computer exists because it has introduced the capacity and capability to perform data processing jobs that would have been impossible through other means. One of the impressive features of a computer is its speed. A fast, modern computer can do more arithmetic in one minute than a person using a pencil and paper could do in a lifetime. The computer thus makes it possible to solve many problems that would be completely impossible to do by hand. Most modern advances in science, engineering, and medicine are made possible by the availability of high-speed computers.

Computers come in many sizes, shapes, and colors. They range from very large computer systems called *mainframe* computers to small *minicomputers* to even smaller *microcomputers*. Regardless of size, all computers work on the same basic principles and perform the same basic functions. Mainframes and minicomputers perform the functions faster and can store and handle more data than a microcomputer; however, they all process the data in an identical manner. The similarities and differences between the three types of computers are discussed in this chapter. We briefly present the binary system used by computers and the ASCII code. Discussions are included on how the microprocessor and other units work and how the job of manipulating data is managed, and some suggestions for the maintenance of the microcomputer system are offered.

In this chapter we also discuss the peripheral devices that can be added to the computer to make up a complete system. The peripheral devices that provide both input and output capabilities for a microcomputer are detailed, along with a rationale as to why teachers should know about these devices.

MAINFRAME COMPUTERS

Mainframe computers are very large, sometimes taking up as much space as the average classroom (nine hundred cubic feet). They can store enormous amounts of information, billions and billions of individual pieces of data. Generally, a large mainframe computer system will cost more than a million dollars. Many large corporations, state and federal agencies, and universities use mainframe computers to assist in the daily operations of record keeping, budget preparation, payroll, personnel data, inventory maintenance, and so forth. The United States Navy uses mainframe computers to help keep track of the movements and locations of its ships and submarines. The U.S. Air Force uses these large computers to keep track of aircraft and satellites.

Mainframe computers usually have many terminals connected to them. These devices are used to send information to, and receive information from, the mainframe computer. Terminals may be in the same room as the computer, in another building, or even in another city. The terminals are interconnected to the mainframe computer via cables, through telephone wires, or by communications satellites. (For a view of a mainframe computer setup, see Figure 2.1.)

Mainframe computers, because they are so large and can store so much information, can do many jobs at one time. For example, the U.S. Air Force has a

FIGURE 2.1 Mainframe Computers
(Courtesy of International Business Machines Corporation)

large computer in Colorado that can communicate with terminals at all Air Force bases in the United States and via satellite with all bases in the world. Large department stores have a computer system that can communicate with terminals in all branch stores around the country.

MINICOMPUTERS

Minicomputers are smaller than mainframe computers. They usually take up only a small space on the floor; some can fit on a large table. They range in price from $10,000 to $150,000. They can store large amounts of information, although not as much as the mainframe computer system. Like mainframe computers, minicomputers can handle more than one job at a time and are interconnected by terminals. (See Figure 2.2.) They are used by medium and small companies as well as by some school systems. A mainframe system may be used to handle

FIGURE 2.2 Minicomputer

(Courtesy of Granite Mill, Salt Lake City, Utah)

information affecting an entire company or agency, while minicomputers are used in the different departments. For example, a government agency may have several departments. Each department handles specialized data that do not concern other departments in the agency. So, rather than use the agency's mainframe system to handle this specialized work, each department has its own minicomputer.

In some medium-sized or small school districts, the minicomputer has the capacity to handle all the varied needs of the district (payroll, pupil records, attendance reports, budget information, and inventory, for example).

MICROCOMPUTERS

Microcomputers, even smaller than minicomputers, are often called personal or home computers because many people purchase them for personal, home use. They are small and light enough to be portable, fitting on a table or desk. A complete microcomputer system usually costs less than three thousand dollars, sometimes considerably less. Microcomputers cannot store as much information as mainframes or minicomputers, and terminals are usually not connected to them. Unlike the larger, more powerful machines, microcomputers are designed to do only one job at a time. In a typical large organization, the mainframe computers and minicomputers are used to handle major computing chores and the microcomputers are called upon to solve smaller, more individual problems.

For the purpose of this text, we will concentrate on the functions and utilization of the microcomputer. Although the functions it performs are identical to those of the minicomputer or mainframe computer, there are differences between these machines in speed, capacity, and ability to perform more than one job at a time.

In general, a device can be classified as a computer if it:

1. performs *arithmetic* operations on data, including addition, subtraction, multiplication, and division;
2. performs *logical operations*—for instance, it can compare data items to determine whether they are equal or unequal, smaller or larger than each other;
3. can be *programmed*—that is, it can be provided with a set of instructions that processes data without human intervention; and
4. can *store* programs internally, rather than relying on wired panels or other external methods.

Basically, a computer used for data processing must be provided with two ingredients: *instructions* and *data*. The instructions (programs) are prepared by individuals known as programmers. The program is essential to the operation of the computer; it provides the precise instructions for the input, arithmetic, logic, and storage operations that the computer must carry out to complete a data processing job. A program is prepared and entered into the computer, then control is turned over to the computer, which executes, or carries out, the various instructions in the program. Under program control (prepared by a programmer), the computer processes the data without human intervention.

BINARY IDEAS

The microcomputer is a digital device; that is, it uses discrete signals in its operation. The two states employed are, very simply, on and off. This is the basis for the binary (*bi* = two) system. The smallest unit of information in the binary system is called a *bit* (short for binary digit). A bit can have the value of 1 or 0; that is, it can be on or off. Although only two signals are possible, many bits can be linked up in various ways and these extensive combinations can then be used to represent different letters, numbers, and symbols.

In order for this approach to be workable, it is necessary to have some kind of code based on the various combinations of on and off. One such code is the American Standard Code for Information Interchange, or ASCII.

THE ASCII CODE

Computers don't speak English (or Japanese or Russian) and people don't speak binary; therefore, some method of translating back and forth is essential if people and computers are to communicate with each other. The code that makes this possible is the ASCII code. The human language input at the keyboard is changed into the 1s and 0s of ASCII by electrical circuitry.

On the outside, a computer keyboard looks much like the ones used on typewriters, but internally it is very different. Electronic elements are provided that, when activated by a keypress, generate the ASCII codes for specific symbols, numbers, and letters. Note that each letter and number in the ASCII chart (Table 2.1) has a special combination of 0s and 1s that is distinctly its own. For example, an *A* is 01000001 (which is the number 65 in binary); and *B* is 01000010 (or binary 66). Each succeeding letter is one number higher, permitting the computer to alphabetize a list of entries quite easily, if this is desired. No two combinations in ASCII are the same; there are more than enough combinations available to represent all of the letters (both upper and lowercase), numbers, and symbols on the keyboard.

MICROCOMPUTER SYSTEM COMPONENTS

All digital computers consist of the same basic components. Let us examine the major components.

TABLE 2.1 ASCII Code (Partial)

A	01000001	W	01010111	a	01100001
B	01000010	X	01011000	b	01100010
C	01000011	Y	01011001	c	01100011
D	01000100	Z	01011010	d	01100100
E	01000101	0	00110000	+	00101011
F	01000110	1	00110001	−	00101101
G	01000111	2	00110010	>	00111110
H	01001000	3	00110011	?	00111111
I	01001001	4	00110100	#	00100011

Microprocessor

The real computer in any microcomputing system is actually no bigger than your thumbnail. It consists of thousands of transistors (electronic on/off switches) that, through the use of microphotography, have been squeezed onto a very small segment (called a chip) of silicon. This chip, encased in a piece of ceramic material, is called a microprocessor (see Figure 2.3).

There are other chips within a microcomputer; the microprocessor, however, has features that set it apart from all the others. Microprocessors differ in construction from one brand to another, but all are similar in one respect: they contain the central processing unit (or CPU), which does the actual computations, comparisons, and so on. Some microprocessors contain varying amounts of memory, and others might even add the capability to perform input and output functions; but all contain, as a minimum, the CPU. Let us examine this remarkable device.

The Central Processing Unit

The central processing unit controls the flow of instructions and data to and from memory or an input/output device. It also performs operations upon the data to change them in some way. The operation of the CPU is managed by specific instructions, which are provided by a program, the nature of which determines just how the data are to be handled. For example, the instructions intrinsic to a word processing program will cause the CPU to proceed in a manner that will be different from the way it works with a graphics program.

The CPU consists of three basic entities—the control unit, the arithmetic unit, and the logic unit. In most microcomputers, the arithmetic and the logic units are combined into one unit called the arithmetic logic unit (ALU). The control unit supervises the sequencing of the work—it handles or controls the operation of all

FIGURE 2.3   Microprocessor

the computer parts—while the ALU actually executes the instructions. It is the CPU that is the actual computer within the computer system.

Memory

One group of chips within the microcomputer provides memory spaces within which the information that the computer is working on is stored. The random access memory (RAM), like other functions within the computer, is located on silicon chips. One chip may be capable of holding thousands of bits of information, stored in the form of an on or off state corresponding to the 1s and 0s of the binary code with which computers work. The memory cells of a computer are arranged so that they can be *written to* or *read from* as needed. Thus, memories operate in two basic modes: read and write.

One disadvantage of semiconductor RAM memory units is that they require a constant power source. Since they rely on electrical currents to represent data, all their stored data is lost if the power source fails and no emergency (backup) system exists. Thus, when you turn off your microcomputer or the power is interrupted (for even a split second), the RAM memory is lost. This is called *volatile* memory because it is not permanent.

You will recall that a character in ASCII is made up of a series of 0s and 1s; each 0 or 1 is called a *bit*. A group of 8 bits is termed a *byte*. A computer that has the capability of working with one full byte at a time is termed an 8-bit computer. The terms *bytes, words,* and *characters* are synonymous in a computer with an 8-bit word length. The capacity of RAM is generally measured in kilobytes (K), or thousands of words. Generally one K equals 1,024 units; thus a computer that has 64K of storage can store 64 × 1,024, or 65,536, characters.

The amount of RAM available in computers today varies from 64K to 512K in small personal computers, from 512K to 2MB (megabytes, or millions of words) in professional microcomputers, and from 16MB to 128 or more megabytes in large mainframe and super computers.

RAM is still much more expensive than secondary storage (data on diskette, disk, or magnetic cassette tape) on a byte-by-byte basis. As a result, secondary storage is where the vast amount of computer information is held in computer-usable form until required for processing. The capacity of one diskette of secondary storage varies between one hundred thousand and several million bytes of information (more detailed information on secondary storage is presented later in this chapter).

Another group of memory chips provides a place where certain information is stored permanently. This information is built into the computer by the manufacturer and includes such things as instructions that translate a computer language such as BASIC into the only language a computer can understand, the 0s and 1s of machine-language. This type of memory is known as read only memory (ROM).

ROM instructions are "hard-wired"; that is, they cannot be changed or deleted by other stored program instructions. This type of memory is permanent, or *nonvolatile*. The only method of changing its contents is by altering the physical construction of the circuits.

All of the chips, RAM and ROM, are plugged into a plastic board called a *motherboard,* which provides an interconnecting network of circuitry for them. See Figure 2.4 for a complete diagram of a typical microcomputer. This figure details the location of the CPU, the RAM chips, the ROM chips, the peripheral slots, the power supply, the speaker, the keyboard, and the input/output port.

PERIPHERAL DEVICES

As we stated at the beginning of this chapter, teachers may need to know how a microcomputer works so they can, in turn, assist students as they learn about computers. The same reasoning applies to peripheral devices, with several added concerns. A teacher will need to know what devices are available, how they work, and some idea of costs in order to make wise decisions regarding purchasing peripherals to complete a basic system consisting of the microcomputer, monitor, and disk drives. The teacher will also need to know how to hook up these peripheral devices so they can be utilized by the students (as it is unlikely that someone knowledgeable will be available to do this installation for the classroom teacher).

FIGURE 2.4 Diagram of a Typical Microcomputer

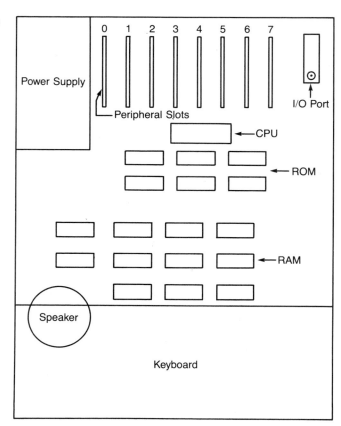

With some basic knowledge, teachers can provide their students with a rudimentary introduction to the operation of these mechanisms.

A microcomputer system comprises several basic components. The physical machinery (*hardware*) includes input units (such as the keyboard), a processing unit (the actual computer) and storage units (such as disk drives), and output units (such as a monitor or printer). The system enables the user to enter data into the microcomputer, allows the computer to process and store the data, and provides a means for the computer to return the processed data to the user. Even though both input and output units are mentioned in other chapters in this text, an in-depth discussion of selected units will be helpful and will provide a better understanding of how a complete microcomputer system operates.

PERIPHERAL STORAGE OF DATA

The fact that microcomputers are limited in the amount of read-write memory (RAM) that is available makes it necessary to provide for the storage of large amounts of data in some other way. External or peripheral storage devices are available for this purpose. Currently, the floppy disk is the most common mass storage medium in use in the schools. As hard disk systems drop in price, however, these are likely to become popular also.

The $3\frac{1}{2}$-inch disk format is becoming very popular as more companies design machines to use it. In the meantime, the $5\frac{1}{4}$-inch (commonly referred to as 5-inch) format is still the most popular for home and educational applications. Hard disks (finely machined aluminum disks coated with a magnetic material and encased in a rigid housing), capable of storing very large quantities of information, are great for record keeping on a school or district level and for other specialized functions.

Two recent innovations, CD-ROM and videodiscs, are available and offer teachers some excellent new options as peripheral storage devices. These two devices provide tremendous storage capacity plus the exciting possibility of adding motion and sound to the interactive capability of the microcomputer.

Most operations can be performed with a single disk drive, but there are times when two disk drives are not only handy but essential. For example, when using an authoring language such as PILOT to write lessons, a lesson disk must be in the second drive to save the program that is written. Although many two-disk programs work fine on a single drive, the inconvenience of switching back and forth from the disk containing the program to the one saving data makes the purchase of a second drive a good investment.

Disks of a common size don't always hold the same amount of information; some computer systems are designed so that they make better use of the storage space on the disk than do others. The most common way to store data is to place it on only one side of the disk in a pattern that is termed single-density. But it is possible to place twice as much data on a single side by cramming it together—this is termed double-density. In order to do this, the disk must have a higher quality ferrite (iron oxide) coating than is necessary for single-density storage, so the cost goes up.

Storage is also increased when both sides are used. This type of disk is used in drives that have two read-write heads, one for each of the two sides. Or, the disk can be flipped over and used in the traditional way in a standard drive. Double-sided disks have been certified on both sides, while the single-sided ones are certified on one side only. It is therefore possible to store four times as much data on a double-sided, double-density disk as on a typical single-sided, single-density one. Whichever type is used, the drive must be compatible with the particular disk format.

It seems appropriate at this point to discuss the care that must be exercised in handling and utilizing the disk drive system. It is very critical that the disk be inserted properly into the drive mechanism (see Figure 2.5). Note the placement of the thumb over the label and the position of the read-write opening on the diskette.

With proper care, diskettes last for a long time. Here are some suggestions that will help extend their lives.

1. Always store the disk in its protective envelope when not in use. Make sure that the read-write opening is covered by the envelope.
2. When handling the disk, do not touch the exposed surface (that portion you can see through the read-write opening). A thumb print on this portion of the diskette can cause the disk drive to misread information stored there.
3. Be careful where you place the disk—never expose it to a magnetic field. Electrical devices such as monitors and TV receivers emit magnetic signals that can damage the program on the disk.
4. When you label a disk, use a felt marker. The pressure from a ballpoint pen or pencil may destroy the data on the disk.
5. Do not leave the disk in your car, particularly on very hot or very cold days.
6. Do not bend the disk: you may damage it.
7. Do not use alcohol to clean the disk surface. Alcohol will cause the magnetic coating on the surface of the diskette to separate from the plastic base.

FIGURE 2.5 Properly Inserted Disk

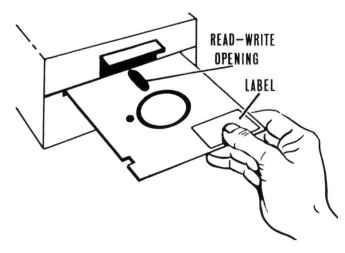

8. Never attach anything to the disk with a paper clip.
9. A good rule to follow when placing the disk in the drive is the "rule of thumb." Place your thumb over the label (on the top) and carefully insert the disk (never force it) into the drive (see Figure 2.5).
10. Store the disks upright in their original boxes or in cases available commercially for this purpose.

The flexible disk, diskette, or floppy disk (it is called any one of these three names in the current literature) was introduced in 1973 to replace punched cards as a medium of data entry. It can also store programs and data files. The diskette comes in three standard sizes, 8 inches, $5\frac{1}{4}$-inches, and $3\frac{1}{2}$-inches. It is made of plastic and coated with a thin, precisely placed iron oxide coating; the disk is then permanently sealed in a plastic or paper jacket lined with a soft paper containing hundreds of small holes that absorb and contain the dust and dirt particles that may scratch and damage the disk surface.

Diskettes sell for under two dollars in most cases; they are reusable, easy to store, and weigh less than two ounces. A typical floppy disk can store the equivalent of thousands of punched cards.

HARD DISK DRIVES

More and more large schools and many school districts are now making the switch to hard disks for storing programs and data and for "networking" systems (consult Chapter 7, on telecommunication, for additional details). The hard disk devices can hold huge amounts of information, so many schools equipped with a hard disk drive can easily store their entire software collection and associated data files on one hard disk. In addition to the great convenience of having all needed information stored on a single storage device, most hard disk users find that their units are faster, easier to use, and more reliable than floppy disk drives.

Hard disk drive units, called *Winchester drives,* employ fixed cartridges containing a disk formed from aluminum and coated with iron oxide (as in the floppy disk). The fixed cartridge concept means that the heart of the Winchester system—the disk—with its associated read-write head mechanism is sealed in a dustproof housing. Winchester head-disk assemblies are put together in "clean rooms" so that microscopic dust particles do not get on the disk surface. This great care is necessary because the head, unlike that in the floppy disk drive, does not ride on the surface of the disk. The hard disk spins at 3,600 rpm and the head literally floats over the surface on a cushion of air.

The advantages of hard disk drive systems are in their storage capacity, speed of operation, and relative permanency of stored information. An eight-inch hard disk unit can store up to twenty megabytes (millions of characters) of information—approximately four hundred pages, single-spaced, of instantly accessible data. Hard disks can transfer data at speeds up to ten times faster than floppy drives; therefore, a hard disk unit can get needed information into a microcomputer's RAM at lightning speed. The stored information is relatively permanent, so if the system is properly designed, commonly used programs will be instantly available instead of requiring insertion of a disk and loading and executing a desired program.

Many computers come with a hard disk drive as standard equipment. Many schools and districts find that the speed and greater storage capacity are valuable additions to their microcomputer systems, especially when the systems are networked and the need arises for storage of large amounts of data.

THE DISPLAY

The most common output devices used with today's classroom microcomputers are cathode ray tubes (CRTs) and printers. We will discuss the cathode ray tube first.

There are basically two kinds of CRT screens. The first is the regular television set hooked up to a special modulator adaptor that allows the TV to receive computer signals instead of television programs.

The differences between using a computer monitor and a standard television receiver coupled to your microcomputer are in speed of display, amount of data capable of being handled, and quality of the picture. With a standard television, the colors tend to smear together: there is a lack of distinct edges between various colors, and the colors are not pure in hue or saturation. There is also the problem called overscan, in which the picture goes beyond the edges of the screen. This is acceptable with broadcast television but can cause important details on the edge of the picture to be blurred or even omitted in microcomputer utilization.

The slower speed of display and reduced amount of data handled by a standard television set are major drawbacks because these two factors affect color quality. The information handled corresponds roughly to dots of light on the screen; the more dots, the clearer and sharper the image. The total number of dots, or pixels (short for *picture elements*), that can be displayed is limited because of the TV receiver's *bandwidth* (the range of frequencies available for transmission of data). The bandwidth of a television receiver is not sufficient to accommodate all the data that can be sent to the CRT by a microcomputer. In simple terms, the standard television receiver will not handle the data fast enough or clearly enough to be legible and sharp on the screen; therefore, a user gets a poor-quality picture that can cause eyestrain and muscle fatigue after a short period of viewing the screen.

The second CRT device, and one that is much superior to the TV receiver for use with a microcomputer, is a *monitor*. A monitor is like a television receiver minus the front-end electronics. You can't tune to any channels with it, and it won't amplify signals from the antenna. It simply takes the video signal coming from the microcomputer and passes it through to the circuitry that drives the cathode ray tube. With the exception of a channel-selector knob, a monitor has all the usual controls: vertical and horizontal, brightness, contrast, tone, and (in color sets) color. Most monitors have a separate on/off switch, and must be turned on or off independently of the microcomputer (unless you use a central control switch).

A monitor is designed to handle higher and wider bandwidths than those of a standard television receiver. The television signal that most monitors are designed to accept is called NTSC (National Television System Committee) video or *composite* video. This video signal can't be sent over the airwaves on the specific frequencies designed by the Federal Communications Commission for television stations. It is designed to be transmitted via the cable that is hooked from the monitor to your microcomputer. *Composite* means that the picture information that defines the beginning of each horizontal scan line (there are 525 lines needed to fill the entire surface of the screen) and the number of pictures per second are tied together into synchronized pulses that the monitor can understand and translate into a picture. There are thirty complete pictures/displays on the screen each second.

MONITORS

You are likely to encounter three types of computer monitors: monochrome, composite color, and RGB. Following is a brief description of each.

Monochrome

Monochrome means one color, usually green or amber against a black background. Amber screens have become popular because many people believe that they are easier on the eyes. There is no scientific evidence to back up this claim, however; it seems to be a matter of personal preference. Generally, amber monitors cost a bit more than green ones.

Monochrome monitors have quite sharp displays, and they are the least expensive, commonly available for less than $200.

Composite Color

A color monitor is a bit more complex than a monochrome one. A color monitor contains three electron devices (instead of one, as in a monochrome monitor) to create the scan lines on the picture tube. These devices, called "guns," generate the three colors red, green, and blue. The composite color monitors employ, basically, the same technology as used in conventional color television sets except that the speed with which they handle data and the sharpness of the picture are enhanced. This type of monitor has one composite electron signal that controls all three of the color guns; thus the beam of light that strikes the front of the picture tube is a combination of red, green, and blue. Most composite color monitors cost within the range of $250 to $400.

RGB

The sharpest color monitors are the RGB monitors. RGB stands for "red, green, blue"—the basic colors all TVs and monitors use to produce a color picture. With RGB monitors, unlike regular TVs and composite monitors, a separate video signal is used for each of the three color guns. These discrete signals mean that color intensities can be transmitted more precisely and decoded by the monitor more rapidly, making it possible to produce sharper images than those of the composite video monitor or regular TV. The RGB monitor is more expensive than the composite, and can range in price from $400 to $5,000.

Test for Monitor Quality

Once you have narrowed down your choice to a monochrome, composite color, or RGB monitor, you should try one out yourself before making a purchase. You may need to spend time in a few different microcomputer stores, but it will be time well spent. Many vendors will bring a monitor right to your school to let you try it out for a few days. Be sure to ask for this service; if the vendor will let you borrow the monitor you can try it out on your students.

In the store or at your school, there are a few tests you can perform to help determine how good a monitor is and how well it suits your needs.

□ *Convergence* (point at which the beams of light come together in a color monitor). The critical area is around the screen's edges, where the television tube's face curves back and the electron beams are shot at their most acute angle. Fill the screen with one letter—an N, H, Z, M, or E—by pressing down on the key and holding it down. Adjust the monitor so the letters are white; this requires all three electron guns to work at full strength. Now look closely at all the letters around the screen's perimeter, especially in the corners. Are there any colored fringes? How bad are they? If such fringes are present, they are caused by poor manufacturing or design, or improper factory adjustment. The factory adjustment can be corrected; the poor workmanship or design cannot.

□ *Screen loss.* With the text still on the screen, look again to see if any letters are chopped off at the screen's top or bottom edge. If there is any loss, look for another brand or manufacturer's model; the inadequacy of this model is obvious.

□ *Horizontal and vertical lines.* Again, with the text still on the screen, stand about six feet back from the screen and stare at it straight on. Do all the horizontal lines of characters look horizontal? Are the vertical lines in a vertical position? With allowances for the natural curve of the tube's face, you should not see much degree of wavering. If you do, it generally means faulty design or poor manufacturing.

□ *Cursor smear.* Clear the screen and move the cursor across the screen at maximum speed. This is generally accomplished by holding down on the space bar. Do you see a trail, or smear, behind the moving cursor? If you do see this trail, the surface of the monitor may be coated with special phosphors designed to glow longer than others. These long-persistence phosphors prevent flickering but are not suitable for applications that require rapidly changing images as with CAI packages. This smear can be very frustrating to your students and can even cause eye fatigue.

□ *Monitor flicker.* Place a few words on the screen, or even a small figure. Does the image seem to flicker? If it does, it generally means the electron guns are not emitting rays that strike the surface of the monitor rapidly enough to prevent the flicker. In some cases your eyes may be very sensitive and you can detect this problem. In either case, this flicker is likely to get on your nerves and could cause eyestrain.

These little tests will give you a good general idea of the quality of the monitor; still, the most important consideration is your own viewing comfort. Seat yourself in the normal viewing position you would take when using the microcomputer. Now stare at the screen and decide if you like what you see. Do you like the colors or, when necessary, the lack of them? Are you satisfied with the resolution? Do you like the appearance of the characters? How is the brightness? The contrast? Are the controls conveniently located and accessible, or is the access door difficult to unlatch? Do you need to get up to adjust these controls, or are they right in front of you? Make the effort while shopping or previewing a monitor to deal with these questions seriously so you will select a monitor you will be pleased with and can live with for many school sessions.

Before we conclude our discussion on the selection of a monitor, it is important that we suggest the securing of a glare-free screen and a mechanism to hold the monitor that has the capability of being tilted or adjusted for users of varying heights. There are growing indications that the glare and difficult viewing angles experienced by users of a microcomputer monitor are the two major factors causing eyestrain and body fatigue. There are even some indications that extended use of high-phosphor CRTs seems to produce some physical problems and that the ambient radiation from extended exposure to color monitors by young children may enhance such problems as eyestrain, backache, irritability, and neck strain.

Other Monitor Technologies

Flat-panel displays are now on the market. They are the latest innovations that may change the look of the traditional CRT. They are not yet available for most standard desktop microcomputers; however, they are being used in the latest lap-sized portable computers and most likely will become practical as monitors for microcomputers within the next few years.

We will discuss two types of flat-panel displays that seem to hold promise for use with personal computers—liquid crystal and electroluminescent. Both of these new technologies are based on solid-state electronics rather than on electron beams; therefore they are much more rugged and consume less power than a cathode ray tube. Their slim profile and light weight make them ideal for small, portable microcomputers. Another positive feature is that flat screens do not distort images around the edges as CRTs do.

Liquid Crystal Display. Liquid crystal displays (LCDs) have been used in watches, calculators, and other electronic devices for some years now and are currently available on portable computers such as Radio Shack's TRS 80 model 100. To provide this kind of display, a liquid crystal material is deposited between two sheets of polarizing material; this sandwich is in turn squeezed between two glass panels containing thin wire electrodes arranged in a very closely spaced grid pattern.

In a normal state, light shines through the two polarizers and is reflected back to the viewer. When a current is passed between two crossing electrodes, the resulting electromagnetic field aligns the liquid crystals so that light cannot shine through, thus producing a dark pixel on the light background

One drawback to a liquid crystal display panel is that because the LCDs emit no light of their own, there must be a reliance on reflected light to see what is on the screen. This limits the viewing angle to a very narrow range, requiring that the viewer observe the screen straight on.

Electroluminescent Panel. As with the other flat-panel displays, the front panel of an electroluminescent display contains a set of closely spaced vertical wires that are invisible to the eye. The back panel includes a similar set of horizontal wires. A layer of zinc sulfide and manganese is sandwiched between these two panels. When a current is sent through a vertical and horizontal wire, an electrical field is set up at the point where the wires cross and an orange- or yellow-colored pixel is generated. Currently, a 12-by-21-inch electroluminescent panel can provide a resolution of 240 by 320 pixels on the monitor screen. The price has dropped dramatically in recent months, and soon this type of display may be economically feasible for microcomputer use.

PC PROJECTOR

When a teacher desires to show the entire class a spreadsheet, a data base record, or a word processing document, it is difficult for the whole class to gather around a single monitor to view the information presented while the teacher demonstrates some aspect of a current lesson. Until recently, the best solution to this problem was the use of a large-screen projector that cost in the neighborhood of $5,000 and was very large and cumbersome to set up and use. With the introduction of the LCD projection system (commonly called a PC projector) with a cost of between $700 and $1500, teachers have found a practical and effective means to project the images created on their monitors onto a large classroom screen.

The PC projector is a computer output device that is hooked directly into the computer's video output port (the same port that hooks to the external monitor); thus the computer program outputs directly to the transparent LCD screen. This LCD screen is then placed on an overhead projector just as you would place a regular transparency for projection to a classroom screen. The overhead projector becomes the projector that displays the programs that are generated by the microcomputer and normally feed to the monitor. PC projector controls are mounted conveniently on the projector. Users can center the display, adjust contrast, and toggle between standard and reverse video very easily.

The PC projector looks much like a large, framed picture that has a blank area where the picture is normally displayed. Size varies by manufacturer, but the LCD screen and plastic housing are usually no larger than 12 by 18 inches and 1 to 2 inches thick. The device uses the liquid crystal display technology that has been used in watches, calculators, and other devices for a number of years. Using this proven technology, the PC projector is a very reliable and easy-to-use piece of equipment (refer to the discussion on LCDs in this chapter). The PC projector will display black-and-white and color images. The MagnaByte II system produced by Telex Communications, for example, will produce images using the colors yellow, gold, orange, violet, and blue. (See Figure 2.6)

One concern when using the PC projector is the heat buildup that can occur when using it on an overhead projector. It is important that the PC projector have a system for cooling, either a cooling fan or a system that dissipates the heat from the LCD crystals during projection. Check out any system you plan to buy by using it for at least a couple of hours. If the heat buildup becomes extreme, the LCD screen will begin to fade and the images will become indistinguishable.

The PC projector can provide the classroom teacher with an easy-to-use, versatile, and inexpensive method for sharing computer displays with the whole class, thereby opening the door to many creative teaching techniques.

PRINTERS

The two major kinds of printers are impact and nonimpact. Characters are formed in the one case through physically striking the paper surface with the printing element (like a typewriter); nonimpact printers use no such physical action.

The most common type of printer is the dot matrix impact printer, which uses a matrix of tiny wires from which any character can be formed. In this type of printer, characters are not formed by a type element (such as a ball, thimble, or wheel) but are stored as a pattern or matrix of dots in a memory inside the printer. When using dot matrix technology to print, the pattern of dots is retrieved by the output device and transferred dot by dot to the impacting mechanism of the printer. Compared with printing with a formal character set (such as a daisy wheel), dot matrix printing has fewer restrictions on the size or style of characters. Since characters or images are produced by a selected pattern of dots, the software program being utilized can change the number, size, and style of characters. It can even produce graphics and draw pictures, filling in the graphs and images dot by dot. With the addition of multicolored ribbons, the dot matrix printer can produce text and graphs in several colors.

Recent innovations in dot matrix technology have added more print wires to the printhead (as many as twenty-four), thus achieving almost true letter-quality printing. The twenty-four-wire printhead also provides extremely high quality graphic images. This new technology has not added greatly to the overall costs of these printers. They are priced in the range of $150 to $300.

Twenty-four-wire printheads use a staggered two-column layout with two twelve-wire columns, thus reducing the gap between the wires. This reduction of the space between the printhead wires plus the use of smaller diameter wires provide a more compact printhead, which makes higher quality printing possible. Another advantage of this technology is the capability to print many more font styles, even some delicate scripts with fine calligraphic features.

FIGURE 2.6 · PC Projector
System

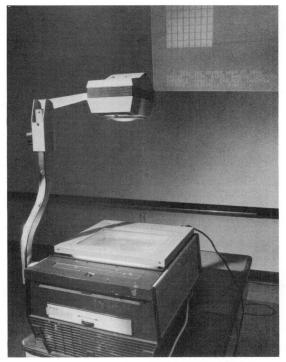

(Courtesy of Instructional Media Services, University of
Utah at Salt Lake City.)

The other common type of impact printer is the daisy wheel printer, which
uses an element composed of "petals" upon whose tips the raised characters are
located. This style of printer is slower than the dot matrix variety and does not
permit production of graphics; however, the daisy wheel printer produces type
that is termed "letter quality." This means that the printed document is of the
same quality in terms of legibility, evenness of print, and formation of letters,
symbols, and numbers as that achieved by an electric typewriter. This is the
quality that is generally required for business correspondence, textbook copy,
advertising layouts, magazine text copy, research papers, and so on. (See Figure
2.7 for samples of dot matrix and impact printing.)

Nonimpact printers use methods other than striking the printing head or matrix
to form characters. Typically, they are quieter than the varieties mentioned
above, and they tend to be more reliable and cheaper.

Thermal and electrosensitive printers burn dots into regular copy paper. Thermal transfer printers use heated wires to melt ink from a ribbon onto the paper
surface. These printers provide high-quality multicolored copy and they are inexpensive to purchase. But the drawback is that the ribbons are costly since they
can be used only once and thus must be replaced frequently.

FIGURE 2.7 Sample of Type
from a Dot Matrix Printer and
Letter-Quality Type Sample from
a Daisy Wheel Printer

dot matrix printer

dot matrix printer

letter quality line printer

letter quality line printer

(© 1983 Burgess Publishing Company, Used by permission.)

Technological advances have brought the prices of inkjet printers down to the point where many schools can afford to purchase them (under $800). It is possible to have multicolor printing just by exchanging the various cartridges containing the desired ink colors. (See Figure 2.8) These innovations and lower costs make the inkjet printer a good choice for schools that desire to print colored materials.

A relative newcomer to the printing field is the laser printer. Even though laser technology is not new, the costs involved have been so high that most schools could not afford to purchase them. Since the introduction of Hewlett-Packard's first desktop laser printer in 1984 (about $3,500), prices have come steadily down, making laser printers affordable for even budget-conscious school districts. Good quality laser printers are available in the $1,500 to $3,000 range.

The laser printer uses the same principles of operation as the photocopying machine, a process called electrophotography. Information is fed from the computer to the laser printer's microprocessing unit, which manipulates the data into a proper format for the printer's use. The main component of the electrophotog-

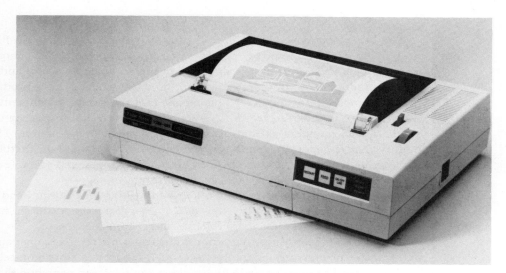

FIGURE 2.8   A Color Inkjet Printer from Radio Shack
(Reproduced by written permission from Tandy Corporation)

raphy printing process is a drum coated with a photoelectric substance. A laser beam is shot at a series of rotating mirrors, which in turn reflect the beam of light onto the drum. Toner (ultrafine graphite powder) is magnetically adhered to the drum in places where it is charged by the laser beams. This toner is then transferred onto the paper. Heat causes the toner to fuse to the paper.

After the image of the page has been transferred to the paper, the drum is rotated past a discharge unit, which eliminates any remaining charges of electricity, and a felt pad removes any traces of toner, preparing the drum for the next image. Printing speeds for laser printers are measured in pages per minute. Most laser printers can print from 6 to 12 pages per minute. (See Figure 2.9).

The great advantage of the laser printer is its ability to print letter-quality characters as well as high resolution graphic images, thus combining the best features of the daisy wheel and the dot matrix printer.

Don't buy a printer before you have tried out a number of different kinds in your price range. Look for qualities such as speed, the nature of the printed character, and noise level. Be cautious that you do not purchase a printer that does not print below the line. Letters such as *p, g,* and *y* need to descend below the level of the printed line. Also, the need for subscripts and superscripts for scientific or math applications is an important consideration, as is the ability to print special characters such as Greek letters or math symbols. Good documentation is certainly an asset if you are unfamiliar with printers. A critical consideration is whether or not there are reliable repair and service agencies available locally.

Some printers produce excellent graphics and others have color capabilities, which are features to consider if such luxuries are needed and can be afforded.

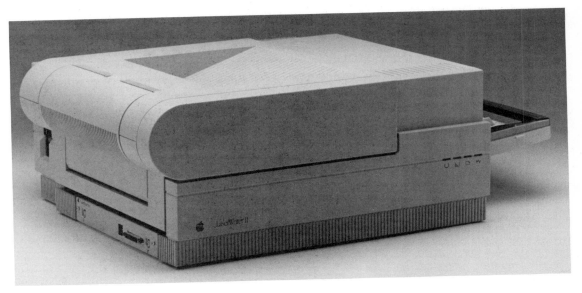

FIGURE 2.9   Laser Printer
(Courtesy of Apple Computer, Inc.)

Even certain low-cost printers have special features such as the ability to print in boldface and to underline—always check for such features before you buy. Graphics are possible with a dot matrix printer *only* if the computer has a graphics-capable interface board. Often users buy graphics software only to discover that to use it they need to replace their text-only interface with a graphics-capable interface such as "Grappler + ."

A printer does not have to be of the same brand as the computer to work. A few modifications may be required to match up the units, such as a different connector from the computer to the printer or a different interface board, but these are normally easy to make.

Printers have different kinds of feed mechanisms. Friction feed is similar to the method used by typewriters, where a single sheet is fed through at a time. The more common method is tractor or pin feed; in this case sprockets are provided whose pins engage the holes in the continuous supply of fanfold paper. The more versatile printers employ both kinds of feed, thereby permitting the user to print a special letter on a sheet of bond paper or to tractor feed numerous pages of cheaper paper for inexpensive hard copy.

Of the several kinds of available printers, the daisy wheel is the most practical for school use when letter-quality hard copy is needed. Most daisy wheel elements can be changed to permit a variety of typefaces and degrees of boldness to be printed.

Although the low-cost dot matrix printer is the most widely used for hard-copy printouts, the quality is not the best. On the other hand, high-resolution dot matrix machines are capable of creating copy that is very nearly as sharp and clean as that produced by character printers. They do this through the inclusion of more and finer dots in the characters. Printers of this kind have the advantage of being able to print out a wide variety of fonts without the need for element changes.

With the price of the laser printer going down every year, this printer offers teachers an attractive option. It provides letter-quality and high-resolution graphic printing with the features of both multiple fonts and fast production of copies.

Printers not only provide hard copy, but some also have a graphics capability. It is a relatively straightforward matter to create colorful, stunning graphics on the computer screen, but it is another problem to do the same thing on paper. Graphics output devices are available, but many are far too expensive for most schools to afford. At the low end, once again, are the dot matrix printers, which constitute the most common hard-copy graphics device, using patterns of dots to create pictures rather than letters and numbers.

Printers other than impact varieties are also available for hard-copy graphics production. Inkjet printers produce nice graphics because the ink tends to blend, for a softer effect.

PLOTTERS

A different breed of device for the production of hard-copy graphics is the plotter. These machines are quite different from printers in appearance and construction, but this seems to be an appropriate place to mention them. They contain from one to eight pens of different colors that descend and ascend in concert with signals from the computer to place marks upon a moving sheet of paper. Basically, a plotter is much like an electrocardiograph in the manner in which it works, but the signals are coming from the computer rather than from a human heart.

A plotter produces the image on paper by controlling the motion of the pen carriage that draws the lines. The output medium of paper is utilized by the plotter as a series of x, y coordinates. If you were to plot similar coordinates on a piece of graph paper and then draw lines connecting the points, you would have an approximate visual metaphor of how a plotter draws lines. The microcomputer sends the plotter a series of numbers that represent x, y coordinates in the desired pattern. The pen carriage then moves to the different positions while holding the pen or pens on the surface of the page. Curves are drawn by linking together a series of short straight lines, much in the same way curves are produced on the monitor screen. Figure 2.10 shows a plotter from the Houston Instrument Company.

MODEMS

Several data base networks operating in various places around the country can provide a wealth of information to those who are set up to access them. (See Chapter 7, on telecommunication, for details.) The major problem at present, at least for many schools, is the cost. There is typically an initial network membership fee and an hourly on-line fee, which varies in amount from one system to another. The Source, CompuServe, and Dow Jones are among the larger, better-

FIGURE 2.10 A Plotter from Houston Instrument Company

known companies, but others have been established at universities and colleges that offer information of value in many subject areas.

The advantage of telecomputing for students is obvious: it's as if they had a first-class library right at their fingertips, without the inconveniences. By hooking into the system through a modem and a microcomputer, students can access the extensive data base directly from the classroom, and the information is always as current as today.

The *modem* (for modulator-demodulator) is used to convert the digital 0s and 1s of the machine language of the computer into voice signals for transmittal over telephone lines. There are two types of modems—the acoustic coupler and the direct-connect varieties. The acoustic coupler employs the telephone handset, while the direct-connect type is attached within the computer or between it and the telephone jack. The latter type costs more than the acoustic coupler, but the advantages are most likely worth the extra cost. Some microcomputers come with a built-in modem.

Along with the modem, it is necessary to have the appropriate software to run it. The software takes care of the problem of getting information from the computer to the modem and vice versa.

ALTERNATIVE INPUT DEVICES

The keyboard is the most common device for getting information into the computer, but a number of alternatives allow one to accomplish the same purpose without knowing how to type. Young children can't type, and neither can many adults; also, people with various kinds of handicaps find it difficult or impossible to communicate with the computer through the keyboard. Even those who can type find certain of these options to be highly attractive for various applications.

Alternative input devices are not meant to replace the keyboard entirely but to supplement it. You will use the keyboard to input text for the printer or to write a program in most cases, but there are a few special devices that actually permit the input of textual material.

No attempt will be made here to describe all of the available alternative input devices; rather, a selection has been made of those that appear to have the greatest utility for the largest number of readers.

The Mouse

An input device that was popularized when introduced by Apple's Lisa computer, the mouse is the "electronics marvel" of the input function on microcomputer systems. [It has been estimated that at least one-third and possibly over half of all computer work stations, and especially microcomputer stations, are using the mouse technology for input functions.]

Why the excitement over the mouse? Simply because the mouse is a versatile cursor-mover that helps make a computer vastly easier and faster to use. With a mouse you can move the cursor to any point on the screen virtually as fast as you can point with your finger. You simply move the mouse around on your desk and with the click of the button on the top of the mouse, you can delete, move, save, scroll, or otherwise manipulate text and graphic data. You can even draw with a mouse, though not the detailed work that can be done with a graphics tablet (described later in this chapter). The mouse is a perfect tool for picking up symbols, words, sentences, figures, textures, and so forth and carrying them to other locations in your text or drawing.

Now that the mouse is being used with the popular Macintosh (Apple Computer Corporation) microcomputer, we may well see a mouse population explosion and the introduction of additional kinds, shapes, and sizes of mouse accessories that could make microcomputers totally understandable in human terms, or *user friendly*. (See Figure 2.11.)

Light Pens

Some types of light pens work in much the same way as the mouse, but they are very different in appearance. A light pen looks like an ordinary fountain pen with a cord attached to it that connects to your microcomputer (see Figure 2.12). Some models of light pens are used to direct the cursor through movements that are traced on a surface; others are touched directly to the screen surface to do such things as draw lines, move icons, and so on.

The light pen lets you interact directly with what you see on the monitor, turning the microcomputer screen into a canvas or sketch pad for drawing or painting. Working with a light pen is very similar to coloring with a crayon or pointing a finger, thereby enabling children to interact quickly and easily with the microcomputer. Children do not need to be able to read or recognize shapes that utilizing the keyboard demands of them.

The quality of a light pen is usually determined by its resolution, or its degree of accuracy. One other factor that determines the light pen's overall performance is the quality and accuracy of the on/off switch. This on/off function can be either a mechanical part of the light pen or a part of the software program. With a

FIGURE 2.11 A Mouse

(Courtesy of Apple Computer, Inc.)

FIGURE 2.12   The Gibson Light Pen from Koala Technologies
(Courtesy of Koala Technologies Corporation)

mechanical switch, you usually push a small button on the side of the pen, touch a specific key on the keyboard of the microcomputer, or touch the tip of the pen to the monitor screen to select a location on the screen. With the on/off function as a part of the software program, the program constantly checks the screen location and assumes you have selected a specific location when you stop moving the pen.

When choosing a light pen, you will want to consider at least three factors. First is the degree of resolution the particular application requires. If the light pen will be used to create designs, play games, make menu selections, or introduce children to microcomputers, a light pen costing from forty to sixty dollars (including pen and software) will do the job very nicely.

The second factor is the quality and variety of software that works with the pen. A slightly more expensive pen that comes with plenty of software is probably a better value than a less expensive pen with only one application.

The third factor that must be considered when using the pen with elementary age children is how easy it is to use. For young users, a pen with a software switch where the pen is pointed to get a reaction may be the best. Mechanically triggered pens, however, do give more control over the input of information to the microcomputer. These pens require a child to find the correct key on the keyboard or push the trigger while aiming the pen. Although pushing a button on the side of the pen is simple to do, the act of pushing the switch may move the pen. The push-tip (push the pen tip on the monitor screen surface) is probably the most efficient method, but it is only available on the most expensive pens and can cost as much as $150.

As a teacher in the classroom, responsible for a computer literacy program, you should consider the purchase of a light pen. This can be a very worthwhile investment that can keep the lines of communication open between the students and the microcomputer.

Touch Screens

Imagine sitting in front of the computer screen examining a list of activities that you can do. This is common practice, to be sure, but if your machine is equipped with a touch screen, the next steps are quite atypical. For example, if word processing is the choice, a simple touch of your finger on the screen at the location of the word processing option will put you in this mode.

The word processing functions are also activated by the touch of a finger. If editing is needed, this can be done without the need to type in commands. As mentioned previously, there are numerous applications for which touch screens can be used. Despite this, they are infrequently seen in the schools; perhaps the lack of fine discrimination between detailed points is a factor.

Some very interesting applications of touch screens are used in entertainment and business enterprises. For example, Walt Disney's EPCOT Center combines infrared touch technology with color video monitors to create an interactive visitor information system. Visitors to the amusement park can secure a wide variety of information about the park, its various attractions, their locations, and special features by touching one of the many video monitors located throughout the park. These monitors are a great attraction to people who visit the EPCOT Center.

The Apple Computer Corporation uses infrared touch technology to provide its dealers with an interesting electronic point-of-purchase sales technique. The dealer can place the freestanding display system in a prominent location in the store where customers can use the system to view one or more displays of information about various microcomputer systems.

Many teachers are exploring the use of the touch screen, especially with young children. This technology provides yet another way for students to bypass the keyboard while effectively inputting data into their microcomputer.

Graphics Tablets

Electronic drawing is possible on a sensitive surface called a graphics tablet. Most graphics tablets are a one-quarter to one-inch-thick plotting board that is generally six to twelve inches on a side. Some varieties have a pen or arm attached to this plotting board that is utilized in the drawing operation. Others employ a stylus for pointing and drawing. As the pen or arm contacts the surface of the plotting board, a difference in electrical charge is detected, and the drawn image is stored in the memory of the microcomputer. (A specific device known as a digitizer converts the analog measurements into digital form.) One type of tablet contains a horizontal and vertical grid of sensor wires, usually covered with a thin plastic overlay to protect the wires from pen or stylus movement. As the pen or stylus moves over the grid, it makes contact with specific points and these points are correlated with points on the display screen; thus a screen graphic is created that replicates the combination of movements on the tablet. The data from the graphics are stored in memory so the completed drawing can be converted to hard copy on a printer or plotter or stored on a data disk for later use in a program.

One of the popular graphics tablets is the KoalaPad (see Figure 2.13). This is a slender, hand-held, six-by-eight-inch pad with a touch-sensitive surface. To use the pad, the student selects an option from a menu (much the same as with the touch screen mentioned above) and then proceeds to create various kinds of displays by using commands that are defined in the menu. This device emphasizes a discovery approach to learning. It permits the user to design an endless array of graphic pictures quite simply. Other kinds of activities are also possible with this affordable and intriguing device.

Another of these devices is the VersaWriter, which has an arm that can be moved about on the tablet. Commands are entered on the keyboard, and the movement of the arm causes lines to be generated that reflect the nature of the command. For example, different line widths can be selected and the nature of the line will vary in response. Routines such as circle generation and color fills are also provided.

The VersaWriter is a digitizer consisting of a one-quarter-inch-thick plotting board with a clear plastic overlay. Attached to the plotting board is the double-

FIGURE 2.13   A KoalaPad from Koala Technologies
(Courtesy of Koala Technologies Corporation)

jointed drawing arm with digitizers/potentiometers at the elbow and top locations and a magnifier lens with a dot in the center at the end of the arm.

The VersaWriter also has a two disk software package that provides several interesting features and capabilities. Disk one displays a menu that will allow you to draw, calibrate the system (tablet), recall a picture from a disk, catalog the disk, add text to a picture, calculate area and distance, and display a set of electrical schematic symbols. The software allows you to draw in different scales (125 × to 4 ×), so the original drawing can be reduced or expanded on the monitor screen. Six colors are available, and five different line widths, from a thin line to a paint-brush effect, can be chosen. Other options on the "draw" menu allow you to create a shape tablet, store a picture, or recall a picture that has previously been drawn. The finished graphic design, including the printed text, can be produced in hard copy on a printer or plotter and could be inserted into a software program that you have created. The plotting board, arm, and software sell for about three hundred dollars.

We have included a rather detailed discussion of KoalaPad and VersaWriter, two of the more popular graphics tablets, to give you an idea of how they work and their capabilities for producing graphic images that could be utilized in a computer literacy program or in a school-produced package.

Voice Input Devices

Voice input technology is merely in its infancy, but some rather astounding results are being seen. Most of the voice input devices are quite expensive, but a few are within the range of affordability for many schools.

For about one thousand dollars it is possible to purchase a unit that enables the computer to learn up to one thousand words, which are divided into twenty-five groups of forty words each. This system, called Shadow/VET, is produced by Scott Instruments of Denton, Texas. The system includes a headset, a small interface box, and a peripheral card that interfaces the system to the computer. This system has its own memory on the interface board so as not to use any of the computer memory space. A master vocabulary allows the user to switch back and forth between all of these forty-word lists without even touching the keyboard.

Another device, called Apple Voice Input Module, comes complete with an interface board, a microphone, a utility desk, and an instruction manual.

Having the computer understand verbal input is termed "speech recognition." The opposite transaction—having the computer speak to the user—is called "speech synthesis." Although the latter is not an input operation, this is an appropriate place to mention it.

The categories of voice input are speech recognition and speaker verification. Most input devices are of the speaker verification type; that is, the microcomputer is only capable of recognizing a voice that has been preprogrammed into the memory of the computer. When someone talks to the computer, her speech is converted into digital information and stored in memory. When the user says that word again, the computer takes that digital data and compares it to words in memory. In essence, the computer develops a pattern for each word and then searches through the memory to see if there are any other patterns of the same size and shape. If one is found, the computer then follows the instructions associated with that word.

The uses of voice input devices in the field of special education are promising, to say the least. One use is as a reader for those who are blind, and a second application is as a voice for those who are unable to speak. Consider those who cannot speak distinctly, for example, but who can make consistent sounds. The computer will recognize those sounds just as it will recognize English, French, Russian, or Latin. Attach a speech synthesizer, such as the Votrax Type 'N Talk (Maryland Computer Services, Inc., Forest Hill, Maryland), and the microcomputer will translate these sounds into plain English.

The Votrax system uses a synthesizer board that is capable of producing or vocalizing sixty-four different phonemes—phonetic sounds such as *th, sh,* and long and short vowels. The on-board microprocessor converts letters and groups of letters into digital code corresponding to these phonemes, employing English pronunciation rules; for example, the silent e rule tells the microprocessor that an e is silent when it is followed by a space or by punctuation and preceded by a combination of one or more vowels and a consonant. Approximately four hundred such pronunciation rules enable the system to produce intelligible speech. The system provides the capability of reading aloud a single character or symbol, a full word, a line, or an entire page. Its full speech capability allows it to pronounce any word, no matter how the word is spelled.

One last consideration is for those who cannot talk at all. With any form of physical movement, they can train the microcomputer to recognize Morse code or any other combination of sounds. The possibilities are endless, and the future holds great promise for devices that will be less expensive, easier to use, and more human-sounding in character.

Joysticks

The name *joystick* comes from the steering device used in older airplanes, but the resemblance stops there. Electronic joysticks are used to move the cursor around on the screen. When a game is involved, the cursor may be replaced by a movable configuration that can take the form of a rocket ship or just about anything else. A button on the joystick serves as a firing device, which triggers a response when the screen cursor or other symbol is in the proper position in relation to other display elements. For example, when the cursor is positioned over an option on a menu in a word processing program, a push on the button activates that option. Or, by moving the cursor to various points on the screen and pressing the button, it is possible to create graphics of various kinds. (See Figure 2.14.)

The electronic construction of joysticks is very simple. They consist basically of two channels corresponding to the x and y coordinates of a two-dimensional grid or graph. By moving the joystick, you move an electrical potentiometer (like the volume control on a stereo music system) that changes an electrical current from high to low voltage. These currents must be converted from analog mea-

FIGURE 2.14 A Joystick from Kraft Systems
(Courtesy of Kraft Systems)

surements to digital form. The electronics logic for this process is built into the microcomputer, not the joystick, and is activated when the joystick is plugged into the joystick port on the computer.

A few inexpensive joystick designs do not use potentiometers. Instead, contact switches are mounted in a circle around the joystick handle. Moving the handle closes one of the switches and thus indicates the general direction of motion.

The joystick "fire" buttons are simple on/off switches. Input from the joystick can be read almost instantaneously by the microcomputer. Most microcomputers can read the button inputs 100,000 times per minute; thus the microcomputer can react very quickly to any shots a user may make while using the joystick.

Optical Mark Readers

A device that is being utilized by many schools, the optical mark reader (OMR), has been around for many years. Optical mark readers are devices that detect marks in predetermined locations on a document (generally a card or sheet of paper). As the document is fed into the unit, the OMR's transport mechanism moves the document past a light source (often a laser beam). Timing marks printed in a track on one margin of the document tell the OMR when to read and examine the reflected or transmitted light. This information is fed into the micro-processor as digital data that the microcomputer can interpret and process.

In test scoring, the answer key is first passed through the unit. The OMR will then compare all the rest of the documents with this key. Most marks are made as dark lead pencil marks; however, some OMRs can read punched cards.

Schools and districts have used OMRs to grade objective tests automatically for several years. Recent developments in technology have made it possible to attach OMRs to microcomputers, eliminating the time delay previously encoun-tered when the marked cards had to be sent to a large mainframe computer for processing—a mainframe generally located out of the city and sometimes even out of the state. By linking the OMRs to the school's microcomputer, it is possible for students to get immediate feedback about test results and for problems of individual learners to be detailed quickly. OMRs also save teachers a great amount of time in the process of paper correcting.

Connecting an optical mark reader to a microcomputer is a simple process. Some OMR models come equipped with an interface board for a given microcom-puter model. In some cases, no additional equipment is necessary. Just plug the interface board into a peripheral slot and connect the cable from the OMR to the board. If the OMR unit is not designed to interface directly with a certain micro-computer model, then a serial or parallel interface and appropriate cable must be purchased. Once the unit is connected to a microcomputer, appropriate soft-ware designed to compile the data will be needed.

In addition, you will need special cards or sheets for students to use in marking their answers to standardized tests and surveys or for other applications. Cards can be purchased that are marked for letter answers (*a, b, c, d, e*) and for number answers (1, 2, 3, 4, 5). Also, special-purpose cards—such as those for attendance, absence verification, ballots, inventory, scheduling, and class registration—can be obtained.

Depending on the software package purchased with the optical mark reader, other common applications (besides test checking) of OMR technology include monitoring of achievement objectives, keeping attendance, reporting grades, scheduling media equipment, keeping library records, and recording inventory for textbooks, films, and other equipment.

CD-ROM

Many classroom teachers have wished they had an entire encyclopedia available in some format so students could use the capabilities of a microcomputer to do their research papers. Now, using the technology of compact disk read only mem-ory (CD-ROM), Grolier's *Electronic Encyclopedia* is available. Many other soft-ware publishers are making available data bases, music, picture files, and atlases, gazeteers, and science files. What is this technology, how does it work, and can schools afford to add this peripheral to their computer systems?

The technology behind CD-ROM was a direct outcome of the development of mass-produced lasers. For the CD-ROM to work, a technology had to be per-fected by which light is generated in regular waves, so that it can be focused into a very tight, ultra-small beam. It was also necessary to contain the whole mechanism into a small, compact package that could be connected easily to a microcomputer.

CD-ROM drives are able to read digital information from the disk by interpreting the laser beam as it is reflected off the shiny surface of the disk. As the disk is manufactured, tiny pits are cut into the surface. These pits and the smooth areas between them are read as the 0s and 1s that computers process as digital information.

A CD-ROM disk is very durable. It measures $4\frac{3}{4}$ inches across. The lower surface is etched at the factory with the lands (smooth areas) and pits, and then the whole surface is covered with a thick coating of clear plastic. This transparent surface can be penetrated easily by the laser beam but protects the lands and pits from wear and abrasion. CD-ROM disks can be handled without damage by students using reasonable care, unlike magnetic diskettes, which are more easily damaged.

CD-ROM disks can hold a great deal of information. One disk has a storage capacity of 550 to 600 megabytes. This huge storage capacity means that one disk can store 15 hours of audio and 15,000 color images or combinations thereof. The entire 20-volume, nine-million word version of Grolier's *Electronic Encyclopedia,* with its extensive index, does not completely fill the capacity of one disk.

Drives for the Mac and Apple IIe and IIgs computers, the CD-ROM drive for Tandy/Radio Shack's computer, and IBM PCs are available for between $550 and $1200. The price has been steadily declining and soon the price for a reliable CD-ROM drive should be under $500. This price range makes it possible for many schools to consider the purchase of this exciting peripheral device.

CD-ROM disk technology has advanced to the point where it is possible to purchase disk drives with the capability to record locally produced programs. This technology makes it feasible for programs originating in your school district to be recorded on a CD-ROM disk and incorporated into the local school curriculum. The only drawback to this technology is that it is a bit more expensive than a nonprogrammable CD-ROM drive, but as the technology continues to evolve, the price will continue to drop.

Videodisc Technology

"Today's students have become sophisticated consumers of imagery. Videodisc technology is one way to bring imagery to the classroom." This statement by John Phillipo typifies educators' views on this new technology. Just what is a videodisc and why would teachers be interested in them?

The laser videodisc player looks much like a standard record player except that it only plays laser-encoded videodiscs. Unlike the needle on a record, the laser system does not touch the disc, thereby protecting and preserving the disk surface, which in turn maintains the high quality of the medium.

The technology of the videodisc is much like that of the CD-ROM discussed earlier in this chapter. The player retrieves information from a laser beam that is projected on the lands and pits forming the 54,000 concentric grooves on each side of the disk. The lands and pits are interpreted as the 0s and 1s that computers process as digital information. The disc spins at 1,800 revolutions per minute and one revolution can play back one frame/image of video information. Thus the player is capable of playing back approximately 30 frames (images) per second during normal play.

The playback speed can also be altered by a Still/Stop command, which stops the disc on a single frame allowing the laser to read one revolution again and again, thereby creating a high resolution "freeze" or still frame. Other motion controls include Slow Motion, a process in which the playback is done frame by frame, and Scan, which moves the disc at a fast rate of speed and allows for identification of the various video images contained on the disc. As most videodiscs come with a printed frame and chapter index and the player has an Index/Frame Display function, the user is able to see which frame or chapter of the videodisc is being displayed.

Videodisc programs and players have available the use of two separate and discrete audio tracks. The videodisc player can be controlled to play back both tracks at once or either audio track independently. This feature allows for great flexibility in presenting audio materials.

Videodisc players can be interfaced with most makes of microcomputers and are priced between seven hundred and one thousand dollars. This technology provides an exciting alternative to teachers who desire to couple the microcomputer to a device that presents motion and sound with the interactive capability of the microcomputer. Videodisc players have proved reliable and user-friendly. Teachers generally have little difficulty hooking them to a microcomputer and using the various features. (See Figure 4.1.)

There is one drawback with this technology. The laserdisc is currently read-only; you cannot program your own materials onto the disk without the addition of a very expensive (fifteen to twenty thousand dollar) laserdisc recorder. However, erasable videodiscs are now appearing that will allow the teacher to "master" her own discs.

MAINTENANCE AND REPAIR

Now that you have been introduced to the computer, how it works, and the peripheral devices that can be added to make it a complete system, it is time to discuss some principles of computer maintenance and repair.

The following are some specific measures you can take to keep your microcomputer system in operation.

Troubleshooting

1. Repeated heating and cooling caused by turning the computer on and off can cause chips to work their way out of the sockets—push them down periodically. Be sure to "ground" yourself by touching the power pack before you touch the chips.

2. Keep the ventilation slots clear of obstructions. If you add a number of interface boards to your microcomputer, you increase the chances of heat buildup. This is especially true if you are working with a Macintosh computer. Do not let anything cover these ventilation slots.

3. When putting an accessory of some sort into an interface slot or a chip socket, be very careful not to bend one of the small chip leads. A good procedure is to push the chips or leads halfway into the socket and stop. Carefully examine all the pins to see if they are entering the socket straight. If they are, push the chip or lead completely in.

4. Periodically clean chip leads with a cotton swab dipped in alcohol. Oxidation and dirt are the main causes of chip problems.

5. Periodically use a can of compressed air to clean between the keys on your keyboard.

6. Do not slam the little door after inserting the diskette into your disk drive. Slamming may cause crimping of the center of the hole of the diskette. When this happens, the disk may start to give input/output errors. Open the drive door carefully so you do not cause it to drop out of alignment.

7. Periodic cleaning of your printer is messy but a good troubleshooting procedure. Clean the printhead, the "rails" on which the printhead travels, and the platen (or roller assembly) with a cotton swab dipped in alcohol.

8. Do not connect or disconnect power devices while the computer's power is on. (Power devices are peripherals that get their power directly from the computer itself.) Do not even open the lid of the computer with the power on.

9. We strongly suggest that you do not use double-sided disks. First, you must cut a notch on the other side of the diskette in the exact same place as the original notch. Second, most diskettes, even though certified as double-sided, do not have the same quality control on both sides. Third, when you turn the disk over, the good (certified) side of the recording medium is now coming in contact with the pressure pad. If this pad is dirty or contaminated, you're transferring this dirt and grime to the good (recorded) side with the great possibility of destroying the good side along with your stored data. We think it is much better to spend an extra dollar or so on another disk.

Preventive Maintenance

Preventive maintenance can prevent, or at least delay, breakdowns that can be costly and inconvenient. An ounce of prevention is worth more than five pounds of cure when working with microcomputers. When something goes wrong with a microcomputer, someone has to bundle it up and take it in for repair, where it might be tied up for days or weeks.

The first rule of preventive maintenance is to avoid causing problems by your own actions. If it isn't broken, don't tinker with the mechanism just because you think it's fun. If it is broken, find out what you should do before you start to fix it. A careful look at the operating manual that came with the computer is a good first start—be sure to read it thoroughly before you do anything else.

Cleanliness is one of the cardinal rules of prevention. *Never* permit food or drink to come near the computer. The smallest amount of coffee or cola can put the keyboard out of action. The keyboard is really a series of little switches. As you push a key, you make a contact and complete a circuit. A small drop of liquid can short out the circuit and destroy the keyboard circuitry.

If you should get a small amount of grease or oil (from fingerprints, for example) or human hairs on the surface of your diskette, that segment will be effectively isolated from the reading mechanism of the disk drive. This will prevent the data stored in that area from being accessed; you might lose thousands of words of information from one single fingerprint. Precautions in handling the disk are listed earlier in this chapter.

Try to keep dust at a minimum in your environment. Dust is a hazard to the computer, but the main problem is a layer of dust that may collect on the surface of diskettes. If this occurs, there may well be segments from which data cannot be successfully accessed. One effective way to control dust is to cover the disk drives and computer with dust covers when not in use. Such covers are inexpensive and are available from many computer stores. If you do not have the budget to purchase a dust cover, construct one from butcher paper, newspaper, chart paper, or something similar. Just a few minutes of your time to make or secure a dust cover may prevent problems later when a diskette, disk drive, or computer fails because of accumulated dust and dirt. Always be sure to cover your computer system before the cleaning crew comes in to stir up the dust on the floor. Chalkboard dust can also cause serious problems.

Tobacco smoke can cause a disk drive head to read and write erratically. Each smoke particle is a small ball, and it can lift the head off the diskette sufficiently to keep it from sensing the data magnetically arranged on the surface. Some commercial centers forbid smoking in computer rooms, even though the air going to their disk drive systems is filtered. Microcomputer disk drive systems do not have filters on them; these are installed at the request of the user. If you plan to use a computer extensively, this may be incentive enough for you to give up the smoking habit.

The hair of pets (as well as of humans) seems to gravitate naturally to keyboards, as do other small particles such as paper shavings, strands of clothing, or chalk dust. You can remove them with a strip of masking tape simply by holding the tape so the sticky side faces the offending items, pressing lightly, then pulling away. The hair or other particle will be securely adhered to the tape and your problems should be solved. Never use a liquid spray cleaner on the keyboard; the liquid may be forced into the contact areas and the keyboard will not function.

A magnetic field, which can exist in unusual and unexpected places, can raise havoc with your diskettes. Any magnet can cause problems, and all motors produce a magnetic field. A small vacuum cleaner or electric drill used in close proximity to stored diskettes, for example, has the potential to destroy the stored information. Most screwdrivers and other tools are slightly magnetic and should not be used around diskettes. Never place your diskettes on top of the television or monitor: the field within the monitor can affect the data on the diskette. If you have an auxiliary fan or a surge protector on the computer (this add-on is discussed later in this chapter), do not lay a diskette on top of the running fan. The magnetic field created by the fan motor can alter the data on the diskette.

Static electricity is another enemy of data stored on diskettes and can also be a potential destroyer of a chip. You may need to modify your classroom or other facility if you find that static electricity is a problem. For example, you may find it necessary to cover a carpet with an antistatic pad or to place the computer on a grounded antistatic pad. You may even need to obtain a pair of shoes with soles that cut down on the potential of static electricity generation. It is possible for a charge of electricity to be strong enough to wipe out data on a diskette or destroy a chip in a disk drive or microcomputer instantly. Humidifiers may be useful: moist air seems to help cut down the amount of static electricity that is generated. When you remove the cover of the computer to examine the motherboard or to place an interface board in a peripheral slot, be sure to touch the power source pack (see Figure 2.4) so you will discharge any static electricity before touching any of the RAM or ROM chips and the other interface boards. A large charge of static electricity is capable of completely destroying the CPU.

While you are examining the inside of the computer, it is important that you take off any metal rings or dangling bracelets. *Do not* allow metal jewelry to touch inside parts of the computer: it can damage chips or other parts of the microcomputer.

Some disk drives frequently damage the hole in the center of floppy diskettes; diskettes that are used frequently also suffer from wear around the center hole. If the wear is excessive, the diskette will not work properly and will eventually become useless. You can repair the hole with an attachable reinforcing ring that extends the life of the diskette, but a better approach is to attach the ring before the damage has occurred or, even wiser, purchase only diskettes that have a reinforcing ring already built in.

Even if you are using reinforced diskettes, it is a useful precaution to close the door to the disk drive only partially at first, thus sliding the diskette one way or the other toward the center of the drive. After this brief hesitation, the door can be completely closed; the hub of the drive should be precisely aligned with the hole in the diskette.

Another concern in preserving your diskettes is to store them always in a vertical position. You should not stack one on top of another or allow anything heavy to press down on them. It is a good idea to store the diskettes in a strong plastic, fiber, or metal box. Your archival copies should be played at least once each year: if the diskette is not rotated slightly, there is a possibility, after prolonged storage, that magnetic distortion may occur. An important item to add to the computer system to help prevent component breakdowns is a unit containing a surge protector, a cooling fan, and a heavy-duty switch.

During a month's time, a personal computer that is plugged into the 120-volt power outlet will be subjected to up to a hundred jolts of electricity of over 500 volts each. These power surges are devastating to a microcomputer. Power line glitches, which are very common, can be caused by such things as a storm, a refrigerator cycling on and off, or a printer being powered up. These high-intensity surges last only billionths of a second, but they measure between 400 and 25,000 volts. Sudden surges in electricity can instantly erase the computer's memory or ruin an entire diskette filled with data. About 80 percent of all microcomputer malfunctions can be attributed to power line glitches.

To protect your microcomputer from these glitches, it is critical that you purchase a safety device known as a surge protector. It is also advisable to purchase an auxiliary fan to push cool air inside the microcomputer. Microcomputers run at relatively cool temperatures compared with mainframe computers; however, if the machine is used constantly for long periods of time, and if several interface boards are plugged into a peripheral slot in the motherboard, overheating can be a serious problem. This overheating can be aggravated by the external environment—a hot summer day, for example, or poor ventilation.

You can purchase a unit for under sixty dollars that provides a surge protector, a fan, a heavy-duty switch, and a receptacle that allows you to plug in both the computer and the monitor. This unit is a very good investment and could save the life of a chip or diskette (see Figure 2.15).

Now that we have considered several aspects of preventive maintenance, we will detail what you might do to actually fix some of the problems that could go wrong with your microcomputer.

HANDS-ON MAINTENANCE

First, let's look at cables. Any piece of equipment connected to another by a cable is certain to experience some trouble from time to time. If a cable connector becomes unplugged, the equipment will not operate. If it becomes partially unplugged, all kinds of odd happenings can occur. If your computer is acting strangely, or if it won't function at all, check all of the connections. This sounds

FIGURE 2.15 Surge Protector, Fan Switch Unit

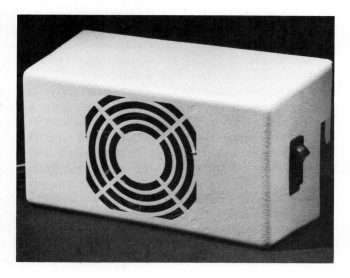

too simple even to mention, but often a connection that appears to be tight and sound is not, and a bit of wiggling will again mate up the two connectors and put your computer back in running order.

Most plug problems arise from lack of contact between the mating plugs, and the most frequent offender is an edge connector. Some circuit boards have notches at one edge that allow a plug to make contact with a number of circuits on the board. These circuits are manufactured from copper, which corrodes when exposed to the atmosphere. Expensive computers have gold-plated edge connector contacts, but most microcomputers use bare copper to cut down on expense. Periodically, or when a problem arises, unplug the computer from the power line, disconnect each edge connector, and check to see if any corrosion has occurred on the contact areas. If there seems to be a residue (it will look darker than the rest of the surrounding copper area), you can generally remove it by carefully rubbing a red pencil eraser over the surfaces (one that is clean and not covered with graphite from paper erasing). In effect, you are erasing the residue from the contact points. The resulting eraser crumbs must be removed before the surfaces are reunited: blow carefully on the surfaces, taking care that you do not spray moisture on the contact points as you blow away the eraser particles. A can of compressed air, available at a photo store, can be used for this purpose, as well as for removing particles from the keyboard and other areas of the computer.

You can polish the contacts by obtaining a can of Cramolin spray from an electronics supply house and applying a very small amount to the contacts. *Do not* use the ordinary oily television tuner or contact cleaner and lubricant: this cleaner picks up dust and can cause intermittent problems.

You should make it a point to check all the cables periodically to make certain that they are not bent or kinked in ways that might lead to wire breakage. Whenever you move or reroute a cable, take the time to straighten it and to smooth out any twists that might have occurred. Also, look carefully for frayed insulation, which most likely indicates damage to the wires. In some cases these frayed areas can be repaired with electrical tape, but you may need to replace the cable if the damage is extensive. Inspecting the cables regularly is the kind of preventive maintenance that can extend their life significantly.

After a microcomputer system has been in operation for several years and a number of peripheral devices have been added, you may have accumulated several different cables to connect a printer, disk drives, synthesizers, modems, extra monitors, and so forth. These cables look somewhat alike, but most of them are different—in the number of internal wires or edge connector pins they contain, for example. Sometimes these differences can lead to system failure if a cable is reversed or is plugged in at the wrong place. Also, forcing a plug into a connector could do serious damage to pins or housings. It is a good idea, to prevent any disastrous damage to a plug or component, to label both ends of each cable. If a cable can be inserted two ways, label the top or right side. If there is space on the plug, place the label directly on the plug; if not, place the label on the cable.

After you use your disk drive for a period of time, iron oxide from the surface of the diskettes will build up on the face of the read-write head. This residue buildup must be removed if first-rate operation (accurate reading or writing of data) is to be maintained. To accomplish this, a liquid cleaning solution is applied to a head-cleaning diskette made of a plastic mesh; the diskette is then rotated against the head for a few seconds (usually *only* thirty seconds). There are a few operational safeguards that you should observe when using the head-cleaning diskette. Because you cannot see when the oxide is removed, the tendency is to use the cleaner for too long a period of time; but thirty seconds is sufficient. Also, it is possible to insert the diskette upside down, which will not clean the head. The label on the cleaning diskette should be up, with your thumb on the label, just as when inserting a regular program diskette. It is good practice to read the instructions that come with the cleaning diskette carefully before using it. Incidentally, if you are using a cassette recorder rather than disk drives, you can obtain a cleaning cassette that does the same job as the diskette cleaner.

It is possible to clean the read-write heads on your disk drives by actually opening up the case and going directly to the heads. This is the best way, but it involves an element of risk. In some cases, warranties may be voided if you open the equipment, so be sure to check on this aspect. If the warranty has expired, however, this is no longer a factor.

If you intend to clean the heads directly, you will need a kit of materials—the kind used to clean audio tape recorder heads—which you can purchase from an electronics or sound store. Be sure that you know how to open the disk drive case before you begin. The technical manual provided by the manufacturer of the disk drive system will spell out precisely how to do this. Read this manual carefully so you do not damage the case or internal mechanisms of the disk drive. For most disk drive systems, the procedure is a simple matter of removing a few screws and sliding off the case.

Locate the head; if there is a red smudge on it, indicating a buildup of iron oxide, put some of the cleaning solution on one of the cotton swabs in the kit and wipe off the smudge, being careful to touch only the head with the moistened swab. The residue should come right off with little effort. Use only the cleaning solution—*not* the lubricant that comes with the kit, which is designed for tape, not for diskettes. Finally, put everything back together, being careful to line up all holes properly and to replace the screws and other parts you might have disassembled.

Major Repairs

If you need to have repairs done to your computer beyond the simple preventive maintenance and hands-on techniques outlined above, here are a few words of advice.

If you must ship your computer for service, using commercial methods (for example, U.S. Parcel Post, United Parcel Service, or a freight line), be sure to ship it in the original boxes in which it was sent to you, along with all of the original packing material. These containers are designed to protect the equipment from damage while in transit. Many hundreds of microcomputers are damaged each year because they were packed inadequately. Be sure to send all the parts that may be giving you trouble. In case of doubt send everything. Write a brief explanation of the malfunction, even though you may have called the repair agency detailing the problem before you sent the equipment. The note of explanation will help the technician to diagnose and correct the difficulty more accurately and quickly.

When you have adequate local service, do not ship the equipment from your area. Be especially careful in transporting the microcomputer system to the repair agency: occasionally, additional damage is inflicted by a sudden stop, a sharp turn, or other traffic problems en route to the store. Tell the technician as precisely as possible what the malfunction is, how often it occurs, and so on. An intermittent problem is hard to track down, and the service department may have trouble duplicating it in the shop. Your verbal or written description will help.

Following are some additional suggestions that may make the repair or servicing of your computer system less painful and less costly.

1. Join a users' group, if available, and possibly get free service. Most users' groups have engineers, technicians, or others capable of solving system problems. However, you generally get what you pay for, and if the service is free you can't expect much in the way of a warranty on the workmanship. In addition, part-time technicians may have trouble getting certain specialized parts.
2. Try to find out which service centers are the best. Get referrals from users who know. Your state department of public instruction (microcomputer division), the local microcomputer department at the state university or college, or a trusted friend can help here.
3. Get an estimate on how long the repair is likely to take. Some repair shops have facilities to provide one-day service. The normal repair will take two or three days, or it may take weeks if a special part must be ordered from the factory. In such cases it may pay to shop around to see if another repair agency has the special part in stock.
4. Check into the availability of loaners. Although this is generally not standard procedure, if you protest loudly enough you may be able to have the use of one while your system is being repaired.
5. Cultivate a friendship with the people at your local computer store. If you consistently purchase printer ribbons, diskettes, cables, diskette storage cases, and other equipment from them, chances are good that they will give you preferred-customer treatment on repairs.
6. When you pick up the repaired system, ask the service center to list in detail exactly what was done. Talk to the service manager or service technician if possible. Beware of motherboard or interface board swaps that fix your problem by substituting a used board that may have its own problems. (Jot down serial numbers of your boards before sending the equipment in for service, then check to see if an unauthorized substitution was made.)

7. If a motherboard, interface board, or other component such as a disk drive is replaced, the warranty on the new component should match that of the original. If the component fails within the warranty period—usually ninety days or, in some cases, one year—you shouldn't have to pay for repair or replacement.

8. Have the service shop call you if the repair will exceed a certain amount. Just as with repairs to your automobile, if you feel that the estimated charge is unreasonable, take the system somewhere else.

9. When you pick up the repaired system, try it on the spot. This will take some additional time and, perhaps, cause some frustration, but the inconvenience will be worth it because it is possible that a subtle problem may not be fixed. If your original problem occurred intermittently, ask the service people if they operated the system long enough to see if the problem reappeared after the repair. You don't want to take the microcomputer system back to your school or home only to have the problem reappear the first time the system is used.

SUMMARY

At the beginning of this chapter we discussed the fact that teachers need to know how a microcomputer works so they can, in turn, assist students as they learn about computers. Although one can operate a computer without knowing about the mechanics involved, teachers have special concerns that are quite different from those of the typical computer user. Because they are called upon to respond to the needs of students and to provide a wide range of information in response to questions that are often spontaneous, teachers must have at their command a considerable store of knowledge. Knowing something about how a computer manages data and instructions, and how it is constructed internally, will better prepare the teacher to build upon student curiosity as it relates to these matters. Additionally, if a unit on computer literacy is undertaken, the subject of how computers work is quite appropriate; it is also very interesting to most students. We discussed the differences and similarities between the three classes of computers—mainframe, minicomputer, and microcomputer—and included some idea of basic costs of each.

The binary system that is used by all computers to process data was illustrated, including a discussion of bits, bytes, and the ASCII code. The methodology utilized in the binary code to represent different letters, numbers, and symbols was explained, including samples of several letters and numbers. All digital computers consist of some basic components, which were discussed in detail: a central processing unit that contains a control unit, an arithmetic unit, and a logic unit. The types of memory, RAM and ROM, were presented, along with a detailed discussion of why one kind is volatile (RAM) and the other nonvolatile (ROM).

We discussed the peripheral devices that can be purchased to make a complete microcomputer system. A minimum system typically consists of the microcomputer, a monitor, and a cassette or disk drive for external storage of data. To this basic system can be added a number of peripheral devices that will add capabilities and special functions deemed essential for a particular program. Peripheral devices, although increasing costs, provide the means for bringing the total world of microcomputing into the school and individual classrooms.

In an introduction to the peripheral storage devices, it was noted that cassette drive systems are losing favor because of the slow speeds at which data is accessed and that the floppy disk is the most common mass storage medium in use in the schools. Procedures for handling and utilizing the disk system were presented in considerable detail. The advantages and disadvantages of a hard disk drive system were outlined.

The three types of monitors—monochrome, composite color, and RGB color—were discussed and contrasted with a regular TV receiver modified for use with a microcomputer. This discussion included strengths of the monitor, such as speed of display and amount of data handled. Five tests that can be applied in the evaluation of a monitor to help ensure the selection of a high-quality device were described. Flat-panel displays (liquid crystal and electroluminescent panel) and the PC projector were also discussed.

The strengths and weaknesses of the two major kinds of printers—impact and nonimpact—were discussed, including samples of what the printing looks like and the capabilities of each type of printer.

The use of the modem to enable the computer to access remote data bases was described. In this chapter and in the chapter on telecommunication, we detail how a school can utilize the services of an information utility and a computerized bulletin board system to bring the world outside into the classroom.

Alternative input devices that supplement the keyboard—including the mouse, light pens, touch screens, graphics tablets, voice input devices, joysticks, optical mark readers, CD-ROM, and videodiscs—were considered from the standpoint of how they function and how they can be used in classroom or school computer programs.

We also included in this chapter some suggestions for the maintenance and repair of a microcomputer system. It is important to protect the microcomputer system and diskettes from dirt and dust, tobacco smoke, and the harmful effect of static electricity. Some suggestions on procedures to facilitate major repairs on the computer system were advanced.

SELF-TEST

1. Describe the differences and similarities between a mainframe, mini, and microcomputer.
2. What is the ASCII code?
3. Discuss the three functions performed by the CPU.
4. Describe the differences between RAM and ROM.
5. Discuss what is meant by *K* and why it is important to have sufficient K in RAM. In your discussion include what sufficient K is.
6. Describe the various components that comprise a typical microcomputer.
7. What is peripheral storage? List the various types of peripheral storage, and discuss why it is important to provide peripheral storage.
8. Describe in detail how to maintain diskettes. Include the proper method for inserting a diskette into a disk drive.
9. What is a hard disk drive?
10. Describe the three types of monitors, and include the strengths and weaknesses of each.
11. How do you test for monitor quality?
12. There are two major types of printer. What are they and what is an example of each? In this discussion, detail the strengths and weaknesses of the various types of printer.
13. What is the difference between a plotter and a printer?
14. Describe the function and operation of the following input devices:
   a. the mouse
   b. light pens
   c. touch screens
   d. graphics tablets
   e. CD-ROM
   f. videodiscs
   g. joysticks
   h. optical mark readers
15. What kinds of preventive maintenance should you do to protect your disk drive? Your diskettes? Your connecting cables? Your computer circuitry?

REFERENCES

Alessi, S. M., and S. R. Trollip. *Computer-based Instruction: Methods and Development*. Englewood Cliffs, N.J.: Prentice-Hall, 1985.

Bitter, G. *Computers in Today's World*. New York: John Wiley & Sons, 1984.

Coburn, E. *Microcomputers: Hardware, Software, and Programming*. Indianapolis: Bobbs-Merrill, 1984.

Kolb, A. "Which Keyboard Should We Use?" *Classroom Computer Learning* (September 1984): 66–69.

McCarthy, R. "Stop the Presses: An Update on Desktop Publishing." *Electronic Learning* (March 1988): 24–30.

McGinty, T. "Text Crunching." *Electronic Learning* (March 1986): 22–26.

Olivas, J. "Laser Printers." *Classroom Computer Learning* (November/December 1987): 49–53.

Olivas, J. "Seeing the Big Picture with the New LCS Screen." *Classroom Computer Learning* (October 1987): 32–37.

"Optical Disc Technology." *Technological Horizons in Education Journal* (November 1988): 58–60.

Phillipo, J. "A Unique Synthesis of Traditional Teaching Tools." *Electronic Learning* (May/June 1988): 60–62.

Phillipo, J. "An Educator's Guide to Interactive Videodisc Programs." *Electronic Learning* (September 1988): 70–75.

Phillipo, J. "Videodisc Players: A Multi-purpose AudioVisual Tool." *Electronic Learning* (November/December 1988): 50–52.

Phillipo, J. "Videodisc's Impact on the Changing Needs of the Learner." *Electronic Learning* (October 1988): 50–52.

Pogue, L. "18- and 24-Wire Printers: A Good Compromise." *Electronic Learning* (October 1987): 61–62.

Pogue, L. "Laser Printers Are Quiet and Fast, But They Do Have Limitations." *Electronic Learning* (March 1988): 34–37.

Pogue, L. "Time and Money Savers: EL Looks at Six Scanners." *Electronic Learning* (February 1988): 20–22, 47.

Powers, M., P. Adams, and H. Mills. *Computer Information Systems Development: Analysis and Design*. West Chicago, Ill.: South-Western Publishing Co., 1984.

Radin, S., and F. Lee. *Computers in the Classroom—A Survival Guide for Teachers*. Chicago: Science Research Associates, 1984.

Reeves, P., and S. Glyer. "Videodisc Applications Bring New Promise to Schools." *Technological Horizons in Education Journal* (September 1988): 68–70.

Salpeter, J. "CS-ROM Update: A Report from the International Conference on CD-ROM." *Classroom Computer Learning* (May/June 1988): 78–81.

Salpeter, J. "Archival Videodisc: A Multi-media Library You Can Hold in One Hand." *Classroom Computer Learning* (January 1987): 49–51.

Salpeter, J. "Interactive Video: The Truth Behind the Promises." *Classroom Computer Learning* (November/December 1986): 26–27.

Spencer, D. *The Illustrated Computer Dictionary*, 3d ed. Columbus, Ohio: Merrill Publishing Co., 1986.

Stallings, W., and R. Blissmer. *Computer Annual*. New York: John Wiley & Sons, 1984.

Stanton, D. "Enhancing Your Image: Three Projection Systems." *Electronic Learning* (April 1988): 44–46.

Stanton, D. "Laser Printers Light the Way to Desktop Publishing." *Electronic Learning* (February 1987): 26–27.

Sullivan, D., et al. *Computing Today: Microcomputer Concepts and Applications*, 2d ed. Boston: Houghton Mifflin Co., 1988.

Tanner, D. and R. Bane. "CD ROM: A New Technology with Promise for Education." *Technological Horizons in Education Journal* (August 1988): 57–60.

Trainor, T. *Computer Literacy: Concepts and Applications*. Santa Cruz, Calif.: Mitchell Publishing Co., 1984.

Tyre, T. "Erasable Optical Media Is Closer to Being Real." *Technological Horizons in Education Journal* (October 1988): 68–72.

Tyre, T. "New CD-ROM Drive Offered for Apple IIs and Macintosh." *Technological Horizons in Education Journal* (May 1988): 56–63.

CHAPTER 3

Instructional Software

CHAPTER TOPICS
☐ The disk operating system and its function
☐ Three modes of instructional computing
☐ The primary kinds of instructional software
☐ A description of computer-managed instruction
☐ Approaches to the evaluation of instructional software
☐ The software evaluation form and how it is used
☐ Help from the publisher: software documentation
☐ Suggestions for previewing instructional programs
☐ Software warranties: protecting your investment
☐ Alternatives to purchasing single programs at full price
☐ Copy protection: ways publishers lock their software
☐ Backup policies
☐ Public domain software: free and inexpensive programs

Over the past few years the quality of computer-based instructional software has undergone considerable improvement. Many of the early programs were written by computer buffs who had little background in learning theory or pedagogy. As educators became familiar with programming techniques, they began to create lessons that met their instructional needs but were far from being technically elegant. Today, however, educational software is typically created by teams made up of educators, programmers, and frequently instructional designers.

This happy coalition has come about for a number of reasons. For one thing, some of the large textbook manufacturers are getting involved, bringing their considerable resources to bear on the problem. Software producers have come to recognize the sales potential of good educational packages for both the school and home markets and have geared up to meet the need. The substantial demand for these programs is attested to by the sales to U.S. schools in 1988, which amounted to approximately 250 million dollars and is increasing all the time.

The distinction made between *software* and *courseware* is worth mentioning here, since you will encounter these terms repeatedly. Software refers to the computer program stored on a medium such as a disk or tape. Courseware is an educational term used to refer to instructional materials consisting of computer-based lessons (or software) together with related print materials such as guides, workbooks, worksheets, appropriate maps and diagrams, teacher's manuals, and perhaps other traditional kinds of media (Figure 3.1).

FIGURE 3.1 Courseware Includes Disk-Based Programs and Various Print Materials (Copyright National Geographic Society)

THE OPERATING SYSTEM

Before moving on to the discussion of the applications programs that permit the computer to change its character and functions, let us consider some little-known, special programs whose sole function is to manage the computer and its peripherals. These essential programs, some of which were built into the computer as special integrated circuit chips at the time it was manufactured, are referred to as *system software*. When programs are stored in the ROM, they are often referred to as *firmware*. (Many kinds of programs, including word processors and graphics programs, are available as firmware.)

The system software most important to the user is the DOS (*disk operating system*). Perhaps you are familiar with this term, having encountered it in articles or in conversations centered around computers. Possibly you have had the occasion actually to use DOS in one way or another. The term MS DOS is close to being a household word in our society; it is the programs that enable the IBM PC and related computers to operate. Basically, the DOS is a collection of instructions designed to do things such as translate the lines of program code into the binary language the computer "understands." When you instruct the computer to save a program you have written, the DOS comes into play; the same is true when you initialize a brand new disk so it can store data.

The operating system is typically stored on a disk that comes with the computer when you purchase it. It is sometimes placed on a disk along with the CAI program. This arrangement enables the user to simply insert the disk in the drive, start the computer, and go immediately to work. All programs written for the Apple II series computers are arranged this way. However, with many instructional and application programs for MS DOS computers, such as the IBM, you must first load the DOS before the instructional program can be run. This is because the computer cannot interact with a program in the disk drive without first having access to the special instructions contained only in the DOS.

Although the different types of DOS are not as numerous as they were a few years back, there are still too many to please most people. The differences in operating systems constitute the most basic reason why a computer of one brand cannot run software written for one of another brand.

Because the DOS is large and complicated, it requires considerable data storage space in the computer. This is one reason it is generally placed on a diskette rather than within the computer. However, with the large ROM capacities of modern-day microcomputers, this is not the concern it once was. More important is the fact that disk-based operating systems are much easier to replace when upgrades are issued. Because of the need to remain on the cutting edge of the technology, manufacturers are constantly upgrading components and programs, including operating systems. You can simply exchange your older version for the newer one, pay a modest fee, and go back to work with your new DOS disk in the drive. You can see that the process would be more complex if the programs were chip-based and located within the computer.

Although you won't be aware of the operating system because it does its work so unobtrusively, the converse is true of the instructional programs that you will run. These are the applications programs that put all that information on the screen, ask for input, give feedback, instruct you, and sometimes frustrate you. Our principal concern in this and upcoming chapters will be for these kinds of programs. Programs of this nature typically are part of a package that includes documentation and, in many cases, textual materials such as workbooks and worksheets. This software (or courseware) makes a special purpose device of the general purpose microcomputer. There are basically three broad categories of instructional software, each of which has a number of unique features.

THREE MODES OF USE

Microcomputers seem to have unlimited uses in education: teachers, administrators, and students discover new applications almost daily. Students create musical works using computers. Aspiring artists replace brushes with keyboards, canvases with display screens. Using the computer as a drill master in math or languages is a common practice. And writers find the word processing functions—composing text, editing it, and printing it—both timesaving and convenient.

The many seemingly unrelated applications make more sense when they are considered within the context of some kind of classification scheme, such as that devised by Robert P. Taylor of Teachers College in New York. This scheme uses three broad headings: the *tutor* mode, the *tool* mode, and the *tutee* mode. When the computer is used to instruct in traditional subject matter areas, it becomes a tutor; when used as an aid to performing a task, it is a tool; when it becomes the object to be studied and programmed, it is a tutee.

The Tutor Mode

Appropriate software enables the computer to tutor the student in a broad range of subjects. The efficiency with which this is done depends upon how expertly the specific program was designed; thus, the more accomplished the instructional designer and the programmer, the better the program. One of the problems intrinsic to teaching programs is that of individualization: whereas a human teacher is able to respond to the needs of the student on the basis of observation and interaction, a programmer must anticipate potential needs and build strategies for dealing with them into the program.

The term computer-assisted instruction is commonly used to describe what takes place in the tutor mode. The broad view of CAI typically includes a number of different program formats, among which is the tutorial. Although drill-and-practice programs, simulations, and instructional games are also classified as types of CAI, confusion can be avoided if the term *tutor* is understood in the broad sense of *teacher*. Thus the teacher (or tutor) may use a tutorial approach when new concepts are being taught but may use drills to reinforce what has been learned during the tutorial sequence (Figure 3.2).

The tutor mode at its best includes diagnostic capabilities to determine the needs of the particular student, prescription functions that provide appropriate content and activities, tutorial functions to assist the student through the program, and assessment and record-keeping capabilities to manage instruction. Although increased interest is being given to other kinds of CAI programs, drill-and-practice activities continue to predominate in the classroom. This condition is bound to change, however, as other kinds of activities, such as word processing and discovery programs, gain in favor and availability.

FIGURE 3.2 Computers Being
Used in the Tutor Mode

(Courtesy of Commodore Electronics Limited)

The Tool Mode

A tool is defined as an instrument for doing work or accomplishing a task. Once
a worker becomes proficient with it, the tool then becomes an extension to be
used intuitively, without the need for premeditation. To observe instances of the
computer being used as a tool it is only necessary to visit a bank, a typical office,
or almost any other place where information is being processed or created—
including the schools.

In the tool mode the computer is not looked upon as an aid to, or surrogate for,
the teacher, as it is in the tutor mode; nor is it an object to be studied, as in the
tutee mode. Rather, it serves a utilitarian function in getting a job done. The
particular program that is working within the computer determines the nature of
the tasks that can be accomplished. When the computer becomes a tool, it assumes
a variety of identities. It may become a paintbrush, enabling an artist to create
colorful graphics; it may change into a magical typewriter that permits the aspiring author to manipulate words and paragraphs with the press of a key; or it may
be transformed into an electronic spreadsheet capable of reflecting constantly
changing data.

The widespread acceptance of tool applications such as word processing and
data base management has caused schools to rethink the meaning of computer
literacy. Where once this term implied programming, it is rapidly coming to mean
the competent use of a variety of computerized tools (for a discussion of this
application, see Chapters 5 and 6).

The Tutee Mode

For a third computer use, the roles are reversed: the machine becomes the tutee
and the student become the tutor. The student teaches the computer by program-

ming it (Figure 3.3). In this approach, learning about computers is seen as a discipline unique unto itself. The subject matter is the computer, rather than a more traditional subject such as English, math, or biology. Students learn first and foremost how to program, but they may also learn something about how the computer works.

Whereas using the computer as a tool can be thought of as an extension of the CAI approach, the idea of programming (the computer as subject matter) is quite a different thing. Software is the essential ingredient in both the tutor and tool modes: it converts the computer from a math to a science teacher or changes it from a special kind of typewriter into an artist's electronic canvas. But when the computer becomes the subject for study, as in the tutee mode, the software, though indispensable, is unobtrusive. The student seems to interact directly with the computer. Where formerly the essence of the machine was masked by the software with which the student interacted, now the machine obeys only those instructions that come directly from the student.

THE KINDS OF CAI SOFTWARE

In the pages that follow, emphasis will be placed upon the varieties of instructional software, that is, software for use in the tutor mode.

No standard classification scheme for educational software or courseware has yet been adopted, and some confusion exists because of this. Some authors place simulations in the larger category of instructional games; others accept drill and

FIGURE 3.3   Programming: The Computer as a Tutee

practice and tutorials as types of CAI programs but place all other types into some other category.

In this text, the system as outlined by P. Coburn et al. in *Practical Guide to Computers in Education* is used with modifications. These authors classify drill and practice, tutorials, simulations, and instructional games as computer-assisted instruction, and they place applications such as word processing and telecomputing into a category they call "instructional/learning tools."

Drill and Practice

Some authors (see Dennis and Kansky) point out that there is a distinction between a drill lesson and a practice lesson. They prefer to use the terms separately, while acknowledging the fact that both share a common purpose: "to fix concepts previously learned." Drills, according to this approach, should be used "to describe activities which seek to fix simple associations such as the names and symbols of the chemical elements." In contrast, a practice activity will lead to "the smooth execution of some process or procedure." Although such a fine distinction does exist, we will follow the popular trend and lump the terms together. If we were involved in the development of instruction and the authoring of lessons rather than in evaluating courseware, a separation of the two activities would definitely be in order.

The drill-and-practice program encourages the improvement of skills that have been previously learned. For example, the design of a math-based program is such that speed and accuracy will be enhanced through its use. Because a certain degree of familiarity with the set of concepts being stressed is required before a student can successfully interact with most drill-and-practice CAI lessons, numerous activities typically precede and accompany the computerized instruction.

Most educators are quick to admit that many of the computer-based drill-and-practice exercises could be carried out just as well and much more economically with such aids as handouts and workbooks. This situation has caused some to feel that drill and practice is not a legitimate use for computers, the argument being that the computer's potential far exceeds running programs of this nature, so other uses should be found that take advantage of the machine's untapped capabilities.

There are certainly compelling arguments, on the other hand, in favor of the drill-and-practice approach. Teachers commonly spend an inordinate amount of time drilling students—which the computer can handle very effectively—when they could be putting their energies into more creative activities. Much of the new drill-and-practice software is designed to take advantage of computer capabilities that were overlooked in the first round of program production. An example of a drill-and-practice program is Basic Math Competency Skill Building from Educational Activities (Figure 3.4). It offers a range of options from rounding off numbers to generating means, medians, and modes and, as with many programs of this kind, provides more than just straight practice—useful tutorial features help students master potentially difficult principles.

Often the drill-and-practice component is built into a game format. An example with a geography theme is Coast to Coast (Mindscape). In this program the stu-

FIGURE 3.4 Two Screen Shots
from a Drill on Fractions

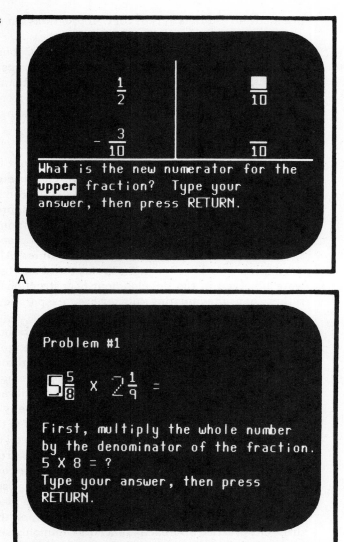

(Courtesy of Educational Activities, Inc.)

dents use a keyboard containing the abbreviations of state names. The objective
is to match the state (by pressing its designated key) with facts displayed on the
screen.

Mention should be made of the increasing use of speech-based drill-and-practice software. This approach is particularly useful for drill programs in reading.
In all areas where young students or those with reading problems are involved,

the use of software of this kind makes understanding directions and instructions much simpler than if students had to read them (Figure 3.5).

Tutorials

In the tutorial mode the computer assumes the role of the teacher who, like Plato of old, involves the students in a one-on-one dialogue that increases in complexity as the lesson progresses. Unlike drill-and-practice programs, which stress the enhancement of known facts, tutorials teach new concepts as they build on old ones. Although a few tutorials require teacher intervention, most are entirely self-contained. A typical lesson of this type begins with an assessment of the student's knowledge, followed by a set of instructions or other essential information so the lesson can proceed.

The nature of the student's response determines what the computer does next. If the response is correct, some appropriate reinforcement occurs and the program moves ahead to the next sequence. If the response is only partially satisfactory, additional information is provided and the student is again questioned. In the case of a totally incorrect response, the computer will present a review sequence before moving ahead.

Students are often confounded by the human-like qualities of a well-designed tutorial: the computer seems to tailor its responses personally. Indeed, the machine seems to be interested in no one but the current user and directs every response to that person alone, even using what may be perceived as a kind of bedside manner—this is really one-on-one instruction at its best.

FIGURE 3.5 Speech-Based Software Enhances Learning for Young Students

(Courtesy of International Business Machines Corporation)

Among the excellent tutorials are the Earth Science Series and the Physical Science Series from Educational Activities. These programs make good use of colorful graphics, provide helpful prompts, and include a record-keeping feature. Interaction is provided by having students manipulate various components on the screen to achieve the proper relationship of one to another. For example, in The Structure of Matter, part of the Physical Science Series, students build atoms and molecules from subatomic particles as shown in Figure 3.6.

Machines, Work, and Energy is another of the Physical Science series of programs. The six basic machines are covered using simulation sequences within the tutorial. An example illustrating the concept of input and output forces is shown in Figure 3.7. At the conclusion of each exercise the student's knowledge of the subject is evaluated, enabling the teacher to decide whether remedial work is necessary before moving on.

Simulations

Programs in the simulation category are designed to represent real-world events in an encapsulated form. Simulations are highly interactive and involve the student as an essential element in the "real-life" situation that is set up. Many excellent simulations are available, but the more complex ones require that a considerable amount of prior study be undertaken before they can be successfully used. For example, the program Three Mile Island is accompanied by a booklet that explains the essentials of operating a nuclear power plant; this supplemental material must be rather thoroughly understood if the computer-based lesson is to be meaningful.

A simulation is typically the central component in a broad-based lesson that includes active student input as one of the major characteristics. By varying the nature and magnitude of the input, students are able to determine what effect such variables would have on an actual system. Through the use of simulations,

FIGURE 3.6 A Screen Shot from the program The Structure of Matter

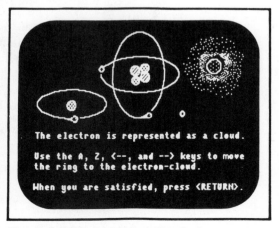

(Courtesy of Educational Activities, Inc.)

FIGURE 3.7 A Screen Shot from Machines, Work, and Energy

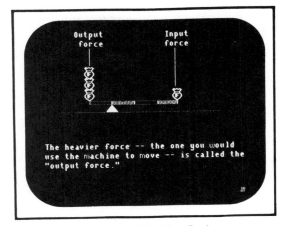

(Courtesy of Educational Activities, Inc.)

students can crash an airplane, go bankrupt, melt down a nuclear reactor, or run a tanker aground on a sandbar without the actual loss of a drop of oil or a human life. Conversely, they can become wealthy, balance an ecosystem, land a lunar module on the moon's surface, or bring a tanker into home port without earning a cent or getting moondust on their shoes.

An excellent example of a flight simulator is Flight Simulator II (see Figure 3.8). A full-screen, three dimensional window view simulates the movement of the plane over varying terrain. Flight controls and instrument panels for visual and instrument flight are included, so that once a student feels comfortable with the controls, she can indulge in an aerial trip to test her flying skills.

A challenging simulation is Car Builder, a product of Optimum Resources. The student is called upon to build a car from various mechanical components and then to create a custom body for it. Next, the car is run through a complete diagnostic test, which includes a wind tunnel. After completion of the road test, a full report on the car's performance is given. Using this information, the student makes decisions on what additional design changes to make. The student must get involved, in the manner of a real car designer, in making decisions as to which features to emphasize. He or she must consider such things as size of the engine, styling, fuel economy, and aerodynamics. Screen shots from this program are shown in Figure 3.9.

A powerful simulation is Balance of Power (Mindscape), in which students become world leaders on whose shoulders rests the burden of maintaining a shaky peace. The setting is the United States or the USSR; the time span is 1986 to 1995. The objective is to attend to the enhancement of your country in various ways while at the same time maintaining peaceful relations with the rest of the world. You are called upon to make numerous decisions regarding other countries, the consequences of which can lead to enigmas of various kinds. Working with simulations such as this leads to worthwhile class discussions and a sensitivity to events taking place throughout the world.

FIGURE 3.8 A Typical Screen
Display from Flight Simulator II

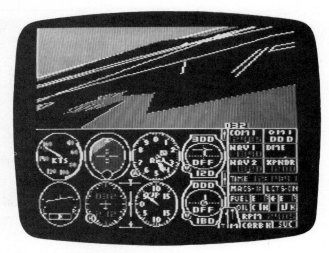

(Courtesy of SubLOGIC Corporation)

Simulations are valuable primarily because of the real-life problem-solving activities they present to the students. Although some games seem to be simulations, as a general rule, simulations attempt to replicate real-world situations whereas games do not. Another effective use of simulations is for experiments, such as those that would require expensive, specialized equipment in the actual setting or that are too dangerous to be carried out in the classroom.

Unlike some other varieties of CAI, simulations can be adapted for group use; as a matter of fact, many educators prefer this approach. Complete lessons can be successfully built around a microcomputer simulation, possibly extending over several weeks, with suitable supplemental activities introduced at appropriate times. Most simulation packages—the Minnesota Educational Computing Corporation (MECC) simulations, for example—include extensive supplemental materials such as maps, workbooks, and manuals. With materials of this nature, students are able to spend considerable time between computer sessions on related activities, the end result frequently being a thorough and complete understanding of the concepts and principles involved.

Games

Most computer-based games resemble games in general: they involve competition, and there is a winner and a loser. Some computer-based varieties pit student against student; a more common approach is to have the student play against the machine. Challenge is another feature. A challenge exists when there is a degree of uncertainty involved: if the outcome is predictable there is no challenge and therefore no reason to play. Players will soon figure out a fail-safe way to win if the program presents the material in an identical manner each time. To afford the greatest challenge, a game should be designed to randomize the sequence of presentation. Games also have rules that the players must understand and follow.

FIGURE 3.9 An Example of a Car Designed by a Student Using Car Builder

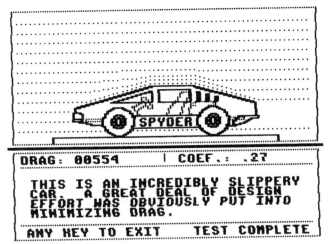

DRAG: 00554 | COEF.: .27

THIS IS AN INCREDIBLY SLIPPERY CAR. A GREAT DEAL OF DESIGN EFFORT WAS OBVIOUSLY PUT INTO MINIMIZING DRAG.

ANY KEY TO EXIT   TEST COMPLETE

(Courtesy of Optimum Resource, Inc.)

An innovative approach to educational game construction is to permit more than one player to cooperate in a collective effort to triumph over a series of obstacles. This is an excellent way to encourage socialization and represents a computerized equivalent of team games.

The newer collaborative games give sections of the display to different players, who must work in harmony to make their strategies effective. The opponent in this type of game is not another student but the computer. Perhaps the developers of this format are reflecting the feelings that many groups express as they band together to resist collectively what they perceive to be the sinister threat of a dehumanizing technology; then, on the other hand, they may simply be tired of seeing students involved in competition among themselves. The better games provide for different skill levels by permitting the player to select succeeding levels of difficulty until the game presents a challenge or by automatically upgrading the level of difficulty as the player improves.

Some educators use games as rewards for work well done—they can be very effective as reinforcement if used judiciously. Games can also reduce the feelings of apprehension that some individuals have toward computers (this is seldom a problem with children, however).

Some programmers have been criticized for incorporating too much violence into the games they create, whether designed for instruction or for entertainment. The violence-action format has been cited as one reason traditional video games seem to appeal more to males than to females. Fortunately, this situation has been recognized, and as a result, considerable effort is being made to modify the philosophy underlying this type of CAI.

Many varieties of games are available as microcomputer programs. Although a large percentage cannot be classified as educational (they are primarily meant for entertainment), there is a growing list of games that have utility in the classroom. These fall into several categories, three of which are described here.

Adventure Games.   Adventure games are intriguing not because of any direct competition between parties, but because of the challenge that arises as a student tries different strategies in an effort to resolve a dilemma. An adventure game presents the dilemma in the form of environments and choices selected from real-world instances; in this respect, they are related to simulations (as a matter of fact, some refer to simulations as "simulation games").

A classic series of adventure games is based on the travels of a mythical character named Carmen Sandiego. Several titles are available so students can learn about various countries as well as the world itself. A typical program is Where in the World is Carmen Sandiego? (All the games use this title format, substituting specific locations such as Europe for World).

The master thief, Carmen Sandiego, has stolen a priceless national treasure and students in the role of detectives must track her and her band down and solve the mystery. They visit great cities throughout the world as they chase the elusive crooks. A World Almanac and Book of Facts are provided to help interpret clues. Included are ten suspects, thirty cities, and close to a thousand clues, all of which relate to characteristics unique to each location. This program is a product of Broderbund Software. A screen shot is shown in Figure 3.10.

Arcade Games.   Some instructional games are patterned after the familiar arcade variety—they incorporate rocket ships, androids, laser guns, and the like, and the objective is to blast the enemy and avoid getting blasted.

Two popular instructional arcade games are Math Blaster and Word Attack. Both present the student with drills and sets of questions, then culminate with tests in the form of action-filled arcade segments. The student gets points for shooting down the word that matches a definition (Word Attack) or the correct

FIGURE 3.10 Carmen Sandiego Leads Her Pursuers to Places All Over the World

(Courtesy of Broderbund Software Inc.)

FIGURE 3.11 A Screen Shot
from Word Munchers

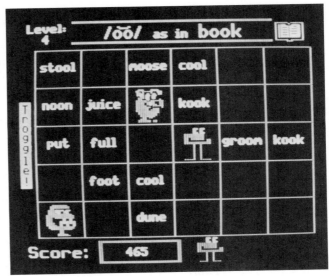

(Courtesy of MECC)

answer to a math problem (Math Blaster). Various levels of difficulty are provided
in both games, and students or teachers can add their own problems if desired.

Word Munchers from MECC is another popular arcade game. It is designed
for use in the language arts area by students in grades 1 to 3. The objective is to
help young readers distinguish words with different vowel sounds. Players move
a word muncher around a game board, where it eats words containing the target
vowel sounds. When an incorrect word is munched, a turn is lost. There are also
"Troggles," which must be avoided if possible because they eat the word munchers. An illustration from this program is shown in Figure 3.11.

Logic Games. Logic games are often referred to as problem-solving software.
The player must approach this type of game analytically—it takes more than
mastery of a simple list of rules to win at this game.

A perennial favorite from the Learning Company is Rocky's Boots. This program is designed to help students build logical thinking skills and develop creative
problem solving strategies. Students use the principles of electronic circuitry and
circuit design to practice logic. The challenge involves designing "machines" to
solve each of over forty problems that are presented by using the electronic parts
provided by the computer.

A second program from the same company is Think Quick, which is designed
to develop reasoning and thinking skills as the student roams through the many
rooms of the Castle of Mystikar. Students learn to interpret maps, decipher codes,
design strategies, manage their resources, and make decisions quickly as they
interact with the computer.

In another popular game, The Factory, students select various kinds of machines (some of which are shown in Figure 3.12) to make up the production line

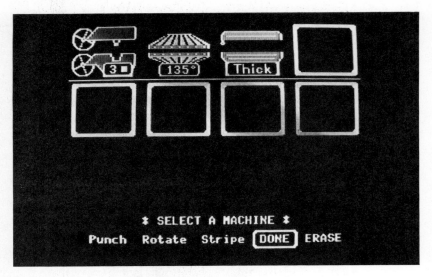

FIGURE 3.12 The Factory Gives Students a Logical Challenge
(Produced by Sunburst Communications, Inc.)

in a factory. As a piece of raw material passes along the line, the machines leave their imprints on it—drilling holes or painting patterns, for example. When the finished product emerges, the other players' task is to create machines that can duplicate that product.

Quiz Shows. A well-designed program of the quiz show variety is The Game Show from Advanced Ideas. This is a versatile game in which individuals or teams compete in an environment that simulates a television quiz show. The master disk contains forty topics in math, science, language arts, and social studies. It also provides a built-in authoring system for use in customizing programs to meet special class needs. Animated color graphics add action to the game and help to make it interesting for users from ages six to adult. A typical display from this program is illustrated in Figure 3.13. Note the host in the center who controls the activities and the players on either side, with the points they have earned displayed below their names.

Before leaving this discussion of the types of CAI, it should be noted that most programs typically incorporate more than one variety in their design. For example, a program might be basically a tutorial but have drill-and-practice segments interspersed throughout. Simulations frequently offer game-like interludes, and some games are essentially simulations. Shortly you will be introduced to an evaluation form that requires an identification of the type of CAI involved. Because more than one type can be included in a given program, you should attempt to identify the *primary* type of CAI, which may not be the exclusive one in every case; for some programs, though, you may wish to mark more than one kind of CAI.

FIGURE 3.13 A Typical Display from The Game Show
(Courtesy of Advanced Ideas)

COMPUTER-MANAGED INSTRUCTION

Prior to the advent of the microcomputer, the large-scale management of instruction was performed by mainframes or minicomputers that were frequently located in a district office. A few systems were so designed that a centrally located computer could service schools in several states, providing them with an analysis of student performance and prescriptions for appropriate follow-up instruction. Today microcomputers are capable of performing many of the CMI functions that were formerly the domain of the mainframes. Although they cannot store the massive amounts of data that larger systems can handle, the rapidly decreasing cost of hard disk systems is making microcomputer use possible for those who need more storage.

The microcomputer is capable of performing many of the management tasks related to individualized and group instruction and has become an important tool in the effort to meet the growing demands for accountability in education. The management function has become all the more important as educators have found themselves under increasingly heavy criticism from various constituencies. The emergence of the "back to basics" movement, and the concomitant call for improved documentation, has magnified the need for better ways to conduct the business of education. Computer-managed instruction can provide at least a partial response to these growing concerns.

Unlike CAI, computer-managed instruction is not used to instruct students directly; rather, it is a computer-based tool for gathering and analyzing data on student performance (record-keeping), developing student profiles (reports), and determining appropriate learning activities (prescriptions). CMI may be used in conjunction with any instructional approach; it is not limited to computer-based activities. The management function is just as useful for traditional classroom instruction with text and workbooks as it is for CAI.

More information on CMI software and applications is found in Chapter 6.

SOFTWARE EVALUATION

At some point you may find it necessary and desirable to evaluate a selection of instructional programs. Where do you begin? How should you proceed? What criteria are used? These questions will be addressed in the following sections.

The business of evaluating computer-based teaching materials appears to be new and different, but in actual practice it is not very far removed from evaluating materials in other mediums. However, there are a few dimensions that are unique to the computer and its attendant software and must therefore be taken into account in an effective evaluation.

As you evaluate software, there are certain steps you should take to ensure that nothing escapes your critical judgment. Make it a habit to start from the beginning every time the program is run. Much of the current software goes through exactly the same sequence with each use, which is not really the best design. The only way to tell if different problems are randomly generated on each run is to reboot each time (that is, turn the machine off and start from scratch). This involves a bit more time and effort, but it is the best way to check things out.

Plan to change roles each time you use the program. The first time through you can be the teacher: do everything correctly and look at things from the instructor's perspective. Next, take the role of the bright, serious student who wants to have an enlightening experience with the computer. Check to see if the program is friendly: it should be easy to run, the vocabulary should be appropriate for the particular learner group, and the instructions should be clear. Answer the questions as correctly as possible, but try different versions of the correct answer to see how the program responds: some programs output such phrases as "that's wrong" if an answer is misspelled, but a good program will be able to handle such an error in a better way. Also, examine the nature of the reinforcement: a program that says "greeeeat, that's right" every time a correct answer is given will not maintain student enthusiasm for very long. On the other hand, the feedback for wrong answers is often even more deadening: "That's wrong, stupid" will certainly not encourage a student who is having problems. Finally, try it as a "heathen"—do your best to make it crash. Enter any far-out answer that comes to mind. If the program can't handle input such as this, it probably isn't worth considering any further. Some programs simply crash if the answer is inappropriate, and you can be sure that sooner or later a student will type in a wrong answer.

DOCUMENTATION

The nature of the documentation is one of the more important considerations in any decision to purchase software. Although this aspect of program evaluation is mentioned later, it merits additional attention. The following discussion will be helpful as you consider this important software feature.

A Description

Fortunately, documentation is improving. There was a time not too long ago when the instructional package consisted solely of the disk (often a cassette tape), a licensing agreement, and a plastic wrapper. Nowadays a variety of well-conceived printed materials—the documentation—typically accompanies the disk. The documentation's functions are to teach you in the most direct manner how to use the program and to inform you of its characteristics (Figure 3.14); once this has been accomplished, it should serve as an ongoing reference.

FIGURE 3.14   Documentation Gives Instructions on Using a Program

Some courseware, such as that from MECC and Control Data Corporation (PLATO), also includes workbooks and other related materials that students use directly as part of a total lesson; these materials are often accompanied by teacher workbooks. Although educators commonly refer to all of this printed material (and to similar materials that might be included in the computer program itself) as documentation, to purists, the term is used to describe only those materials that relate to the operation of the program and to its characteristics; curriculum materials constitute another category and are thus not considered part of the documentation.

Development

Although much current documentation is not yet as good as it might be, it is so greatly improved over the earlier versions that comparisons are difficult to make. There are several reasons for the poor quality of early documentation (and some that is current). The early material (sparse as it was) was often written by the technical people who created the programs. After the exhilarating challenge of conceiving, writing, and debugging a program, compiling a written set of directions in lay language was an exercise for which few had any enthusiasm. Manuals were written as an afterthought; they were typically poorly planned and illustrated, frequently incomplete, and couched in confusing technical terms (at least for the user). Today the trend is to hire people who have a background in writing and to bring in illustrators and designers to dress things up and clarify concepts through graphics. In some cases producers go to considerable trouble to develop a profile of the typical user; documentation is then created systematically, with this person's needs in mind. This is a more pragmatic approach than the one used by those who hold that writing documentation is more of an art than a science.

Regardless of the philosophy involved, the finished product is now more polished than was formerly the case (see Figure 3.15). The new materials are visually appealing—they emulate commercial packaging in their attention to design and aesthetics. But external appearance is far from being the only improvement.

Printed documentation need not be comprehensive if the program itself has some of this information built into it (often in the form of a tutorial). The popular word processing program The Bank Street Writer has an outstanding tutorial as part of the program; Rocky's Boots is another example of this approach, and there are many more. In addition, help options are available in many programs: in response to a typed command (such as an *H* or a *?,* for example), material will appear on the screen to help you solve your current problem. Although building documentation into a program is gaining favor, there are those who maintain that there simply is no substitute for well-written printed documentation, citing the ease with which a manual can be used—it can even be taken home if necessary, and it requires no electronics. Of course, many would argue that the computer itself should be available for checkout, but the scarcity of machines makes this idea unfeasible in most cases. The ideal situation is probably one that combines the best features of both the disk-based and printed formats.

FIGURE 3.15 An Example of Attractive Packaging

(Courtesy of Broderbund Software Inc.)

Evaluating Documentation

As you set out to purchase software, be certain to put the documentation to the test. Take time to read through the manual to determine how understandable it is; if it is overflowing with computerese, beware. The documentation should include the names of those who designed and wrote the program. The producer or company that distributes the program, along with addresses and telephone numbers, should appear somewhere in the materials. Dates are also useful—they give the previewer an indication of how current the materials are. The brand of computer and the particular model for which the program was designed must also be part of the documentation; the brand name alone often isn't sufficient because of the tendency of some companies to create new lines of machines that are incompatible with the older models.

The description of the program is perhaps the most useful part of the documentation. It should be complete, including a statement of the objectives, the grade levels covered, what the user can expect to see as the program runs, and other such considerations. In addition, information should be provided on how to get the program up and running, how to call up a help screen, ways to get out of the program before it terminates, and how to use cursor movement keys (for word processing and graphics programs).

The kind of output the user should expect when the program is running might also be described if it is of an unusual nature: illustrations of typical screen displays are often useful. If supplemental materials (such as workbooks) are included as part of the total package, they should be mentioned. Data pertaining to any field testing that was part of program validation procedures may also be of interest to potential users, so this should also be included. Documentation is a most important factor when considering software for purchase—it is worth a second look.

THE SOFTWARE EVALUATION FORM

Guidelines for the evaluation of courseware have been developed by a number of organizations, including the Northwest Regional Evaluation Laboratory (NWREL), the Educational Products Information Exchange (EPIE), and the Minnesota Educational Computer Corporation. NWREL provides a useful evaluation form and an evaluator's guide through its MicroSIFT clearinghouse. EPIE/Consumers Union also publishes an evaluation form that is widely used, and TESS (The Educational Software Selector) is also a useful tool. In addition to providing excellent CAI programs to the schools, MECC has been engaged in courseware evaluation for many years. They, like the other organizations mentioned, have developed an evaluation model that is quite useful for educators. Additional versions of evaluation forms can be obtained from school districts, textbooks, and periodicals oriented toward instructional computing.

The form presented in this text (Figure 3.16) is a composite one that has evolved over time. It has proved useful in various versions to hundreds of students in our classes and to numerous educators. Some individuals, however, will prefer to create one to fit their own needs. In any case, this form can be valuable, not only to the one who evaluates the courseware, but also to others who desire a quick overview. Obviously, total consensus is seldom possible in any kind of evaluation—what is useful to one individual may not have the slightest utility for another. On the other hand, usefulness and quality are not synonymous—a poor program is poor whether or not it can be used in a particular setting. It is thus possible to determine, on the basis of the information on the evaluation form relating to overall quality, if a preview will be worthwhile.

When evaluating any kind of instructional medium it is useful to have a list of things to consider; the evaluation form arranges these in a logical format. However, the brevity of the typical evaluation form makes it advisable that some kind of supporting material be provided to define the meaning of the terms more completely. The following explanations, therefore, relate to items on the form and are presented in order (please note that self-explanatory items are not included).

Program title. The program title is generally displayed prominently on the documentation as well as on the support materials such as workbooks and teacher guides. It will also appear in a smaller format on the disk's label. Some sample titles are "Money! Money!" (Hartley), "Metric System Tutor" (Cygnus Software), and "Science: Human Body" (BrainBank).

Producer. You should be able to locate the producer's name in the documentation or on the title screen when the program is run. Typical producers' names are Baudville; Opportunities for Learning, Inc.; Pelican Software; Hartley Courseware; Mindscape, Inc.; and The Learning Company.

Cost. Cost is often difficult to discover—the documentation virtually never includes the price of the package, and it isn't indicated in the program either. Don't leave the space blank. If you can't determine the cost, write "unknown" or put in a question mark. People referring to the evaluation later might think blank spaces indicate a slip on the part of the evaluator; at least a question mark eliminates this possibility. If invoices or software lists such as those from MECC are available, you will be able to come up with a price, and evaluations in journals also list prices. Although this criterion may not seem important, it often is. Most courseware packages are rather modest in price, but occasionally an expensive one appears: a price tag of $250 is likely to discourage a teacher who would otherwise waste her time previewing an unaffordable program.

Copyright date. A program's copyright date, which typically appears on the title page of the documentation, can be most helpful: although some older programs are fine, many not only are outdated from the standpoint of content but also may be low in quality.

Required hardware. If the program will run on the equipment at hand, the available hardware is obviously adequate. But once again, the documentation should provide the brand and model of the appropriate computer.

In addition to the computer, required peripherals (joysticks, game paddles, and so on) should be listed, as well as the preferred type of monitor (a color monitor to make some programs more attractive or effective, for example, or a monochrome display for word processing).

Storage Medium. The smaller $3\frac{1}{2}$ inch disk in its hard cover is becoming more common all the time and is now standard equipment on many microcomputers. But the $5\frac{1}{4}$ inch format continues to be used in most schools since it is compatible with the machines already available. Hard disks are a favored medium which, if available, should be listed as "other" on the evaluation form. A very few schools still use older computers having cassette tapes for storage; this medium should also be listed in the "other" category. Cartridges that plug into a slot in the computer are infrequently encountered; place these in the "other" category also.

I. Program Characteristics

1. Subject matter area. Typical subject matter areas are math, language arts, art, biology, music, and social studies. Specific topics are metrics, algebra, and binary arithmetic in the subject matter of math, or verbs, nouns, spelling, and capitalization in the area of language arts.

2. Grade level. If grade level is not indicated in the documentation, make an educated guess. The term "pre" is used in the evaluation form to indicate pre-

FIGURE 3.16   Software Evaluation Form

SOFTWARE EVALUATION FORM

Program title _____

Producer _____ Cost _____ Copyright date _____

Required hardware _____
       (Include microcomputer brand and any special requirements)

Storage medium: 3½″ disk _____   5¼″ disk _____   Other _____

Name of reviewer _____ Date _____

Address or school _____

I. PROGRAM CHARACTERISTICS

1. Subject matter area _____ Specific topic _____

2. Grade level(s) Pre   K   1   2   3   4   5   6   7   8   9   10   11   12   Adult   College

3. Objectives: Clearly stated? _____Yes _____No   If stated, list them. if not stated, described what you perceive them to be: _____

_____

4. Is documentation provided? _____Yes _____No   If provided, describe briefly: _____

_____

5. What prerequisite skills should the student have? _____

6. Appropriate number of users _____ individual _____ pairs _____ small group _____ entire class

7. Nature of the program (check as many as apply)
   Drill and practice _____   Problem solving _____
   Tutorial   _____   Simulation   _____
   Game   _____

   Other (specify_____

_____

II. DESCRIPTION: In your own words, describe the program. Tell what it is about, how it is

structured, etc.

FIGURE 3.16 *continued*

Key: Y = YES   ? = NOT SURE   N = NO   NA = NOT APPLICABLE

III. CONTENT

1. Y ? N NA   The content is accurate.
2. Y ? N NA   The content is appropriate for the objectives.
3. Y ? N NA   The content is consistent with expectations of school district.
4. Y ? N NA   The content is free of bias.

IV. RUNNING THE PROGRAM

1. Y ? N NA   The instructions are clear and easy to understand.
2. Y ? N NA   Instructions and help screens are provided.
3. Y ? N NA   The program will tolerate inappropriate input without malfunctioning.
4. Y ? N NA   The screen display is well designed.
5. Y ? N NA   The material is well organized and presented effectively.
6. Y ? N NA   Appropriate interaction is provided.
7. Y ? N NA   Feedback is appropriate in nature and amount.
8. Y ? N NA   The program is self-paced.
9. Y ? N NA   Graphics and sound are used to enhance the program.
10. Y ? N NA   The program represents an appropriate use of a computer.

V. MAJOR STRENGTHS AND WEAKNESSES
Identify the major strengths of this program:

Identify the major weaknesses of this program:

List/indicate teaching strategies/uses for this program:

VI. RECOMMENDATION (Check One Only)

Excellent program; recommend purchase _____
Good program; consider purchase   _____
Fair program; might wait   _____
Poor program; would not purchase   _____

school, and "adult" refers to noncollege adult students. Note that more than one grade level may be marked if appropriate.

3. Objectives. Although objectives sometimes appear in the program, they often will be included in the printed materials. If the objectives are not specified, simply note what you feel they should be (you may have to wait until you have finished your evaluation to do this).

4. Is documentation provided? Refer to the documentation section earlier in this chapter for an in-depth discussion of the subject.

5. What prerequisite skills should the student have? Determining necessary prerequisites may call for a guess, but this will not be difficult once you get into the program. Students frequently encounter problems because the programmer assumed they would possess certain prior skills. The question to ask is, "What skills do I need to work with this lesson successfully?" (for example, does a grammar program assume that you know the parts of speech?).

6. Appropriate number of users. Good documentation will indicate the number of users the program is designed for, but an educated guess will suffice if such information is lacking. Do you see the program as being useful for only one person or possibly two at a computer? Might it be used with a small group? Or a large one?

7. Nature of the program. For a description of the different varieties of software (tutorials, drill and practice, simulations, and games) see the section earlier in this chapter. As you attempt to identify the nature of a particular program, note that it might incorporate more than just one type.

II. Description

In your own words—short and to the point—tell what the program is about, how it is structured, and whatever else you feel is necessary to describe it.

III. Content

Examine the key on the evaluation form before you proceed; circle only one symbol for each item.

1. The content of the program is accurate. Is the material free from factual errors? Are spelling and grammar correct?

2. The content is appropriate for the objectives. Consider what the software will be used for and ask if it will accomplish the task. Also consider the setting in which it will be used; if other quiet activities are taking place in the same room, for example, sound generated as part of the program might be disruptive. In addition, determine how much time a student will require to derive some benefit—a lengthy program might take more time than is normally available. (Some programs of this type, however, permit you to store the results, so the program can be continued at a later time.)

3. The content is consistent with expectations of school district. Many school districts have curriculum guides that are meant to serve as outlines for a particular unit of study. If the program seems to diverge too radically from the prescribed guidelines, it might not be suitable. (If you are uncertain about this one, circle the *?* or the NA.)

4. The content is free of bias. Biases—such as stereotyping or representing racial groups inappropriately—might be reflected in the way the language is used or in the actual words used.

IV. Running the Program

1. The instructions are clear and easy to understand. Words common to everyday discourse should be used in the language of the program rather than computer jargon. Such phrases as "input error," "reenter," and "illegal quantity" can be frustrating to the user; it is better to substitute phrases such as "please type your answer again," "the number is too large," or "try a different word." Many programs force the user to pass through a sequence of instructions with each use—this becomes very boring after a few times. A better approach is for the computer to ask, "Do you want instructions? Type Yes or No." If you answer "No" the instructions are skipped.

2. Instructions and help screens are provided. Menus, submenus, and other information screens should be available whenever needed to help guide the user through a program. Students thus will never be left dangling: if they get lost or confused, an appropriate display is only a keypunch away.

If a student reaches an impasse while working through a lesson, he should be able to get help immediately. Many programs offer help screens containing essential information, such as constant values in a math program or conversions in a tutorial on metrics. A graphics program might list the number keys and the colors they represent, along with the cursor moves and special key functions. A program on map reading may display the map when prompted to do so.

3. The program will tolerate inappropriate input without malfunctioning. A common format used when designing courseware is multiple choice, with the choice restricted to a set of letters or numbers. At times, however, it is useful to have the input consist of words; a problem arises, though, if the answer is correct but the spelling is not. Some programs are designed to tolerate errors in spelling up to a point: if one error is allowed, for example, then "Warshington" (with an *r*) would be accepted.

Routines to redirect the user after an incorrect response can be quite useful. For example, one program consists of multiple-choice questions with the selections numbered from 1 to 4. Lacking directions, some students type in the word rather than the numeral, and the response is immediate: "That is not correct." But those who make this mistake are given no indication of why the response is incorrect. To remedy this situation the programmer should anticipate the problem and provide for it with a message such as "Please type in the number 1, 2, 3, or 4." Programs should not crash, (that is, stop dead) if the wrong keys are pressed. It is wise to input some incorrect responses when evaluating courseware to see how the computer reacts.

4. The screen display is well designed. The quality of the text display is of great importance. Many schools use television receivers for the display, and fine resolution of the characters cannot be taken for granted. Even when a monitor is available, clarity will suffer if the design is not good. Text should be uncrowded, and the format should be consistent throughout the program. Each *frame,* or individual screen display, should contain a complete idea. Rather than presenting a math problem in a fragmented way over several frames, for example, the program should break the problem into logical steps and present them one per frame.

Often the screen goes blank when a program is being loaded from a disk. Students frequently believe that something is wrong with the system and begin to punch keys. Some kind of display should therefore be on the screen during this period to reassure the user that nothing is wrong. (Some programs use phrases such as "Loading Metric Tutor" or "Gassing up.")

5. The material is well organized and presented effectively. The material should be presented in small segments; the sequencing should be logical and should reflect a consistent pattern of progression. Definitions should be given when appropriate, and examples are useful. The user should be able to select from various levels of difficulty to accommodate his or her ability. The number of questions presented should also be flexible. Computer-based games that are too easy or too difficult are not very popular with students—if the computer wins every time, it is intimidating; if the human invariably wins, there is no challenge.

6. Appropriate interaction is provided. Interaction is among the more important attributes of CAI; the program should take advantage of this feature. If the user merely sits as a passive viewer, a textbook might do the job as effectively. (Note that simply pressing the space bar does not constitute interaction.) The student's response will determine the next output from the computer if the program is properly designed. The student should be the controlling factor in the direction the program takes. Different responses should elicit different kinds of output.

Appropriate means for student response should be provided. Voice input and output aid children who cannot read. Devices such as the trackball and the mouse are favored over the keyboard by many students. Menus from which selections are made can make input easier than typing on the keyboard. Response time should be rapid; nothing is more frustrating than having to wait for the computer to respond to input so the user can proceed with the program.

7. Feedback is appropriate in nature and amount. From research on learning we know that feedback is most useful when it informs the learner of an incorrect response. This should not be done in a demeaning manner, of course, but rather should use helpful and instructive language. The feedback should follow the response immediately and should give whatever information is needed to clarify the problem. If a string of correct responses has brought about numerous positive comments, reinforcement should become less frequent; it is better to use positive feedback sparingly than to overdo it.

In some programs the reinforcement for an incorrect response is more rewarding than it is for a correct one. One in particular makes sounds and displays colorful graphics for a wrong answer but simply moves on to the next question if the response is correct.

An incorrect response should not elicit insulting feedback. A curt "wrong" is not as good as something like "close, but not quite." Also, the prompt "try again" is not particularly useful if the student simply does not know how to work a problem. After a certain number of incorrect responses, helpful information should appear so the student can move on.

Some programs include tutorial-like screens and sample programs to help the user. In a math program a cue such as "that number is too small" may be helpful initially. An approach used in a grammar program is to give the definition for a part of speech when the student gives an incorrect response; for example, if the student is asked to respond with a verb and types in something else, the computer responds with "remember, a verb shows action, try again."

8. The program is self-paced. Students often complain that they are tied into a program and can't jump around; they must start at the beginning and work straight through to the end. Some programs are modularized, enabling the student to move backward or forward to any module desired. Menus, directions, problems to be worked, and other displays should be left on the screen long enough for the user to attend to them and respond as needed. Using a prompt such as "press space bar to continue" is helpful.

Some programs have an extensive set of directions that scrolls up the screen. Although this technique is commonly used to list credits for a motion picture or TV program, it is generally a poor practice in CAI.

9. Graphics and sound are used to enhance the program. In the 1950s and 1960s researchers proved that embellishing films and filmstrips with colorful, purely decorative graphics did not improve the educational value of the medium and, in fact, often diminished it. These findings are as viable today for microcomputers as they were years ago for films. Embellishments frequently do nothing more than detract from important content.

Many highly embellished programs receive positive ratings because they are so colorful and attractive. An in-depth analysis, however, frequently reveals a dressed-up drill-and-practice program of questionable instructional value: don't be fooled into giving a program a high rating when in fact it may be relatively worthless.

Sound can be used to enhance a program, but it should be employed judiciously. One program uses a sound much like a Bronx cheer when a mistake is made—needless to say, kids hate it. If sound is used as a prompt, it should precede the display of textual material rather than occur at the same time.

10. The program represents an appropriate use of a computer. As you evaluate the program, ask yourself if the objectives might met be as effectively through some method other than CAI. Be sure to consider the logistics involved: although a teacher working one-on-one with a student might be as effective as the computer-based tutorial, or even more so, in large classes only minimal individualized instruction is possible. Programs that might be considered inappropriate use of computers are some of the simple drill-and-practice programs.

V. Major Strengths and Weaknesses

After you have run the program, you should have a good feel for its strong and weak points: list the most important in each category. A major strength, for example, is "good graphics and text displays"; "unable to break out of the program" is an example of a weakness. You might also wish to list several uses for this program.

VI. Recommendations

To indicate your recommendation, simply place a mark in the blank opposite the rating you feel to be most appropriate.

Now That It's Over

Using an evaluation form can be a challenging experience the first time through—the process seems overly complicated, perhaps even needlessly so. But after the form has been used once or twice, applying it to subsequent evaluations becomes almost routine.

As mentioned previously, the form is useful in two respects: first, it furnishes the reviewer with a logical and thorough evaluation procedure, and second, it provides information to others with an interest in a particular courseware title, either for purchase for a school or for checkout from the resource center for use in the classroom.

The completed evaluation forms should be shared with others. Many schools, districts, and state organizations have established courseware libraries or preview centers to house these and other computer-related materials. People who use the facilities and the courseware are urged to complete a standardized evaluation form—available at the centers—for each preview; this practice has led to the establishment of libraries of evaluations. Educators are using the collections widely and find the evaluations to be highly informative and a time-saving substitute for the actual preview.

SOFTWARE PREVIEW

No one likes the idea of buying a commodity unseen and untried, but there was a time when this was about the only way to acquire the software you wanted. Producers as a rule did not offer provisions for examining their products before purchase, but review policies are now becoming much more liberal. In the past, many companies resisted sending their products out for review for fear they would be copied. In contrast, it is now common for them to send disks to schools for a 30-day preview period with the stipulation that the school must either send the program back or purchase it when the period is over. This arrangement provides schools with ample time to put a program through its paces and determine whether or not it fits their needs.

Another method is for producers to distribute demonstration disks and video-tapes containing selected segments of the complete program. The potential buyer is not able to use the program for anything but review purposes since essential segments have been left out, but a good overview of its content and capabilities can be obtained from the demonstration.

If a decision is made to acquire a particular program even though previewing is not possible for one reason or another, there are still things a prospective buyer can do to get some idea of what the program is like. A good first step is to contact another educator who is familiar with the courseware in question. A look at what reviewers have to say can also be helpful: such journals as *Classroom Computer Learning* and *Electronic Learning* offer in-depth reviews of a number of different packages in each issue, including pictures of typical screen displays so the physical features of the program can be better appreciated. There are also organizations specializing in reviews that offer extensive information on various selected titles in such publications as the EPIE reports, the microSIFT reviews from NWREL, *Software Reports* from Allenback Industries, and *Software Reports* from Trade Service Publications. Lists of additional journals and other sources of software reviews are included in appendixes C, D, and E.

Certain producers are well known because of ongoing advertising in top-flight journals or because of numerous positive reviews in various publications—this is a good indication of the general credibility of the firm. Also, good programs become highly visible through the plaudits they receive from satisfied users. Another consideration is the manner in which producers typically develop their materials: if a field-testing program is in place, for example, you can feel confident that the materials will be of better quality than if they have never been tested. Although there are some unreliable software producers, a fairly large corps of reputable companies has evolved that offers the educator a consistently good product supported by ethical and fair backup policies.

If you should desire to preview a specific program and it is not available at the time, you can get a feel for the general quality of the line of courseware by previewing other products from the producer of the preferred program. If all efforts to obtain a preview have failed and the program is not available locally, it may become necessary to resort to the mails. The products and service of mail-order vendors should prove satisfactory if the company advertises month after month in the journals: certain vendor names have become virtual household words because of this continuous exposure.

SOFTWARE WARRANTY

The warranty specifies the period of time the software, if defective, will be replaced without charge. Most warranty periods are ninety days, but some extend to one year while a few give protection against defects for life. At the end of the warranty period you can still obtain a replacement by sending back the disk and paying a modest fee. In some cases, the fee is increased to the full price of the item after a certain period of time. An example of a warranty policy that has been made more liberal is that offered by Scholastic Software. This company originally offered a replacement for 10 dollars, but only within a ten-month period. Under the new policy, the 10-dollar charge is applicable for the lifetime of the software. Also included is a free replacement for defective disks for a period of ninety days after purchase.

SOFTWARE PURCHASE OPTIONS

Software producers are paying more attention to the needs of users than they did in the past. Liberalized warranties are one example of this trend; the packaging of software in a number of formats to serve the differing needs of educators represents another sign of increased producer concern.

Until recently, educators were required to pay full price for each of the several copies of a given title they ordered. Today, several plans for acquiring software for multiple usage in the schools have been formulated. Among these are the distribution of lab packs at a discount rate, site licensing agreements, and networking arrangements.

Lab Packs

Lab packs are multiple copies of a specific program bundled together with a single set of printed materials, including the documentation, which are sold as a package at a package price substantially below that for multiple complete sets.

The standard number of copies in a lab pack is generally five, but packs of ten are also common. A typical price for the five-pack is twice that of a single disk, while that for a ten-pack is three times the cost. An example of this arrangement is Blockers and Finders from Sunburst Communications. The price for a single disk is $65, while that for a ten-pack is $195.

A variation on the standard lab pack is the AppleWorks package offered by the Computer Literacy Press. Included are ten sets of textbooks and workbooks, a copyable disk containing a number of AppleWorks files, more than sixty blackline masters for making handouts, a selection of transparency masters, and a wall chart showing commands for the program.

Site Licensing

Site licenses are arrangements between a software producer and a school or district in which programs are provided to the purchaser for use only at a specified site. As a general rule, the programs are not protected, and can be copied for use in multiple computers. At times, the number of allowable copies is specified.

Often the documentation is also provided at a reduced cost. Because this material is frequently quite voluminous, it is inconvenient to copy. Having the company furnish copies is a convenient alternative preferred by most schools.

MECC is a pioneer in site licensing. A special copy program is provided with the membership that permits the school to duplicate a specified number of the titles in the MECC collection. The membership fee is $150 for schools and $300 for a district.

Springboard Software provides members the option to purchase as many programs of one title as they wish for ten dollars each. If documentation is desired this can be had for eight dollars per copy. The membership cost for each title is about twice the price of a single program, so the greater the number of disks purchased the greater the savings.

Milliken offers a plan called the 18/8 Site Membership Plan after the cost of the software involved. A program disk costs eighteen dollars while there is an eight dollar charge for replacement and backup disks. Orange Cherry Software provides unlimited copying of its programs by a single member school. An increasing number of producers are finding the site licensing approach to be a practical answer to educators' requests for multiple copies of software.

Networking

This practical approach to the multiple use of a given program involves hooking several computers to a central disk drive (generally a hard disk drive) from which the program is distributed. Again, this arrangement is popular with software producers, over 70 percent of whom now offer networking agreements for their products. Amounts charged for networking licenses vary from one publisher to the next, some charging rates that vary with the number of computers being used in the network.

An option to a true network, which can be quite expensive to install, is the disk sharing system. Unlike the network, this kind of system is not hooked to a hard disk, so the capability is much reduced. Floppy disk drives are used, and the number of programs that can be accessed is considerably fewer than with a standard network. Nevertheless, this is a good alternative to a local area network (LAN) when one is not available. For more information on networks, refer to the chapter on telecommunications.

It should be emphasized that making multiple copies of a program without explicit permission from the publisher is clearly against the law. On the other hand, the practice of loading a program into several computers from a common disk is seen as acceptable by many teachers. Some companies regard this as illegal and make their position clear; however, others give permission to multiple load a program. In the absence of a published policy stating that this practice is acceptable, teachers should avoid using a single disk-based program on multiple computers.

COPY PROTECTION AND BACKUP POLICIES

Under the copyright law the purchaser of a program has the right to a second, or archival, copy of that program to put aside for use in case of problems with the original disk. If the software producer fails to furnish such a copy, or fails to specify how this can be obtained, the purchaser can proceed to make one of his own, a simple task unless a copy protection scheme is involved.

There are many ways to protect a program from being copied. At one time, almost all producers put some kind of an electronic "lock" on a disk to protect it from illegal duplication. This practice made it impossible for legitimate owners to make a backup copy when they needed one, which brought an outcry from users and stimulated programmers to develop "lock-breaking" programs that could overcome the copy protection system and make copying possible.

The adversarial relationship arising from this state of affairs was not productive for either the user or the producer; something had to be done. Producers responded with several schemes, including the simplest one of all: in many instances they did away with copy protection altogether. For disks that are not copy protected, the publishers expect the user to obey the law and make no more than one copy of the original program. Educators, in return, are doing a better job of respecting the rights of the publishers. They have become more sensitive to the damage that is done to a company when a large percentage of its product is used without compensation.

The move toward dropping copy protection was stimulated by at least two factors. The first was that knowledgeable pirates have little difficulty in duplicating software, even if it is copy protected; the second had to do with the increasing popularity of hard disk storage systems. In order to use a system of this kind you must be able to load your programs onto the disk; this cannot be done with copy-protected software unless special provisions are made, so those with hard disk drives tended to avoid the purchase of products that could not be copied.

Various other schemes have been devised to satisfy the need for duplicate programs. For example, you can make a single backup copy from the Fantavision (Broderbund) program. If additional copying is attempted, the backup routine fails to work.

Producers have also made lenient provisions for making more than one copy for classroom use. The Society for Visual Education (SVE) has designed its software to allow the purchaser to make a maximum of five copies of a given program, after which a built-in feature locks the disk. At no extra cost, the J. Weston Walch Company allows the teacher to make as many copies as needed for use in her own classroom.

For more information on copyright law refer to Chapter 10.

PUBLIC DOMAIN SOFTWARE

Most of the programs discussed in this chapter are commercial ones. To acquire a good library of software of this type, a school must be willing and able to expend a considerable amount of money. But what of those schools that, for one reason or another, cannot justify such expenditures? Must they simply go without? Fortunately, free or inexpensive programs are widely available: the public domain software. The quality of this type of material ranges from extremely good to terrible, as you might expect. The problem is one of finding it and sorting out the good from the bad.

Many of these programs have been written by professional programmers in their spare time and have simply been passed around. Others are the products of teachers who, not knowing how to market them (some are not marketable) or not caring to, have shared them with other educators. Programs that have been in circulation for a time frequently benefit from the alterations made by users; although not always the case, it is generally legal to alter these programs in any way.

Locating public domain software is often a kind of treasure hunt at which you may come up empty-handed. Various user groups (see Appendix E) are noted for the free software they pass around among their members; these individuals are known to the local vendors, who can usually give interested parties information on how to contact them.

Chapter 7, on networking and telecommunications, has information on how to access the electronic bulletin boards that are spread across the country. This is an excellent source for free software—you acquire it electronically using the telephone lines and a modem. In addition, various publications list public domain software. For example, hundreds of free programs for the IBM PC, ranging from business applications to games, are listed in a software guide from the PC Software Interest Group.

Perhaps the most useful source for educators is SOFTSWAP, a mail-order service that offers over two hundred public domain programs of an educational nature. Individuals who wish to copy any of these need only visit the center (located in San Mateo, California) with a blank disk—the programs are free. If you prefer to use the mail, you can purchase any set of programs for a given computer, subject, and grade level on a single disk for ten dollars. Most programs have been donated by teacher-programmers; all have been evaluated, edited, and modified by volunteers so that standards are maintained.

SUMMARY

This chapter examined the kinds of instructional programs—drill and practice, tutorials, simulations, and games—and gave examples of each; in addition, it discussed computer-managed instruction.

When used as a tutor, the computer assumes many of the duties traditionally performed (though sometimes reluctantly) by the human teacher. Computers can provide the student with a variety of individualized drill-and-practice lessons indefinitely, without losing patience. Tutorials start with a concept that is unfamiliar to the student and, through interactive input and output, guide him through to mastery. Simulations provide a realistic situation with which the student interacts; her decisions result in consequences, but none have the potentially disastrous impact of a real-world decision. Through simulations, a student can engage in experimentation and make mistakes without the expenditure of anything more than a little time: he can fly and crash an airplane, melt down an atomic reactor, or cause a business to go bankrupt, and then try it again—nothing is lost, much is gained.

Instructional games provide a learning experience within the context of rules, competition, winning, and losing. Games are also used for reinforcement when this is appropriate. And computer-managed instruction enables the teacher to maintain records, score tests, diagnose needs, and prescribe instruction in a very efficient and effective manner.

A systematic approach to the evaluation of instructional software was outlined in this chapter, including a useful evaluation form.

Also discussed were topics of concern to educators who wish to maximize the use of software in their classrooms. Several alternatives to the full-price purchase of single programs were described, including lab packs, site licenses, and networks. The chapter concluded with a discussion of copy protection and backup policies.

SELF-TEST

1. Why was early software often poor in quality? Why is it getting better?
2. Describe the disk operating system. Tell what it is used for.
3. List Taylor's three modes of computer use; describe a characteristic activity for each mode.

4. Summarize the major differences between drill-and-practice programs, tutorials, simulations, and instructional games.
5. How can a computer assist with classroom management chores?
6. When you evaluate an instructional program you should assume three different roles. Name them.
7. In what ways can a carefully completed software evaluation form aid teachers?
8. What is documentation? How is it useful?
9. In what ways are software preview and software evaluation different? In what ways are they similar?
10. How long is the typical software warranty period? What is the maximum period?
11. Describe three ways producers have packaged software to make multiple use more convenient and less expensive.
12. Why is copy protection being discontinued by many producers?
13. How does public domain software differ from commercial software?

REFERENCES

Allessi, S., and S. Trollip. *Computer-based Instruction: Methods and Development.* Englewood Cliffs, N.J.: Prentice-Hall, 1985.

Dennis, J., and R. Kansky. *Instructional Computing: An Action Guide for Teachers.* Glenview, Ill.: Scott, Foresman, 1984.

Dunathan, A. "What Is a Game?" *Audiovisual Instruction* (May 1978): 14–15.

Eiser, L. "What Makes a Good Tutorial?" *Classroom Computer Learning* (January 1988): 44–51.

Eiser, L. "Solving Math Word Problems." *Classroom Computer Learning* (April 1988): 60–68.

Field, C. "In Search of Software Treasures." *inCider* (June 1989): 46–50.

Hannafin, M., and K. Peck. *The Design, Development, and Evaluation of Instructional Software.* New York: Macmillan, 1988.

Lehrer, A. "A Network Primer: When Is a Network Not a Network?" *Classroom Computer Learning* (February 1988): 39–47.

McCarthy, R. "Educational Software—How It Stacks Up." *Electronic Learning* (April 1988): 26–30.

Mandell, C., and S. Mandell. *Computers in Education Today.* St. Paul, Minn.: West Publishing Company, 1989.

Parham, C. "Computers that Talk." *Classroom Computer Learning* (March 1988): 26–35.

Sloane, H., et al. *Evaluating Educational Software.* Englewood Cliffs, N.J.: Prentice Hall, 1989.

Salpeter, J. "Have It Your Way: How Software Publishers Respond to Your Needs." *Classroom Computer Learning* (January 1988): 34–39.

Solomon, M. "Microcomputer Site Licensing: Concepts and Problems." *T.H.E. Journal* (October 1988): 34–39.

Taylor, R., ed. *The Computer in the School: Tutor, Tool, Tutee.* New York: Teachers College Press, 1980.

CHAPTER 4

Computers in the Curriculum

CHAPTER TOPICS
☐ An emerging trend: integrating computers into the curriculum
☐ Some approaches to integration
☐ Ways to use computers in selected curriculum areas:
  Early learning and readiness
  Mathematics
  Reading and language arts
  Science
  Social studies
☐ Hardware and software for use in selected curriculum areas

If you studied Chapter 2 and Chapter 3 before arriving at this point, you now have some understanding of the nature of the hardware as well as a knowledge of the kinds of software available to educators. Knowing these things is helpful, but a logical question to ask is "How do I use this technology in the classroom?" There are many ways. In this chapter we will consider ways in which traditional subject areas can be enriched by the introduction of computers and appropriate courseware into the curriculum.

You will recall that one of the topics discussed in Chapter 1 was the trend away from the study of the computer (the computer as subject) to using the computer as an aid to teaching traditional subjects such as science, math, and reading. In this view the emphasis is placed on curriculum objectives, and the computer is of secondary concern. In other words, the computers and courseware are regarded as another medium for enhancing learning, taking their place alongside more familiar instructional mediums such as transparencies and overhead projectors, videotapes and players, films and projectors.

Software producers have recognized the reality of this trend, and have started to respond. For example, Decisions, Decisions, from Tom Snyder Productions, consists of discussion-oriented software designed around the established social studies curriculum in grades five through twelve. Scholastic Software is pursuing a similar approach with its reading programs. These programs are meant to be used in the curriculum as it exists rather than as a curriculum unto themselves. Many additional examples could be mentioned.

Other companies are designing software packages that are correlated to textbooks and include not only drill components but often simulations and even tools such as word processors and data bases. Such related materials enable the teacher to select the appropriate medium at the proper time to enhance the achievement of course objectives.

In view of the current integration efforts, the idea of the totally computerized classroom in which the structure of the curriculum is modified to fit the electronic medium hardly seems viable any longer. Computer-based learning should be provided within the context of the regular curriculum when it is seen to be the most effective of the available instructional modes to use. The computer, when used imaginatively, is excellent for problem-solving activities. Good simulation software can provide students with a contrived slice of the real world when the actual phenomenon is too dangerous, expensive, or remote to duplicate in the classroom. Tool software such as word processors and data bases, among others, have characteristics making them desirable for use in writing and social studies. Drill-and-practice programs have proved effective in a number of areas, notably mathematics.

Teachers who successfully integrate computers into their curriculums attest to the value of the CAI approach. They cite increased pupil enthusiasm for study, enhanced social skills, and fewer disciplinary problems. Additionally, children overcome any apprehension they might have had toward the technology, and become knowledgeable about it at the same time through actual hands-on experiences. This amounts to a kind of computer literacy training without the formal structure.

INTEGRATION SCHEMES

Among the problems preventing more rapid integration of computers into the established curriculum are a lack of training on the part of teachers and a serious lack of equipment in most schools. Some of the steps being taken to deal with the first problem are described in Chapter 1. Three approaches to the second problem are outlined below.

Whole Class Instruction

Although nearly every school in the United States has computers, some have only one or a few. To compound the problem, many programs require that students be on task for as much as a half hour to 45 minutes at a time, a difficult situation even when multiple computers are available. The best that some teachers can do is to acquire a single computer for permanent use in their classroom. Although this might seem little better than none at all when the numbers of students in a typical class are considered, there is a way that a single system can be used to benefit every student in the class. Collis (1988) suggests that the computer be attached to a large monitor and used by the teacher as a demonstration device. She refers to this approach as whole-class instruction.

We use this approach, together with hands-on activities in our lab, and find it to be very useful. We have three large monitors arranged around the classroom and attached to an Apple IIe at the instructor's desk, and a single black-and-white monitor attached to a Macintosh. However, we are finding that an LCD display panel used with an overhead projector (as described in Chapter 2) is proving to be even more satisfactory.

Collis, speaking of graphing software used in the whole-class manner, says that the program serves "as an intelligent blackboard or filmstrip" and that "the advantages of class-teacher interaction are maintained, while the demonstration materials generated by the computer are probably of better quality than those that the teacher could produce on overhead transparencies or on the blackboard." These advantages would likely apply to most other kinds of programs in all subject areas.

Selecting Teachers

While the ideal would be to have a sufficient number of computers in every classroom, the reality is that finances will not permit this situation to prevail. There are options to the whole-class approach, but they tend to be more controversial. Another strategy, for example, is to concentrate computers in the classrooms of those enthusiastic, technology-oriented teachers who will get the most use out of them. You can see that this approach might not appeal to some parents, who would feel (perhaps with some justification) that their children were being discriminated against if they did not end up in the classes using computers. On the other hand, merely introducing computers into classrooms (or into schools, for that matter) where there is no incentive to experiment and innovate is not going to make much of a difference in the nature of the teaching and learning taking place. Although controversial in some eyes, perhaps the most productive approach is to provide computers primarily to schools in which both the administrative and teaching staffs are committed to improving instruction and are willing to put in the time and effort necessary to make certain that this happens.

Selecting Problem Areas

A third way to get the most out of a scarce and costly resource is to identify areas within the curriculum where problems are occurring and where computers might make a difference, and then concentrate the technology there. One area that might be chosen is math. Research studies show that computer-based drill can be quite effective, particularly with students who are performing below grade level and with accelerated students. Other areas are candidates for a new approach to teaching also. Much has been said and written about the lack of geography and science knowledge among American students; perhaps computers and related technologies might help these young people acquire greater proficiency in these subjects. Students need to write more, but the demands placed on a teacher who must correct the countless themes resulting from writing assignments are overwhelming. There are excellent writing programs available that encourage writing and relieve the teacher of much of the mundane drudgery that is a product of the usual ways of teaching writing. Because traditional approaches to instruction have not done the job, many policy makers and educators are eagerly searching for a better way to do things; to many, introducing computers into the curriculum is a gamble worth taking.

Some school districts, notably in California, have adopted this last approach. They have used various techniques to identify problem areas, and have then proceeded to train personnel, revise curricula, and introduce the hardware and software. As part of this effort, California has implemented a software development partnership with several software companies. This program was designed with the goal of having software producers create materials in harmony with ongoing curricular guidelines established by the state. Money has been provided to support software development in areas that might not be economically attractive to commercially oriented companies. This amounts to a subsidy, of course, but producers cannot be expected to operate at a loss.

Alabama, another state involved in curriculum integration efforts, uses funding provided by the legislature to support a consortium of educational institutions in the development of software tailored to fit the established curriculum. Both states decided on this course of action when it became apparent that existing commercial software could not readily be adapted to meet their instructional needs. It will be interesting to see what the long-term effects of these experiments are. In any case, efforts of this kind represent steps in the right direction. America cannot afford to stay with the status quo while students from other countries continue to outperform our own.

SOFTWARE, HARDWARE, AND INTEGRATION

As noted earlier, many software producers, having recognized the trend toward the integration of computer technology into the existing curriculum, have begun to respond in a variety of ways. For example, guides have been introduced by various companies to assist teachers in selecting the best software for a range of subjects. These booklets show the software title, description, publisher, and other helpful information for a wide selection of top-rated programs. The information is logically arranged within a curriculum matrix that is consistent throughout the guides, making them easy to use.

To make classroom utilization more convenient, some companies furnish special school editions of their consumer versions of software. These typically consist of the same software as the consumer editions but with teachers' guides, lesson plans, masters for making handouts for student activities, and a scope and sequence chart showing how the programs fit into the curriculum.

Also available are lab packs of multiple copies of a given program. These are sometimes accompanied by lesson plans, tests, and related items. (Lab packs were discussed in detail in Chapter 3, as were other approaches to the multiple-use of software.)

Another useful innovation is the comprehensive instructional package that provides a range of applications from basic skills training to advanced study in specialized areas. This software reinforces fundamental skills in language, reading, writing, and mathematics. It typically consists of a series of content disks containing lessons, tests, quizzes, and sometimes record-keeping features for use by individual students or entire classes.

Advances in hardware have also made integration more practical. One shortcoming of the computer as a whole-class instructional device has been the small size of the display screen. This problem can be overcome to a large extent by using one of the special display panels which, when positioned on the stage of an overhead projector and connected to the video port of the computer, projects an image large enough to fill a large wall screen. Anything you do at the computer is projected onto the large screen, so you can create graphics, change figures on a spreadsheet, interact with a game, and your students can see it all clearly.

Other varieties of hardware in the form of networks, CD-ROM drives, and interactive videodisc players, all hooked to computers running the essential software, can enhance the teaching of a variety of subjects. Networks, when used in an integrated learning system (ILS), provide lessons on demand to a broad audience. CD-ROMs afford users with mass storage of archival data, while interactive videodiscs let teachers create their own illustrated lessons using an authoring language and stored images and sound.

Integrated Learning Systems (ILS)

Integrated learning systems (ILS) are now coming on line in schools with networking capabilities. A network is an arrangement whereby many microcomputers are hooked to a central device such as a printer or, in the case of an ILS, a central micro- or minicomputer with a hard disk, or a CD-ROM drive as these become more widely available. In an ILS, the hard disk or CD-ROM contains carefully planned sequential lessons in various subject areas. Students are provided appropriate activities based on their prior performance, which is documented by the computer. The student's progress is tracked as she or he moves from one lesson to the next. Pertinent information regarding performance is generated in the form of a report for the teacher's use. You can readily appreciate the advantages of such a system: there is no need to maintain and manipulate a large collection of floppy disks, no need to try to patch together available software to form a coherent lesson, no guess work as to which lesson should be used next, and no cumbersome grading and record-keeping for the teacher. A range of activities in a broad selection of subjects is offered by the various companies providing integrated learning systems. For example, Wicat, of Orem, Utah, provides kindergarten through grade 12 coverage in language arts, English as a second language (ESL), and math, together with various special programs. Other companies that offer integrated learning systems are Wasatch Educational Systems, Jostens Learning Corporation, Computer Systems Research, Ideal Learning Systems, Computer Curriculum Corporation, and Computer Networking Specialists.

CD-ROM

CD-ROM technology can also help to make integration more practical by providing any of a multitude of different programs, hundreds of which can be stored on a single disk, available to the teacher on demand. An example of this use is The PC-SIG Library on CD-ROM, which is a collection of several hundred public domain programs for the IBM computer on a single compact disk. Another collection of this kind is Public Domain Software on File for the Apple II series of computers. Information in the form of dictionaries, encyclopedias, and almanacs is available on compact disks from companies such as Ztek, of Lexington, Kentucky. The massive storage capability of CD-ROM makes it useful in creating data bases of various kinds. An example of this application is Science Helper K-8 from PC-SIG, which includes about one thousand science lessons.

Laser Videodisc

The laser videodisc is yet another medium that shows great promise for enhancing instruction in subject areas. Thousands of images together with text can be stored on its surface and can be accessed randomly and rapidly without the linear search required by videotape. Because the data are read by a laser beam and there is no physical wear involved, a laserdisc will last virtually forever. When a computer is hooked to a videodisc player and the proper software is used, an interactive system results. An example of such a system is shown in Figure 4.1. This arrangement combines the power of the computer with the features of video to provide an exciting new tool for educators.

Teachers can use available authoring software to create their own lessons, using combinations of the images encoded on the disc in combination with text and sound. Such programs can present material, offer a review of selected parts of the lesson, give a quiz, and provide remedial help.

The images can be played back in any combination desired, including still frame, slow and fast motion, and normal speed. You can program a lesson so that it allows students to bypass segments they are familiar with, or branch to other parts of the lesson if they wish. Text frames can be created and inserted as desired, and sound can be used to enhance the presentation. Some publishers provide the programs necessary for interacting with the disk, saving teachers from having to develop their own. This kind of software provides users with a method for accessing whatever topics they desire without the need to use a printed index. The preceding discussion is of a level three system, or one that involves a computer and provides interactive capabilities. Actually, you can use the videodisc player without a computer; this approach is referred to as a level one system. The user relies on the traditional remote control to move from frame to frame on the disc; however, since the electronic index provided by the computer is not in place, a print index must be used. You can see that such a system is not nearly as convenient nor as fast as a level three system, but it still has many applications.

Some subjects have been omitted in the following discussion of computer use in the curriculum. Because space was not available for complete coverage, the areas deemed to be of the broadest interest were included. Problem solving is frequently included as a separate category in any discussion of the curriculum. Since most problem-solving programs are related to one traditional subject or another, we chose to integrate discussions of problem-solving activities into the subjects where they seemed to fit best.

The content of this chapter was not meant to be all-inclusive. The hope is that coverage will be sufficiently broad that readers will find ideas that are useful to them, regardless of their field of specialization.

FIGURE 4.1 A Videodisc System

(Courtesy of Sony Corporation)

EARLY LEARNING AND READINESS

There are so many excellent traditional materials available, both commercially produced and teacher-made, that educators often find it difficult to say for certain if there is any room left for the computer in the early learning curriculum. If the computer served only as an electronic version of blocks, beads, and pictures, perhaps there would be room for speculation of this kind. But the computer has the potential to challenge children in special ways and to achieve difficult learning objectives with greater predictability than was possible in the past.

Seymour Papert, author of *Mindstorms* and developer of the Logo language, perceives the computer as being particularly useful in the teaching of defined or abstract concepts. "My conjecture is that the computer can concretize (and personalize) the formal," he states, and further "I believe that it can allow us to shift the boundary separating concrete and formal." The formal nature of so many essential ideas is a decided impediment for young learners to overcome, and many never succeed in doing this to the extent that they should. As a result, an adequate foundation upon which to build higher level learning is never established.

In addition to the ability to concretize the abstract, computers hold a fascination for young learners. Children love them. They are fascinated by the screen images and sound, and by the fact that they can elicit an immediate, personalized response with a simple key press. Software is becoming better all the time, and simpler for young students to use. With the increased utilization of speech synthesis and digitized speech, the ability to read text on the screen is no longer a critical consideration. Many of the better programs for preschoolers employ a game-type format that is both attractive and fun to use, with the content to be learned so neatly integrated that children enjoy staying on task longer than would be the case with straight drill-and-practice software. The range of subjects covered in the current software selection is broad, ranging from learning the alphabet to developing perceptual skills.

Software and Hardware for Early Learning Activities

Various peripheral equipment has been designed for use by young children and others who might benefit from input devices other than the standard keyboard. The Muppet Learning Keys Keyboard is one such device (Figure 4.2). It consists of a colorful set of large keys that plugs into the joystick port on the computer. Features include upper- and lower-case letters arranged in normal sequence, action buttons (Stop, Go, Erase), keys that select the upper and lower case options, and a print button for hard copy. Many early-learning programs are designed to be used with this keyboard. If you lack a special keyboard, you can make a regular keyboard easier for the students to use if you mark the most frequently used keys in special ways. For programs that use the return key to advance to the next frame you might place a green piece of tape with the word "GO" printed on it over this key. Put a strip of yellow tape (for "CAUTION") on the keys the children should use only for special purposes, and a red piece (for "STOP") on the key used to terminate the program.

Another input innovation is the touch screen. Rather than using keys to communicate with the computer, children merely touch their selection on a display of options and the computer responds. Made up of a frame with sensors positioned around its inner edges, the touch screen is simple to install and easy to use. The position of a child's finger is "read" by the sensors as a coordinate and the information is then sent to the computer for processing.

If you would like your computer to talk, you can install a speech synthesizer such as the Echo+ or Cricket from Street Electronics. Again, these are simple to hook up to the computer and often come packaged with speech-based programs such as Talking Text Writer from Scholastic. Speech-based software can offer a decided advantage over nonspeech versions in many instances. Children learning prereading skills can benefit greatly from this technology. Lacking the ability to read the text displayed on the monitor, and possessing little familiarity with the meaning of many of the words even if they could identify them, children receive critical help from clear, well-pronounced speech output.

In addition to having speech capabilities, programs for young learners are typically very colorful, have an abundance of graphics, employ large letters, and use considerable variety in presenting content. Programs designed for young children must be childproof in that a random press of a key does not cause unwanted consequences such as the lesson terminating prematurely. They should also have various provisions for ongoing input and feedback so the child is an

FIGURE 4.2 The Muppet
Learning Keys Keyboard

(Courtesy of Sunburst Communications Inc.)

active participant in the learning process. Programs that have various levels of difficulty provide children with challenges commensurate with their abilities, so they do not get bored with lessons that are too easy or discouraged by those too difficult. Reenforcement should be appropriate for the audience and designed in accordance with sound learning principles.

Computer-Based Learning in Early Childhood

The variety of activities children need in order to develop a strong foundation for the more formal curriculum to come is broad indeed. In order to prepare for the formidable mathematics activities they will encounter from the primary grades on, they need to be competent in shape recognition, classification skills, number recognition, counting, and many other related skills. In the language arts area they will require familiarity with the alphabet, functional language skills (important in all areas), and later, the ability to form letters and to recognize strings of them as particular words. The list is virtually endless and makes one wonder how young children can cope with what looks like a hopeless overload.

Teachers and parents do their best to create a rich environment by providing experiences and materials to stimulate young minds. In addition to the more traditional materials such as parquetry blocks, sequencing beads, felt board figures, alphabet posters, feely boxes, pictures, cut puzzles, figure-ground activity cards, and other such items, there are now computers.

Software producers have been quick to recognize the need for excellent software that appeals to young learners while at the same time stimulating them to learn critical skills. As you might expect, early learning software tends to reinforce the activities that are stressed in early childhood educational activities. These tend to be clustered in the traditional areas of math and reading and language arts, although lesser emphasis is given to writing, art, and perhaps one or two other subjects. While a few programs can be said to emphasize problem solving, this activity exists as a strand running through most software of this genre. Let us begin with a consideration of programs that teach math-related concepts.

Mathematics Software for Early Learners

Developing Basic Concepts.   Among the skills children must possess before they can graduate to more formal mathematical activities is shape recognition. Along with more traditional kinds of media, programs can be used to provide young children with practice in the discrimination of like and unlike shapes. Some programs use speech to communicate with the user: the instructions are frequently spoken by an animated character as a personalized touch. Children get involved in selecting shapes, manipulating them, and then asking the character to name the shapes. Some programs include a feature that lets the user create toys and other constructions from any combination of shapes desired.

Other programs are designed as games in which the learner positions and manipulates figures such as circles, squares, rectangles, triangles, and diamonds. Reenforcement for correct choices typically consists of different animated full-color pictures on the screen. An example of this type of program is Sticky Bear Shapes (Optimum Resources), in which the concept of opposites is taught by a bear on a unicycle, in a car, in a hot air balloon, and in other conveyances that enable him to move around to illustrate concepts such as in front of and behind, up and down, and full and empty.

The programming language Logo can also be used to teach various basic concepts. In one classroom, the teacher developed Logo procedures that could be called up with the press of a single key on the keyboard. Shapes of all kinds were displayed, and activities devised to involve the user in manipulating them, learning to identify and name them, and recognizing their positions on the screen.

Developing Number Concepts.   Counting and number recognition are stressed in number concept programs. In one such program various groups of colorful devices and creatures such as birds, airplanes, and trucks are used in numerous combinations to challenge the user's ability to use simple number skills. This use of animals and vehicles to enhance early learning math games is very common. Animated cartoons tend to be favorites as well, and often turn up in such programs. Muppetville, from Sunburst Communications, is an example. The objective is to develop identifying and classifying skills in young learners. The main character is Kermit the Frog, who takes a unicycle ride through the town, stopping at such places as Gonzo's Zoo and the Muppet Factory. Each time Kermit stops, one of the Muppet characters presents an activity in which the child works with shapes, numbers, and other items to develop perceptual skills. This program can be used with the Muppet Learning Keys or the Touch Window.

While many programs concentrate on a specific concept, other courseware packages are designed to teach more than one skill or concept in a particular area of the curriculum. Programs of this kind are described below.

Multiconcept Courseware Packages.   A common format for multiconcept software is the learning game. Various levels of difficulty are generally available, and operation is simplified so that the game can be played by pressing very few keys (frequently only the space bar and return key). Math Rabbit is typical (Figure 4.3). The concepts covered are counting, less and more, number recognition, addition, subtraction, identifying equivalencies, and number relationships. The setting is a circus ring of animals and performers such as clowns. There are four games, each of which provides different challenge levels that are structured so that they build on one another. Lively music and a dancing rabbit, with whom the children readily identify in this and other editions of the Rabbit series, make programs such as this favorites of young learners.

Another example of multiconcept courseware is Puzzle Works: Readiness, a series of three programs that deal with math and several others that deal with additional early learning activities. The math programs stress visual discrimination, association and classification, and numbers. Teacher support is excellent: the package contains a single disk, six pages for reproduction, a teacher's guide, a chart for keeping track of students' progress, and a teacher's key.

The programs listed do not lend themselves conveniently to whole class instructional strategies. Rather, they are best used by students sitting at the keyboard, working at their own pace through the exercises. This feature limits the time that students have to interact with the programs, but you can get more of

FIGURE 4.3   A Screen Shot from Math Rabbit

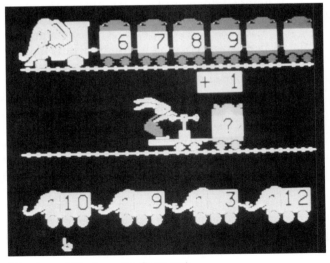

(Courtesy of The Learning Company)

them involved if more than one student is placed at a computer. This approach stimulates and encourages interpersonal sharing of ideas, and has been found to be a highly desirable plan even where sufficient equipment is available for individual student use.

Reading and Language Arts Software for Early Learners

Early learning activities in language arts are heavily oriented toward the development of prereading skills. Software producers have responded to signals from the market place and have issued an extensive selection of programs that provide training in this area. Software of this kind not only appeals to those in organized preschool and kindergarten settings, but it is popular with parents of young children who own a computer. Although preschoolers are the typical audience for which prereading software was developed, some versions are also used with special education students, adults with learning difficulties, and students in ESL classes. Software of this type is designed to develop the learner's oral vocabulary as well as reading readiness skills.

The range of specific academic skills covered by such programs is broad indeed, and includes practice in spelling, vocabulary development, letter-pattern recognition, and several reading skills including sight word acquisition, decoding, phonics, and comprehension.

In general, most programs in this area are of the drill-and-practice variety, although some have tutorial features. They generally involve the user in game-like activities, and all use color intensively. Some have speech capabilities; others have animation features. Because learning to read involves so much repetitious drill, programs incorporating such features can be very useful. They help to make the learning process less tedious and engage students longer than many traditional approaches do. Because the programs generally include tutorial features, a minimal amount of intervention is required. Teachers are thus able to spend more of their time dealing with problems that require human involvement.

The MECC Early Learning Series contains three reading readiness programs designed to help young children develop skills in letter identification, letter sounds, alphabet sequencing, vocabulary, and letter and word discrimination. The programs are titled First Letter Fun, which stresses matching the proper letters with the initial sounds of selected words, Fun From A to Z, which is an alphabet game, and Paint with Words, a vocabulary builder. The last title, illustrated in Figure 4.4, is typical of the series. Children have fun creating computer pictures from words they choose and manipulate. The words are selected and positioned on a background where they change into images that represent the words. A voice system made by the Jostens Company can be attached to the computer to create natural sounding voice output, which is a further aid to word recognition. After the screen picture has been "painted" the child can print it on paper in color using an AppleScribe ImageWriter II printer. Management options built into the programs permit teachers to modify the lessons to fit the individual needs of students.

FIGURE 4.4 A Screen Shot from
Paint with Words

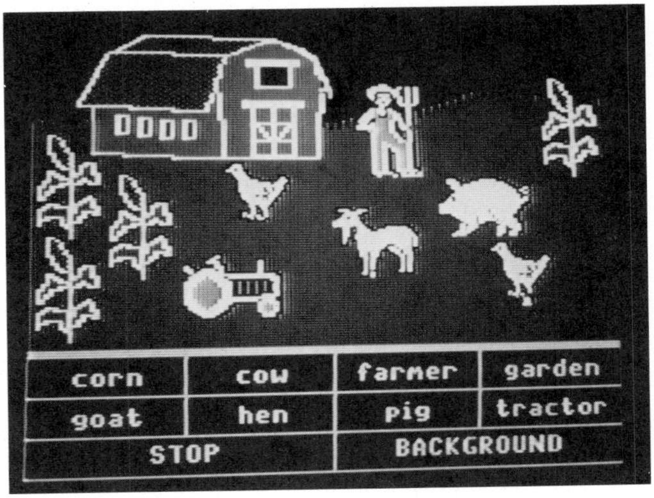

(Courtesy of MECC)

A program that stresses letter recognition is Easy As ABC. Large, easily read letters are displayed on the screen in various combinations. The student is challenged to select the letter appropriate to a given problem, such as that of sequencing as shown in Figure 4.5. Various kinds of reinforcement are provided when the correct letter is pressed. In the case illustrated, the middle frog develops a grin of satisfaction and leaps about on the screen. Soaring rockets and other types of animation are also used to keep children fascinated as they learn letter concepts.

FIGURE 4.5 A Screen Shot from
Easy as ABC

(Courtesy of Springboard Software, Inc.)

As a rule, prereading courseware employs sequenced game-like activities in such areas as letter and word recognition, memory building, and vocabulary development. Many are matched to reading curriculums common to the schools. Colorful screen pictures are used to illustrate concepts and supply reenforcement. A customizing option that enables teachers to tailor lessons to meet individual student needs and a record-keeping system for maintaining an ongoing record of the progress of each member of the class are frequently provided.

Talking Word Processors

In addition to the various early learning drill tutorials that are speech-based, a number of talking word processors for use by children have been developed.

Combining speech with the traditional word processor has provided a tool that enables the youngest of students to become involved with activities formerly reserved for older children. As the learner's skills expand, he or she is able to take advantage of the higher level capabilities possessed by the program, and can continue in this fashion until a move to a more sophisticated program is feasible.

Dr. Peet's Talk/Writer (Figure 4.6) is simple enough that it can be used by the youngest students. The program is introduced by an uncomplicated tutorial in which the computer sings the ABC song and letters are identified. Then the user moves on to more traditional activities such as typing letters, words, and sen-

FIGURE 4.6 Dr. Peet's Talk/Writer is a Popular First Level Word Processor

(Printed with Permission from Hartley Courseware, Inc., Dimondale, Michigan)

tences (if he or she has reached this stage). As the letters and words are entered, the speech synthesizer sounds them out. A menu is provided for use by the teacher to modify the pronunciation of selected words, control the sound feature, and set the program up so it can be used by visually impaired individuals.

Speech Synthesizers

To enable a computer that lacks speech capabilities to speak, a speech synthesizer in the form of a special circuit board must be added to the computer. These devices typically include an attached volume control and a port for earphones. Adding any kind of card (or board) is easy to do. Slots for peripherals are typically provided within the computer so that its capabilities can be expanded. It is in one of these that the synthesizer is positioned. The procedure is illustrated in Figure 4.7, although the card shown is not a synthesizer.

Some synthesizers come packaged with the speech versions of programs, but in other cases you might have to buy one separately. Fortunately, the cost of this kind of device has dropped considerably, and is easily within reach of both individuals and schools. Low cost and availability have made speech technology a favorite of software producers and users alike. With the addition of the voice feature to early learning programs, one of the ongoing problems with this kind of software has been largely resolved. This is the necessity for an adult, or at least a student who reads, to interpret instructions and other text material for the young learner who cannot read. In the future, virtually all software designed for reading readiness applications will have speech capabilities, and the technology promises to become ever more sophisticated and capable of producing better and more realistic speech output.

FIGURE 4.7 Inserting a Card into an Empty Slot Within the Computer

(Courtesy of Apple Computer, Inc.)

MATHEMATICS

As noted previously, one of the greatest success stories in computer assisted instruction, using improved student performance as the measure, has been in the area of mathematics. Perhaps this is the case because the greatest instructional use of the computer has been in math education. This is understandable in light of the fact that most mathematics teachers have had some experience with computers and feel unintimidated by them. Indeed, the math department in the secondary school is the place where the computer has traditionally been found. Math and computers have always been perceived as "going together," and, indeed, there is much to be said for this assumption. The logical structure of mathematics, its emphasis on procedures, and its problem-solving characteristics are precisely those features that characterize computer operations. In addition, the algorithmic nature of programming languages represents a high degree of correspondence to many mathematical procedures.

In the conventional mathematics curriculum, the major effort continues to be the mastery of a defined set of skills rather than an emphasis on developing problem-solving strategies, although increasing attention is being paid to the latter approach. Because the mathematics curriculum continues to be traditional for the most part, software producers have responded with traditional kinds of software that support this orientation. Consequently, most mathematics programs are of the drill-and-practice variety with some having various kinds of tutorial features. There are, however, increasing numbers of programs that involve the user in logical thinking exercises frequently referred to collectively as problem-solving software. In this section we shall examine examples of each type of program, describing representative titles. Many are very effective and are highly regarded by mathematics teachers. It should be emphasized, however, that there are many situations in which traditional paper and pencil operations are the most efficient way to do exercises in math. As with other disciplines, the computer should be utilized when its capabilities make it the best of available alternatives.

Software and Hardware for Mathematics Instruction

Special peripherals such as alternative input devices, probeware, and MIDI musical instruments are not essential acquisitions in mathematics as they are in some other disciplines. Virtually all CAI math activities can be carried out with a standard system and appropriate software. From the standpoint of numbers, the range of programs for the teaching of math is a broad one indeed; there are literally hundreds available. The most straightforward format is that of drill-and-practice. There are also tutorials, many of which are coupled with drills and thus might be termed drill/tutorials. There are also various simulations, most of which are not listed as math programs, that have a degree of usefulness in the mathematics curriculum. One early simulation fitting this description is Lemonade Stand, in which estimates are made as to the number of glasses of lemonade and signs to produce given varying circumstances such as weather and road construction. The cost of production is then compared with the number of glasses sold (as calculated by the computer) to determine whether or not a profit or loss resulted.

Tools such as spreadsheets, data bases, and graphing software are also used in varying degrees in mathematics education. Both the Logo and the BASIC programming languages have applications in the math class, the former being useful in teaching geometry because of its graphics capabilities.

There is much that is repetitive in learning mathematics. As mentioned, drill programs have been developed in large numbers to fill this need, but many simple computer-based drills do little that cannot be done with paper and pencil. This powerful technology should not be wasted on mundane operations of this nature. But there are also many excellent drills available, and they continue to improve all the time. Programs of this type are useful for several reasons.

To begin with, much of what constitutes math is factual and skills oriented and these kinds of things can only be internalized through practice and more practice. Such practice becomes routine and monotonous, challenging young and old learners alike to stay on task until mastery is gained. Computer-based drills, if imaginatively designed, can add variety that makes the activity more interesting and less tiring.

Such software can also tutor the student, helping him or her to progress through passages that might be difficult or even impossible without additional help. A human teacher can do this also, but not as intensively or continuously as a computer, which is always available. A human teacher will also praise the student for work well done, but the praise might be late in coming or it might be overlooked. The computer can present reinforcing feedback at precisely the proper moment, and while it might not be as warm and personal as that from the teacher, it can be very effective if well designed. These features, among others, can help to make the essential drill-and-practice sessions, often remedial in nature, much less boring than they might otherwise be.

Along with drill-and-practice software, there are also many packages designed around the tutorial format. Students can continue at their own pace until a problem is encountered; at that point they can ask for help, which is provided in various ways. For example, in a procedural problem such as solving an equation, the computer might illustrate the sequential steps involved in the solution. In another instance, computers might use graphics instead of theorems to explain the basics of geometry. Such displays can be evolving and active, demonstrating the nature of various figures in a dynamic form.

CAI Software in Mathematics Instruction

To represent a broad sampling of software used in the mathematics curriculum, we have selected several diverse areas for our discussion. These are computation skills, fractions, problem solving, algebra, and geometry. Another area, math readiness, was discussed in the preceding section on early learning.

Teaching Computation Skills. There are more drill-and-practice/tutorial programs available for the teaching of computation skills than for any other area of mathematics. Many of the drills are made more appealing and interesting by using animated characters with whom young children can identify, such as the Stickybear Math I and Math II computation programs. Game-type formats are widely used for older students.

An interesting approach with appeal for girls is found in Fay, That Math Woman. In this program, the action is carried out by a female figure rather than by the more traditional cartoon or animal character. A small animated female figure is positioned on a number line, where she moves in appropriate ways to illustrate the meaning of the various mathematical operations the child has to identify (Figure 4.8). For example, in the addition component the problem might be to add 2 + 4. To demonstrate this, Faye will walk two units, then stop briefly, and then walk four units before ending at six. Other operations are illustrated in a similar manner.

An intriguing change of pace is offered in the program Piece of Cake Math. The setting for the five learning modules is a "magical computerized bakery" in the words of the publisher. One of the activities involves students in addition and subtraction activities in which cakes are the elements manipulated. One approach to subtraction involves showing the total number of cakes produced by the bakers and indicating the number sold. The student is asked to indicate how many are left. The approach to addition, which is similar, is illustrated in Figure 4.9. If the answer is correct, the display changes to reflect this; if it is not, a series of approaches to tutoring the student in subtraction is undertaken. The varied methods used for this constitute one of the strong features of the program: the effects become increasingly concrete, and employ graphics and animation until the child understands the concept clearly. Note that the lower levels of this program can be useful in early learning activities.

Games are also used widely in the teaching of computation skills as well as other math concepts. Many are in the arcade game format, and involve the kinds

FIGURE 4.8 The Arrangement of the Number Lines in Fay: That Math Woman

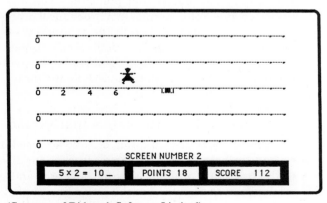

(Courtesy of Didatech Software Limited)

FIGURE 4.9 A Screen Display
Showing a Problem in Addition
from Piece of Cake Math

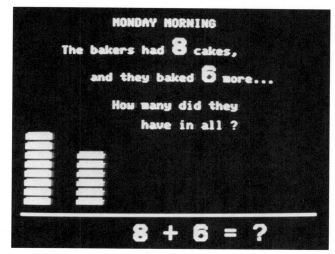

(Courtesy of Springboard Software, Inc.)

of action activities for which these are noted. A very popular arcade game is Math
Blaster, mentioned in Chapter 3.

Teaching about Fractions.   The computer's graphics and animation capabilities can be used to great advantage in making clear the difficult ideas involved
in dealing with fractions. For example, one program incorporates a candy bar,
which is cut into halves, quarters, and eighths to demonstrate how the parts of a
whole are related and how they are identified. The candy is sliced as the students
work at the keyboard, then each segment moves to a different position on the
screen. The parts can be recombined and recut as desired. The action takes place
within the context of a story in which the owner of the candy bar is called upon
to share it with varying numbers of friends. This activity has proved to be very
effective in actual practice.

A 10-store shopping mall is used as the setting in a program designed to teach
about fractions and other math skills. When working with this program, titled
Math Shop, students become clerks in the various stores where they must use
various math skills as they attend to the needs of their customers. In one store
they must add decimal numbers, in another they must multiply fractions, while
in yet another they are called upon to figure percentages. The problems become
more difficult in each shop, but ongoing assistance in solving them is provided by
the computer. A screen shot from Math Shop is shown in Figure 4.10.

Problem Solving Software.   An early award-winning program in this category
is Rocky's Boots from the Learning Company. This program induces students to
think logically as it requires them to construct "machines" that use, among other
things, a kind of logic common to computers. In order for the machine to work,
its logical structure must be correct. Students must first learn to identify the
components available to them (logic gates, sensors, wires, and a boot); then they

FIGURE 4.10 In This Example from Math Shop by Scholastic Software a Customer Has Just Paid One Dollar for an Item and Is Waiting for You to Make Change

must plan the machine, making it as efficient as possible. Building the machine comes next, followed by a test run to determine if there are any problems. Fixing the problems is often an intensive problem-solving challenge involving a certain amount of trial-and-error testing of alternatives. Students learn procedural skills as they pass through the various phases described. They also develop problem-solving skills that might be generalizable to other learning situations.

A popular tool for use in problem-solving activities is Logo, a programming language, which is discussed later on in this section and also in the chapter on programming.

Algebra and Geometry. The development of software in algebra and geometry has been fairly straightforward, since the content and pedagogy in both subjects are fairly well established. With this to guide them, software producers have proceeded with the design of numerous selections that fit readily into the established curriculum. Most of these are in the drill/tutorial format, although a few have simulation and game features.

A typical approach is illustrated by Algebra Shop, the companion to Math Shop, mentioned previously. The setting is a store in which students take the role of workers whose job is to assist customers using different algebra-related concepts. Customers are taken one at a time by workers who must use proper solutions to solve a given problem before the next customer can be served. For example, finding the common factor of several numbers is required when the "clerk" is asked to find the proper number and size of containers for a particular order. Various levels of difficulty are provided for, increasing from one customer to the next, but the student might also elect to move from one shop to the next for different challenges. Slower students can spend as much time as needed to master a concept; by staying in only one store, the challenge is further simplified. Instructions accompany each problem and, if an error is made, appropriate and helpful clues are provided to help the user over difficult spots.

Geometry lessons in four areas are combined in The Geometric Supposer, a highly rated series from Sunburst. In addition to programs on triangles, quadrilaterals, and circles, there is also one called The Geometric preSupposer, which provides a foundation for geometry by presenting such concepts as congruence, similarity, and parallelism. Also available as adjuncts to the disk-based material are blackline masters and videotapes. Geometric figures can easily be constructed to demonstrate theorems using the graphics features of the programs; students can more readily construct triangles, quadrilaterals, and circles using the computer than they can with traditional methods. This encourages experimentation and inquiry, and stimulates students to conjecture on the theorems involved.

Spreadsheets in Math Instruction

Students learning to use a spreadsheet should be spared the rigors of designing the necessary formulas until they have gained confidence in using the various calculation features. Templates are predesigned spreadsheet formats containing the necessary formulas to do the required calculations on data entered by a user. By preparing the templates ahead of time, teachers provide students with a tool for performing various mathematical functions as it stimulates thinking about the logical connections among values, number patterns, and other concepts. Later, when they are ready to do so, students can be challenged to enter their own formulas, simple ones at first, and then more complex ones.

As a beginning, students can work with a spreadsheet using an appropriate template. The activity might involve data from the members of the class, such as height or weight of all the members. The template might be so designed that it contains the formula for obtaining the mean weight for the class, the high and low extremes, and the total weight of all students. From this modest beginning, activities can become more complex.

For example, a spreadsheet might be designed to calculate the area of various geometric figures. Input would be in the form of dimensions, which would vary according to the desires of the user. The input for a square would be a single number, the length of a side; for a rectangle, two numbers, and so on. Students would be called upon to design the formula for area so that it conformed to the format required by the spreadsheet. Exercises of this kind are very useful in helping students understand the structure and functions of a formula.

Problems of immediate interest to students, such as those having to do with automobiles, can create considerable excitement. For instance, a spreadsheet might be constructed to examine the relative costs of making a given trip in cars of varying gasoline consumption. Formulas can be designed so that the length of the trip as well as the average mileage obtained by a particular model of automobile can be entered to derive the total cost for the trip. Other refinements might be added by students working together in teams, and ideas from the various teams might then be incorporated into a master template of considerable versatility.

Most spreadsheets have graphing capabilities and can produce paper copy in the form of line, column, and pie graphs from the data displayed on the screen.

Thus, graphics can be prepared that support a term paper or other such project, enhancing the material and making it more understandable.

Programming in Math Instruction

Mention was made previously of the close correspondence between many mathematical activities and those involved in programming. For example, the algorithmic approach used in solving math problems is precisely that employed in writing a computer program. The two activities are more or less interchangeable: the step-by-step approach of solving mathematical problems is readily applied to the development of programming algorithms; the algorithmic approach helps students think through the steps needed to arrive at the correct solution to a mathematics problem.

Intrinsic to programming languages are various mathematics functions that make possible the writing of routines to solve an assortment of advanced problems. In the BASIC language these include the following: ABS (absolute value), INT (integer), SIN, COS, LOG, and RND (random number). The RND function is also useful when programs are being written for areas besides mathematics, since it generates a variety of output in a random fashion. Thus, questions can be posed in a different fashion every time the program is used; reinforcement messages can be randomized to add greater variety and appeal to a lesson, and so on.

Logo is a programming language frequently used in the teaching of geometry. In his book *Mindstorms,* Seymour Papert speaks of Logo in terms of a way of doing geometry that is simply a different approach from that of Descartes or Euclid. He goes on to speak of the similarity between Euclid's point and Logo's turtle which are, as Papert sees it, fundamental entities in each system. Beyond this, turtles can be said to have properties the point lacks. Turtles are dynamic and have a heading. "Children can identify with the turtle and are thus able to bring their knowledge about their bodies and how they move into the work of learning formal geometry." The turtle "understands" commands given to it in the Logo language, and, if the syntax is correct, will respond in predictable ways to them.

For example, typing FORWARD followed by a number will cause the turtle to go forward in the direction of its heading a distance specified by the number. Therefore, FORWARD 30 will cause a line to be drawn that is 30 "turtle tracks" in length. To change the heading of the turtle the command is RIGHT or LEFT followed by a number that expresses degrees of turn in this fashion: RIGHT 90. Typing this will cause the turtle physically to turn to the new heading. Repeating these commands four times will cause a square to be drawn.

After learning the rudiments of Logo, students can be called upon to generate various kinds of geometric figures using the REPEAT command. Regular polygons are easily formed this way. Students must figure out the different angles required to construct the various kinds of polygons; this is a relatively simple matter for a square, but becomes increasingly more challenging as the number of sides increases. An even greater challenge is to figure a procedure for generating a circle.

Logo is a natural tool for teaching coordinate geometry because a pair of co-ordinates are used to define the location of the turtle and other elements on the screen. The concept of negative numbers can also be taught in conjunction with the activity of plotting points on the screen.

Because of the graphic nature of Logo, students find working with it fascinating. They are encouraged to experiment with geometric shapes, which are displayed with progressive animation and in bright colors, much to the delight of the user. In their efforts to teach the turtle to execute various configurations, students get involved in using logic and problem-solving skills that may carry over to other kinds of math activities. Additional information on Logo, including a description of various commands and how to write a program, is found in Chapter 8.

Graphing Programs

Mention was made in the preceding section of the graphing capabilities of spreadsheets. Other programs are devoted exclusively to the creation of such graphics. For example, Exploring Tables and Graphs Level 1 and Level 2 (Optimum Resource) provide an introduction to the nature of tables and graphs. Level 1 is designed for ages seven to ten while Level 2 is for learners from ten years on up. Level 1 involves students in experiments with tables and three varieties of graphs: picture, bar, and area. Both real-life and game applications are provided. The line graph is added to the other three varieties in the Level 2 program. Various real-life topics of interest to modern students are used in the applications exercises. Both programs provide a tutorial on one side of the disk and hands-on activities on the other side, which provides practice in applying the principles covered in the tutorial. Students can construct their own graphs using various kinds of data, modify them on the screen, and then print them on paper. Other graphing programs are described in Chapter 6.

Data Bases

A data base provides a tool for storing data collected from a number of sources. Once the data have been obtained and organized, they can serve as the basis for generating graphs using a graphing program. One common source of data is the survey, in which a questionnaire or interview is used to obtain information on a particular topic. The group questioned is typically made up of a sample randomly selected from a larger population. The data are stored in a data base to be retrieved and transferred to a spreadsheet, where the statistics such as means, medians, standard deviations, and the like are calculated. These are used in further activities to describe or make inferences about the larger population. A discussion of spreadsheets and data bases is provided in Chapter 6.

READING AND LANGUAGE ARTS

Proficiency in reading and writing is the most important factor in how well a student succeeds in school. Little wonder that so much emphasis is placed on the language arts curriculum in the elementary and middle schools and, later, on English in the senior high school. Although the approach to teaching language proficiency is changing from a product approach to one that stresses process, in most schools the traditional orientation prevails. The product approach in language arts, as in mathematics, stresses the mastery of various subskills that lend themselves to concentrated study apart from other related subskills. As competence grows, a clustering of these into larger units occurs, permitting products of greater complexity to be generated. In such an approach, the emphasis is on getting correct answers, examples being identifying the parts of speech, capitalizing the proper words, or punctuating a sentence correctly. Software producers have designed the bulk of their offerings around the product model; thus, an abundance of drill-and-practice programs are to be found.

An estimated up to half of the available language arts software is of this kind. On the other hand, teachers who lean toward the process approach will employ various kinds of tool software in their teaching. The word processor is a favored instrument for encouraging students to write more, while related tools such as spelling checkers and the thesaurus are also widely used.

In process writing, teachers seldom engage in the well-known routine of marking misspelled words and incorrect verb tenses with a red pencil. Instead, they assist students in refining their compositions by making suggestions directly in the document using the computer. With pen and paper, or even a typewriter, most students find the revision process boring and frustrating. Having creatively composed their piece, they must now labor over it to correct the mechanics involved. Electronic tools permit students to respond to the teacher's comments embedded in their work by using spellers, style checkers, and related aids. As they use such tools, students learn many skills they might otherwise have given up on. The speller constantly presents correct spellings for problem words, and the thesaurus reveals meanings they might never see using traditional writing methods. Electronic writing tools permit young writers to concentrate on content—the result is that they enjoy writing more, and consequently will likely do much more of it.

Software and Hardware for Teaching Language Arts

The same concerns prevail for language arts drill-and-practice software as for that in mathematics: many of the activities could be carried out just as well using paper and pencils or other established methods. As with mathematics, a certain amount of drill is important to establish the skills base needed for more creative activities. The challenge is to make this as interesting as possible; here is where the computer can help. Many language arts programs in the drill format make good use of the unique capabilities of the computer.

Because the nature of a drill is such that it is best used in a one-on-one fashion, the utility of even superior programs is somewhat limited without sufficient equipment. In such cases, the program could be used for remedial applications, but this might relegate both the user and the computer to a lesser status in the eyes of the other students.

Another approach is to identify specific passages in certain drills that are worth having all students experience. This can be accomplished by having them rotate through the exercise as other class members engage in workbook or related activities. Sometimes a passage in a drill can be adapted to the whole-class instruction approach employing a computer and large screen monitor or projection panel. Certain tutorial segments placed in the program in the form of HELP screens meant to be called up by the student as problems are encountered can be used this way. By sharing these with the entire class you can cut down on the individual time students need to spend at the keyboard, thus making the computer more available.

While the drill-and-practice format is favored for those who use the product approach in teaching language arts, tools are most useful when process is stressed. The predominant tool in process writing is, of course, the word processor. Also useful for certain activities is the data base. Students can create their own data bases or can use those, such as banks of synonyms, that are available commercially.

Of special importance is a display of sufficient size and clarity to enable the user to read the materials without difficulty. While adequate for many CAI programs, perhaps the least suitable display for text is a color TV receiver. Inexpensive monochrome monitors are a much better choice where text output is involved. On the other hand, improved color monitors that have sufficiently high resolution to permit text to be displayed with great clarity are now becoming more popular. This is due in part to the fact that some word processors are able to work in full color.

Printers are also important. Inexpensive dot matrix varieties are suitable for draft copies of a document, and most are also capable of generating graphics, a useful feature when printing products such as newsletters. More capable printers of this kind provide, in addition to the "dotty" draft copy, near-letter-quality output that looks very nearly like the printing from an electric typewriter. Other types of printer, including the popular laser, are discussed in Chapter 2.

Although we elected to consider reading and writing separately, in actual practice the division is not so distinct. As Douglas Clements (1985) points out, "Experiences that help children to write also help them to read. Activities that develop speaking vocabularies of students simultaneously develop their ability to comprehend oral and written communication of others." Although Clements was referring specifically to the early and primary grades, his statement holds true for learners at all levels.

Before considering activities and associated software for teaching writing, we will examine approaches to teaching specific language skills of a type that collectively make up the product-oriented curriculum.

Software and Activities for Basic Language Skills Development

An examination of almost any educational software catalog will reveal the extent to which producers have committed themselves to developing basic skills programs. Among the language arts courseware is the highly rated series titled Words at Work, which includes various self-explanatory titles such as Contraction Action, Prefix Power, Suffix Sense, and Compound It! Each of the titles is self-contained, addressing a separate area to be studied, and can be used individually if desired. Contraction Action is representative of the titles in the series. Recognizing, spelling, and matching contractions and their corresponding words are the activities stressed in this program. A record is maintained of the student's progress and various features can be tailored by the teacher to meet individual needs. A printing option is available. Various formats are provided within the program, including a concentration game and a spelling feature that has students spell contractions when their corresponding words are shown, or spell the words when the contractions are shown.

Suffix Sense encourages students to practice the recognition and identification of suffixes and root words and to learn the meanings of words containing suffixes. Four games provide the format for learning common suffixes, one of which is illustrated in Figure 4.11. Problems are generated randomly from a problem pool designed by the teacher. Graphics are used throughout. Several useful management features are provided, including automatic maintenance of student records, variable performance levels, and an optional use of context sentences.

There is no lack of exotic settings and colorful characters used in programs of this type to make them more attractive to young learners. For instance, Wizard of Words, a spelling and vocabulary program, is designed as a medieval world filled with a collection of animated and colorful medieval personalities, including knights, heralds, a princess, and a dragon. The program consists of five word games, each containing eight learning levels. The Wizard is in control of activities, providing appropriate words throughout the game from a list of 38,000 entries. The teacher can tailor the program to the desired level and can use a built-in authoring system to add words or lessons. The games will accommodate individuals or several students at a time (Figure 4.12).

Another program with an unusual setting is Grammar Gremlins. One segment consists of a fast-paced game set in a haunted house. Displayed with the house is

FIGURE 4.11   Suffix Sense Is a Concentration Game from MECC

FIGURE 4.12   The Wizard Is an Animated Character Who Controls the Learning Activities in Wizard of Words from Advanced Ideas, Inc.

a sentence containing blank spaces or a question on some aspect of grammar. Possible answers to problems float out of the windows like so many ghosts, and the player must indicate whether the answers are correct or incorrect by pressing various keys. When the Gremlin emerges from the window, extra points are awarded. The faster the player identifies a correct answer, the higher will be the score. The areas covered are subject and verb agreement, contractions, parts of speech, sentence structure, plurals, punctuation, and possessives. An easy to use editor enables the teacher to add his or her own practice sentences.

Writing Software and Activities

Teachers who emphasize process writing in their classes are quick to admit that basic skills and concept acquisition is an important part of learning to write well. They agree that process writing does not mean that students are simply turned loose to do their own thing. Both drill programs aimed at skills enhancement and concept acquisition and writing programs (as well as word processors) used in process writing are discussed in this section.

Teddy Bear-rels is highly graphics oriented. Young learners can select from over 200 ready-made pieces of art and borders to create just about any kind of illustration they desire. Original backgrounds, border designs, and other graphics are easy to produce with the aid of a graphics tablet. The graphics can then be used along with a variety of letter styles to write stories, make captions, design headlines, and produce titles. The Text Writer is an easy to use feature with various type faces and sizes. This approach is calculated to encourage students to have fun composing, and to do much more of it as a consequence (Figure 4.13).

Various schemes and models are commonly employed to provide a framework for the activities in which learners engage. One such model in Writer Rabbit uses the "W" words (What, did What, When, Where, Why, and How), to present the parts of speech. Rewards are animated and colorful, and have considerable appeal for young learners. For example, for a correct answer the first time around, a three-scoop carrot ice cream cone is provided on the screen. The size diminishes as more guesses are taken, with the empty cone finally being displayed along with the correct answer.

A popular and effective approach to motivating young creative writers is the story starter. Once a subject has been selected from the list of titles a "what if?" branching procedure assists the student to develop an original story. Word processing capabilities permit changes to be made as the story progresses. Additional story starters can be created and stored on the disk by the teacher or student.

Also useful are outliners or idea processors, which store ideas as they are typed in. The user composes at the keyboard as he or she would with a regular word processor, but each idea is listed separately. These are selectively arranged to serve as outlines for compositions.

Some programs provide the capabilities of a regular talking word processor as well as a word bank feature that stores words as they are formed. These programs support either typed or dictated input and also display words on the screen or speak them as output. Each word is saved in an alphabetized list that can be used by the writer to create additional compositions.

FIGURE 4.13 Teddy Bear-rels of Fun Is a Graphics-Oriented Writing Program from DLM, Inc.

Complete writing programs containing regular writing tools, such as a word processor, a spelling checker, and a thesaurus, as well as several specialized tools for organizing a document, are also available. Features include such things as an "outliner" to assist in developing an outline and a "notetaker" which is used to generate notes. The notetaker provides data-base-like features such as searching and sorting.

Several distinct stages are common to the process of writing. An early step is prewriting, and a considerable number of programs are devoted to this activity. Then comes the writing stage in which ideas are refined and ordered. Finally, the document is revised and edited until it can be said to be finished. Various programs designed to lead the user through the various stages of writing are available. Programs of this kind typically provide modules devoted to the key stages in composition: prewriting, organizing, composing, and editing. The prewriting module helps students develop ideas for stories by using techniques such as free writing. Prompted activities help students organize the prewriting materials in the arranging module. A word processor is included in the composing module to enable students to convert the work from the preceding two modules into a composition. Style checkers and spelling checkers provide writers with tools for refining their work and adding the finishing touches.

Word Processing Activities

While many of the programs described above provide word processing capabilities of varying degrees of sophistication, these are but part of a larger package that includes such features as story starters, idea processors, and outliners. In this section we will discuss dedicated word processor programs: those lacking CAI features and used strictly as tools. This kind of program is devoted to productivity rather than to learning as such, although learning occurs, as it does even when writing activities are undertaken with tools as basic as paper and pencil.

A wide array of word processing programs is available in varying levels of sophistication. Several that are useful in early learning activities are described in the previous chapter; various others are covered in detail in Chapter 5, while exercises are provided in Appendix G.

All word processors have five features in common: text entry, text editing, formatting, saving and using files, and printing. The first two features are typically combined to the extent that you can both enter information and make corrections at the same time. However, the two modes are readily apparent in the early version of Bank Street Writer, which requires that the user switch from write mode to edit mode by pressing the escape key on the computer keyboard.

The formatting function lets you change features such as margins, line width, and spacing to customize the document. As the document is being composed, you should save it periodically as a file on the disk. Files thus stored are then retrieved as needed. The print feature provides the means for producing a paper copy of the document.

Once students have become familiar with these several features, they can begin to concentrate on the process of writing unencumbered by such problems as poor handwriting, or by the fear of making mistakes, since corrections are so easy to make. They can brainstorm at the keyboard, quickly saving ideas that show promise while erasing others with a few keystrokes. Words and blocks of words can be moved about and inserted at any point in the document. Spelling errors are found by the speller, to be corrected or changed as desired. And the dreaded revision task becomes relatively easy when a word processing program is being used. The finished document is easily printed in a clean, attractive format sure to please student and teacher alike.

While many commercial programs provide writing exercises of various kinds, creating your own lessons using a word processor is quite easy to do. For example, you might type a series of sentences using only lowercase letters. The students are required to capitalize the proper words by making the changes on the computer and saving their corrected lesson for you to check. This same approach can be used for just about any grammar activity. You might also scramble a literary selection and challenge students to rearrange it so that it is syntactically correct.

LogoWriter is a program that combines a word processing feature with programming, sound, and graphics capabilities. (Logo, the precursor to LogoWriter, is mentioned in other chapters of this text; a detailed discussion is provided in the chapter on programming and authoring.)

As its name implies, LogoWriter stresses writing. The graphics features of the earlier Logo are maintained, but text capabilities are greatly expanded in the newer version. Students can type words any place on the screen; they can even label illustrations they have created, moving the words so they correspond to parts of the graphic. LogoWriter can also serve as a 40-column word processor, providing capabilities similar to other word processing programs. Several students can write individual compositions on a topic using the word processing feature and can then use the programming component to write instructions so the computer will link all the separate files together into a single document. This multitalented software can provide an endless array of activities for language arts teachers and their students.

Data Bases and Activity Files for Writing

Programs are available containing information on a range of subjects along with various prewriting and writing activities for use with a word processing program.

BookWorm is a program from MECC that teaches fundamental data base concepts while serving as a tool for writing book reports. Users provide the computer with information about books they have read. The program organizes this into records that can be searched and edited to provide the basis for the report. A printing option provides a paper copy of the finished report.

Scholastic offers several disk-based writing activity files for use with their Bank Street Writer III word processing program. Ready To Write is a bank of writing activities for younger students using the 20-column large-type feature of Bank Street Writer. The twenty activities include developing sentences, working with story structures, and enhancing writing and storytelling skills.

Another title in the series is Writing Skills Bank. Containing 40 lessons and 150 writing activities, this instrument also provides the teacher with the means for building customized lessons.

Those mentioned are but a small sample of the many writing banks available. With a bit of effort you should be able to find files on just about any subject in which you have an interest.

Other Writing Tools

In addition to word processors and data bases, several other useful aids to writing are available. Among these are spelling, style and grammar checkers, and the electronic thesaurus. All are designed to be used in conjunction with a word processor. The usual method for using a program of this kind is to remove the data disk (the one containing the document you are working on) from its drive, then to insert the checker or thesaurus disk and strike certain keys to call it up. After the document has been checked, you return to the normal word processing functions, remove the checker disk, insert the data disk, and continue to work on the document. Hard disk systems have enough memory to install the checker and thesaurus permanently.

Spelling checkers compare words in the document with a stored dictionary of up to 100,000 words. In a typical program of this kind the computer moves through the document searching for misspellings, double words, and certain other problems depending upon the kind of checker being used. When a misspelled word or word not recognized is encountered, it is highlighted and a list of possible words are presented on the screen. Several options are available at this point, including correcting the word, or skipping it or adding it to the dictionary (if it is a correctly spelled word not already in the dictionary). Various brands of applications software are available for school use; one such program is shown in Figure 4.14.

Grammar checkers are convenient proofreading tools used to locate common writing mistakes. Thousands of the most frequently misused English phrases provide the search clues for the program. Phrases that are pompous, informal, cliches, vague, wordy, repetitive, or sexist are quickly located and the errors displayed in context. Replacement wordings are suggested, which can be quickly substituted for the problem phrases. A typical screen shot from a program of this kind is shown in Figure 4.15.

Style checker programs let writers examine their documents for problems such as wordiness, redundancy, overuse of passive voice, and so on. Students might also use them to study the writing styles of noteworthy authors. Style checkers also find common mistakes in punctuation and various grammatical errors such as incomplete sentences. Once a problem has been identified, the style checker, like the other checkers, makes suggestions for correcting errors and improving overall writing quality.

The electronic thesaurus represents a valuable addition to the writing tools mentioned. The problem of finding just the right word to express an idea is solved

FIGURE 4.14   Sensible Speller Is
a Popular Spelling Checker

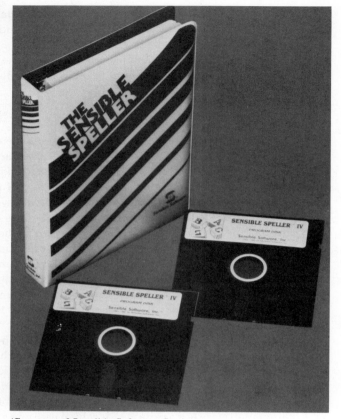

(Courtesy of Sensible Software, Inc.)

when you put the thesaurus to work. As you compose the document you can stop
at any word and request a list of synonyms from which a more satisfactory alternative can be selected.

Publication Systems

Desktop publishing programs provide the means for creating attractive newsletters, newspapers, books, and other materials that formerly required special skills
and a printing press for their production. With programs of this kind you can
involve students in every phase of the publishing process including composing,
editing, typesetting, illustrating, layout, and printing.

An excellent program for school use is Print Shop, a product from Broderbund
Software. This tool provides a variety of clip art (pictures), several different letter
designs (type fonts), typesetting functions, formatting options, and a freehand
drawing feature that lets you modify existing art or create your own.

Desktop publishing programs are discussed in detail and examples shown in
Chapter 6.

FIGURE 4.15   Sensible Grammar for the Macintosh Searches for Cliche Expressions.

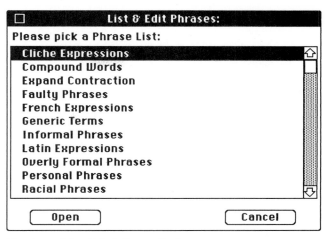

(Courtesy of Sensible Software, Inc.)

Reading Software and Activities

Various kinds of tools are available for teaching reading in addition to the ubiquitous drill/tutorial software. For example, speed reading programs with features for adjusting the rate at which the text is presented are used by many teachers. Comprehension tools present a written selection, which the student reads, followed by a series of questions to determine the extent of comprehension.

Much reading software, like that used in the product approach to writing, concentrates on the development of subskills which, once mastered, are amalgamated into products of greater complexity. Again, the emphasis is on getting correct answers; that is, on identifying a word, pronouncing it correctly, deriving the "right" meaning from a statement. All this is necessary and important, and good software is of considerable help in achieving proficiency in the many subskills that combine to make a capable reader.

Software producers have developed a wealth of materials for use in the reading area. Because of the close relationship between reading and writing, it is not surprising that many programs incorporate both activities into their structure. One example of a program of this kind is Writing To Read, from IBM. In learning a fundamental skill, students progress from one stage to the next aided by a multimedia approach that includes voice output, audio recordings, and interactive CAI.

An example of the way the system works follows: To begin, a picture of a cat might be shown while, at the same time, a voice directs the child to repeat the phonemes that make up the word as he or she types it at the keyboard. This activity is reinforced by an audio recording of the word or words and their phonemes followed by hands-on activities at the computer.

Writing To Read has been adopted by many schools and districts. For example Mississippi, a state with a very high illiteracy rate, recently selected this program for inclusion in every public elementary school at the kindergarten and first grade levels. Implementing such a plan will cost the state several million dollars, a large part of which will be donated by foundations. Mississippi obviously feels that the benefits that will come from making readers out of those who might otherwise be illiterate are worth the costs.

Although programs such as those mentioned cover a range of reading skills, most tend to concentrate on a single area such as vocabulary building or sequencing. We will consider several single-skill packages in the following discussion; the reading skills areas selected are not inclusive, but are representative of those contained in any comprehensive reading curriculum.

Reading Skills Software

Vocabulary.   The game format is widely used in most subjects to make essential drills more palatable to students. The strategy is frequently employed in language arts software. Various games have been designed to introduce students to antonyms, homonyms, synonyms, and other vocabulary concepts. For example, Word-a-Mation (Sunburst) uses six special machines to transform words. For instance, when the machine is asked for the antonym for rich it responds with poor; when asked to provide a homophone for poor, it answers with pour.

Some programs use a multilevel series of high-interest questions to help students to identify synonyms, antonyms, homophones, prefixes, suffixes, and words with multiple meanings or to define unknown words using contextual clues. Additional exercises can be added to expand such programs, tailoring them to the varying ages and skills of individuals or groups.

Sequencing.   This reading skill is among the most difficult for students to master. Various programs are available to aid teachers, many of which use the computer's unique features to great advantage. In a program titled Those Amazing Reading Machines, strange machines engage students in various activities. Separate programs at four levels provide appropriate challenges for students from third through sixth grade. Reading Machines I (third grade) is a typical program in this series. There are three "rooms" serving different functions. The Graphics Room and Editing Room provide practice in reading for detail; the Cut and Paste Room uses a word-processor-like feature to teach sequencing. In this room an animated machine is presented along with a scrambled description. Students read the scrambled paragraphs and put them in correct order (Figure 4.16). To strengthen students' reliance on contextual clues in the text, teachers can use a Teacher Option to limit access to the machine. Text is designed for students reading at a third grade level; teachers can select from up to six skill groupings to match student needs.

A popular approach to teaching sequencing is to show three or more pictures out of sequence. The student numbers these in the correct order to tell a story such as how to prepare a bowl of cereal for breakfast or how to feed the goldfish. Pictures are gradually phased out in favor of text as higher levels are reached.

FIGURE 4.16 Students Work with Animated Machines to Improve Reading Skills in Those Amazing Reading Machines from MECC

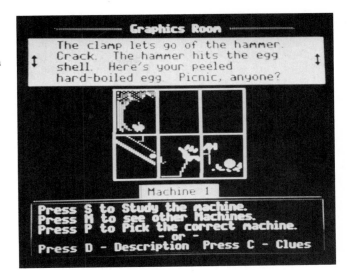

For example, text might be used to replace two of the pictures at the second level while at the third level all three frames would display text to be sequenced.

Spelling.   A program that integrates reading and writing while stressing spelling is S-P-E-L-L: The Reading/Writing Connection, from Sunburst Communications. This is a complete course that can be used for the entire school year. It includes sections in which students practice spelling new words, play word games, take tests, and compose with a word processor. An excellent feature is the optional ECHO speech synthesizer, which can be used to reinforce auditory skills. A built-in management system keeps track of performance and enables the teacher to modify the program to meet individual student needs. The word list can be added to as desired. The Teacher's Guide provides reproducible worksheets and suggestions for activities off the computer.

Reading for Comprehension

Comprehension comes about when an individual has mastered various capabilities such as those mentioned in the foregoing sections. Because all are closely connected, some teachers as well as certain publishers would prefer to consider them in a related fashion rather than individually. Several software companies have developed programs integrated into complete sets of related skills that together constitute a total approach to reading comprehension. Most programs provide a complete set of skills software including such topics as forming inferences, facts and opinions, identifying the main idea, recognizing important details, and sequential order.

In Getting the Main Idea, from Mindscape, students practice identifying the main idea as they take a graphic trip around the world. Context Clues involves students in understanding the meaning of words in a given paragraph as they gain entry to a treasure chest and obtain the riches inside, while Drawing Conclusions challenges readers to uncover secret messages as they discover hidden meanings in various selections. School is the theme in Inference and the challenge is to work your way from elementary school all the way through college. Reading for Detail asks the questions Who, What, Where, and When as race horses speed around a race track in an attempt to reach the finish line first. Predicting Outcomes involves students in using analytical and critical thinking skills in a colorful graphics setting. Following Directions engages students in an automobile race which they will be unable to complete unless they understand the sequence and purpose of the directions and follow the rules. Finally, Sequence develops organizational skills by having students arrange scrambled words, sentences, and paragraphs in proper order. There are two versions in this series, the first of which is for the younger learner while the second is designed for use in grades five to twelve.

Another program that permits you to use built-in stories or create your own to build comprehension skills is Sticky Bear Reading Comprehension, from Optimum Resources. Thirty stories suitable for children ages seven through nine are available on the disk, but the program can be expanded for a wider range of ages and skills by adding more stories. After reading a selection, the student is asked to respond to comprehensive questions for which the number of tries and level of difficulty can be set by the teacher. Children are automatically advanced to more difficult levels if their performance warrants. A report card option tracks and stores the assignments and maintains progress reports for a total class.

SCIENCE

Leaders in education, government, and other fields continue to express alarm at the apparent loss of interest in science among young people. This situation tends to be true not only for the brightest students, who might become professional scientists, but also for others who could benefit from being knowledgeable about things scientific in a world where the progress of nations rests in large degree upon the extent of their scientific prowess. Science classes were once quite popular. What has gone wrong?

One of the authors, who taught science classes at the junior high level years ago, clearly recalls the enthusiasm engendered in his students by various experiments conducted in class, some of which were quite simple in nature. One such experiment was the air pressure demonstration, in which a large can is heated to drive out air and then is capped to be crushed slowly by the outside air pressure. The class would gather around and watch expectantly as various experiments such as this evolved. These days activities of this kind seem less exciting to students.

As with most of society's shortcomings, the finger of blame is pointed directly at the schools and those who teach in them when the subject of lack of interest in science is discussed. In some ways, this attitude is justified. In schools where strong science programs exist, the emphasis tends to be on training students to be professional scientists. This approach alienates large numbers of students who lack either the aptitude or interest required for careers in this discipline.

In addition, simple experiments that once attracted students are now unexciting compared with what goes on in science fiction spectaculars shown on television and at the movies. Also, science teachers find it difficult to prepare and conduct experiments in poorly equipped classrooms. Even an activity as basic as the air pressure demonstration is difficult to conduct for many teachers. There is the problem of finding a sufficient number of suitable containers so each of several classes can participate. A burner must be available, and some way to cool the can to speed up the process is helpful. Multiply these difficulties by the number of experiments to be conducted over the school year and a sense of the magnitude of the problem can be obtained.

Many teachers are thus discouraged from engaging in activities that could add interest to the textbook-oriented curriculum prevailing in all too many science classes. Although not a panacea by any means, computers have the potential to help science educators enhance their teaching, motivate students to learn, and perhaps reverse current negative trends.

Computer-based simulations make highly effective substitutes for actual demonstrations, and the range of activities is greatly expanded over those usually possible in a classroom setting. For example, experiences with nuclear reactors and space craft, while not practical in actuality, are possible using simulations.

Perhaps the most exciting innovation is the microcomputer-based laboratory (MBL), frequently referred to as probeware, that turns the computer into an extremely accurate tool for conducting real-time experiments. In this application the computer collects data as they are generated by the ongoing experiment using special probes and interfaces. The data are interpreted and displayed on the screen in the form of charts or graphs that actively reflect evolving changes in the experimental setup.

Traditional computer-based tools such as data bases and graphing programs also have potential in science teaching, and there are good drill/tutorials for teaching terminology and principles available in all science areas.

Although computers show considerable promise for use in science education, the same problems that hinder widespread use in other subjects exist in this one as well. There are far too few computers available to use them consistently in individual drill-and-practice and tutorial activities. A second problem is the large amount of time necessary to carry out many activities. Simulations are notorious for requiring extended interaction time to arrive at a point where the results are sufficiently complete to allow termination of the program.

On the other hand, experiments conducted with probeware can be projected for the entire class to see using a PC Projector hooked to the computer. This approach overcomes the problem of shortage of equipment and enhances visibility. With a change in the philosophy of science education, including modifying the curriculum to reach all students, and with greater use of the computer, perhaps some of the old excitement can be reintroduced into the science classroom.

Hardware and Software for Science Education

Special equipment is required when the computer is used to collect and analyze data from a real-time experiment. A typical selection of probeware will contain the program and data disks plus probes, interface boxes, a circuit board or card that is inserted into an expansion slot within the computer, and cables to hook everything together.

If you desire paper copies of the graphs or charts that the program creates, a printer capable of generating this kind of output is required. Just about any dot matrix printer of the kind found in most schools will do the job, but character printers such as those having daisy wheel elements will not work since they cannot produce detailed graphics. Laser printers and ink jet printers will work very nicely if available.

Most science programs, regardless of category, are designed to be viewed most effectively on a color monitor, although a monochrome version will generally produce satisfactory images. Color monitors have come down in price dramatically and can be purchased for what monochrome varieties used to cost, and most schools have one or more monitors of this kind. Color projection panels for use on the overhead projector are also available.

You might also wish to connect with remote data bases to take advantage of the massive banks of information offered on many subjects, including science. To do so, you will have to have some kind of modem to translate the computer's signals into a code that can be carried over the telephone lines. For more information on this technique refer to Chapter 7.

Drill and tutorial software is used when the product approach to learning is stressed, but simulations are more appropriate in process-oriented activities. Much simulation software has been developed for the use of science teachers, particularly in the upper grades. Simulation programs are designed to imitate the various ways real world processes or systems work. Simulations allow students to make comparisons between two or more processes without having to set up an experiment physically. For instance, the rate of expansion for different metals at varying temperatures can be determined using a simulation simply by entering the specifications into the computer. A graphing feature displays the changes as they occur in the form of an ever-changing graph on the computer monitor.

Having students collect data as an experiment unfolds, and then having them analyze it at a later date is a useful approach, but it is often prohibitively time consuming. Using probeware for this purpose permits students to focus on the higher order activities of forming hypotheses and interpreting information rather than on the less challenging process of data gathering.

While simulations and probeware are both popular in progressive science classes, they differ in a significant way. Glen Fisher (1987) points out that "While simulations allow students to 'practice science' probeware encourages them to behave like scientists—to inquire, to experiment, to question."

Standard tool software such as data bases and spreadsheets are also useful in certain kinds of science activities. A description of how different teachers have used data bases in their science classes is given later in this section.

Science software is discussed in detail in the following section. The programs selected represent but a small cross-section of those available.

Software and Activities in Science Education

Drills and Tutorials. A knowledge of certain basic concepts is important if the student is to perform successfully in the more process-oriented science activities. For instance, if he or she is to fully comprehend what is taking place in a temperature experiment using probeware, the concepts of Fahrenheit and centigrade should have been learned previously. Drill and tutorial software is useful in presenting and strengthening important vocabulary, rules, concepts, and principles.

M-ss-ng L-nks Science Disk is a program similar to the social studies version of the same title that presents passages about science topics that have patterns of letters and words missing. The student can choose the desired pattern from a list that includes words having every other letter missing, or passages with every other word missing. She can also select more challenging deletion patterns, or no specific pattern at all. Subjects include a variety of science areas such as anatomy, animal life, and astronomy.

Another game presents the complex formulas that govern motion in a game-like format. The student begins by trying to move an object around a track. He or she must decide whether to give the object a boost or merely let it coast on its own. The track can be positioned on the earth or in outer space or next to the sun. The effect of these various positions on motion can then be examined.

Simulations. A physiological simulation designed to teach the functioning of the heart to older students is available for use in health sciences, physiology, and related classes. The program is a mathematical and graphic simulation of the mechanical behavior of isolated heart muscle that allows control over several muscle variables. An overall picture of the muscle's performance is graphically portrayed on the computer screen.

Computer Investigations: Plant Growth (Focus Media) lets students design experiments involving a computer simulated corn crop. The students decide what the variables will be by selecting such things as the time for the experiment to run, the number of plants that will be grown, and such growth factors as soil type, temperature, fertilizers, and so on. The plants "grow" on the screen using a colorful graphics display. If all goes as planned, the plants will flower, be pollinated, and produce a nice crop of corn.

Simon and Schuster offers a program in a laboratory setting for older students called CHEM LAB. Three levels of difficulty are provided within fifty scenarios that require experimentation to solve a problem. In the lab are various containers and two robot arms. A problem is presented together with a list of available substances. In the experiment called "Seeing the Light," for example, the student produces nitroglycerin using chlorine, nitrogen, and carbon dioxide together with water, sulfuric acid, glycerin, and nitric acid. The student is required to determine the proper quantities and combinations. Feedback messages inform the student of results from various combinations.

Probeware.   Among the more promising applications of the computer is the microcomputer-based laboratory (MBL). The name derives from the MBL Project undertaken at the Technical Education Research Center in Cambridge, Massachusetts. Other names are used to describe this approach in which the computer becomes an instrument for collecting, analyzing, and graphically displaying the on-going activity of a real-time experiment. Broderbund Software uses the title Science Toolkit to identify its MBL series, and this name is frequently used in a generic way by science teachers. Another widely used term is *probeware*, which is perhaps the most common of the several terms used.

The MBL Project series consists of three separate programs including Heat and Temperature, Motion, and Sound. Each of the three programs employs effective approaches to data collection using probes attached to a card installed within the computer. In the Sound module are an amplifier and microphone, which are encased in clear plastic so students can see how they work. The sounds that are generated are visible on the computer screen in the form of continuous output similar to that shown on an oscilloscope. These can also be frozen as permanent sound patterns to be used for in-depth examination.

A sonar device similar in principle to that used by submarines is used in the Motion module. The computer sends out sound waves which are reflected back by an object and the return time is measured to determine distance. The graphing feature displays motion in the form of lines of predictable character. By studying the graphs, students are able to interpret the precise motion of an object from the nature of the recorded lines (Figure 4.17).

In Heat and Temperature, a graphing program draws a graph based on input from a thermometer and the elapsed time of the experiment. The result is a graph showing these features on two axes. This module includes a heat pulser, which is controlled by the computer to generate just sufficient heat to raise the temperature of a fluid the exact number of degrees desired.

A second series of this type is Science Toolkit from Broderbund Software. Included in the Master Module is an interface box that plugs into the game port on the computer, two probes (a temperature sensor and a light sensor), the software to enable the elements to work together, and a manual. Figure 4.18 shows how the master module controls are displayed on the screen. The three modules in the series are Speed and Motion, Earthquake Lab, and Body Lab, which is designed to provide biofeedback to users.

In Speed and Motion students can record and analyze acceleration, thrust, wind resistance and centrifugal forces using features such as a highly accurate on-screen speedometer and tachometer as well as a light probe and balloon-powered car. Earthquake Lab provides an actual seismoscope, which is used in conjunction with the on-screen seismograph to measure harmonic and wave motion. The program can be used in many interesting ways; for example, students can determine who in the class walks most heavily, or the extent to which the school building shakes as buses and trucks pass by. A built-in plotter permits students to print the results of their experiments in a form similar to an actual seismogram.

FIGURE 4.17   The HRM Motion Module Employs a Sonar Device to Determine the Distance of an Object

(HRM Software from Queue, Inc.)

FIGURE 4.18   The Master Module Controls for Science Toolkit

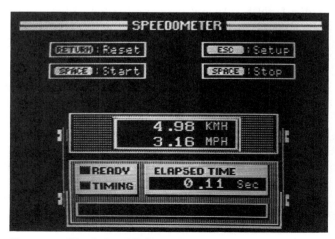

(Courtesy of Broderbund Software Inc.)

With the Body Lab module students can observe their own heart rate on the screen and can then plot the results and print them out. A response feature measures the rate at which students respond to varying kinds of stimuli; and a spirometer measures lung capacity and other respiratory functions. By watching the computer display, you can actually see the changing effects on the heart brought on by exercising. In the same fashion, you can observe the effects of cooling or heating by watching the strip chart recorder in the master module as you physically feel the fluid you are measuring change temperature. This feature assists students to correlate a physical phenomenon with its graphic representation.

The instruments used in software of this kind are highly accurate. For instance, the thermistor in Broderbund's package records temperatures in hundredths of degrees, while the timer is accurate to hundredths of a second.

Graphing Software. Some graphing programs require that students collect their own data and enter them at the keyboard while others use the data collected by probeware to generate graphs automatically, as in Body Electric (Figure 4.19). In either case, graphs are created quickly and accurately, saving the user untold hours of hard work at the drawing table. In addition to the program and the components that make up a probeware system, hardware in the form of a graphics printer is needed to produce a paper copy of a graph or chart. Some graphics programs permit full-color copies to be made, but this requires a printer with color capabilities as well.

Project Zoo is a graphics package designed to give students an opportunity to build skills in graphing, measurement, map making, and research in a problem-solving context. A tutorial approach helps students learn how information is represented in graphic form and how to interpret tables and graphs. A printing option permits graphics created on the screen to be printed as paper copy (Figure 4.20).

Data Bases. Because such a diverse collection of information is involved in the study of science, the data base management system (DBMS) or file management system are most useful tools for categorizing and organizing data collected by students.

For instance, one class involved in a unit on ornithology elected to use a file manager to store all the data they had collected on local birds by categorizing it in fields that would assist them in recognizing birds in their natural environments. Among the fields selected were size, shape, color patterns, flight characteristics, and habitat. These same features served as the basis for notes taken during field trips, making searches through the data base easy to conduct. Identifying unknown birds became a relatively simple process using this approach. This same technique might be used to organize information on a variety of animals, plants, minerals, or other kinds of science-related objects and events.

Jennifer Brawer (1988) describes a way that one teacher used a DBMS in the study of algal species in a local bay. The students collected samples of algae and used a microscope to identify them. They then used a data base to maintain a record of the types of algae found in different areas of the bay. Next, they determined the pH and salinity of the water using a probe attached to a computer,

FIGURE 4.19 Students Collect Data from each Other in Body Electric

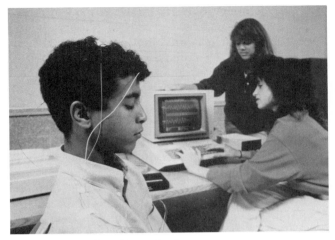

(HRM Software from Queue, Inc.)

which then generated graphs showing the correlation between algal species and water conditions. Polluted and unpolluted water samples were taken, and the computer was used to determine the extent to which these conditions affected the numbers of species in the samples. An in-depth analysis of the findings followed the experiments. Needless to say, the project represented a very positive experience for those involved.

Various prepared data bases for the sciences are available from a number of software producers. Among the subjects available in the data base format are animal life, endangered species, space, climate and weather, astronomy and many others. Animal life data bases, for example, contain information on characteristics, behavior, food, and habitats.

FIGURE 4.20 Project Zoo is a Program Designed to Teach Students About Graphing Techniques

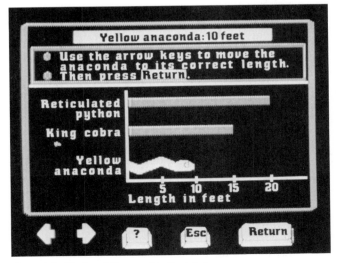

(Copyright National Geographic Society)

Some programs permit use of a modem, which connects the computer to the telephone lines to access remote data bases containing science information. An example of such a data base is Accu-Weather Forecaster which provides current information such as that used by professional weather forecasters. You can display the information as tables and graphs or weather maps as desired. As with most online utilities, you are required to subscribe to this service in order to make use of it.

Videodiscs. There are many videodiscs available that are suitable for use in the science classroom. As you recall, this medium is capable of storing thousands of images as well as sound, and these can be combined in various ways using an authoring language to create tailor-made lessons. For example, still images can be sequenced and timed to operate at the desired speed in the fashion of a traditional, projector-based slide show, and animated sequences can be incorporated to add variety to the presentation. Students might sequence images to illustrate reports, and while the equipment is not commonly available in the schools as yet, students and teachers will soon be able to record their own images and sound on the erasable videodiscs now entering the market.

The multifeatured program HyperCard, which comes bundled with the Macintosh computer, has a feature that serves as an authoring language for use in creating videodisc-based lessons. You can create your own "stacks" (a term used to describe the set of directions created with the program) or you can get them ready-made from companies such as Optical Data Corporation. The stack is made up of "cards" which can be arranged in various ways to control the selection of visuals such as slides, film clips, and diagrams that are displayed, as well as the sequence in which they are displayed.

SOCIAL STUDIES

The social world is the source of ideas and activities for this area of the curriculum. By engaging students in activities relating to social issues, teachers hope to impress them with the importance of being worthwhile, contributing citizens. Additionally, stress is placed on the development of skills necessary for making reasonable decisions about the social world. An important element is the study of the value structures of different societies. Also involved are skills of a more academic nature, such as map reading (identifying and naming the states) and interpretative skills (discussing the ramifications of the Bill of Rights).

Throughout this chapter mention has been made of the importance of learning essential facts. In math, children learn to count, then study basic computation; in prereading they learn the alphabet, followed by words. In social studies, among other things, they will study maps, learning where states, nations, and continents are located. Leslie Eiser and Judy Salpeter (1987) make a case for this approach in their article titled "Where on Earth Is Washington DC?" They observe that "Until young students can place themselves on a map and understand the relationship among towns, states (or provinces), countries, and continents, they'll have trouble putting information about far-off people and places into any meaningful perspective."

While for social studies there is not the diversity of software found in areas such as language arts, nor the quantity found in mathematics, many excellent drill-and-practice programs as well as simulations are available. Drills are most useful in teaching factual information such as names and places, while the simulation is an ideal instrument for the study of different societies and the development of social awareness. Indeed, simulation has come to be the primary computer-based tool in the teaching of social studies. Other kinds of software, such as word processors, can be used in this area also. Their use depends in large part on the orientation of the instructor.

Although the shortage of computers continues to be a problem, this is perhaps not as critical in the social sciences as in other areas. In most subjects teachers do their best to involve students in individual activities at the computer because much of the software requires this approach. But in the social studies, where interaction among people is one of the fundamental ingredients, it makes sense to stress this orientation by putting it into practice in the classroom. Many simulations, such as The Other Side (mentioned below), engage students in group activities. Older programs that were not designed specifically to be used by teams can nevertheless be incorporated into a group-oriented unit that involves the use of other media and activities.

Hardware and Software for the Social Sciences

Little in the way of hardware beyond what is commonly found in the average classroom is required for social science instruction, although a modem will be required if you plan to connect to a remote data base.

The simulation is the preeminent kind of software in most social studies classes. Activities become highly personalized because they deal with the fate of individuals and even nations. Even though the experience is artificial, students tend to get caught up in what is taking place, and often come away concerned and exhausted. All simulations have characteristics in common, but many of the newer ones in the social studies area are unique in that they involve groups of students, rather than individuals or pairs, as players.

Typical drills and tutorials stress such things as naming states and countries, identifying symbols used on maps, and developing a knowledge of the Constitution of the United States. A few such programs are available in a game format, which makes them a bit more attractive to students who find drills difficult to stay with.

Social scientists rely on data from many sources for making their decisions. The data base management system (or the simpler file management system), are useful tools for storing and categorizing quantities of data and are rapidly catching on among social studies teachers. This is an ideal way to store the collective information from many sources, including the students themselves. When used in conjunction with a graphing program, information can be organized and printed out as attractive graphs and tables in various formats.

Software and Activities in the Social Sciences

Drill-and-practice and Tutorial Programs. Scholastic Software publishes a drill program in the game format, which challenges students to respond to drill questions about the seven continents and their characteristics. Students may play as individuals or may team up for a competitive challenge. As the game progresses, the computer keeps a running score. At the end, winners receive reinforcement in the form of medals on the screen. The subjects include population, location, history, rivers, lakes, mountains, and cities.

Various tutorials devoted to different social studies topics are available from a number of vendors. In one such program, the entire Constitution is covered. Each unit consists of a tutorial and a test; the instruction mode provides a complete explanation for each question. Questions can be selected by topic or by level of difficulty.

Other programs engage students in different kinds of challenges using animation and colorful graphics. One such program, based on the geography of the United States, displays a map with a set of answers to the question posed. Students have control of a cursor, which can be moved to any point on the screen to make a selection. A score card on the screen keeps track of correct and incorrect answers, and a screen timer ticks away as you contemplate the problem. An editor provides the means to prepare custom maps to add to those in the program.

The Carmen Sandiego series (one title is shown in Figure 4.21) is among the most popular geography programs. Carmen is an ex-secret-agent turned thief who, along with her notorious gang, roams the world in search of adventure and ill-gotten fortune. From the clues provided, students are challenged to track her and her accomplices down using their crime computer and an almanac. This series consistently shows up at or near the top of the sales charts.

Simulations. Discover the World is a simulation program that challenges students to find a route to the Orient under trying conditions; the time is 1412, and the setting is one of five ports in various locations. Many problems beset the adventurers, including pirates, icebergs, reefs, and even mutiny. The ship must be provisioned with sufficient goods to enable it to reach its destination, which can be nearer or farther away depending on the route chosen. You must make decisions throughout the trip, including whether to fight or run away when pirates appear. Variables such as wind velocities and currents influence progress. Sets of questions appear at intervals throughout the trip; by answering correctly you can earn points to be added to the score obtained at the end of the voyage. If questions are too difficult, you can call up a tutorial feature for more information. Although designed to be used by one or two students, you can involve larger groups by having teams make the decisions and by letting students rotate at the keyboard. Figure 4.22 shows a screen shot from this program.

Another challenging simulation in which two countries (two teams of students) try to build a "peace bridge" between themselves is The Other Side, from Tom Snyder Productions, an innovator in the development of social studies simulations

FIGURE 4.21 The Carmen Sandiego Series is Among the Most Popular of Geographic Programs

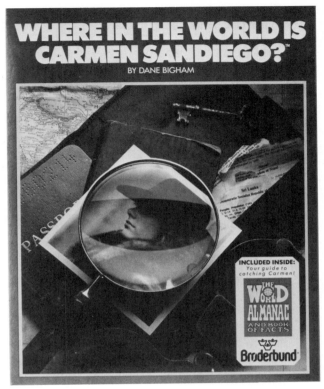

(Courtesy of Broderbund Software Inc.)

and other instructional software. The countries cannot succeed at this task unless they are willing to put the quest for peace above their own selfish interests. The package includes two disks, two student guides, and cables to hook two computers together, so the teams, like real-life countries, are remote from one another. The immediate objective is to explore for fuel, which comes in three varieties (orange, green, and blue) and can be mixed together and exchanged for money. In order to obtain the proper mixtures, it is necessary for the two countries to exchange fuel. This calls for trust and cooperation. The money obtained through selling fuel is used to buy bricks to build the bridge of peace.

To complicate matters, each side has a computer-assisted defense system that takes over control if the economy appears to be in trouble. This can precipitate the unleashing of bombs, in which event the game will be terminated and neither side will have won. The overall objective is to collaborate to avoid war and to complete the bridge, thus establishing peace in the world. The computer can also be connected via a modem. This means that the game can be played between teams in different schools, or even different states.

FIGURE 4.22 In Discover the World Students must Overcome a Variety of Challenges as they Plot a Course to the Orient

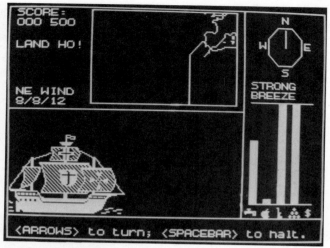

(Printed with Permission from Hartley Courseware, Inc., Dimondale, Michigan)

Another example of the way social studies simulations can involve students in cooperative efforts is illustrated by National Geographic's multimedia kit titled *The Golden Spike: Building America's First Transcontinental Railroad*, which includes a filmstrip, audio cassette, and two computer diskettes. Student teams assume the leadership of the two railroads involved in the venture, the Union Pacific and the Central Pacific. As they did in 1860, the two teams compete to see how fast they can join the east and west sections of track together. They are continually confronted with problems similar to those of the original builders: tight budgets, time constraints, supply decisions, and selecting workers. Much emphasis is placed on reading maps properly so the railroad will follow the specified route. The goal is to reach Promontory Point in the time allowed without going broke in the process; the reward is, as you might have guessed, a golden spike (Figure 4.23).

In using simulation programs, the teacher is central to the use of the software in that he or she conducts activities in much the traditional fashion, involving students in discussing and analyzing the problems and then making decisions collectively. The computer serves to maintain a record of the decisions that are made; these are analyzed and the consequences determined. The students are informed of the effects of their decisions, and new activities are prescribed. The teacher exercises control over the time spent making decisions, and she can also stop the simulation when desired, saving the data to be used when the activity is renewed.

Data Base Management Programs. Data base management programs are without equal when it comes to storing ethnographic data collected by students. Any data base can be used; even very simple ones have utility in the social

FIGURE 4.23   Students Compete To See How Fast They Can Build a Railroad in The Golden Spike: Building America's First Transcontinental Railroad

(Copyright National Geographic Society)

sciences. Create-A-Base from TIES, a useful data base designed just for school use, is mentioned in Chapter 6. A planning sheet for use with this program, which shows the fields selected for storing data on each of the U.S. presidents, is found in the same chapter.

Data can be collected from populations if they are small enough, or from samples taken randomly from larger populations using questionnaires or interviews. Students might use resource materials such as books, newspapers, and other publications to obtain information on a particular group or nation. You can also obtain a working data base on a disk, already formed. Data bases containing a preformed matrix into which the user types data are called *templates*. Numerous social studies data bases and templates are available containing a wealth of information on just about any topic that interests you.

Sunburst offers a selection of up-to-date titles that include information on North America, Colonial times, and the United States. The North America data base includes files on the people, climate, demography, culture, economy, and government of each nation in this part of the Americas. These programs are designed to be used with the Bank Street Beginner's Filer and the Bank Street School Filer, two data base packages that let you create your own files or use premade ones such as those mentioned.

A data base from Mindscape, titled Quest for Files: Social Studies, provides students with information so they can compare historical events and the people who were involved in them. A tutorial and file manager are available as components in the program for assisting students to succeed in their data retrieval efforts. Families of the World: The Melting Plot, one of three titles in the series, provides sets of questions along with the profiles of 29 families, which students use to find answers to the questions. The families were specifically chosen to stimulate discussions on immigration.

The program titled Immigrant: The Irish Experience in Boston provides another premade data base. The files include a passenger list of immigrant ships arriving in America along with various kinds of personal data, information on conditions in the adopted city such as housing specifics, and job and transportation information. Students use the data to make decisions for the immigrant families. They help them find appropriate housing and jobs; they determine the best and least expensive means of transportation, and, using the spread sheet capability, they calculate living and related expenses for the families. This program, developed at the Educational Technology Center at Harvard University, is in the public domain, which means that it is inexpensive and can be copied freely. It is used with the Appleworks integrated program described in the Tools Chapter.

Other Software.   The use of a spreadsheet was mentioned in the discussion of the Immigrant program. It is used in this program to calculate such things as income and expenditures for the Irish families, but it could be applied in many other social studies activities. For example, one of the favorite things to do around election time is to conduct simulated elections. The spreadsheet, with its ability to store, organize, and analyze data, is invaluable at this time. Votes on any number of candidates can be sorted and stored, a formula can be designed to enable students to predict outcomes, percentages are easily calculated, and the principle of the electoral college is readily illustrated.

Another useful tool is the word processor. Everything from ballots to political speeches can be produced for use in the election unit. In his article "The Computer-Infused Social Studies Classroom," Robert Vlahakis (1988) tells how he uses the word processor and a desktop publishing program to create a "Colonial Age newspaper" for one of the original thirteen colonies. As Vlahakis points out, projects such as this "allow students to look at history from a more personal point of view, getting behind the scenes and expressing personal opinions and anecdotes from a particular era."

Survey Taker (Scholastic) lets students get involved in conducting actual surveys in the school or community. When the data are typed in, the program analyzes the information statistically and displays graphs and tables of the results. Students use questionnaires based on the program format as they conduct a survey; this approach makes entering the data much simpler. In the process, they learn to design a survey instrument, which can be printed for use in the field. They also learn to read graphs and tables as they develop insights into how statistics work. This program is also valuable in mathematics education.

SUMMARY

The trend away from studying the computer as subject to using it as an aid to teaching traditional subjects is growing. Teachers are more likely to use the technology if it is integrated into the established curriculum than when it is used to serve other purposes. In this chapter, approaches to bringing integration about were described and factors that support this movement, such as software design, were identified.

Five curriculum areas were discussed including Early Learning and Readiness, Mathematics, Reading and Language Arts, Science, and Social Studies. The software in each area has characteristics unique to the learning activities in that area. Early learning programs stress the development of basic skills through an approach that is highly concrete, and synthetic speech is used extensively to compensate for the young learner's lack of reading skills. Problem-solving software and programming activities in which logic skills are enhanced are popular in mathematics. Tool software such as word processors is a mainstay in the Reading and Language Arts curriculum. The Microcomputer-Based Laboratory gives science students experiences in conducting real-time experiments in a safe, tidy environment. Students in Social Studies gain insights into world problems as they get involved in realistic simulations of various kinds.

Integration efforts show promise of bringing about a wider and more positive use of the computer as teachers recognize the potential that exists for enhancing teaching and learning in all areas of the traditional curriculum.

SELF-TEST

1. Describe the concept of computer integration.
2. List three approaches to computer integration.
3. Identify several ways software producers are providing support for integration efforts.
4. Describe several characteristics of software designed for use in the Early Learning area.
5. What is a "talking word processor"?
6. Why is drill-and-practice software so commonly used in mathematics instruction?
7. What is the value of programming in mathematics instruction?
8. In which of the curriculum areas are word processors most common? Why?
9. Describe probeware. In which area is it most commonly used?
10. What is a simulation?

REFERENCES

Barbour, A. "Computerized Speech: Talking Its Way into the Classroom." *Electronic Learning* (January 1987): 87–88.

Barbour, A. "A Cemetery Database Makes Math Come Alive." *Electronic Learning* (February 1988): 12–13.

Bitter, G., and R. Camuse. *Using a Microcomputer in the Classroom. 2d ed.* Englewood Cliffs, N.J.: Prentice Hall, 1988.

Brawer, J. "From the Ocean to the Prairie." *A+ Magazine* (October 1988): 24–25.

Brownell, G. *Computers and Teaching.* St. Paul, Minn.: West Publishing, 1987.

Buckleitner, W. "Software for Preschoolers—Giving Your Youngsters a Head Start." *Family and Home Office Computing* (August 1988): 20–21.

Char, C. "Videodiscs in Art and Language Arts." *Classroom Computer Learning* (January 1987): 50–54.

Charp, S. "Writing to Read: A Program for Literacy." *T.H.E. Journal* (May 1989): 57–60.

Clements, D. *Computers in Early and Primary Education.* Englewood Cliffs, N.J.: Prentice-Hall, 1985.

Clements, D. *Computers in Elementary Mathematics Education.* Englewood Cliffs, N.J.: Prentice Hall, 1989.

Collis, B. *Computers, Curriculum, and Whole Class Instruction—Issues and Ideas.* Belmont, Calif.: Wadsworth, 1988.

Dugdale, S. "Computers: Applications Unlimited." in *Computers in Mathematics Education, 1984 Yearbook,* ed. V.P. Hansen and M.J. Zwing. Reston Va.: National Council of Teachers of Mathematics.

Eiser, L., and J. Salpeter. "Where on Earth Is Washington, DC?" *Classroom Computer Learning* (November/December 1987): 28–29.

Fisher, G. "Where Computers Work Well Is Not Always Where They'll Do the Most Good." *Electronic Learning* (February 1987): 6.

Hoelscher, K. "Computing and Information: Steering Student Learning." in *Computers in Education: 1988.* ed. J. Hirschbuhl. Guilford, Conn.: Dushkin Publishing Group, 1986.

Lehrer, A. "A Network Primer: How They Are Used and How They Could Be Used." *Classroom Computer Learning.* (April 1988): 41–47.

Linn, M., et al. *Establishing a Research Base for Science Education: Challenges, Trends, and Recommendations.* Berkeley: University of California Press, 1986.

McCarthy, R. "Making the Future Work: The Road to Curriculum Integration." *Electronic Learning* (September 1988): 42–45.

Marville, J. "Meet the Winners." *A+ Magazine* (March 1988): 83–87.

Morrison, D., and J. Walters. "The Irish Immigrant Experience." *Classroom Computer Learning* (October 1986): 40–43.

OTA. *Power On! New Tools for Teaching and Learning.* Washington, DC: Office of Technology Assessment, 1988.

Papert, S. *Mindstorms.* New York: Basic Books, 1980.

Parham, C. "Computers that Talk." *Classroom Computer Learning.* (March 1988): 26–31.

Phillipo, J. "Videodiscs as Information Archives for the Classroom." *Electronic Learning* (May 1989): 42, 44.

Phillipo, J., and S. McCarty. "Ideas for Integrating Videodisc Technology into the Curriculum." *Electronic Learning* (April 1989): 38, 40.

Riedesel, C., and D. Clements. *Coping with Computers in the Elementary and Middle Schools.* Englewood Cliffs, NJ: Prentice-Hall, 1985.

Roberts, N., R. Carter, S. Friel, and M. Miller. *Integrating Computers into the Elementary and Middle School.* Englewood Cliffs, N.J.: Prentice Hall, 1988.

Salpeter, J. "The Archival Videodisc: A Multi-Media Library You Can Hold in One Hand." *Classroom Computer Learning* (January 1987): 49–51.

Thornburg, D. "Learning Curve." *A+ Magazine* (September 1988): 57–58.

Trautman, A., J. White, and F. Breit. *The Micro Goes to School: Instructional Applications of Microcomputer Technology.* Pacific Grove, Calif.: Brooks/Cole, 1988.

Vlahakis, R. "The Other Side: Snapshot of a Social Studies Simulation in Action." *Classroom Computer Learning* (May 1987): 42–45.

Vlahakis, R. "The Computer-Infused Social Studies Classroom." *Classroom Computer Learning* (November/December 1988): 58–61.

Watt, D. "Software for Preschoolers." *Popular Computing.* (March 1985): 46.

White, C., and G. Hubbard. *Computers and Education.* New York: Macmillan, 1988.

CHAPTER 5

Tools I: Word Processors

CHAPTER TOPICS
☐ Some advantages of using a word processor
☐ The features of a word processor
☐ How a word processor works
☐ Selected word processing programs for school use
☐ The spelling checker and thesaurus
☐ Keyboarding programs
☐ Classroom activities using word processors

Word processing programs have become the most common of all the varieties of tool software, and with good reason. We live in an information society in which words are the traditional vehicle for storing information and communicating ideas, so anything that makes writing easier is bound to have wide appeal for those who work with words.

The word processor makes the creation of error-free documents much less of a task than it used to be by providing the operator with convenient ways of dealing with the mechanical problems of writing. Composing on a word processor has many advantages over using a typewriter or pencil and paper. Words placed directly on paper during the creative process seldom represent thoughts in their clearest form; subsequent changes of varying magnitude are nearly always called for.

The revision process can become so involved as to discourage young writers (and many older ones), who either settle for a less than adequate product or simply give up the struggle altogether. But the word processor, whose output is in fluid form on the computer screen, permits you to make any changes desired with the press of a few keys. Not until the document is satisfactory in all respects is it printed onto paper. The printing process, like the other functions of the word processor, is straightforward: turn the printer on, give the computer the command to send the document to the printer, and relax while the equipment does the rest.

In the classroom, the net result of using word processors is an increase in the productivity of students, who approach the writing task with a more positive attitude than they ever had before.

There are, however, certain difficulties inherent in the use of these programs, the primary one being that of economics. A few computers are available to greater numbers of students if they are used primarily to run drill-and-practice and tutorial courseware. Students working with a word processing program, however, are likely tie the equipment up for hours. Allocating identical or extended blocks of time to each user does not solve the problem, either—ideas might just begin to jell as time runs out.

Although not a total answer to the problem, the whole class approach, as described in Chapter 4, is very practical when the mechanics of word processing are being stressed. By attaching the computer to a projection panel placed on the overhead projector, you can demonstrate the various functions of the program for all the class to see. In the final analysis, however, nothing can take the place of hands-on experience when writing with the word processor is the goal. This kind of activity does not necessarily require one student per computer, although at times this is appropriate. You can devise ways that enable pairs and groups of students to experience keyboarding and other activities when computers are in short supply. A variety of such activities is described later in this chapter and in Chapter 4.

HOW THE WORD PROCESSOR WORKS

A word processor consists of the software (generally on a diskette, a hard disk, or built into the computer in ROM) and the appropriate hardware to take advantage of the program's capabilities. A critical part of the package is the documentation, which describes in detail how the various key combinations are used to activate different functions. Along with the printed materials, most word processors include a disk-based tutorial as part of the package; working with such programs can be a great help in learning to use the word processor.

Getting started involves following the same steps common to other types of stored programs: insert the disk and wait for the program to load, or, in the case of programs in ROM or on a hard disk, use the appropriate commands to load the program. Although one disk drive is adequate for many of the word processing programs used in the classroom, some of the more powerful ones are best left in the drive during use and thus require two disk drives (or a hard disk drive and a floppy drive), one to hold the program and the other the data disk. After the word processor is loaded various prompts will appear on the screen; responding to these puts you in the insert mode, where text is typed in and the document composed.

The process of typing the text does not differ much from using a standard typewriter, but instead of appearing as print on paper, the text shows up on the display screen as light letters on a dark background (or occasionally dark letters on a white background, as in the Macintosh). The arrangement of characters, spaces, and even mistakes corresponds exactly to what is typed in. Some word processors display fewer than the normal seventy to eighty characters per line. The basic version of Magic Slate, for example, displays very large letters in a twenty-column format that appeals to children (Figure 5.1).

The uniqueness of the word processing approach becomes apparent as the revision of the material proceeds. Correcting a typo or two is not too difficult on a typewriter, particularly if the machine provides correction features, but changing a word or more, or inserting an entirely new passage, necessitates retyping entire sections of the document. Inserting additional text is no problem with a word processor—as the insertion is made, the text simply moves ahead to make room for it. Editing the text is one of the principal functions of a word processor,

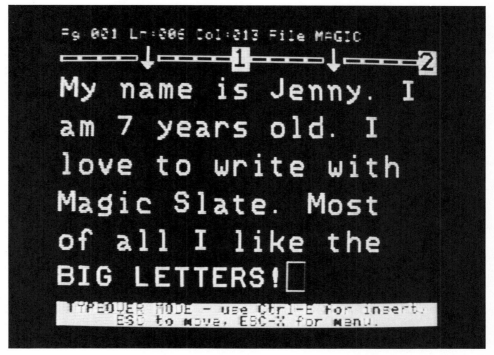

FIGURE 5.1   A Screen Display from Magic Slate Showing the Twenty-Column Large Letter Format
(Produced by Sunburst Communications, Inc.)

along with formatting, file management, and printing. We will examine each of these processes in the following pages.

Text Editing

This process includes such operations as defining blocks, deleting and inserting text, and using the search and replace functions. Most programs are designed so the text can be edited as it is typed in. Often glaring errors are corrected as the composition progresses, and major modifications are made and minor errors corrected the second time through.

Cursor Movement.   The common way to move the cursor around on the screen is to press the directional arrow keys. To move in greater increments, say from the beginning of a line to the end, you would press a second key together with the arrow key. In the case of the WordPerfect program, for instance, you would press the Home key and the right or left arrow key to jump to the end of a line; you would use the Open-Apple key and arrow keys to move in increments of more than a single character or line in AppleWorks. The combination differs somewhat from one program to the next. In addition, some programs are designed so a mouse can be used for cursor movement.

As the cursor is moved up or down through the document, the lines scroll rapidly off the bottom or top of the screen. You will have several lines to work on at any one time. These vary in appearance according to the kind of program being used. The most satisfactory arrangement is to have a screen display that represents the full page layout as it will appear on the final printed sheet. As mentioned, a printed page is typically from seventy to eighty characters in width, but some programs display fewer characters than this while others allow you to adjust to different numbers of characters as desired. This feature is useful when young children are working with the program and fewer letters of a larger size are needed.

Inserting Text. The insertion process alone is enough to make the word processor worth the investment. Unlike a document printed on paper, the screen-based word processing document can readily be modified, regardless of the magnitude of the changes required, before it ever appears on paper. Inserting text is a simple, straightforward process. The cursor is moved to the point in the document where a character, word, or other addition is needed and the material is typed in. The text moves to make room for the addition.

Also useful is the overtype mode, which allows you to simply type right over unwanted material, replacing it with the new letters. Thus, if you wished to change "feet" to "foot" you would move the cursor to a position in front of the first *e*, press the key(s) to put the computer in the overtype mode, and type the letter *o* twice to make the correction.

Deleting Text. When you start the program it will typically be in the insert mode, which means that the words typed at the keyboard appear on the screen automatically. If you should need to make a correction, the letter or word is deleted by positioning the cursor at the point of correction and pressing the proper key or keys to remove the unwanted material. As you make a deletion, the resulting space is filled as the text moves backward. You can delete anything from a word up to large blocks of text (see Block Function). A character is typically deleted by pressing the back space or some other key. To remove words, lines, or larger segments of text, various key combinations are used, or the block function is activated and the delete option used to remove the block.

However handy the delete function is, it should be used with caution since the results of much effort can be lost with the stroke of a key. Fortunately, most word processors temporarily save the text that has been deleted. Thus, if material is removed inadvertently, it can be retrieved once again and no harm is done.

The Block Function. Moving entire sections, or blocks, of text as a unit can be very useful. To do this you define the beginning and end of the block by positioning the cursor on the first letter in the passage to be cut or copied. Next, the computer is placed in the block mode, again by pressing the prescribed keys; you will be informed that the block function is in operation by a prompt on the screen. WordPerfect, for example, displays the flashing words BLOCK ON in the lower left corner of the screen. As you move the cursor through the material with the arrow keys (or a mouse) each line of words will be highlighted. Once the desired material has been defined in this way it can be cut or copied as desired.

Cutting a block removes it entirely from the text and places it in temporary memory; copying a block leaves it intact on the screen but also stores a copy in memory. In either case the stored text can be retrieved and inserted into the current document or an entirely different one. When inserting the block, the cursor is moved to the position in the manuscript where you want the block to appear, the retrieve command is typed, and the block instantly appears precisely where you wanted it. This operation is often called cut-and-paste, a reference to the laborious, old-fashioned process of trimming a passage from a typed manuscript and pasting it in a new location using rubber cement or tape.

Search and Replace.   Although they are often used together, search and replace are actually two separate functions. The search function, when used alone, positions the cursor at the first occurrence of the specified word; the computer then awaits further orders (continue the search or abort). If the search is continued through the entire document, the cursor comes to rest at each succeeding occurrence of the word. More commonly, the search and replace functions are used together, as illustrated in Figure 5.2. The text editor searches through the file

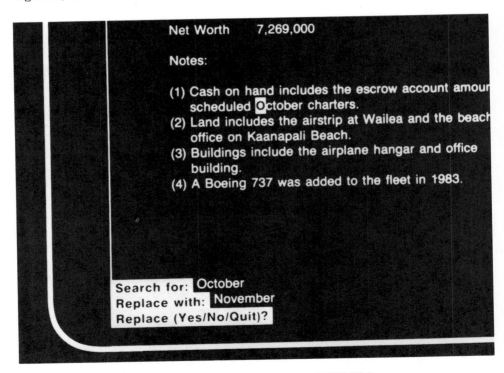

FIGURE 5.2   Using the Search and Replace Feature of PFS:Write
(Courtesy of Software Publishing Corporation)

until the first occurrence of the specified word is found; at this point, a press of a key inserts the replacement word. This process continues until every occurrence of the old word has been found and replaced with the new word or the search has been terminated. Automatic search and replace performs these functions without intervention.

The value of this feature becomes immediately evident if, for example, you discover that a word has been consistently misspelled throughout an entire document. All that is necessary to correct the error is to evoke the search and replace function and then direct the computer to substitute the correctly spelled word every time it finds the misspelled version. The search (or find) function is very handy when you wish to locate a specific word or passage in a lengthy document. Lacking this function you would have to read through the document until you found what you were looking for. But in the search mode the computer can locate the desired information quickly and accurately.

Formatting

Formatting includes (among other things) setting margin widths, selecting the spacing between lines, choosing the number of lines per page, and sometimes changing the typefaces. Some word processors display formatting and other options as icons (small pictures) on the screen. MacWrite, a display of which is shown in Figure 5.3, is a program that uses this approach.

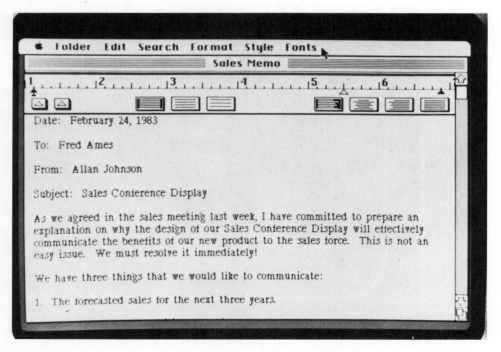

FIGURE 5.3 The Layout of the MacWrite Word Processor Screen
(Copyright Claris Corporation. All rights reserved.)

Two methods for setting the format of a document—menu-based and text-embedded—are available with some programs. The first and most common of these involves typing in changes to a basic set of commands that are displayed as a menu. For example, you may wish to have wider margins than the preset (default) format displayed in the menu. You simply select this option from the menu and then type or select the new value.

The second method permits you to type formatting instructions as part of the manuscript. They may look peculiar on the screen because they appear as coded characters right in with the text, but only the results of the commands, not the text-embedded commands themselves, appear in the final printed copy.

Formatting considerations are important because they determine how the finished, printed document will look. Whereas text-embedded instructions must be entered as the document evolves, menu-based instructions need only be defined once and can be changed quickly anytime you want to alter the appearance of the document. If, for instance, after having completed a composition, you decide wider margins would enhance its appearance, simply typing in new width measurements for both the left and right margins immediately changes the formatting of the entire document.

Some word processors use icons to display certain formatting options. Note that three boxes in Figure 5.4 show the spacing arrangements available to the user. The first box is single space, followed by space and a half, and then double space. To select an option you simply move the cursor to that box and press the mouse button. Any typing on the screen is automatically reformatted, and new text that is typed will conform to the specific option selected. Several of the formatting options common to all word processors are discussed below.

Justification.   Printed material—whether from a typewriter or a computer—is usually left-justified, that is, it is aligned on the left. You can change this in several ways, however, if a different layout is desired. Probably the most common option is fill-justify, which the computer achieves by inserting spaces between

FIGURE 5.4   The Spacing Options in MacWrite

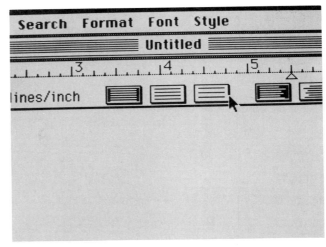

FIGURE 5.5 (a) An example of Right-Justified Text; (b) an Example of Left-Justified Text; (c) an Example of Fill-Justified Text

IN THIS EXAMPLE, THE RIGHT JUSTIFY (RJ) OPTION HAS
BEEN CHOSEN. THIS IS PERHAPS THE LEAST COMMON OF
THE VARIOUS FORMATS, HOWEVER, THERE ARE TIMES WHEN
IT CAN BE USEFUL.

A

THIS IS AN EXAMPLE OF A PARAGRAPH THAT WAS PRINTED
USING THE LEFT JUSTIFY (LJ) OPTION. THIS IS THE
PRESET (DEFAULT VALUE) FORMAT OF MOST WORD
PROCESSORS.

B

THIS SAMPLE SHOWS HOW SETTING THE FILL JUSTIFY
OPTION CAUSES BOTH THE LEFT AND THE RIGHT MARGINS
TO BE ALIGNED. NOTE THE UNEQUAL SPACING BETWEEN
THE WORDS. THIS IS A COMMON PROBLEM WHEN THE FJ
OPTION IS USED.

C

words to spread the lines out so they are flush with the right margin as well as the left. This sometimes creates sizeable breaks between words; thus, the effect is not quite as pleasing as when the spaces are equal throughout the line. A fill-justified page does, however, have a nicely balanced feel about it. A third alternative is to justify the lines on the right. Figure 5.5 shows examples of the three different options.

Although most word processors provide a printed menu from which the various justification schemes are selected, some use icons for this purpose. Note that the four boxes to the extreme right on the Macintosh screen (Figure 5.6) represent the justification options provided by the MacWrite program. The first of these is the normal left-justified layout; following this are the center, right, and fill-justified options.

Margins. Margins should be set before input begins if you elect not to use those already set by the program. All word processors have built-in values for the various settings; these are termed *default values,* and they are generally a good compromise for most purposes.

FIGURE 5.6 The Print Justification Options for MacWrite

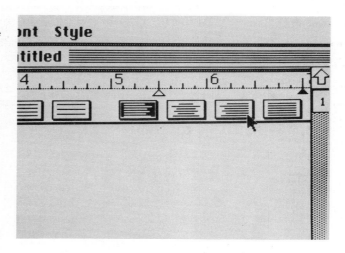

Some programs display the margin and other data on a ruler along the bottom or top of the screen (Figure 5.7). Others permit you to call up the format values menu whenever a quick check is desired. Incidentally, word processors have a feature called *word wrap,* which works like an automatic carriage return and prevents you from having to worry about margins as you type: instead of breaking a word when it runs into a margin, the word processor simply shifts the full word down to the beginning of the next line.

Centering. A document often can be made to appear more attractive when major headings are centered. This option is also useful when titles are required. Various approaches to centering are used by different programs. MacWrite, for instance, provides an array of icons showing different formats, one of which is centered text; selecting this option positions the cursor so words typed will all be centered. Other programs activate the centering function with the press of a function key or some key combination.

File Management

A file is a unit of information stored on the disk under a specific name. For example, if you have typed a form letter that may be used again, by giving the letter a name and saving it on a disk you have created a file. It is wise to save the

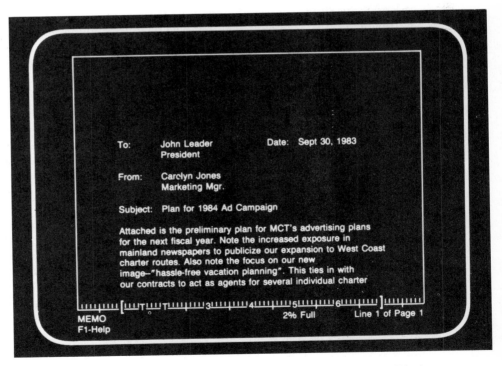

FIGURE 5.7 PFS:Write Has a Useful Data Line at the Bottom of the Display
(Courtesy of Software Publishing Corporation)

document being composed every ten or fifteen minutes to avoid accidents. Since information such as text, programs, graphics, and anything else currently being composed is stored in the volatile RAM, in the event of a power loss, the information will be erased. Disks, however, are permanent storage mediums—the material saved on them remains intact regardless of what happens to the computer.

You can save your work any time you wish and then return immediately to the document to continue working on it. Assume for example that you have established a routine of saving every 15 minutes or so as you compose at the keyboard. All that is required when it is time to save is to press the save key (or the appropriate key combination) and respond to the screen prompt that appears. As a general rule, if this is the first time you have saved the current document, the prompt will simply be the word SAVE. You respond by indicating the drive where the storage disk is located followed by the name of the file.

If you have saved part of the document before, the SAVE prompt will be followed by the name you have given the file. The computer, when instructed to save a file under a name it finds already on the disk, will ask if you really want to replace the old file with the new one. Since you are actually replacing the file on the disk with an updated version (the results of the past 15 minutes of typing have been added to the document in the RAM) you will reply in the affirmative (perhaps pressing the Y key for "yes") and the replacement will occur. As soon as the prompts disappear and the drive stops running, you can proceed with your writing activities, confident that you now have everything that you have typed to this point saved on the disk. The saving process varies somewhat from one program to another. Another approach is to provide a menu from which various options, including saving, can be selected. To save in this case, simply position the cursor on SAVE and press the mouse button.

Printing

The ultimate reason for using the word processor is to obtain high-quality printed copy; the printer, therefore, is an essential component in the word processing system. The various kinds of printers are discussed, along with other peripheral devices, in Chapter 2.

During the processes of text entry and editing, the printer sits quietly; once the document has been composed and corrected, saved on a disk, and formatted, however, the printer goes to work. Some printers have features that must be physically selected and adjusted on the printer itself. For example, a printer might offer options such as pitch and line that permit you to alter the copy's final appearance. If such adjustments are needed, they are performed before the actual printing begins.

The program will provide a command to activate the printer; once the process has started, very little human intervention is needed unless single sheets of paper need to be fed manually.

WORD PROCESSORS FOR SCHOOL USE

There are currently so many excellent programs on the market that an entire book would be needed to describe them all. Rather than attempt to cover every suitable title, we have selected a sample of proven, popular programs that are representative of what is available. We elected to include several titles designed specifically for use in the schools along with others that have utility both in and out of the classroom.

Dr. Peet's Talk/Writer.   A program from Hartley, Dr. Peet's Talk/Writer is simple enough that it can be used by the youngest students. The program is introduced by an uncomplicated tutorial in which the computer sings the ABC song and letters are identified (Figure 5.8). The user then moves on to more traditional activities such as typing letters, words, and sentences (if he or she has reached this stage). As the letters and words are entered, a speech synthesizer sounds them out. A menu is provided for use by the teacher to modify the pronunciation of selected words, control the sound feature, and set the program up so it can be used by visually impaired users.

Talking Text Writer.   Talking Text Writer can be used by early learners or those with greater sophistication. Like the Talk/Writer this program has the computer speak the individual letter as the beginner types it, or the word as this is composed. Later, entire lines of words are sounded out as they are created. Talking Text Writer permits word definitions to be typed into a talking dictionary, thereby

FIGURE 5.8 A Screen Shot from Dr. Peet's Talk/Writer.

(Printed with Permission from Hartley Courseware, Inc., Dimondale, Michigan)

permitting the user to create a collection of words that are important for one reason or another. Other useful features are the adjustable reading speed and the capability of displaying 20-, 40-, or 80-character columns of text. A screen shot of a student exercise is shown in Figure 5.9.

Talking Notebook. Talking Notebook (First Byte) takes advantage of its sound capabilities by using voice not only in the production of text but also to give instructions and feedback. The voice can be tailored to sound like a male or female, speak faster or more slowly, and the tone and pitch can be altered as desired. This feature appeals to more advanced students who can modify the voice so that it corresponds to the personality of the passages being read. The user can also create his or her personalized dictionary with this program.

Muppet Slate. A product of Sunburst Communication, Muppet Slate is another word processor for use by young children. Either the Muppet Learning Keys mentioned in Chapter 4 or the standard keyboard can be used with this program; however, since it is designed for use in kindergarten through the second grade, the large, colorful Muppet Keyboard is the odds-on favorite.

This program has been termed a "picture processor" because, like other programs to be mentioned, it provides graphics and borders which young writers can use to decorate their compositions. There are 126 available pictures and ten decorative borders available from the "picture book" for use in various combinations. The text is large and easy for children to read, and important commands remain at the bottom of the screen for quick reference. Colorful Muppet characters are used throughout the program.

There are built-in customizing features that permit you to fit the program to individual or group needs, and 24 lesson plans to help you to familiarize young writers with the various stages of writing. All the main features of more complex word processors are available, including editing, file management, printing, and

FIGURE 5.9 A Screen Shot from Talking Text Writer Showing the Large-Size Letters

(Courtesy of Scholastic Software)

others that provide young students with a sound foundation in the use of the word processor.

Bank Street Writer.   A venerable program, long a favorite in the schools, Bank Street Writer is now in its third edition. Bank Street Writer III (Scholastic) has many features the earlier versions lacked, including a spelling checker, a thesaurus, and pull-down menus such as those used by the Macintosh. Many schools still use the original version, however, and find it quite satisfactory for most of their needs.

An excellent disk-based tutorial makes the use of the written documentation unnecessary for many students, although the quality of the documentation deserves a word of praise. A student guide and a reference guide are included, as are a question-and-answer segment and a collection of ideas for using word processing in the classroom. Another feature that appeals to young students is the large print format of the screen display. This program also has word-wrap and block movement features, search-and-replace capabilities, and text highlighting features, among others, so it is suitable for most word processing applications.

LogoWriter.   LogoWriter is a program that combines word processing with programming, sound, and graphics capabilities. The programming language features of Logo, the precursor to LogoWriter, are discussed in detail in Chapter 8, Programming and Authoring.

As its name implies, LogoWriter stresses writing. The graphics features of earlier versions of Logo are maintained, but text capabilities are greatly expanded in LogoWriter. Students can type words any place on the screen; they can even label illustrations they have created, moving the words so they correspond to parts of the graphic. Or, LogoWriter can serve as a 40-character column word processor, with characters twice the size of the usual 80-character column, providing capabilities similar to other word processing programs. Several students can write individual compositions on a topic using the word processing feature and can then use the programming component to write instructions so the computer will link all the separate files together into a single document. This multi-talented software can provide an endless array of activities for language arts teachers and their students.

GraphicWriter.   GraphicWriter from DataPak was specifically designed to take advantage of the excellent graphic capabilities of the Apple IIGS computer. Like LogoWriter, it has graphics capabilities for use in illustrating manuscripts. Unlike LogoWriter, the graphics are created using an environment very similar to that of MacPaint and similar programs based on pull down menus and icons. The mouse is used for graphic generation, the keyboard for text input; both can be used for cursor movements and the selection of commands.

Both black-and-white and colored graphics can be created and positioned any place in the document. The program permits the user to create various page formats, so graphics and text can be arranged in different patterns for the best effect. These and other features make GraphicWriter similar to a first-level desktop publishing program.

MultiScribe. A versatile word processor from Scholastic, MultiScribe provides an operating environment similar to that of GraphicWriter, displaying Macintosh-like menus and other features. Unlike GraphicWriter, however, this is strictly a word processor without graphic features.

Unlike some word processors, which do not display features such as underlining as they will appear on the printed page, MultiScribe provides a screen display that is the exact equivalent of the printout. Words to be underlined will be identified with a line under them rather than with some other feature such as highlighting (an approach common to many programs). A change to a different letter style will also be mirrored precisely on the screen. A font editor is supplied, which enables you to modify existing letters or create your own.

Although a mouse is supplied, you can do all work at the keyboard if this is your preference. Beginning users might find the mouse convenient for accessing the pull-down menus, but after learning the keyboard commands, they can generally work faster by simply typing the key combinations to activate the various functions. Easy to learn to use, with many built-in letter fonts and a spelling checker, this program is a good choice for use in most classrooms.

FrEdWriter. FrEdWriter is short for *Free Education Writer*, a word processor for educational use that has become a popular alternative to more expensive programs. The fact that this program was developed from a public domain word processor does not mean that it is second-rate; indeed, a number of useful features make this a quality tool. For instance, FrEdWriter uses ProDOS, the updated version of the Apple II operating system, and it has built-in help features that you can call up if information is needed on features of the program. Rather than confusing combinations of keys, single control characters are used to access the various functions. The choice of two screen formats (40- and 80-character) provides options for students with differing capabilities. An extremely useful feature called "prompted writing" permits the teacher to include prompts on the screen that serve as guides for the student to follow as he or she composes at the keyboard. Although these are visible on the screen, they are not printed when the hard copy is made. There are also eight lesson plans included on disks that come with the package.

Despite the title, a modest charge (twenty dollars) is made to cover costs such as production, packaging, and mailing. The program may be freely copied by teachers for use by their students. The documentation comes on the disk itself, although for a slightly higher price printed documentation can be obtained. The source for the package is CUE SoftSwap of Concord, California.

AppleWorks. AppleWorks (Claris) is an integrated program containing three applications modules: a word processor, spreadsheet, and data base. This program is designed around the concept of the desktop environment. In this scheme the desktop is represented by the computer screen; folders holding various kinds of tools and things to do are positioned on the desktop. Folders have a title and a list of the contents (a menu) printed on the front. To retrieve something from a folder you make a choice from the menu. Prompts are provided to help you each step of the way.

Thus, when you get AppleWorks up and running, the first thing you will see is a folder with the words "Main Menu" printed on it. The available options are listed so you can make choices and then go immediately to work. At the top of the screen are the same words as those on the first folder: Main Menu. These indicate your location in the stack of folders. As you move through the folders, the caption at the top of the screen changes to reflect your new position, so you can never get lost with this system. Also helpful are the short instructions at the bottom of the screen that inform you of the way to move or make selections.

Making a selection from the main menu immediately causes a new folder to appear on top of the current one, giving you a new set of options to choose from. For instance, selecting the Add Files option places a folder with this label on top of the Main Menu folder. The selections on the Add Files menu let you get a file from a disk or create a new file. You can choose to work on the word processor, the data base, or the spreadsheet, all of which are listed as options on the folder (Figure 5.10).

Moving the cursor to the Word Processor caption and selecting it will enable you to use that application. The workspace (the space on the screen where you will work) is blank except for a line of information at the top and one at the bottom. These contain the name of the file you are working on, prompts telling you how to get to the main menu, and other information of this kind. You position the cursor where the first letter is to appear and begin to type.

Commands are identical throughout the three modules in the program and you soon find them easy to use. For instance, pressing OA-D enables you to delete material in a word processing document, and it works the same way in the data-base for deleting a record.

The newer AppleWorks GS Word Processor has several features not present in the earlier versions of the program. Among these are an easy to use option for switching from uppercase to lowercase letters, menus from which different fonts of letters can be selected, greater cursor movement within the document, and a more visual approach to displaying various features (such as the spaces, called headers and footers, at the top and bottom of each page). Also available as a separate application within the program is a page layout feature that allows you to combine text and graphics, format a page into columns, and use different type fonts to achieve effects normally associated with desktop publishing programs. For more on using the AppleWorks Word Processor, refer to the exercise in Appendix G.

MacWrite. This classic for the Macintosh, from Claris, set the stage for an entire generation of icon-based word processors for every brand of microcomputer. The mouse is used to select a specific function from the display of options or from menus that are "pulled" from the top of the screen like window shades. This approach is consistent with all programs of this kind, including paint and draw versions. Pictures can be created using a paint program and can then be transported into a MacWrite document to illustrate the text.

There is a second way to access the various functions: you can use key combinations to circumvent the mouse. Many users find this approach to be a bit faster, but others like the freedom of movement the mouse affords. Printed copy

FIGURE 5.10 The Word Processor Is One of Three Applications Available in the AppleWorks Program

is an exact duplicate of the screen display minus any visible formatting features such as rulers. The letter style is easily changed by selecting from the font options; sizes are just as readily selected. Some of the lettering options are illustrated in Figure 5.11.

Many programs are now available for use on the Macintosh that rival this aging standard. For example, Microsoft Word is an outstanding program that is also available in an MS DOS version. It provides several features lacking in Mac-Write, and in some ways is more convenient to use. However, the latter program continues to be a favorite and is still widely used.

WordPerfect. An outstanding program of great power, WordPerfect continues to be a favorite for both business and school use. The MS DOS version requires that you use special keys to activate its various functions. To make this approach simpler, keyboards are used that contain an array of function keys (Figure 5.12), each of which provides several functions when combined with other keys such as the control or shift keys. WordPerfect is also available for the Macintosh and the Apple II line of computers including the IIgs. In the Mac and IIgs versions, menus are used in the same fashion as in MacWrite; thus, you have the best of both worlds.

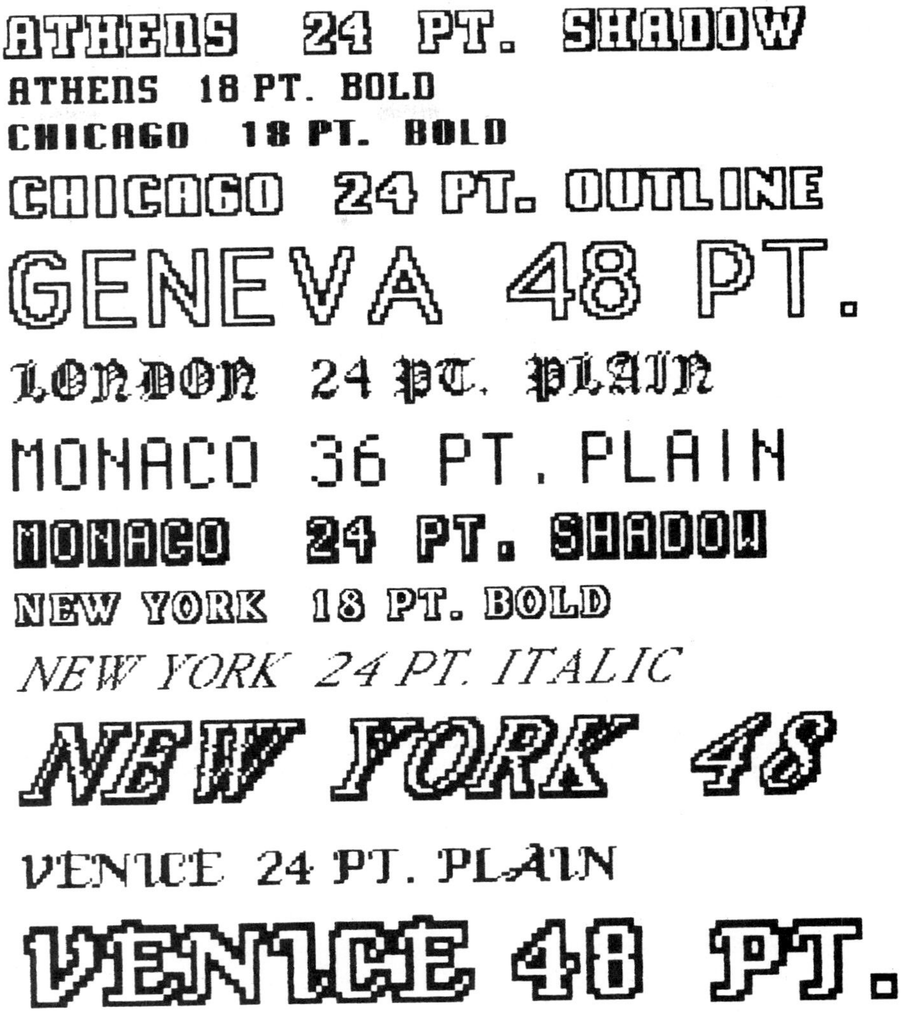

ATHENS   24 PT. SHADOW
ATHENS   18 PT. BOLD
CHICAGO   18 PT. BOLD
CHICAGO   24 PT. OUTLINE
GENEVA   48 PT.
LONDON   24 PT. PLAIN
MONACO   36 PT. PLAIN
MONACO   24 PT. SHADOW
NEW YORK   18 PT. BOLD
NEW YORK   24 PT. ITALIC
NEW YORK   48
VENICE   24 PT. PLAIN
VENICE   48 PT.

FIGURE 5.11   Some Examples of Fonts and Styles Available for the Macintosh

In this short discussion we will consider only the characteristics of the MS DOS version of this program, since this is the one most commonly encountered. The WordPerfect package comes complete with an extensive spelling checker, a thesaurus, a demonstration disk, a lesson disk, and the word processor. Also included is an extensive manual covering every aspect of program use.

The screen display is very similar to the printed document—a feature not shared by all word processing programs but one of considerable importance to most writers. Those with color monitors can take advantage of the color coding features to customize the display; this approach is becoming more common as the quality of color monitors continues to improve.

FIGURE 5.12   An Enhanced Keyboard Showing the Row of Function Keys along the Top

(Photo Courtesy of Tandy Corporation/Radio Shack Advertising)

WordPerfect does an excellent job of using the function keys. Commands can be easily activated and deactivated using the same key(s), and information is constantly available on the screen to keep you informed of which function is currently operating. Color-coded templates that fit neatly over the function keys are available to remind you of the key combinations needed to call up various commands. Versions 5.0 and 5.1 provide the user with various desktop publishing features such as combining graphic images with text, using various sizes and fonts of letters, and selecting from a greater range of formatting options.

RELATED SOFTWARE

Spelling Checkers

The principle underlying the spelling checker involves an approach that people, if they had to do it, would find very cumbersome. It consists of matching, one at a time, the words in a document with words stored on a disk. If computers did not operate so rapidly, this approach would be impractical. At that, waiting for the checker to move through a document of any size can take a relatively long time.

When a word is encountered that cannot be matched with the stored dictionary, the computer will stop scanning and will highlight the suspect word. This occurrence does not always mean that a misspelling has been found; many words are flagged simply because they are not in the current dictionary. Most spellers provide a means for dealing with this problem: you simply select the option that provides for an addition to the dictionary and type the word in; from this point on the computer will not stop on that particular word (unless you misspell it).

A word that is truly misspelled can be corrected by choosing the "correct word" option. Typically, the highlighting disappears and the blinking cursor, which can be used to delete letters, is provided. Changing the spelling and pressing the enter key replaces the misspelled word with the corrected one and reactivates the search. When a correctly spelled word (one not in the dictionary) is highlighted you can use the skip command to leave it intact and continue searching. Most spellers will also flag double words, such as "the the" or "and and"—common mistakes that everyone makes as they type.

A good spelling checker will include the 10,000 most commonly used words plus up to 30,000 or 40,000 additional ones, for a total of up to 50,000 words. The size of the dictionary alone does not, however, denote a quality program. The checker should also provide a list of words similar to the misspelled one to serve as models for making the correction.

Although this type of program is very convenient it does not relieve you of the responsibility of proofing the document the old fashioned way. You still must read through your work with an eye for words that are correctly spelled but wrong in the context. For example, the phrase "their were too birds" would be accepted and skipped by a spelling checker program because no words are misspelled. Figure 5.13 shows a screen from Sensible Speller, a program for the Macintosh.

Thesaurus

A thesaurus can also be a handy tool for writers. Programs of this kind provide a list of synonyms for words you might wish to replace because they have been used too frequently in a document or for other reasons. They may also provide antonyms, homonyms, and often homophones. A typical thesaurus sits quietly until a word is identified as needing replacement. Then, the cursor is placed on that word and the thesaurus is called up. This is accomplished in different ways by different programs. A list of synonyms is then displayed; selecting one of the

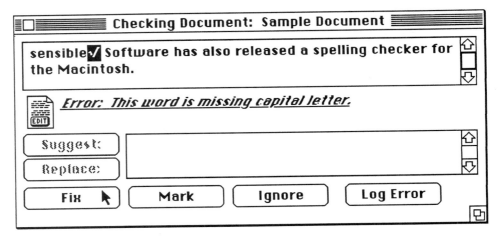

FIGURE 5.13 A Typical Display from Sensible Speller
(Courtesy of Sensible Software, Inc.)

words automatically deletes the old word and replaces it with the new one. If none of the words in the list quite suit your needs, you can select the one that seems best and obtain a list of synonyms for that word. This process can be continued—obtaining synonyms for synonyms—up to a depth of several levels.

Keyboarding Programs

For all the benefits provided by word processors, some teachers argue that there is a risk children who lack keyboarding skills will develop undesirable typing habits. To answer these concerns, software developers have issued a selection of "typing tutors" that teach proper keyboarding techniques (Figure 5.14). Some include features for strengthening punctuation skills and improving students' spelling and grammar.

Among the excellent programs of this kind are Type! (Broderbund Software), Typing Tutor IV (Simon and Schuster), Type To Learn (Sunburst), and Mavis Beacon Teaches Typing (Software Toolworks). Although these programs differ from one another in detail, a general idea of how keyboarding software is designed and how it works can be obtained from the examination of a single selection; we will look at Mavis Beacon.

Approximately thirty lessons designed to help students with specific typing problems are available, but additional lessons can be created if those on the disk are not adequate. Graphics are lavishly used throughout; these include shadow-like hands on the monitor that mimic the movement of the actual hands at the keyboard, and graphs that display the user's performance on each key.

After the initial sign-on procedure you are asked to take a short typing test, then you can move on to one of the three different teaching and testing modes. In the classroom mode an illustrated keyboard is used for drills and instruction; in the workshop numerous interesting "tools" are provided to help build typing skills. In the game mode the speed of race cars is controlled by the typing rate of the user. Many different kinds of practice material are provided, including short riddles and jokes, business letters, and resumes. You can follow the computer's suggestions, which are based upon the diagnosis of your performance, call up different activities, or even create your own lessons. An open typing mode is also available, so material from any source can be typed in to be analyzed for accuracy and speed.

WORD PROCESSORS IN THE CLASSROOM

Although playing with a program to discover how it works is often the best approach, there may be times when a more structured strategy is desired. The three Moby Dick exercises in appendix H, which include a number of typical mistakes to be corrected, represent an effective way to introduce students to word processing. These exercises were designed to be used with three popular word processors, each of which operates on a different type of computer. We selected the AppleWorks Word Processor for the Apple II, WordPerfect for the IBM and clones, and MacWrite for use on the Macintosh. It is hoped that one or more of

FIGURE 5.14 Typing Tutor IV Is a Popular Program for Teaching Typing

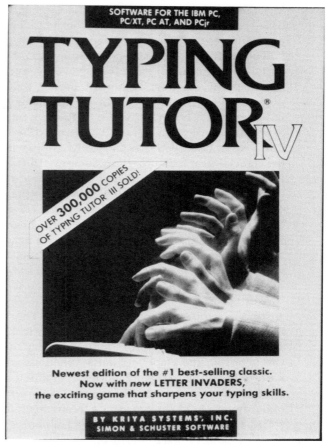

(Used by Permission of Simon & Schuster, Inc.)

these programs and computers is available to you and your students; however, if this is not the case the exercise can easily be modified so it can be used with any word processing program.

   The exercise is generally placed on a disk, mistakes and all, to be loaded into the computer as the session begins. The student has a printed copy of the manuscript and a line-by-line description of the commands to use and the steps to follow in correcting the errors. Note that the original document is retained as a file on the disk to be reused whenever needed; the corrected material exists only in the computer's memory and will be erased (or saved or printed) when the session is over.

   Students do not necessarily have to work in isolation when engaged in word processing—small group activities are practical and appropriate. A group can write collaborative stories and manage the editing activities by taking turns at the keyboard; the final draft can then be saved on a disk in preparation for printing onto paper. Word processing activities become more meaningful if actual projects—research papers, notices, school newspapers, or anthologies of student compositions, for example—are produced.

The production of a school newspaper is a particularly useful activity because of the diverse functions involved. Not only must the text be composed and edited, but blocks of text must be defined, moved about, and inserted in the appropriate places to fill the various columns. Formatting becomes a challenge as young editors figure out how to create a traditional newspaper layout. Although few inexpensive word processors will generate different varieties of type, students can design their own headlines and subheadings with transfer letters. They might also use special graphics programs such as Print Shop and Fontrix to create fancy letters. Spaces can be included in the layout to accommodate student-produced line drawings. The end result of an activity such as this is an interesting collection of reports on a variety of subjects in an error-free and attractive format.

Almost any project that involves writing can be undertaken on a word processor. The basic material for a lesson—such as words to be used in the creation of a poem, a limerick with the lines mixed up, a half-finished anecdote, a list of words to be alphabetized, a letter outline to be personalized by each student—can be placed on a disk to be loaded by the student.

Word processors are especially valuable when process (as opposed to product) writing is being stressed in language arts. There are many ways to use these tools in process writing. Students can type in words and phrases associated with a particular object or event as individuals, or the entire class might participate in this activity. The block and move functions are then used to choose and manipulate selected phrases and words, combining these into a verse for all to enjoy. Just about any subject will work, although some have greater potential than others. A favorite of ours just after a fresh snowfall has covered everything is "snowstorm." Students, excited about the happening, readily respond with a multitude of words and phrases. From the common ones such as "cold" and "white" the terms expand to "blanketing," "hushed," and "enfolding." Phrases show a range of descriptive imagination also: "soft winter's hand," "white arms enfolding," "silence speaking." You can see how easily interesting poems might be constructed from an extensive, student-generated list of this kind.

Another group activity involves the members of a class in writing a novel. The teacher can stimulate the process if, after the class decides on the subject, he places starter sentences for each chapter on the disk for students to examine and use as they wish. Or, the story might evolve in a random fashion as each student adds a sentence or paragraph that builds on the preceding one. This process can continue as long as the class desires, or it can terminate when each student has had a turn, or even on a certain date. A Christmas story, for example, might be initiated some time before Christmas to be concluded on the last day of school before vacation time. The finished story would be printed and duplicated for each student to take home and share with his or her family.

Jack McGarvey (1988), in an article in *Classroom Computer Learning,* tells how he helps students write better by using the find function. In the revision stages he has students use this function to locate words that tend to make their writing less specific and therefore less stimulating. A list of words such as "good," "nice," and "interesting" is posted for all to see. Students are encouraged to have the computer locate each instance of use for each word to see if changes can be made to strengthen the meaning. He also displays a chart of weak verbs for students to search out with the find function so they might determine if stronger verbs need to be substituted.

Various word processing programs offer a range of type fonts and sizes which can be used selectively to illustrate a story. A style of letter is chosen for its ability to enhance meaning in a visual way. For example, the word *power* is printed in bold letters, *ballerina* in graceful ones. A composition constructed in this manner is delightful to read. This activity encourages young authors to analyze and interpret word meaning with greater care than when unembellished words are used.

Having a composition on a disk makes critiquing much simpler for the teacher than if it were on paper. Correction and comments are typed and saved as the document is reviewed. When the student views her work at a later time, the suggestions are there for her to follow. Students might review each other's work in this fashion also, with both the author and critic benefitting from the activity.

Word processing is not restricted to student use exclusively, of course—some innovative teachers have adapted it to their own needs. For example, several English teachers have devised an interesting approach to correcting student themes. They have their students compose on the word processor and then save the compositions on individual disks—one disk per student. The teachers check the themes on the computer, inserting information on needed corrections and changes, then resave the material, including the suggested refinements, back onto the disk. Students can edit their work, making corrections where noted, and then print the final draft if desired. Thus, unlike the traditional approach—where the teacher red-pencils the final product—corrections are suggested and carried out in the formative stage of composition. Students feel much better about their work and the product itself is obviously of higher quality. One problem with this approach, however, is that if the themes are of any length, they require substantial effort for the teacher to edit them.

While many commercial programs provide writing exercises of various kinds, creating your own lessons using a word processor is quite easy to do. For example, you might type a series of sentences using only lower-case letters. The students are required to capitalize the proper words by making the changes on the computer and saving their corrected lesson for you to check. This same approach can be used for just about any grammar activity. You might also scramble a literary selection and challenge students to rearrange it so that it is syntactically correct.

Experience indicates that students love to use the word processor. Although it has not been clearly proven that their writing improves as a consequence, studies reveal that students write longer documents and revise more extensively with word processors. The fact that documents tend to improve qualitatively in proportion to the number of revisions leads to speculation that word processing will indeed have a positive effect on the quality of student writing.

Other classroom applications of word processing are discussed in Chapter 4.

SUMMARY

The ease with which word processors permit students to edit and revise their compositions has made this task much less formidable than it used to be. As a consequence of this and other factors students using computers tend to write more than when typewriters or paper and pencils were the primary tools. While they are involved in writing creatively, students also build their skills in punctuation, grammar, vocabulary, and other essential areas.

In addition to the convenient editing features of word processors, several other capabilities were discussed in this chapter. These included formatting, which can be easily tailored to fit various page layout needs; file management; and printing the document as paper copy. Several special capabilities found in programs of this kind were also mentioned. Included were the find function, search and replace, defining and moving or cutting blocks, and cursor movement. Spelling checkers are useful for finding misspelled words, which are then highlighted so corrections can be made; the electronic thesaurus provides numerous synonyms to replace a word that is deemed inappropriate or has been overused.

Keyboarding programs are used to teach proper keyboarding techniques so students can function maximally at the computer keyboard. Good software of this kind provides a broad selection of activities to lead students through essential drill-and-practice activities in a challenging and interesting fashion.

Many brands of word processors are available for use in the classroom. For very young learners, the talking word processor is a good choice. A current trend is to incorporate graphic capabilities in word processing programs to enable students to illustrate compositions they have written; various programs exhibiting this feature were mentioned. A selection of programs with advanced capabilities for use by older students was provided, and a public domain word processor called FrEdWriter was discussed. In conclusion, various activities built around writing with a word processor were suggested.

SELF-TEST

1. List three advantages of using a word processor.
2. Describe the search and replace function.
3. What is a block?
4. How might you use a word processor for whole-class instruction?
5. What are the function keys? Why are they useful?
6. List several features of a document that can be changed using the formatting function.
7. What is the difference between a menu-driven and a command-driven program?
8. What is the purpose of a keyboarding program?
9. Talking word processors are popular for use with very young learners. Why?
10. Each brand of word processor has its own unique features. Discuss at least three such features you consider to be noteworthy.
11. How do the spelling checker and the electronic thesaurus work?
12. Describe several ways to use the word processor in the classroom.

REFERENCES

Bitter, G., and R. Camuse. *Using a Microcomputer in the Classroom.* 2d ed. Englewood Cliffs, N.J.: Prentice-Hall, 1988.

Blissmer, R., and R. Alden. *Introduction to Computers and Application Software.* Boston: Houghton Mifflin, 1986.

Boudrot, T. "The Thesaurus of Course." *Teaching and Computers* (January/February 1988): 60–64.

Collis, B. *Computers, Curriculum, and Whole-Class Instruction.* Belmont, Calif.: Wadsworth, 1988.

Eiser, L. "I Luv To Rite." *Classroom Computer Learning* (November/December 1986): 50–57.

Grauer, R., and P. Sugrue. *Microcomputer Applications,* 2d ed. New York: McGraw-Hill, 1989.

Grupe, F. *Microcomputer Applications Using WordPerfect, Lotus 1–2–3, and dBase III PLUS.* Dubuque, Iowa: Wm. C. Brown, 1988.

Howell, R., and P. Scott. *Microcomputer Applications for Teachers.* Scottsdale, Ariz.: Gorsuch Scarisbrick, 1985.

Jaroslovsky, R. "The IIe/IIc Word Processing Challenge." *A+ Magazine* (July 1988): 72–76.

Lockard, J., P. Abrams, and W. Many. *Microcomputers for Educators.* Boston: Little, Brown, 1987.

Markowitz, M. "Just My Type." *A+ Magazine* (October 1988): 52–57.

McGarvey, J. "The Magic Fingers of Find." *Classroom Computer Learning* (March 1988): 50–52.

Riedesel, C., and D. Clements. *Coping with Computers in the Elementary and Middle Schools.* Englewood Cliffs, N.J.: Prentice-Hall, 1985.

Solomon, G. "A Free Word Processor that Stands Up to the Crowd." *Electronic Learning* (January 1987): 30–31.

Troutman, A., and J. White. *The Micro Goes to School.* Pacific Grove, Calif.: Brooks/Cole, 1988.

Turner, S., and M. Land. *Tools for Schools: Applications Software for the Classroom.* Belmont, Calif.: Wadsworth, 1988.

CHAPTER 6
Tools II: Spreadsheets, Data Bases, and More

CHAPTER TOPICS
☐ The nature of and uses for electronic spreadsheets
☐ Spreadsheet programs for school use
☐ Classroom applications of the spreadsheet
☐ The organization of a data base
☐ How a data base works
☐ Data base programs for school use
☐ Classroom applications using data bases
☐ The varieties of graphics software
☐ Some educational uses for graphics
☐ Classroom activities using graphics software
☐ Ways to create hard copy graphics
☐ How to use a desktop publisher
☐ Desktop publishing software for school use
☐ Classroom activities using desktop publishing software
☐ Useful teacher tools for classroom management
☐ How to use electronic gradebooks, test generators, and attendance software
☐ The characteristics of a typical integrated program
☐ Some integrated programs suitable for use in the school

The word processor, most ubiquitous of all the electronic tools, was discussed in detail in the previous chapter. Additional tools are covered in this chapter. Included are spreadsheets, data bases, graphics software, desktop publishing programs, teacher tools, and integrated programs.

Electronic spreadsheets provide a convenient means for recording and manipulating numerical data. Programs of this kind perform various calculations using built-in formulas or those designed by the user. A data base is useful when large amounts of data must be organized and stored, and then portions of it retrieved according to a predetermined structure. The design of a data base has a parallel in the old fashioned file cabinet, with folders containing related items of information, but the similarity ends here. Unlike a hand search through manilla folders, computer-based searches are simple, fast, and extremely thorough. Graphic tools enable users to produce neat, attractive images of various kinds even though their artistic skills might be quite limited. Among the varieties of graphics software are painting and drawing programs, animators, programs for printing posters and banners, graph-makers, and presentation tools. Desktop publishing software provides teachers and students with the means to create published materials from inception to final printout. The page layout capability is used to design the basic page; illustrations can be imported from a clip art file or created by the user.

Attractive text is easily composed using a wide range of different letter styles and sizes.

Many different tools have been designed to make the mundane tasks of classroom management easier for the teacher to carry out. These include electronic gradebooks, computerized test generators, and attendance programs. When word processors, spreadsheets, and data bases (and frequently other kinds of tools) are combined, the result is an integrated program. With software of this kind you can create a document in one module and move it to a different one for further modification.

SPREADSHEETS

The computer-based spreadsheet is an electronic representation of the extensive record-keeping, planning, and projecting activities that were formerly carried out laboriously with pencil, paper, and a calculator. Indeed, the first electronic spreadsheet, VisiCalc, was created by Dan Bricklin and Robert Frankston, students at Harvard and M.I.T., respectively, to help take the drudgery out of business applications. When the electronic spreadsheet is displayed on the screen, it appears as a grid made up of horizontal rows and vertical columns as shown in Figure 6.1. Wherever a row and column intersect, a *cell* is formed that accepts information typed in by the user. Two types of information can be entered into a spreadsheet: words (called *labels*) and numbers and formulas (called *values*).

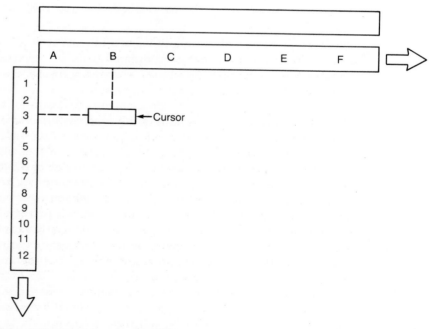

FIGURE 6.1 A Typical Spreadsheet Arrangement with the Cursor on Cell B3

Some programs provide hundreds and even thousands of columns and rows. One popular spreadsheet has 256 columns and 8,192 rows; others have even more than this. Large capacities such as this are necessary for business applications, but for most classroom uses smaller spreadsheets are adequate. Obviously, because of its size, the total spreadsheet cannot be viewed on the screen all at once— it is necessary to scroll both horizontally and vertically as the work progresses. In most programs the columns are identified with letters and the rows with numbers. This permits each cell to have a distinct letter/number code to identify it from all others. Cell D2, for example, is located in column D on row 2.

In Figure 6.2 a spreadsheet designed for an experiment in nutrition using rats is shown. Labels are seen across the top of row 1 while values are distributed in the columns and rows throughout the sheet. Formulas have been entered in cells where a calculation is required (for example, cell I3, where an average is computed, and cell K3, where a weight loss is computed). Although the formulas themselves do not show, the results of the calculations do.

Perhaps the single most important reason for using a spreadsheet is the *recalculation* feature. Once the relationship among values has been specified, any change in one or more of them causes all dependent variables to be recalculated to reflect the change. In Figure 6.2, a change in the weight entered in cell E3, for example, would bring about a recalculation of the average weight for column E, the final average weight, and so on for all dependent variables. Most modern spreadsheets are capable of generating graphs from the numerical data that is entered. Data from the spreadsheet can be displayed on the computer screen or printed out as hard copy. Various kinds of graphs can be produced, including line, bar, and column graphs, and sometimes circle or pie graphs.

It is not necessary to start and design a spreadsheet for every application. The alternative is to use a *template,* a predesigned file stored on a disk that defines the form of the spreadsheet. It is only partially complete, however, since the data will be entered by the user. What is in place are all the labels, formulas, and formatting necessary to perform a specified job. A template in common use in schools is the gradebook. Gradebooks contain spaces for student names and test scores as well as other entries. Formulas are in place to calculate means, standard deviations, averages, and final grades. Templates are favored by many educators because so much of the time-consuming work has already been done for them; all that is necessary is to load the template and data can be entered immediately.

Some Features of Spreadsheets

Editing.   Spreadsheets allow the user to make changes on the data being typed before it is entered into the spreadsheet. As the material is typed, it is displayed on an edit line below the worksheet for you to examine. If the information looks correct, you can enter it with a press of a key. You can also edit information already in a cell by using a slightly different procedure.

Calculation.   In addition to labels and values, the spreadsheet has built-in (preprogrammed) formulas or functions. You can also design your own formulas using

File: Nutrition   REVIEW/ADD/CHANGE   Escape:

=====	A=====	B=====	C=====	D=====	E=====	F=====	G=====	H=====	I=====	J=====	K=====	L=====
			Beg. Wght. (grams)		Week 1		Week 2		Week 3		Week 4		Ave. Wght.		Gain/Loss

1	GROUP I								
2									
3		1	272	271	270	268	268	269.25	-2.75
4		2	348	340	338	335	330	335.75	-12.25
5		3	353	352	345	344	336	344.25	-8.75
6		4	360	357	351	346	340	348.5	-11.5
7									
8	Ave.		333.25	330	326	323.25	318.5	324.4375	-8.8125
9									
10	GROUP II								
11									
12		1	303	304	307	312	317	310	7
13		2	349	343	348	350	353	349	10
14		3	340	341	345	354	354	347.5	7.5
15		4	352	357	362	367	372	364.5	12.5
16									
17	Ave.		333.5	336.25	340.5	345.25	349	342.75	9.25
18									
19									
20									

FIGURE 6.2 A Spreadsheet Designed with AppleWorks

the functions provided. As numbers are entered, the computer performs the mathematical calculations defined by the particular formula being used and displays the results in the cell containing the formula.

Recalculation. You can change numbers as desired when using a spreadsheet. The program immediately recalculates all values in every cell related to the figures being changed.

Formatting. Like the word processor, certain changes can be made in a spreadsheet to make it more versatile as well as more attractive. For instance, you can make columns wider so longer words can be entered.

Copying and Cutting and Pasting. You can copy and move data in operations similar to those of the block function on the word processor; however, rather than defining a block you merely select a cell to be copied or cut from the spreadsheet and pasted somewhere else.

Graphing. Most spreadsheets are capable of generating various kinds of graphs from the numerical information in the worksheet.

Printing. Not only can the worksheet itself be printed, but the graphs generated from the information can also be printed as hard copy. You will recall that some spreadsheets provide thousands of rows, all of which might conceivably contain data. How can such an extensive document be printed? Such documents cannot be printed as a single, continuous copy since standard printers are not capable of producing output wider than the 80-character width of the screen; however, you can print out sections of the spreadsheet as desired.

Help Options. On-screen features provide immediate assistance right on the screen—a much more convenient way to get needed information than searching through lengthy documentation.

Sorting. The sorting feature permits you to rearrange information already on the spreadsheet into alphabetical or numerical order.

Spreadsheets for Classroom Use

The spreadsheet in AppleWorks is the one most commonly used in the classroom. The spreadsheet is accessed in the same fashion as the other applications in the program—from the Menu of Options (Figure 6.3). The spreadsheet is designed along the same lines as the word processor and data base, using the same kinds of files, prompts, and commands. The display is composed of the standard rows and columns; moving among these is as simple as pressing the arrow keys. You can move more rapidly using the Open-Apple and arrow keys in combination.

Several useful features are provided to help you view the spreadsheet, parts of which are normally hidden. You can use the zoom feature to zoom in to examine cell formulas and out again to see the values derived from the formulas. You can command AppleWorks to fix the titles across the top and on the left side of the screen so they remain visible regardless of how far down or to the right the cursor

FIGURE 6.3 The Menu of Options from AppleWorks. The Three Applications Are Shown at the Bottom of the Menu

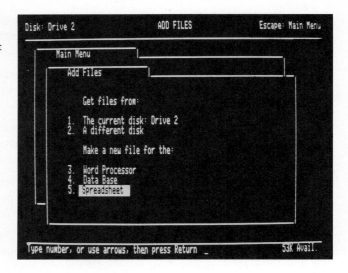

```
Disk: Drive 2                 ADD FILES              Escape: Main Menu
┌─────────────────────┐
│ Main Menu           │
│ ┌─────────────────────┐
│ │ Add Files           │
│ │
│ │    Get files from:
│ │
│ │ 1.  The current disk: Drive 2
│ │ 2.  A different disk
│ │
│ │    Make a new file for the:
│ │
│ │ 3.  Word Processor
│ │ 4.  Data Base
│ │ 5.  Spreadsheet
│ │
└─│
  └──────────────────────────────────────────────
Type number, or use arrows, then press Return _        53K Avail.
```

is moved, and you can split the spreadsheet so that two remote parts can be compared and examined. All the other regular spreadsheet features are available to AppleWorks users; they are easy to access and easy to use.

The newer AppleWorks GS spreadsheet has many more functions for use in calculating than the older versions. These are displayed in a box and are selected in Macintosh fashion by positioning the cursor on the one to be used and clicking the mouse button to automatically place the function in the formula being designed. Also, the display is much more graphic than in the older versions, using more icons to show options. Other features of the AppleWorks program are described in the word processing chapter, as well as in the discussion of data bases in this chapter.

Figure 6.4 shows some of the files generated with AppleWorks and stored on a data disk. Note how the application that was used is identified; you can readily find the files created on the spreadsheet.

Many other spreadsheets, some relatively inexpensive, are suitable for school use. Practicalc II, for the Apple and Commodore, is a low-priced, capable program that includes a feature for placing prompts within the worksheet that solicit specified input from the user. It also provides graphing features and sorting capabilities.

SynCalc, for the Atari and Commodore, is menu-driven and simple to operate. Multiplan (Microsoft) is an excellent tool that is available for several makes of computers. The price starts at a low forty dollars.

Microsoft Works is a popular standby that came bundled with the school version of the IBM computer; it is available for other makes of computer as well. Various public domain spreadsheets are available at minimum cost from different sources.

FIGURE 6.4 The Method of Displaying the Names of Files Created with AppleWorks

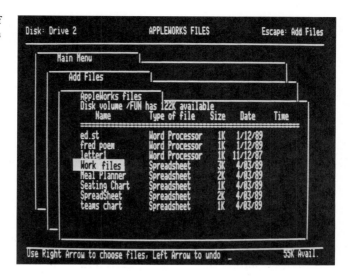

Classroom Applications

After learning how spreadsheets work, students will devise many ways to use them if encouraged to do so. Although traditional applications should not be downplayed, one of the most useful and exciting ways to use this tool is in the realm of speculation, the what-if scenario. Spreadsheets enable users to construct a complete set of interrelated information that can represent a profile of an aspect of a business or other enterprise. The real strength of the electronic spreadsheet is in its what-if capabilities: changing the value of any cell automatically causes related values to be modified.

A traditional use of the spreadsheet is shown in Figure 6.2. A junior high school science class decided to find out how diet might affect weight gain or loss. They obtained eight laboratory rats of similar weights to use as subjects in the study. Using published nutritional information, they devised two diets, similar in weight, one of which was high in saturated fats while the other was similar to a diet prescribed for patients with high cholesterol. The amounts the rats ate were carefully controlled so that overeating would not be a factor in weight gain. Using AppleWorks, the students designed the spreadsheet illustrated. They divided the rats into two groups, each containing four rats. Group I rats were fed the low-fat diet; those in Group II were fed the high-fat diet. Some cells of the spreadsheet were set aside to accept data (weekly weights) while formulas were typed into others. To obtain average weights, the averaging function in AppleWorks was used. This function is typed in this fashion: @ AVG(list or range). The other arithmetic functions in this program use a similar format (example: @ SUM(list or range) to obtain the sum of several cells). By entering the formula @ AVG(C3 . . . C6) in cell C8, the students directed AppleWorks to figure the average beginning weight for the four rats in Group I (represented by cells C3, C4,

C5, and C6); note that it turned out to be 333.25 grams. If, for any reason, one of the rats had to be replaced, substituting the weight of the new rat would immediately cause the average to change. You can examine the spreadsheet to see how the experiment turned out. Of course, the final averages should be analyzed statistically to determine whether the difference between the two is significant; this can be done with another kind of program, the statistical package, if one is available.

Spreadsheets are particularly useful in the social studies area. They make possible a kind of educated prediction that could only be labeled pure speculation using older methods. The kinds of information that can be managed by a spreadsheet are virtually without number; any sort of table can be constructed. What if, for example, nations should suddenly renounce war? The implications are much more far-reaching than one would expect. How many microcomputers could be purchased for the schools using the money earmarked for the construction of ballistic missiles? If the price of computers was going down at a constant rate while the price of the missiles was rising at a different rate, how many more computers could be purchased each year? On the other hand, how many new jobs would have to be created to accommodate those who worked in war-related industries and are now unemployed? Other problems might involve situations such as the relationship of changing world populations to food production or energy resources to current and projected consumption.

Additional uses for spreadsheets in various subject matter areas are described in Chapter 4.

DATA BASES

Data bases are designed to provide a convenient way to store large quantities of data in an organized manner. The data can be arranged, or sorted, according to a number of schemes including alphabetical and numerical listings. A data base management system (DBMS) is a program that provides an efficient way to access and manipulate the information in a data base. When information is needed the computer is directed to conduct a search for a specific subset of data, which is defined by one or more search keys, and then to display this and perhaps to print it as paper copy.

Most classroom programs are simplified versions of a full-scale DBMS and are generally referred to as *file management systems*. While not full-featured, such programs have several characteristics that make them convenient for school use. They are generally menu-driven, providing lists of options from which the user makes a selection, which greatly simplifies the operation. They are also relatively inexpensive, many being available as public domain programs. They provide all the features most teachers ever need, including such things as creating original record templates, searching, sorting, and printing hard copy. On the other hand, record keeping at the school or district level requires a more capable DBMS to manage the large amounts of data involved. To enhance the access and retrieval of information, electronic data bases use a logical method for organizing data.

Actually, the system is not really unique; it is much the same as a teacher might use if he or she were filing traditional paper-based material.

A common teacher responsibility is to create and maintain records for each member of a class. Typically, this involves filling out sheets with such things as the student's name, birthdate, and other personal data. Generally, a standard form is provided into which the unique information for each student is entered. When complete, all the sheets are collected and organized in some order (generally alphabetical) and are then placed in a binder of some kind. Later, when information on a specific student is needed, the teacher searches through the binder for that student's record, which is then scanned to find a specific bit of information. This is essentially the same way that an electronic data base is organized and used. The smallest item, such as a birth date, is termed a *field* in the electronic data base. The term *record* is used to define the sheet containing all the information for a single student, and the binder with all the records inside is called a *file* (Figure 6.5).

Electronic data bases search a file just as the teacher might, looking for a specific bit of information designated with a keyword (birthdate, address) but they do this infinitely faster than is possible for any human.

Templates of the kind discussed in Chapter 4 are also available for use with data bases. Certain publishers offer templates designed for use in various subject-matter areas that can be used with existing data base programs.

Creating a Data Base

A planning sheet can be very useful when designing a data base. Figure 6.6 shows one such sheet in its completed form for use with the Create-a-Base program from MECC. When the planning sheet with its different fields appears satisfactory, it is used as the pattern for a template in the data base you are creating. The template is formed by typing titles, spaces, and other necessary dimensions into

FIGURE 6.5 How the Elements of a Data Base are Related

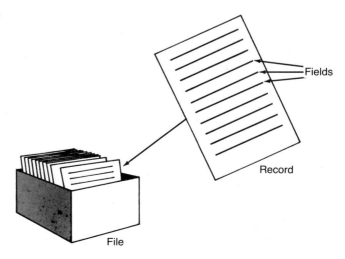

Fields

Record

File

FIGURE 6.6   A Planning Sheet
for Designing a Computerized
Form for a DataBase on the U.S.
Presidents

Planning Sheet

Name(20 max.)   [Presidents_____]

Field Name (12 max.)	# of Input spaces (23 max.)	Numbers only (Y/N)
Field 1 [President___]	[23]	[N]
Field 2 [President_#_]	[02]	[Y]
Field 3 [Party_____]	[23]	[N]
Field 4 [Years_served]	[02]	[Y]
Field 5 [Vice-Pres.___]	[23]	[N]
Field 6 [Birth_state_]	[23]	[N]
Field 7 [Occupation__]	[23]	[N]
Field 8 [Year_died___]	[04]	[Y]
Field 9 [Other_facts_]	(56 max.) [56]	[N]

(Courtesy of MECC)

the computer. The amount of information that a record will hold varies from one program to the next. Note that Create-a-Base, which was designed specifically for classroom use, provides nine fields with a specified maximum number of characters in each. The more professional programs provide considerably greater space for data than this.

Having defined the various fields, you are now ready to enter the specific information for each of the presidents to create a collection of records, which will become, collectively, a file. If you were creating a data base on presidents, a good place to start would be with George Washington, the first president. The record with the field names (president, president number, party, and so on) will be displayed on the screen, followed by blank lines. The pointer will be on line 1, the line labeled "President"; you simply type "George Washington" to fill the space. If the name is spelled correctly, move to the next line and type "01" (president number one) and so on until all the spaces have been filled. Once this is done the computer will ask "Is this record O.K.?" If the answer is no, you can move through the various fields to correct them. If the record is correct, typing "Yes" will cause it to be entered into the data base.

Once the records have all been completed, you can take advantage of the various functions that make a data base so valuable. You can search for any record desired, using a search key based on the names of the fields used to create the basic record. You can sort alphabetically or numerically and you can print out the information as paper copy. For example, you might want to know how many presidents were lawyers; or how many people in the data base, both presidents and vice presidents, were named Adams. The computer will quickly provide this information. You can also delete records that are no longer needed, leaving all other records intact. This short discussion could not possibly cover all aspects of creating a data base, but it should be adequate to give you some insights into the process.

While using a data base is a fairly straightforward and uncomplicated process, there are two functions that are somewhat complex and require further explanation. These are searching and sorting.

Searching

Neither filing cabinets filled with printed materials nor computerized data bases containing electronic records are of much value if you can't find what you want in a reasonable amount of time. Both systems are arranged and accessed in rather standard ways. With a traditional file cabinet, however, a person frequently must search laboriously through all the files to locate an incidental bit of information. An electronic data base, on the other hand, permits you to specify a wide range of sort keys that can be used to find what you are looking for instantly. Data bases typically provide the user with several search options. One of these is a match that conforms precisely—the keyword (the word typed in) and the word in the record are identical. Another option allows a certain latitude by permitting the user to type a word, along with some simple code, that tells the computer to find any records containing that particular word in a designated field: the word *tree,* for example (along with the code peculiar to the program being used), might locate *family tree* and *maple tree.*

Many programs permit you to be very explicit in what you wish to find. For example, you might want to locate French artists, but only those who painted in the impressionist style—this is an example of a two-level search (artist and style). A three-level search might include the addition of a specific year of birth, which would further delimit the search. Only the more powerful data base programs permit searches on multiple levels.

Sorting

The sorting feature permits you to enter the data base and rearrange the records in some specified manner. For example, information might be more useful if arranged in alphabetical order, or according to date or zip code. In the case of a data base on artists, you might want to sort records according to painting style. The most common ways to sort are by alphabetical or numerical order; thus the abstract expressionists would come before the surrealists. Multiple sorts arrange information according to more than one criterion. The keyword used in the sort described above—*style,* for example—is a major sort key. But some data bases can sort according to several criteria simultaneously. If the sort key *artist* were used along with *style,* this would be an example of a minor sort key. The result of this multiple sort would be the alphabetization of the artists within each style category. Depending upon the nature of the data base, you might wish to use several minor sort keys.

Data Base Programs for School Use

AppleWorks continues to be the most popular tool program in the classroom. You will recall that in addition to the data base, a spreadsheet and word processor are provided in this integrated program. To access the data base, you move back to the Menus, move the cursor to the data base option, and make the selection. You can create a data base from scratch or use one of the many available templates. Files may also be imported from a different but compatible program. As in any data base program, a template is created to accept the data you will enter. As each successive record is completed, a blank one takes its place, and the process continues until all records are complete. Editing features are provided so records can be edited and any mistakes corrected. Once the records have been created, you can delete, copy, move, display, select, and sort them as desired.

The newer AppleWorks GS data base has several features lacking in the earlier module. For instance, you need not confine the data to text only; graphics can be imported from the graphics module and stored as readily as information in the more traditional text format. Creating fields is also different from earlier versions in that they can be resized and moved about. The capacity of the fields is also expanded, with one of them set aside to hold multiple pages of text.

Several other data bases are useful for school applications. DCH Notebook Filer (Collamore/D.C. Heath) provides add-on files containing information for use in conjunction with language arts and social studies textbooks. It is totally menu driven for ease of use.

Secret Filer (Figure 6.7) engages students in creating "computerized index cards" that are filed in a categorical arrangement on the disk and called up when needed. Security is provided as students lock their data away using passwords they invent.

DB Master Version Five is a powerful DBM program for the Apple II. It offers up to 250 characters per field and up to 200 fields per record. A tutorial function is built in to provide on-screen help to users as they operate the program. This is a product of Stone Edge Technologies.

Friendly Filer, as its name implies, is a simple, friendly program for use by young students. It provides a modest seven fields with a maximum of 37 characters per field, an arrangement which obviously limits the amount of information that can be contained. Also available are premade data bases or templates in many subject areas for use with this program. Grolier is the producer.

FIGURE 6.7 Secret Filer Is a Popular File Management Program for Classroom Use

(Courtesy of Scholastic Software)

Another filing program for young learners is Bank Street Beginner's File from Sunburst Communications. Designed for students who are unfamiliar with data bases, this program is ideal for introductory activities. A more capable version is Bank Street Filer. With this program students use a natural English language sentence structure for conducting a search or sort. The creation of the sentences is made easy by a series of boxes containing options from which the student selects only those words appropriate to his or her data base.

Stuff and Fetch (MECC) is a simple data base designed to encourage young researchers to organize data most effectively. A built-in word processor provides the material to "stuff" into the data base. The "fetch" feature is equivalent to the search function. Students learn through hands-on activities how best to use these features.

For grades seven through twelve, Scholastic pfs:File/Report is excellent for organizing data and creating reports containing such features as tables and charts. Capable of storing very large quantities of information, this program is particularly useful in the language arts and social studies areas.

Spinnaker's Easy Working Filer is menu-driven, using on-screen menus with every command. Other programs in this series include Easy Working Writer and Easy Working Planner. All work together to provide a powerful integrated environment for storage, mail merge, advanced calculation, and other functions. Up to 10,000 records can be stored in each file.

Data Bases in the Classroom

Students can be introduced to the concept of data bases by using the analogy of the filing cabinet. Once the concept is clear, the students must make some collective decisions: what the primary subject in their data base will be, what kind of information pertaining to that subject is desired, and how detailed the information will be.

When the format has been selected, the students go to various information sources such as the library, encyclopedias, or perhaps their parents to obtain material for the data base. Once they have gathered adequate information, they are ready for the computer. Several current data base programs are simple enough even for gradeschool children, once they have mastered a few fundamentals. After a short explanatory session to create forms and format records, the students can enter data to complete the records. Because few elementary students are proficient at typing, this process can be very slow. A typing tutorial can be useful at this point, but only if ample time is available for practice. When the records are complete, the data base is ready for use. Printed reports of the information obtained can be generated using the printing option built into the data base program.

Data bases are particularly useful in social studies classes because they make instantly available a quantity of data, which can be updated constantly. They permit comparisons between related variables such as gross national product, population, land area, per capita income, or whatever else might be included in the data base. Students become actively involved with information storage and retrieval and with organizational logic. They also have the opportunity to work together on projects that often become rather complex and extended.

Data bases are also useful in areas other than social studies. Any subject in which research is important, information must be accessed rapidly, organization is stressed, or innovation is desired can be taught more effectively with this helpful tool.

The data bases discussed in this section are local, housed and used within a particular school. Remote data bases, which are frequently extremely large and accessed via a modem and the telephone lines, will be discussed in the next chapter.

GRAPHICS TOOLS

Over the past several years the potential for production of graphic images with the microcomputer has vastly improved. Microcomputers have always provided a capability for output of this kind, but traditionally this involved using a programming language, such as BASIC, to design the product. The development of hardware, in the form of graphics tablets, and software devoted exclusively to the generation of graphics has made the programming approach much less common than it once was. Of course you can still write programs to take advantage of the computer's built-in graphics modes, but this is considerably more demanding than is tracing a line on a graphics tablet with your finger or a stylus. In addition to creating images as works of art, students can use the graphics they create to illustrate relationships in math, science, and social studies. These can then be included as illustrations in research papers developed on the word processor. Some computers have better graphic capabilities than others, including finer resolution of images and more colors. One such computer, the Apple IIGs, has special graphics as well as sound capabilities.

Unless you want your students to learn something about programming, you will likely bypass this activity in favor of using one or more of the excellent programs available for creating graphics. Programs of this kind are so structured that they come close to approximating the artist's canvas, but with certain differences: no actual paints are involved in paint programs, nor are brushes. Drawing programs forego the use of pencils, pens, and ink, using electronic equivalents that neither smudge nor spill. These are but a few of the characteristics that make computer-generated graphics unique; others will become obvious as we proceed with our discussion.

Software and Hardware for Graphics Generation

Some graphics software enables students to select colors and create shapes and lines by using the keyboard to move the drawing cursor around on the screen. A more natural way to draw is with a graphics tablet. These are very convenient to use. The KoalaPad, for instance, permits the user to define various kinds of figures by moving a stylus or finger over its surface. A press of the button at the top of the pad will provide a clear screen for drawing.

Penpad, a sophisticated version of the graphics tablet, has a paper-covered surface upon which the user actually draws in ink with a special pen; the movements of the pen send electronic signals to the computer, where they are translated into a graphic display. A unique feature of the system is that it is capable of reading text that is printed on the pad: a letter (even a relatively crude one) can be recognized and displayed as a precise character on the screen. Combinations of graphics and text can be created in a natural, direct fashion using this system.

The mouse is another friendly device that makes input simple and easy. The Macintosh uses this device to direct the cursor to the various selections shown at the edges of the screen. The selected option is then used as a tool to add its unique qualities to the graphic being created.

An interesting and useful approach to creating computer-based images is digitizing. This involves using a device called a digitizer to translate the lights and darks of the original picture or object into signals that the computer can work with. An inexpensive device of this kind is Thunderscan, a digitizer in the form of a cartridge that fits in the printer in place of the ribbon. In effect, numbers (digits) are assigned to areas in such a way as to tell the computer how dark or how light the value is. The digits are interpreted and pixels on the monitor lighted in varying intensities to replicate the values of the original subject. Colors are produced in a similar way, that is, numbers are assigned in different fashion for different colors. An example of a digitized picture made from an illustration of a giraffe in an old book about animals is shown in Figure 6.8.

In order for graphic devices to operate, the appropriate software must be available. In the case of graphics tablets, this typically comes on a disk that is packaged

FIGURE 6.8   A Digitized Image Made from an Old Book on Animals

with the device. The KoalaPad uses a program called KoalaPainter, for instance. The program for Thunderscan comes on a disk that is furnished with the digitizer. Many programs are available that have been designed to work with the mouse. One such classic for creating graphics is MacPaint, for use with the Macintosh computer (Figure 6.9).

Types of Graphics Programs

Many kinds of programs are available for use in the graphic arts. Desktop publishing packages are highly graphic in nature, although they also include word processing features that are text-based. Programs such as Microsoft Chart enable the user to type in data and receive a graphic display and printout in return. And animation programs let the artist create a form in two separate positions which the computer then automatically ties together using successive images in a process called "tweening" to provide the illusion of motion. Paint programs are the most common of the graphic generators, but those that emulate the drafting environment, called "draw" programs, are also widely used. Printing programs emphasize printed materials such as large banners, certificates, and posters.

Painting and Drawing Programs.   The names chosen for these kinds of software are quite appropriate since they describe accurately the capabilities provided to the user. There is a tendency, however, to lump both kinds together as

FIGURE 6.9 A Graphic Created with MacPaint
(Copyright Claris Corporation. All rights reserved.)

if they were the same thing. Not only do the built-in functions differ somewhat, but the basic philosophy behind the two is different. MacPaint, for example, is defined as a painting program because it uses what is basically a free-form approach to creating images. Varied surface treatments are provided that emulate textures on the canvas or sketch pad. For example, you can use the "spray paint" option to add subtle, spatter-like shading effects to create a sense of form on a figure. Or, you can select a "paint brush" for creating a wide variety of lines and painted areas.

MacDraw, on the other hand, is highly mechanical in the way it works. You use drawing "instruments" such as rulers; the freehand option, so evident in paint programs, is quite restricted. Drawings are created from predefined shapes and lines, displayed as icons on the screen. Rulers are used to establish different scales, and a grid serves as the "graph paper" upon which drawings are positioned. You operate more like a draftsman and less like a painter when using this program. There are several programs available that offer the best of both kinds of graphics software: they combine the paint and draw functions on a single disk, a very handy arrangement that enables you to create a mechanical layout and then use various paint options to enhance its appearance.

Some drawing programs permit you to create illustrations in the third dimension. To use such a program you begin by making a traditional, flat, two-dimensional line drawing. You do not have to know about the rules of perspective at all—the program generates the three dimensional figures from the flat ones automatically. A program of this type is Mac3D from Challenger Software, an illustration of which is shown in Figure 6.10.

Graphics programs tend to have features in common, such as menus and displays of icons illustrating the various tools and processes for drawing or painting. As a general rule, when an option is selected, a window of further choices is provided. For example, selecting TOOLS causes a display to appear on the screen listing such things as text, shapes, paintbrush, and so forth. Choosing one of these options causes a list of further choices to appear. In conjunction with the paintbrush, another menu can be opened which provides different brush sizes and shapes. Blazing Paddles (Baudville) and MacPaint (Claris) are programs that work in this fashion. Selecting the pencil icon causes the cursor to act like a pencil that is moved freely around the screen, drawing fine lines as it goes. If you prefer not to work freehand, you can make selections from a library of basic shapes that can be manipulated in countless ways.

Using the various standard shapes provided is easy to do. For example, you might select the circle option to draw a circle automatically; this can then be enlarged to the desired size, pulled into elliptical shapes, filled with colors (when available) and patterns, and repeated in various positions on the screen. A MacPaint screen showing the various selections for drawing and painting is illustrated in Figure 6.11.

Color options are available in most programs, with the standard selection including a restricted number of hues. Some programs, however, generate tints and

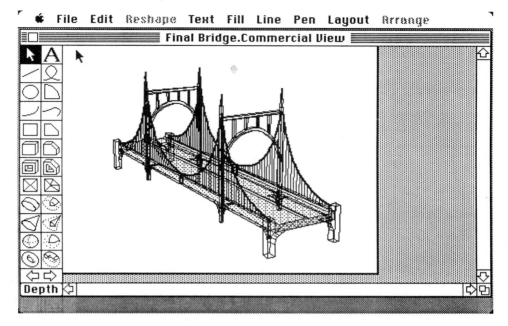

FIGURE 6.10 An Illustration Created with the Mac3D Drawing Program
(Courtesy Challenger Software)

shades of the basic color selection. In most programs, broad areas are filled with color, but in some cases you can color each pixel individually for a striking effect.

Sharper definition is made possible in programs such as Dazzle Draw through the use of double high-resolution graphics. In this process, each pixel is split, so to speak, so the dot pattern appears to be finer. Another approach involves using more and smaller pixels to achieve sharper resolution.

Animation Programs

Animation programs are becoming more popular all the time. This complex art, which was formerly the sacred domain of trained animators using special cameras, becomes much more accessible and simple to do when computer-based animation software is used.

Professional animation is a time-consuming and expensive process. A series of related images must appear and disappear in a succession rapid enough that the eye cannot fix on any individual image, giving the illusion of continuous motion. As many as eighteen images are required for each second of an animated film to give the proper effect. Obviously, few individuals have either the talent or the time, let alone the equipment and materials, to produce even a very short animated film. But computer-based animation software solves the problem of drawing multiple images by providing the necessary frames between two anchor points

FIGURE 6.11 A MacPaint
Graphics Screen Showing Some of
the Tools for Creating Various
Kinds of Graphics

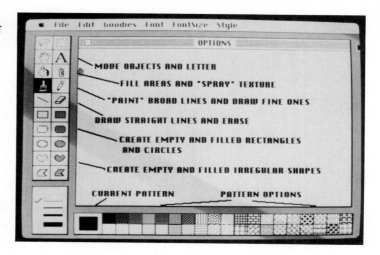

of a given action. For example, two human figures might be drawn (or selected from the built-in library of ready-made images), one of which is standing, the other sitting. The computer will fill in all the in-between positions using a process called "tweening," so that when the segment is run, the figure moves smoothly from a standing to a sitting position in one flowing, continuous action.

Fantavision, from Broderbund, is a popular program for school use. Hayden offers VideoWorks, a very sophisticated and capable animator for the Macintosh. A program titled P11, from P11 Enterprises, is another low-priced animation program with many useful features. An animation series created with P11 is shown in Figure 6.12.

Printing Programs

The printing program, used to produce paper-based materials such as banners, posters, awards, notices, and similar products, continues to grow in popularity. No freehand drawing or lettering ability is required for students to design attractive art products with software of this type. Both letters and graphics are available from libraries of images stored on disks. The development of design sensitivity becomes a by-product as students work to create the most attractive layout using the means available to them.

FIGURE 6.12 An Animation Sequence Created by the Boeing Company with P11
Animation Software to Help Children Learn Sign Language and Written English
(Courtesy of P11 Enterprises)

Once the type of graphic has been chosen and this information given to the computer, you can proceed with the design itself. Choosing from the vast selection of images provided, you move your selection onto the screen and position it where desired. Additional disks filled with graphics are available to supplement the images on the program disk. Given the broad range of subjects covered, you or your students should be able to find images for every need.

Borders of many kinds are also available; these add a professional looking touch to the composition. The images that have been moved to the screen can now be supplemented with text. Choose the font that seems to project the desired feeling best and then type the message. The letters will appear on the screen along with the graphics. Programs with good editing features will provide some of the text layout features of a word processor (such as justifying text and automatic word wrap). All the most versatile programs permit all elements to be moved as desired, thus enabling you to recompose if the design is not quite to your liking.

Most printing programs feature a freehand drawing capability that is similar to, but less extensive than, features of this kind common to paint and draw programs. Various shapes can be selected, modified, and filled with colors and patterns, or you can use the pencil and brush features to create a totally original design. Some programs provide an enlarging feature, permitting the design to be printed in sections that are assembled to make posters much larger than the standard single-sheet size. Comic Works can enlarge a poster to a huge 21 by 26 feet.

Printing Software.   A few years ago you would have had considerable difficulty finding printing software programs, but today they are among the most common computer applications in both school and home; The Print Shop, the pioneer in the field, continues to be among the most popular. Well over a million copies are currently in use, with more being purchased all the time. The Print Shop can be used to create everything from banners up to 30 feet long to small personalized cards and just about everything in between. The package contains a collection of colorful envelopes with matching paper and a helpful teacher's guide. An editor for creating original graphics is provided, as are eight different letter fonts, over sixty borders, and support for over twenty different printers (Figure 6.13).

Print Magic (Epyx) is notable for its powerful graphics editor, which offers features uncommon to most low-cost printing programs. Like much of the paint and draw software, the editor offers a zoom feature for enlarging a section of the graphic, fill features, a set of preformed shapes, cut-and-paste capabilities, a variety of brush shapes, and an array of patterns.

Pull-down menus and a mouse provide the user with a Macintosh-like environment. You can view the finished pages before printing and can make changes much more easily than with many other programs of this kind. Numerous type fonts are provided ready-made, but a useful typeface editor is available so original letter styles can be created.

Create with Garfield! Deluxe Edition (DLM) is a program for students in grades three and up that permits the student to use a graphics tablet to create

FIGURE 6.13 A Design Made
with Print Shop

(Courtesy of Broderbund Software)

original backgrounds, props, and borders. Over two hundred premade borders and figures are also available. Posters up to seventeen by twenty-two inches, personalized letterheads, signs, and items as small as a name tag can be created with Garfield. An easy to use text writer provides seven fonts plus editing capabilities. Over thirty different printers are supported by this program.

Two printing programs dedicated to creating one-page-only documents are Award Maker Plus from Baudville and Certificate Maker from Springboard. These provide a very large number of templates, or incomplete forms, that can be customized by the user to fit specific occasions. You have a choice of 286 templates with Award Maker and 220 with Certificate Maker. With programs such as these, teachers are able to produce attractive, customized certificates on short notice and with considerable ease.

Graphing Programs

Because graphs have utility in so many areas of the curriculum, it is difficult to assign them to one specific place. We elected to locate the main discussion in this chapter, but you will find reference to this type of program in several other places in the text.

Although previously too expensive for everyday educational use, sophisticated programs have declined in cost until they are now well within the budgets of most schools. Although administrators most likely constitute the largest group of users in schools, many social studies and language arts teachers find graphing programs to be just the thing for displaying numerical data in the more meaningful chart and graph formats.

The most striking feature of this kind of software is the ability to construct colorful images, often in three dimensions, from bland input that is not very interesting in its numerical state. Of considerable value is the provision of an analysis feature that enables the user to derive averages, means, and other statistical measures from the raw data.

Graphing Software. Most integrated software lets you generate charts as one of the many features offered, but there are also dedicated graphers that perform this task exclusively. Microsoft Chart, a well-regarded program of long standing, provides nine kinds of data analysis, good graphics definition, and fine documentation. This program runs on the Macintosh and offers the traditional Macintosh environment of pull-down menus and other convenient features. Many producers have incorporated this popular format into programs that run on computers other than the Macintosh. You can purchase graphing and other kinds of programs that run on IBMs, Commodores, and Ataris that look and work just like the Macintosh versions. A column graph created on a Macintosh is shown in Figure 6.14.

For an easy-to-use graphing tool designed for use in grades four through eight you might choose AutoGraph from SVE. Students begin by typing information onto a basic screen form designed with spaces to hold data. Typing the prescribed key combinations causes the computer to display the four kinds of available graphs—line, circle, bar, and pictograph—so that they can be studied. Among the many options offered are changing colors, inserting and deleting captions and other text material, changing the range, and using any of the nearly one hundred pictures to illustrate the pictograph. Pull-down menus and a mouse make using

FIGURE 6.14 A Computer-Generated Pie Graph

(Courtesy of International Business Machines Corporation)

the program convenient and simple. A user's guide includes instructions as well as exercises to help students succeed at graph making.

The MECC Graphing Primer for grades seven through nine is an introductory program for those who have little or no experience with graphs. The program is highly interactive, providing information on terminology and graph construction while emphasizing an analysis of the four basic types of graphs.

Another excellent program, MECC Graph, is designed as a follow-up to the Primer previously mentioned and targets students in the same grade range. Using the program is simple: select the type of graph desired, enter the data, and adjust the scale. The computer then generates and displays the graph, printing it on paper if hard copy is desired.

A final program, pfs:Graph from Scholastic, provides a slightly different selection than the programs previously discussed. The pictograph is excluded while the bar, pie, and line graphs are emphasized. A useful feature permits you to make comparisons by using the various kinds of graphs together. This program is available for both the Apple and the IBM at the same price of less than a hundred dollars.

Presentation Tools

Most of the programs discussed in this chapter can be used to prepare presentation materials of one kind or another. However, certain programs have been designed specifically for this purpose; some of these will be discussed in this section. Presentation (or instructional) materials are used to support and clarify information an individual is sharing with an audience. They include slide shows, using both computer-based images and those on photographic slides, overhead transparencies, video images, and all kinds of hard copy materials such as posters, charts, and handouts. An important part of a presentation is the audio message. This is frequently the teacher's voice, but attendant sound might also be encoded on a tape or disk to be used as part of the presentation package.

The computer-based slide show is mentioned in the section on classroom applications at the end of this section. This approach is becoming quite popular with presenters and audiences alike. Several graphic programs include a slide show feature that allows a series of computer-generated images to be linked together in sequence and timed to advance automatically at prescribed intervals.

Overhead transparencies, once difficult to create and expensive to buy, can now be produced with the computer and printed on plastic using various black-and-white or color printers. Creation of large-format visuals was mentioned in a preceding section. Any of the printing programs used for this purpose would also be suitable for production of presentation materials in nonprojectable format. Making photographic slides from computer-based images is discussed in the following section on hard copy. Slides photographed from the computer screen are amazingly colorful and sharp; this is a good alternative to the traditional technique of making slide art from paper and print materials.

Presentation Software.   Scholastic provides a presentation program titled Slide Shop for creating self-running presentations. Not only can Slide Shop be used for producing teaching materials but students find it useful for illustrating their oral reports. An interesting way to get wider use from the images created with this program is to copy them onto videotape to be played on a videocassette recorder (VCR). You can also use the program to produce titles to add to a video you already have.

The program includes several features worth mentioning. There are pull-down menus to make the selection of various functions convenient. An extensive collection of clip art images is available, as is the capability for creating original images. A library of sounds made up of sound effects, music, and digitized sounds is also included. Many type fonts are provided, as are various types of border, so you can customize each slide you create. There is also a scriptwriter that enables you to experiment with different ways of presenting the slides. You also have the option of using any of forty special effects, including pans, dissolves, wipes, and various types of animation. An extremely useful feature is the capability to print slides either onto paper or as overhead transparencies.

A second program of this kind is Presentation Pro from Strade. Many features are included, some of which are very sophisticated. You can create slides from ready-made templates or create your own. Sixty-four colors and sixteen type styles are available. The editor provides numerous capabilities permitting you to format and arrange the text materials used in conjunction with the graphics. Attractive overhead transparencies can also be produced using Presentation Pro. This program is designed to operate on the Macintosh computer.

ShowOff (Broderbund) operates with the Apple IIGS computer, using a Macintosh-like display of menus to assist the user in selecting options. Like Slide Shop, this program lets you create a slide disk that can be used without the master program disk. In other words, you can simply insert the slide disk into the drive and it will start up and run all by itself. It should be noted that disks you create will normally not operate unless the master disk is available to the computer. You can create overhead transparencies, on-screen slide shows, posters, and handouts. A 35-mm slide projector can be controlled by a feature in the program, permitting this piece of equipment to become an integrated part of a multimedia presentation.

Creating Hard Copy Graphics

Once your graphics have been created on the computer, they can be saved on a disk just like any other program. (This is the way they were stored for the slide show mentioned in the section on classroom activities that follows.) Animated graphics are also stored in this manner. Of course this necessitates the use of a computer for subsequent viewing, and this approach might not be the most practical for many uses.

The most common way to output a graphic in a permanent format is to use a printer to produce a paper copy. Dot matrix printers are generally used for this purpose, but the laser printer (widely used for desktop publishing) and inkjet printers produce excellent images. A comparison between words produced by a dot matrix printer and a laser printer is shown in Figure 6.15. Some programs

LOOKING FOR A PLACE TO GO ?

LOOKING FOR A PLACE TO GO

FIGURE 6.15   A Comparison Between Words Produced with a Dot Matrix Printer (Top) and a Laser Printer (Bottom)

allow you to use a plotter, which provides exceptionally high quality hard copy in color or black and white. Many printers permit you to substitute special films for the paper so that overhead transparencies can be produced.

If you have access to a 35-mm camera, you can make a traditional set of slides by photographing the screen image. Place the camera on a tripod and focus on the screen. Turn out all lights so you will not get unwanted reflections. Use a slow shutter speed and daylight film such as Ektachrome 100. You will have to experiment a bit to find the best combination of camera settings, but once this has been determined you should be able to use them consistently for all of your slide work.

A better way to create slides is to use one of the special camera accessories designed specifically for use with a computer display. The Kodak Instagraphic CRT Imager is one such device. It is a cone-shaped box to which the camera is attached; the other end is placed over the computer screen. A similar system is the Datacam 35; both devices are designed so that the natural distortion of the screen image is to a large extent corrected.

Classroom Activities

Not only can the computer be used for experimental kinds of creative activities; it is also helpful in the teaching of traditional kinds of art skills and principles. An example involves the teaching of the principle of contrast. The importance of this principle is vividly illustrated when students use a limited range of colors to create a design on the computer screen. When light-valued pastel tints are used exclusively, the design appears washed out. The same is true when low value shades are employed. Students experiment to find more effective color combinations and, in so doing, learn about the importance of contrast in visual displays. An advantage of using computer-generated colors is that, unlike colors mixed from pigment, they will always be consistent in hue, intensity, and saturation, provided the monitor is adjusted properly. Also, there is no physical color mixing, which can be messy, and no crayons or chalk sets with one or more missing sticks. Obviously, using "real" pigments is part of the art experience, and no art curriculum would be complete without the wide employment of traditional methods, but if a computer and programs are available they can be used to introduce an exciting auxiliary approach to "doing art."

As a way to encourage students to tell stories graphically, Walt Disney Comic Strip Maker is useful. Students have no trouble becoming cartoonists with this program. They can select ready-made three-frame strips to which they add balloons containing premade captions. They can also use the available illustrations and make up their own captions. Another option is to create a strip from scratch by selecting a combination of backgrounds, characters, and captions. The students can use any of eight Walt Disney characters, which can be changed in size from a distant figure to a close-up. The printing option allows computer-generated material to be printed on paper, which can then be further modified using free-hand methods if desired. This program, produced by Walt Disney Computer Software, is distributed by Sunburst Communications.

Various painting and drawing programs are commonly found in the schools. To become proficient with such programs, students must experiment with the many features provided. An excellent way to familiarize your students with graphics programs of this kind is to have them create "modern art" by combining every option available into an abstract composition. They soon overcome any inhibitions they might have had about using the computer as a creative tool, and many of the projects turn out to be very attractive.

Your classroom and school can be decorated for special occasions using a program such as SuperPrint from Scholastic Software. Anything from small logos to huge posters is easily created and printed by students with a minimum amount of experience. Posters as tall as four feet and banners to stretch above the school's front entry will make student body elections and other functions more exciting and informative. The program provides about two hundred clip art pictures of various kinds. These, along with various letter styles, are combined to form tailor-made visual messages to be printed in a selection of sizes. The printed graphic often looks better when brightly colored. If you have access to a color printer you can print your art in multiple hues, or students can have fun with markers, chalks, crayons, or paint as they add the finishing touches by hand. Examples of graphics made with SuperPrint are shown in Figure 6.16.

Some graphics programs have a slide show feature that enables you to display sequential computer images in any order you choose and for any exposure time you select. One teacher decided to show a series of abstract "paintings" made by his students as they experimented with the KoalaPainter program. He sequenced them, made a title frame and a credit frame, set the built-in timing feature, and synchronized the slides with a musical score. The end result of all this effort was a parade of "modern paintings" created by student artists with the brilliant colors of the computer screen and displayed automatically by the computer to the accompaniment of classical music. If a music program had been available, even the score could have been original.

DESKTOP PUBLISHING

Extremely popular with both students and teachers, desktop publishing programs combine the capabilities of several kinds of software to enable you to create professional looking printed materials that formerly could be produced only by commercial graphics establishments. The program provides composing and editing features, a typesetting component, provisions for the production or importation of graphics, various tools for layout activities, and a printing feature. In

FIGURE 6.16 Visuals of Various
Kinds Created with SuperPrint

(Courtesy of Scholastic Software)

other words, with a desktop publisher you can begin with an idea, generate the
complete layout, and print the finished copy without leaving your desk.

Of course materials such as announcements, flyers, and newsletters are commonly produced on a word processor, but there is a considerable difference in the
appearance of such copy produced by a word processor and that created with a
desktop publishing program. Desktop publishers give a product an appearance
previously difficult to obtain unless professional artists and printers were hired
to do the job. Text and graphics can be combined in a multitude of ways, type
fonts of many styles and sizes can be used, and the layout features provide you
with the potential for developing artistic looking page compositions.

Using a Desktop Publishing Program

The creation of the project to be published typically begins on a traditional word
processor, where the text is typed in with no concern for the format that it will
eventually assume. This typed copy is then imported by the desktop publishing
program from the data disk where it is stored, to be modified in various ways as
the process proceeds.

Illustrations come next. You can use one of the paint programs mentioned previously to create original art work; graphics made this way, like the text from the word processor, can be imported to the desktop publisher also. Large libraries of clip art are available from many sources; again, importing selected items is a good way to save time when illustrations are needed. You can also use digitizers, such as those discussed in the section on graphics programs, to make computer compatible art from available images. However, computer-generated art is not the only medium for illustrating a page. If students with artistic abilities are available, they can make traditional drawings to paste into blank areas reserved for this purpose on the printed layout.

At about this point you will begin to think about arranging the various text and graphic elements into a pleasing layout. This is where the desktop publisher really comes in handy. A good strategy is to make a few "dummies" or rough sketches of ways to arrange the material; this will save considerable time at the computer.

A typical program presents a display of possible page layout designs to choose from, or, you might want to create a layout of your own, an option afforded by most programs. This process includes such things as setting the number of columns, the margins, and other formatting details. Once the selections have been made and the page design firmed up, you are ready to import the text that was composed on the word processor and stored on a data disk. In some cases, the spaces into which the text will be inserted are in the form of "text boxes," which can later be moved about as units if desired. Any minor text editing is carried out at this point; it is generally much more convenient to make corrections with the word processor than with the desktop publisher.

The document begins to display the professional touches that will make it unique as you select headers and text in various sizes and styles from the font library. A few programs, those for the Macintosh in particular, provide features for changing the sizes of built-in fonts as well as for modifying the letters themselves.

Importing graphics involves defining a space or box within which the graphic will be positioned. You can move the box about, resize it, or change the shape as required. Most programs provide an automatic text flow around pictures so no awkward areas of blank page appear. With some programs you can also change the size of the graphic itself. If a graphics editor is provided, you have the potential to make additional changes and additions to the art. Lines, borders, and other features add to the decorative effect of the page. You can use available features of this kind or, with some programs, create your own.

You can view the page being designed in several different ways. When you view the page in actual size, this does not give a view of the total page, only the part currently being worked on. When you activate the overview feature, a full page is provided for you to examine. For a closer look at details, you can use the zoom mode, which provides a close-up of a smaller section of the document (Figure 6.17).

Printing is the last step, if you discount the creation of multiple copies from the master printout. Duplication can be done with an office duplicator or by a

FIGURE 6.17 The Zoom Mode in GeoPublish Lets You Enlarge Portions of a Page

(Courtesy Berkeley Softworks, Creators of GEOS for the Commodore 64/128 and Apple II Computers)

professional printing establishment. Once a good, sharp original is available, the cost of duplication is quite modest. Dot matrix printers generally provide satisfactory print quality, but the laser printer is by far the favored device for use with a desktop publishing program. Note the professional quality of the newsletter printed with the laser printer in Figure 6.18.

While the procedure for producing a finished product with a desktop publishing program seems straightforward and simple, you should be aware that there is frequently a problem with the compatibility of various word processors, graphics generators, and publishing programs. You should make certain that the various programs you intend to use will work together; otherwise, your efforts might lead to considerable frustration. Various programs afford different capabilities; few, if any, have all that you might like. Some are much easier to use than others, providing simple ways to import graphics and text, move around in the document, and carry out editing activities.

Some Desktop Publishing Programs. Once Upon a Time (Compu-Teach) is a simple, first-level program with various desktop publishing features. The student writes a story using the word processing capabilities and illustrates it with combinations of the many graphic images provided. Compositional features are provided so objects can be placed in the most satisfactory relationships on the screen. A printing option lets the student print his or her work as paper copy.

The Newsroom (Springboard) has a built-in word processor for writing text with up to five different letter fonts. Large typefaces enable young editors to create headlines, and a selection of borders and tones further enhances the appearance of published materials. Also provided are a graphic utility for creating original illustrations and a library of more than six hundred pieces of clip art.

by degrees

the newsletter for higher education

fall 1986   *vol.12, no. 3*

College Notes

More College Graduates than Ever

In 1940, the Census Bureau reports, only 38 per cent of those between the ages of 25 and 29 had a high school diploma, and only 6 per cent had college degrees. Today, 86 per cent surveyed said they had high school diplomas and 22 per cent have college degrees.

Getting Extras from Extracurricular Activities

Research now indicates that high school students that do well in extracurricular activites (clubs, sports, student government) more often are successful in college.

The College Board says that extracurricular activities are no substitute for good grades, but such activities help predict students that will do well in college.

by degrees Starts Using Desktop Publishing

You've read about it in *Time*. You've read about it in *Newsweek*. Now you can see it for your own eyes. Starting with the fall 1986 issue, all remaining *by degrees* newsletters will be produced using a Macintosh™ Plus and LaserWriter® Plus from Apple Computer Inc. "We get better results in less time for less money," says Eric Lee, editor of *by degrees*.

New Coalition to Promote Higher Education Goals, Benefits, and Support

by Phyllis Neuman

Can higher education in the West keep getting better? A number of the two- and four-year public and private colleges and universities west of the Mississippi have organized a program to communicate information and to discuss issues pertaining to the future of higher education within the region.

Westerners for Higher Education is the product of more than two years of discussion and planning by both public and independent college presidents. The higher education executives desired to create a campaign to help Westerners understand the current status of regional schools and to present ideas to improve them.

The campaign is sponsored by more than 45 colleges and universities. Each institution contributes non-tax dollars to the campaign program.

Four primary campaign goals have been defined for the public awareness program:

- to maintain the region's commitment and investment in higher education at competitive levels;
- to encourage increased gift support from individuals and organizations throughout the region;
- to discover and develop new opportunities for the education services, high technology, training and research offered by the region's colleges and universities;
- and to stimulate enrollment of recent high school graduates and adults at the region's higher education institutions.

The campaign plans to achieve these goals by managing several projects, including editorial tours, public service announcements, a speakers bureau, college directories, audio-visual programs, exhibits and town forums.

John Smith was hired in August to act as executive director of the two-year campaign. John's background includes nearly ten years as a public relations and community affairs executive with such firms as McDowell Douglas, TTI and most recently with the Aaron C. Pushman public relations agency in San Francisco.

One of the first key projects will be an economic impact study to assess the effect of higher education on the region. It will examine the number of jobs created by colleges, revenues created and other financial gains achieved by the state because of our colleges and universities.

continued on page 2

1

FIGURE 6.18 A Newsletter Created with a Desktop Publishing Program and a Laser Printer

(Courtesy of Apple Computer, Inc.)

If you would like a program with more features, try Medley from Milliken Courseware. Moving from one function to the next is as simple as clicking the mouse button. A full-featured word processing capability permits you to write and edit the entire document within the program. Graphics can be created using the color artwork feature; you can also use this to modify existing clip art or digitized images. A text-wrapping feature causes the text to conform to graphics boxes of various shapes, including ovals, polygons, and rectangles. Also provided are a built-in spelling checker and thesaurus as well as a picture library of over five hundred illustrations.

Pagemaker (Aldus) is among the most powerful of all the desktop publishing programs. Originally designed for use on the Macintosh, it is now available for IBM computers and clones. Features include a large dictionary, capabilities for quick and easy movement of text and graphics from one page to another, and the ability to display up to sixteen miniature pages from a document at one time. Windows containing information and options can be accessed at any time. One window features pens of different sizes for drawing and cropping tools for resizing graphics, which can be used in a fashion similar to actual drawing and trimming instruments. Different ways of viewing a page are provided, including zooms of various sizes. Because it is relatively expensive, Pagemaker and other programs of this sophistication will most likely be found in only the higher grades.

Other programs for use in the schools are Publish It! from Timeworks; Ready Set Go (Letraset), a program similar to Pagemaker; geoPublish (Berkeley Software) for the Commodore 64; PFS First Publisher, a good program for beginners; Springboard Publisher, an excellent choice for the classroom; and MacPublisher, another of the several powerful programs for the Macintosh.

Classroom Activities

Students find writing enjoyable when they assume the role of reporters for the school newspaper. Those responsible for illustrations will read articles thoroughly and carefully in order to come up with the best match between the art and printed words. Students responsible for layout and editing get practice in rewriting articles to make them fit into a given space. They also become more proficient in the careful selection of appropriate words as they are called upon to design effective headlines and subheads in the most direct and succinct manner.

Artistic horizons are widened as illustrations are created for the newspaper. These need not be computer-generated however. If the program lacks freehand drawing features, spaces can be left on the page to be filled later by pasting in drawings the students have created on paper.

Desktop publishing is more than a tool for use in the classroom, however. It provides the school with means to produce any printed matter that formerly required the services of professional typesetters. Not only is the in-house product professional in appearance; it can be designed and printed in much less time than would be required if an outside designer were involved. The financial savings, once the equipment has been paid for, are also considerable.

TEACHER TOOLS

Most of the programs described in this chapter have the potential for use by teachers both in developing materials to aid them in teaching and in managing the instructional process.

Presentation programs, as described in the section on graphics, are an obvious choice for teachers who require visual aids such as transparencies and slides. Desktop publishing programs are useful when illustrated paper-based materials such as worksheets and tests are needed.

Recognizing the need for specialized tools to aid in classroom management, software producers have developed a range of tools for this purpose. Among these are grading programs, test generators, and attendance managers. In this section we will examine several programs of this type.

Gradebooks

Grading software permits the teacher to record grades as they are assigned and uses the accumulated grades to automatically calculate final results when these are called for. Most teachers find grading activities to be among the least desirable of their various responsibilities, but electronic gradebooks take much of the work and effort out of this task.

There are, however, certain steps you must take to set up the gradebook and put it into operation. You still must enter the class roster by typing the information at the keyboard—the computer will not do this for you. On the other hand, scanners are available that can convert a printed page into digitized data for storage on a disk. The computer then displays this data for you to update and modify as you wish.

Typing the names of students into the on-screen gradebook matrix is a bit like entering information into a data base. A limited editing feature permits you to make corrections as the material is entered. Some programs permit you to select a file from one section and place it in another in the fashion of a word processor. A feature characteristic of spreadsheets is the requirement that you place labels above the columns to indicate which assignment is represented. Some gradebooks provide space for longer words than others—this precludes the necessity of using abbreviations and makes the information easier to read and use.

You can also give different weights to different assignments if desired. A midterm exam is most likely worth more than a weekly quiz; and a term paper more than a short essay. The weighting feature provides a way of assigning a greater percentage value to the more important assignments and a lesser value to others. Some programs permit you to cluster related assignments together under various categories, to which weights are then assigned. This feature saves you from the chore of giving a weight to each individual assignment.

Although certain gradebooks accept letter grades, which they convert to number values for calculations, most do not. This means that the numerical equivalent for the letter grade must be figured and entered in order for calculations to be made.

Statistics of various kinds including means and standard deviations, are quickly calculated by most gradebook programs. Other features, such as the generation of histograms, are available in many programs. As with a data base, gradebooks have a sort feature to arrange students into various configurations as defined by a sort key. The most commonly used approach involves alphabetizing a student list, but other schemes, such as sorting on the basis of grades, also have utility.

All good electronic gradebooks offer a print feature, without which they would be much less useful. Printouts are needed for many things, including reports for home consumption. Features are included for individualizing such reports, ranging from a simple space within which the teacher writes comments to extensive lists of "canned" comments to be selected and printed on the report automatically.

Some Gradebook Programs. Gradebook Deluxe (EduSoft), while inexpensive, includes a number of handy features not found in many other inexpensive programs. It provides space for classes containing as many as forty or more students, lets you custom design the display, creates reports in several formats, and provides for missing grades. It also features automatic scoring using a scanner, assignment of letter grades based on student averages, and the option of printing a roster without grades to be used as a grade or attendance sheet.

GradeBook, from Bobbing Software, is designed for use on the Macintosh. The convenient icon and menu environment permits you to interact with the program simply and directly. To enter a name you move the cursor to an empty cell, click the mouse button, and type the student's name. As information is entered, the program automatically recalculates related figures. The cut and paste features mentioned in the word processing chapter are available in Gradebook. These provide an easy way to move student names within and between documents. Histograms and trend lines are generated by simply selecting an assignment column or student row.

Another Macintosh-based program is Gradebook Plus, from Mindscape. Also available for the IBM and Apple II, it uses a spreadsheet-like format for ease in entering or deleting grades and other data. Like many other programs of this kind, different schemes can be used to identify students so their grades can be posted without revealing their names.

With the Kalamazoo Teacher's Record Book from Hartley, you can print bar graphs showing the distribution of scores on any test. Several weighting methods are provided, and means and standard deviations are automatically calculated for all assignments. A full-screen editing feature assists in updating and changing records. Individualized reports are easily made for school and home use. Provisions for extra points on assignments are included in the program.

Other electronic gradebooks include The Teacher's Assistant (Burrowes), an inexpensive (under thirty dollars) program with many useful features, including the generation of seating charts. Grade Management (Bertamax, Inc.) is another economically priced program offering many of the features of higher priced programs. Davidson and Associates provides Classmate, a simple and easy to learn program with several printout options. These include lists of missing assignments, customized student records, a summary of student standings, and a class roster. Grade Manager, from **MECC**, makes tabulating final grades easy. By keeping track of quarterly grade averages, it is able to generate a final average without the need for additional information.

Report Card (Sensible Software) handles up to a hundred students per class, up to ninety graded activities per class, and twenty classes per diskette. It allows you to record, analyze, and rank student marks, providing the information needed to complete report cards with a minimum of effort (Figure 6.19).

Test Generators

Commercially prepared tests are widely available from a number of sources. These are generally based on a textbook series and they may or may not test for what you as the teacher feel to be most important. Many teachers prefer to forgo the convenience of available tests and create their own, but this can be a time-consuming task. Computer-based test generators make test writing a relatively easy, if not pleasant, undertaking.

Some programs of this type resemble a simplified authoring system (see Chapter 8) in that they provide a matrix into which information is entered to form questions. Others provide a kind of data base containing a bank of questions that can be combined in any order to form a complete test.

FIGURE 6.19 Report Card, from Sensible Software, Inc., is a Popular Gradebook Program

Although the output from most test generators is in hard copy form, some programs provide the means for displaying the test on the screen. Students sit at the computer, responding to the prompts and receiving feedback as they take the test. This arrangement is excellent if enough computers are available.

Using a Test Generating Program.   Entering information into a test generator is similar to using a word processor. As you type, text appears on the screen, with words automatically wrapping around when the end of a line is reached. Standard editing functions such as word and letter deletion and insertion are provided so corrections can be made as the typing progresses. A useful feature in some programs is a font library that provides different typefaces and math symbols.

Various test formats are available, including true or false, multiple choice, matching, fill in the blank, and essay. A few also provide a graphics editor so diagrams and other illustrations can be created as part of the document. In the absence of this feature, you must leave a space and then draw or paste in the graphic after the test has been printed. After the questions have been typed, they are saved as files on a disk to serve as a data base from which questions can be retrieved as needed. As the data base grows in size, the potential increases for creating new tests by combining questions from various files. Not only can the questions and their order be randomized but some programs also shuffle the arrangement of the possible responses to multiple choice questions. Finally, the completed test is printed as paper copy to be duplicated for class use. Some programs also provide for other additional printouts, such as answer sheets and study guides. An example of a test generated with TestBuilder (CTB McGraw Hill) is shown in Figure 6.20.

Test Generating Software.   TestRite II from Class 1 Systems is called a "teacher's test item management package," a description that applies to test generators as a group. Several fields of information are available for use including title, identification, date, and pagination. Pages may be arranged in single or double columns, and several optional page sizes can be accommodated. Printing options include pica or elite type, subscripts and superscripts, underlining, and character graphics.

QuickTests (Seven Hills) provides several approaches to selecting questions from the data base. These include choosing by such keys as topic, difficulty, and type of question. You can easily import files from AppleWorks and AppleWriter (a word processing program) into QuickTests if you wish. This feature is useful, since many teachers use integrated programs for the bulk of their composing and record-keeping activities. Using available data for test creation saves considerable time and effort. This program provides a selection of special symbols not found in many others, including graphic characters, math symbols, and accent marks.

LXR.Test (Logic eXtension) is designed for use on the Macintosh and therefore based on the menu and mouse environment. The editor is similar to MacWrite, with many of the same features. Formatting options are extensive, giving you the ability to arrange the material in columns or in regular format as desired. Text

For Items 1-4 read each item and
choose the correct answer.

1 Which cake is cut on a radius?

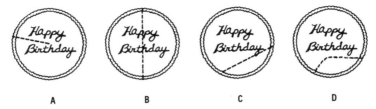

A   B   C   D

2 Which knife is placed across the diameter of the plate?

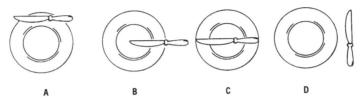

A   B   C   D

3 Which is the right triangle?

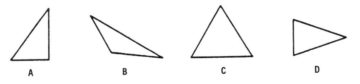

A   B   C   D

4 Which is the scalene triangle?

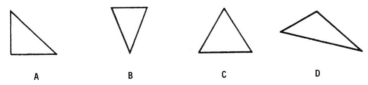

A   B   C   D

GO TO NEXT PAGE

FIGURE 6.20 An Illustration from the *Data Warehouse Item Bank Catalog*
(Reproduced by Permission of the Publisher, CTB/McGraw-Hill, 2500 Garden Road, Monterey,
California 93940)

can be wrapped around graphics, a desktop publishing feature that can make the document aesthetically pleasing in appearance. Graphics can be created using a program such as MacPaint and can then be moved into the layout before it is printed.

Archive III (Collamore/D.C. Heath) provides several question formats including multiple choice, true or false, open-ended, and user defined varieties. A graphic capability allows you to use stored charts and graphs or create your own. Prepared testbanks for use with this program are available in several subjects, including biology, earth science, science, math, and social studies.

Another test generator is P.D.Q. from Micro Power and Light, a menu-driven program for creating multiple choice and fill the blank questions. TestWriter (K-12 MicroMedia) is a capable yet inexpensive program, while Teacher's Pal (South-Western) includes a gradebook along with the test generator. Test It! from EduSoft provides an 80-column format along with excellent question selection features. Easy Quiz Maker (ComPress) is a useful program for generating and storing tests of up to one hundred questions in three test formats.

Test generators for use in specific subject areas include The Earth Science Test Maker (J and S Software), the EA Mathematics Worksheet Generator (Educational Activities), Mathematics Worksheet Generator (Collamore/D.C. Heath), and Math Teacher's Toolkit (Micromatics), which lets you produce an unlimited number of randomly generated worksheets.

Attendance Software

Attendance programs help make the burdensome but necessary task of keeping track of students easier. School Register (Intellectual Software) permits you to record student names, times tardy or absent, and other essential information in a companion program titled Student Data Base. With this software, you can conduct a search using a variety of search keys such as name, homeroom, birthdate, class, and sex. Eleven standard and two open fields are provided, while files accommodate up to 240 students each.

Brewster Software Systems provides a wide selection of utilities for classroom and school management, including Knapsack 2.0, an integrated package containing not only attendance features but also features for grade reporting and scheduling. The program is extremely capable and is designed for use at a school or district level rather than individual class level. Also available for use in the elementary grades is Knapsack-Attendance, a very useful and complete tool designed to maintain records on any number of students. Chancery Software provides a very complete administrative package titled MacSchool Administrator System, a sample screen of which is shown in Figure 6.21.

INTEGRATED APPLICATION PROGRAMS

Integrated programs generally include more than one application on a disk, although a few offer each application as a stand-alone program, the functions of which are compatible with the other programs in the series.

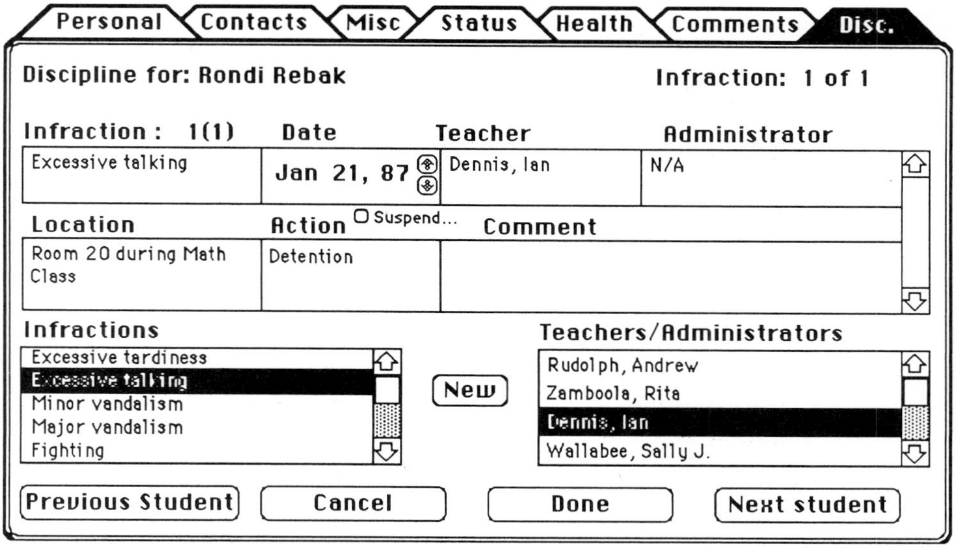

```
/ Personal \ Contacts \ Misc / Status \ Health \ Comments \ Disc.
```

Discipline for: Rondi Rebak   **Infraction: 1 of 1**

Infraction: 1(1)	Date	Teacher	Administrator	
Excessive talking	Jan 21, 87	Dennis, Ian	N/A	⬆

Location	Action ○ Suspend...	Comment	
Room 20 during Math Class	Detention		⬇

Infractions   **Teachers/Administrators**

Infractions		Teachers/Administrators	
Excessive tardiness	⬆	Rudolph, Andrew	⬆
Excessive talking		Zamboola, Rita	
Minor vandalism		Dennis, Ian	
Major vandalism		Wallabee, Sally J.	
Fighting	⬇		⬇

(New)

[Previous Student]   [Cancel]   [Done]   [Next student]

FIGURE 6.21   A Sample Screen from MacSchool Administrator
(Copyright Chancery Software, 1986–88)

Integrated programs make possible the smooth transfer of data from one application or module to another. For example, information from a data base can be transferred (or exported) to a word processor, where it can be modified and then transferred back to the data base. Information can also be moved into a spreadsheet, calculations made, and the results stored in the data base.

Most integrated programs enable the user to print out data in a graphic form—such as a bar, column, or line graph—rather than as tables. This feature was mentioned earlier, in the discussion of spreadsheets and data bases. Once the numerical data has been compiled, a command directs the computer to generate a graph and print it out. This might be incorporated into a document as an illustration, or it might be used as the master for the production of a transparency or slide.

Some Integrated Programs.   Several excellent integrated programs are available for use in the schools, but AppleWorks remains the most popular, according to surveys of computer using educators. The AppleWorks program includes a word processor and spreadsheet and data base applications. Each module is mentioned in some detail elsewhere. We will now consider the program as a whole. All modules are totally compatible, so you can move from one to another as desired. Material created with one application can be moved to another and worked on at any time.

When using AppleWorks you begin with a folder titled Main Menu on the desk top. As you make selections from the contents printed on the front of the folder, other folders appear. As on an actual desk top, each successive folder is placed on top of the preceding one, positioned so that you can see the title of every folder in the array. Other information is provided at the top and bottom of the desktop so you always know where you are in the program and the next steps that need to be taken. For example, the prompt "Press ESC to return to main menu" is a reminder of how to get back to the starting point when this is necessary.

While the older versions are still widely used, the newer AppleWorks GS has many more features than does Version 2.0. Six applications are offered in the GS version, including a word processor, a graphics module, a page layout module, a data base, spreadsheet capability, and a communications module. All six modules are completely integrated, permitting the user to combine features of each to come up with unique products. For example, you can use word processing, graphics, and page layout to create a newsletter that would normally require the use of a desktop publishing program to produce.

The communications module lets you access another computer to bring information from a remote data base, which is then displayed on the screen for you to examine. The text can be saved on a disk and then moved to the word processing module for editing and modification.

The GS version of AppleWorks uses the familiar mouse-icon interface made famous by the Macintosh. A good feature is the ability to open any of the applications at any time regardless of which one is currently in use. This feature provides a convenient way of moving between programs and merging information from one to another. Numerous templates are available for use with AppleWorks. These cover virtually every area of the curriculum as well as school and classroom management and other applications. Clip art collections are available on disks as libraries for use in generating illustrated materials; numerous templates in the social sciences, language arts, and science are available from different producers, and other templates provide assistance in grading, taking inventory, printing progress reports, and other management activities. Test generators are also available, as are report makers and programs for writing individual educational programs.

An excellent integrated package from Spinnaker is Better Working Eight-in-One, an ideal tool for beginners. The eight programs include a word processor, spelling checker, outliner, graphics generator, data base, spreadsheet, communications utility, and desktop utilities. All of these work smoothly together, permitting information generated in any program to be exported to any other to be merged and modified as desired. A screen shot of the outliner is shown in Figure 6.22.

Microsoft Works is a highly rated favorite with an excellent track record. The package includes a word processor, data base, spreadsheet, graphics program, and a communication module. Data is moved quickly and easily from one application to another. The communication module is a useful feature that enables you to send a document you have created to a remote location via telephone lines (see Chapter 7 on telecommunications). As with AppleWorks, there is a consistency of appearance among screens that provides a pleasant continuity from one application to the next. Menus and submenus are used throughout the program, and

FIGURE 6.22 A Screen Shot from Better Working Eight-in-One Showing the Outliner in Use

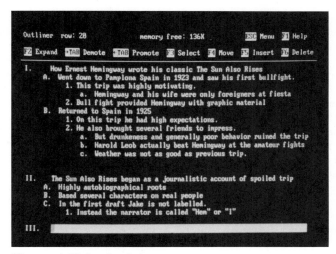

(Courtesy of Spinnaker Software)

these, too, are consistent in the way they are designed. The spreadsheet module in Microsoft Works allows you to create six varieties of charts and graphs.

The popular integrated business program Lotus 1–2–3 (Addison-Wesley), which was formerly both too expensive and too sophisticated for general classroom use, is now available in a student version at a much reduced price. Another program in the same class as 1–2–3 is Microsoft Excel, which runs on the Macintosh.

Trio (Softsync) is available for both the Apple II and Commodore C64/128 computers. First Choice from Software Publishing runs on MS-DOS machines, and the powerful Microsoft Excel is a good choice for those with Macintosh computers.

SUMMARY

Computer-based tools are becoming more popular all the time. Aside from their value in instructional settings, applications such as data base management programs, spreadsheets, and graphics generators have a place in preparing students for activities outside the classroom. Students who have opportunities to use computers in this manner will gain a degree of confidence and skill that will make them better able to adapt to the requirements of the modern workplace. Indeed, not only do such skills have vocational utility, but they are also useful as the student moves on to college or, for that matter, engages in home management.

Spreadsheets permit students to see the results of what-if situations through the manipulation of interrelated variables. Predictions and suppositions are analyzed, and the results made available, to an extent that was previously impossible.

Data base management programs encourage students to practice organizational skills and to get involved in research as they create their own files of information. Programs such as these permit the rapid retrieval of information at a critical moment; enthusiasm for an activity is not diminished by the time lag so common with more traditional kinds of data retrieval.

Creating paintings and drawings with a computer is easy using software designed for this purpose. Flowing action is imported to various images from simple blocks to sophisticated human figures with animation programs such as Fanavision and P11. You can create and print anything from huge banners to tiny greeting cards with special printing software, and graphs appear magically when numerical data are typed into a graphing program.

Presentation tools permit you or your students to generate computer-based "slide shows," or a set of photographic slides to use with a projector can be made from the screen images if you desire. Using the graphics, text, and layout features of desktop publishing software enables you to circumvent the graphic artist and commercial printer, producing your own printed materials entirely in-house.

As a teacher, you will enjoy the convenience of electronic gradebooks, test generators, and attendance software, all of which can make your grading and record-keeping tasks much more convenient to carry out. Integrated application programs such as AppleWorks combine the best of several tools into a single package. Materials created in one application are moved quickly and easily among the various modules. Work can be carried out in one module, moved to another for additional work, and then merged with the contents of a third module.

Various other tools, such as statistical packages and music software, are also available, and it seems as if additional tool uses for the computer are being found every day. The nature and magnitude of such programs make them most valuable additions to any software collection.

SELF-TEST

1. Describe the structure of a typical spreadsheet.
2. List the categories of data that can be entered into a spreadsheet.
3. List and describe five capabilities of a spreadsheet module (example: calculations).
4. Using the filing cabinet analogy, list the electronic equivalents of the following: (a) manilla folder, (b) single sheet of information, and (c) single line of data.
5. Define the terms "searching" and "sorting" as used in data base management programs.
6. What is the difference between a painting and a drawing program?
7. An important feature of an animation program is its ability to carry out the "tweening" operation; what is meant by this term?
8. A graphing program creates graphs from what kind of data?
9. What primary function does presentation software perform?
10. List three different kinds of hard copy.
11. What features typically found in a professional graphics shop are provided by a desktop publishing program?
12. Describe in generalities the way a newsletter or other printed document might be produced with a desktop publishing program.
13. Describe the three teacher tools covered in this chapter.
14. List the three applications found in all integrated application programs.
15. Describe what is meant by an accessory (add-on) as used with a desktop publishing program.
16. What do you consider to be the most significant feature of integrated application software?

REFERENCES

Bertanzetti, E. "Database Detectives." *Classroom Computer Learning* (April 1988): 76–77.

Blissmer, R. and R. Alden. *Introduction to Computers and Application Software.* Boston: Houghton Mifflin, 1986.

Collis, B. *Computers, Curriculum, and Whole-Class Instruction.* Belmont, Calif.: Wadsworth, 1988.

Dunfey, J. "Ready, Set, Publish—On Your Apple II." *Electronic Learning* (September 1988): 60–62, 96.

Eiser, L. "Print It! 101 Things to Print with Your Computer." *Classroom Computer Learning* (April 1988): 76–77.

Eiser, L. "Test Generators: Teacher's Tool or Teacher's Headache?" *Classroom Computer Learning* (May/June 1988): 44–51.

Eiser, L. "Choosing the Right Desktop Publisher." *Classroom Computer Learning* (November/December 1988): 37–53.

Grupe, F. *Beginning WordPerfect*. Dubuque, Iowa: Wm. C. Brown, 1986.

Howell, R., and P. Scott. *Microcomputer Applications for Teachers*. Scottsdale, Ariz.: Gorsuch Scarisbrick, 1985.

Krumm, B. "Getting More from Spreadsheets and Databases (Part 2)." *Family and Home Office Computing* (January 1988): 40–42.

Lodish, E. "Test Writing Made Simple." *Electronic Learning* (February 1986): 28–30, 68.

Nelson, R. "Data Bases Rediscovered (Part 1)." *Personal Computing* (December 1985): 95–101.

Nickles, H., and G. Culp. *The Practical Apple*. Pacific Grove, Calif.: Brooks/Cole, 1988.

Schwartz, R., and M. Callery. "Speaking of Graphics." *A + Magazine* (March 1988): 73–76.

Schwartz, R., and M. Callery. "Desktop Publishing." *A + Magazine* (September 1988): 26–37.

Sluyter, D. "Desktop Publishing for Kids." *A + Magazine* (October 1988): 60–66.

Stanton, D. "Grading the Gradebooks." *A + Magazine* (October 1988): 38–50.

Troutman, A., and J. White. *The Micro Goes to School*. Pacific Grove, Calif.: Brooks/Cole, 1988.

Turner, S. and M. Land. *Tools for Schools*. Belmont, Calif.: Wadsworth, 1988.

Wheeler, F. "The New Ready-Made Databases: What They Offer Your Classroom." *Classroom Computer Learning* (March 1987): 28–32.

CHAPTER 7

Telecommunication

CHAPTER TOPICS

☐ Definition of telecommunications
☐ Modems—acoustic and direct connect
☐ Data communication speeds
☐ Need for terminal software
☐ Information utilities
☐ Computerized bulletin boards (BBS)
☐ Components of a local area network (LAN)
☐ Network configurations
☐ Classroom applications of telecommunications

In many schools across the United States, teachers are starting to make use of the microcomputer in many specialized ways, such as for English and creative writing. In the past, teachers have provided students with traditional stimuli (pictures cut from magazines, plots of television programs, vacation and holiday themes, and so on) for writing papers, themes, or letters. An emerging area of emphasis, however, is the use of the microcomputer linked to an electronic bulletin board system (BBS). Many teachers now access these BBSs by classroom microcomputer to provide students with reasons to communicate with students in other parts of the country. The students are required to compose letters, announcements, reports, or geographical or weather data, for example, during the regular class period; they then send this information to an electronic "pen pal" during the evening, using the telephone lines, a modem, and the classroom microcomputer, and eagerly return to school the next day to see what messages await them.

The use of the electronic bulletin board system is but one exciting application of the microcomputer in the classroom. The emerging area of telecommunication can provide a new type of instructional environment. Consider the advantages of linking two or more computers to impart knowledge usually available primarily in the classroom. Experts can be reached at reasonable rates and the data they impart stored on diskettes for later use; handicapped persons can be educated at home; continuing education can be arranged to accommodate working students' schedules; and campus locations can be used to initiate instruction, with branch campuses or school districts as remote sites.

Besides the bulletin board systems (BBS), information utilities such as CompuServe, Dow Jones, and Educational Resources Information Center (ERIC) are proliferating. To open up the new world now available to your display screen, you will need to add some accessories and peripherals to your microcomputer system. You will also need to be aware of some concerns and problems to make full use of your microcomputer's telecommunication capabilities. This chapter will discuss these peripherals, accessories, and concerns in detail.

Telecommunication: A Definition

Telecommunication is long-distance communication made possible by using a signal like those used in radios and television. The broad scope of telecommunications encompasses transmission of voice, messages (such as telegrams), facsimiles (pictures), and data. Telecommunications can be broken into two distinct areas, teleprocessing and data communication. Teleprocessing, derived from a combination of the terms telecommunicating and data processing, is the processing of data at a distance. Data communication is concerned with the moving of data between terminals and a computer, or even between computers.

Demand for computer information systems (CIS) services have grown continuously since the introduction of the first computers, with the resulting need to conquer distances. Computer users who could talk to distant points by telephone reasoned that computers should be able to communicate with each other by sending data over distances without waiting for the mail or other services dependent on overland transportation and physical delivery. Demand became particularly acute in organizations with geographically dispersed operations, such as large corporations with many branch offices.

MODEM

Although the idea seems simple—combine the two separate electronic technologies, telecommunication and computing—it is not as easy as simply picking up a telephone. Currently, most telephone lines handle analog signals, such as that of the human voice, transmitted as constantly varying voltages over a pair of wires. Computers, on the other hand, are digital devices, with everything they do in binary form. To use telephone lines for data transmission between two or more computers, the digital signals must be changed into analog signals to be sent over the wires (modulation), then reconverted to digital signals at the receiving end (demodulation). This translation is performed by a modem (short for modulator/demodulator) (see Figure 7.1). When you are sending data, the modem changes the stream of digital information from the computer into tones (one tone for 1,

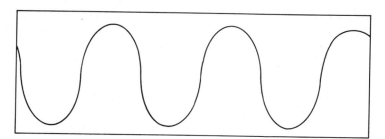

FIGURE 7.1   Analog (Smooth) Signal

another for 0) and sends them out over the telephone lines. At the receiving end, another modem does the opposite, translating the tones back into digital data. For the system to be complete you must have a sending terminal or computer, a modem, an analog signal along a transmission line, a second modem, and the receiving computer (see Figure 7.2).

To be technically correct a modem is only the circuitry that converts digital data to analog tones and back; but because of widespread use, modem has become a generic term for the device that connects the computer and phone, no matter what other devices are added to the system for data transmission.

Two types of modem are available for use with microcomputers: acoustic couplers and direct-connect modems. Most modern microcomputers (produced since 1988) have a direct-connect modem capability built in as part of the internal structure; however, because many schools are still using microcomputers that do not have this built-in capability, we will provide a discussion of both the acoustic and the direct-connect modem.

An acoustic coupler consists of a box (containing a miniature loudspeaker and microphone) with rubber cups into which is placed the handset of any standard telephone. There is no direct electrical connection with the telephone line; the computer and telephone are coupled acoustically (that is, by sound). The modem's circuitry converts the digital signals into analog tones; the microphone then picks up the tones from the earpiece and sends them out via the tiny loudspeaker next to the telephone mouthpiece. The modem transforms the choppy digital signals into smooth tones that can be sent over the telephone line (see Figure 7.3).

The low cost of acoustic couplers—from thirty to one hundred dollars—is possible because they are not connected directly to the telephone line and therefore do not need the special circuitry required to make an electrical connection to the nationwide telephone system. The acoustic coupler is rugged and convenient when traveling, particularly when you do not have access to a telephone jack (needed for a direct-connect modem). Although they have some advantages over direct-connect modems (low cost and ease of use), acoustic couplers have one large and critical disadvantage: the need for an extra microphone and loudspeaker greatly increases the chances for distortion, noise, and error in data transmission. The use of carbon granules in the microphone of the telephone handset is one area of concern. The telephone works fine with normal voice transmission; with the high-speed transmission of tones needed for microcomputer use, however, the carbon granules begin to pack together, causing distortion. After a time,

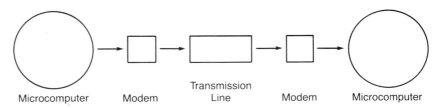

Microcomputer   Modem   Transmission Line   Modem   Microcomputer

FIGURE 7.2   Utilization of Modems in Data Transmission

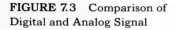

FIGURE 7.3 Comparison of
Digital and Analog Signal

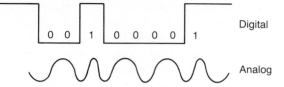

the message is so distorted that garbage will begin to appear on the monitor screen. Regular use of the acoustic coupler requires that you rap the handset on a hard surface to loosen the carbon granules, preferably at the beginning of each telecommunication session. If the compacting of the granules becomes a serious problem, you can purchase (for a nominal cost) a special microphone to replace the element in the handset. When using an acoustic coupler, be sure that the handset is completely encased by the rubber cups of the modem; environmental noise is likely to make the microphone transmission distorted and unclear.

Because of their several advantages, direct-connect modems are preferable to acoustic couplers. Instead of using cups with a microphone and loudspeaker, a direct-connect modem plugs directly into a standard modular telephone jack; it thus attaches directly to the telephone line and is hard-wired to an RS-232c port (the circuit that allows the microcomputer to send information over the telephone lines) on the microcomputer, which is built into most personal computers. The complete system, then, is composed of the microcomputer, the direct-connect modem, a telephone, and the telephone lines (see Figure 7.4). A direct-connect modem is much more error-free than the acoustic coupler because no extraneous noise is introduced. Feeding and receiving tones directly to and from the phone lines is more efficient than using an acoustic coupler.

Another advantage is that direct-connect modems usually take up less space than acoustic couplers; they can sit under the telephone or may even be small enough to be placed right inside the microcomputer. The direct-connect modems, however, cost quite a bit more than the acoustic couplers (from $250 to $450), because they are electrically connected to the telephone system and thus require more complicated circuitry.

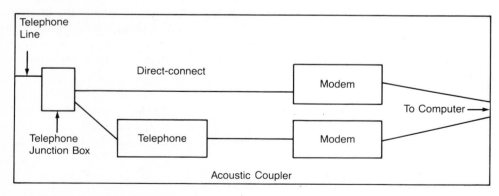

FIGURE 7.4 Modem Hookup

Both types of modem are certified by the Federal Communications Commission (FCC) and can be connected to the existing telephone line. Although the telephone company is very selective about what is connected to the nationwide telephone network, you should not be concerned about connecting your microcomputer to the telephone system via an FCC registered modem—you are legally entitled to do so.

The direct-connect modem is easy to use: upon loading the software that comes with this device, a directory of things to do is usually displayed. The prompts direct you to type in the telephone number of the data base to be accessed as well as the kind of computer being used, the ID number, and your password. Additional menus permit you to select from a wide range of subjects. The many free data bases do not require membership or monthly fees, and you do not need ID numbers or passwords to use them.

Most modems designed for use with a microcomputer have two different transmission modes: answer and originate. You will probably use the originate mode most, especially if your main use is hooking up to information utilities (CompuServe, for example) and electronic bulletin boards (both discussed later in this chapter). When you place the call, the modem must be set in the originate position.

If a friend wants to send something from his computer to yours, you must set your modem to the answer mode. It is necessary for one modem to be set to answer and the other to originate because the frequency of the tones is different in the two modes. The difference is built in, so the system knows which microcomputer is sending and which is receiving the data. You can even purchase a modem with an auto-answer capability. In auto-answer the modem senses the ringing signal on the telephone line and automatically connects itself to the line, so messages can be received automatically, even when you are not present.

Data Communication Speeds

The speed at which data are sent is a concern you must address when setting up your telecommunicating system. Data communications speed is measured in bits per second, which is more commonly referred to as *baud* or *baud rate*. Data are sent over telephone lines in serial fashion (one bit at a time); baud rate is a measure of the total number of bits that pass a given point in a second. The most common speed used with microcomputers produced after 1988 is 1200 baud, or 1200 bits per second.

You may wonder why data cannot be transmitted faster, since a computer that reacts in milliseconds could surely handle data faster than 1200 baud. Unfortunately, several limiting factors necessitate the slower rate. The United States has by far the finest and most reliable telephone system in the world, but even so, it is subject to noise, clicks, echoes, pops and other interference that can garble and distort a telecommunication signal. Thus data must be sent at a comparatively slow rate, so each tone can be long enough for the modem to recognize it in case of interference. The major reason for the slower rate of transmission, however, is band-width. A basic law of electronics or physics is that the faster you send information, the more room it takes up in the electromagnetic spectrum, or, in other words, the broader must be the bandwidth to accommodate the fluctuations in the magnetic cycles. To give you an idea of the limitations imposed by the telephone lines, let's compare the hearing range of the human ear and the range of the telephone network. Most human ears are capable of hearing tones in the range of 20 to 20,000 hertz (cycles per second). The nationwide telephone network, however, consists of voice-grade lines, designed for the range of tones emitted in normal conversations—a range of only 30 to 3,000 hertz. Telephone lines in your home, office, or school can thus handle tones only in this narrow bandwidth. The reliability of data tones transmitted over voice-grade lines is limited.

With most acoustic couplers you are limited to a 300-baud rate, because the system's extra microphone and loudspeaker make it necessary to slow down the rate of transmission so the signals can be heard and interpreted correctly. A direct-connect modem, however, permits the faster exchange of data using voice-grade lines. A standard telephone line can send data at 1,200 baud in one direction at a time. Because a direct-connect modem does not have the extra devices in the system, it can accommodate the increased rate quite adequately.

With many of the new phone systems using fibre optics, it is possible for a direct-connect modem to handle baud rates as high as 2,400 or even 3,600. To make use of more rapid data transmission, you must be sure that both your direct-connect modem and that of the receiving computer are capable of handling these higher baud rates.

TERMINAL SOFTWARE

Once you have chosen a modem and learned how to use it, there is one more essential you will need to hook up to a telecomputing service: terminal software (sometimes called communications software). Terminal software is a program that disconnects some of the internal circuitry of your microcomputer and makes it a terminal of the computer to which you will hook up via the telephone lines. Because most modems use the RS-232c connector on the microcomputer, you will need a means to receive the data and send it out that port. Even if you use an acoustic coupler, the terminal software will still be needed to enable the microcomputer to act as a terminal for the telecommunication process.

A wide choice of terminal software is available, ranging from very basic and inexpensive to sophisticated and costly. Most terminal software costs less than $75, but sophisticated packages selling for up to $300 can dial the phone number and even log on to a system automatically. Some microcomputer operating systems already have terminal packages built into the hardware (CP/M and Radio Shack's TRS DOS, for example), so you would not need to purchase additional terminal software. Be sure to check the manual to see if your microcomputer has this feature.

If you are good at advanced programming (BASIC, Pascal, COBOL, or FORTRAN, for example), you can write a terminal program yourself. Most modem manufacturing companies offer advanced owner's manuals that detail exactly how this is done.

The basic (and least expensive) terminal software allows data to be sent out as you type on the keyboard and information to be received and displayed on the monitor. Although this basic communication software is adequate, most users want additional features, such as software that allows a printer to provide hard copy, for later study, of what is being shown on the monitor.

Some sophisticated (and expensive—up to $250) terminal software packages enable you to use the computer's microprocessor, memory, and floppy disk drive. These packages may be worth the price in the long run (provided you use them on a regular basis) because of the convenience they offer and the savings on long-distance telephone charges. Programs of this type allow you to save the data on a disk for later editing or analysis and to send a file of stored data. Some will even let you store telephone numbers and log-on sequences for a particular data base. You can also purchase an answering feature: the computer can automatically sense a dial tone, answer the phone, log on, and provide some special prerecorded responses (some packages can also turn on a printer and provide you with hard copy).

INFORMATION UTILITIES

Now that you have purchased a modem and checked all systems, you are ready to enter the world of telecommunication. However, after you have all the equipment together, you still need an account number and a password to log on to the big systems (these are not needed for the electronic bulletin boards, as we will explain later). Fees for hooking up to and using telecomputing services can vary widely. In addition to the hourly use charge, most major services charge a first-time hookup fee. We will now discuss the major services, including fees, where they are located, how to secure data, the services they provide, and some basic log-on techniques.

CompuServe

CompuServe, one of the largest suppliers of timesharing services to the business community, became even larger in August 1989 with the acquisition of The Source. With the services of The Source added to those offered by CompuServe, school districts, individual schools, or a university of any size can hook up to mainframe computers via regular telephone lines and use mainframe power to do accounting, payroll, inventory, and many other tasks. The bulk of this activity takes place during the normal business hours of 8 A.M. to 5 P.M. In the past, these mainframe computers stood virtually idle during off-peak hours (5 P.M. to 6 A.M.), using a huge amount of electricity because they must be kept constantly running. To cut down on overhead expenses and to turn this idle time into money, CompuServe started offering computer access to microcomputer users during these slow times. This new service, named MicroNet, offers specialized services such as program swapping, advanced programming, and reference service. With the acquisition of The Source, CompuServe can now provide information and communications geared toward home and business use and also information applicable to classroom use for information retrieval, computer literacy, and word processing. Subscribers can monitor the schedule of current legislative activities in Congress, check the latest changes in airline schedules, and send electronic mail to other subscribers as well as a great variety of other services.

Because of this acquisition, United Press International (UPI) will be one of the most easily accessed of the news services. News stories are categorized using keywords widely used by educators, news reporters, and newscasters. To get news from UPI offerings through CompuServe, you specify one of UPI's broad categories, a range of dates, and the keywords you want to find (for example, Australia, Peru, government, or judiciary). The UPI keyword is further refined (Lima, commerce, July 1990) until the desired information can be accessed.

CompuServe uses a menu-driven system for accessing information. A menu consists of a list of numbered choices from which you select and type in the number to access your choice. These menus are nested, which means that when the general area is accessed, another list of numbered choices is provided to further narrow the field you are exploring. You could be presented with as many as five numbered lists to finalize your choice.

CompuServe is designed to attract users with a wide variety of interests. Highlights include the following:

□ *Newspapers* covers ten large national newspapers, including the *Los Angeles Times, Chicago Tribune, Washington Post, New York Times*, and the *San Francisco Examiner.* The entire text of each newspaper is available the same day the paper is run locally.

□ *Finance* presents reports and services for those interested in stocks, bonds, and commodities. This service includes the *Comprehensive Business Service* and *Standard and Poor's News Service,* a good information source for the "penny stocks."

□ *Entertainment* includes a number of computer games, movie reviews and highlights, current information on videotape and videodisc hardware and software, and the CB Simulation. The CB Simulation allows you to communicate with others logged on to the CompuServe system; it attracts a wide and varied group of people and can be interesting and stimulating to a microcomputer user— access to electronic pen pals.

□ *Communications* offers electronic mail, a service whereby you can leave messages for other CompuServe users; and a national bulletin board, where you can advertise items or services and scan public messages left by others. One of the outstanding features of this service is that if there is any mail waiting for you, a message to this effect appears on the monitor when you log on.

□ *CompuServe users' information* is the clearing house for any information about CompuServe, telling what is new, what is available, and how much it will cost the user.

□ *Special services* contains a great deal of special interest material, such as safety and product information for pilots, information for leather-crafters from Tandy Leather, the *Atari Newsletter* for Atari users, the *Micro Advisor,* and federal reports.

□ *Home information* offers such items as publications from *Better Homes and Gardens, Popular Science,* and the U.S. government dealing with topics such as energy and new products for the home.

□ *MicroNet,* CompuServe's original personal computer users' service is a completely separate part of the data base, designed primarily for those who have intermediate to advanced knowledge of software and programming. MicroNet provides access to technical data on DEC (Digital Equipment Corporation) computers, including technical and service manuals.

□ *CompuServe's Student Forum* is a special educational service that provides a forum for students wherein they can exchange riddles, math and word problems, do word finds, and communicate about topics such as football, baseball, and famous sports figures.

□ *Academic American Encyclopedia* is a service designed to do research on a great number of topics that could range from rare diseases to reports on famous people such as Woolworth, Edison, and Cousteau.

Delphi

A newcomer to the information market, Delphi is a part of General Videotex Corporation. Delphi services are similar to those of CompuServe, and although they are not yet as extensive or broad in their coverage, additional services and capabilities are being added to this data base daily.

Prodigy

Another recent entry to the information utilities market is Prodigy, owned jointly by International Business Machines Corporation and Sears Roebuck and Company. This service is aimed at the mass market and has a flat monthly service charge, instead of the more common hourly usage charge of other utilities. Prodigy features color graphics and emphasizes entertainment, news, shopping, and several other services.

National Geographic Kid's Network

National Geographic Kid's Network is scientific telecommunications project developed by the Technical Educational Research Center located in Cambridge, Massachusetts, and sponsored by the National Science Foundation and the National Geographic Society.

The Kid's Network distributes software and curriculum materials and provides the online network for each project. Elementary schools throughout the United States can participate in ecological studies and relay their data by modem from their school computers to the Society's central computer. A staff scientist evaluates the information, compiles data from participating schools, and graphs the results in the form of a map of the United States. Students then use their school computers to call the Society's computer and see the outcome of their collaborative study. (See Appendix F for the address.)

Dialog

For years major corporations in the United States have earned additional income by sharing research and scientific information produced during research and development as well as by manufacturing and marketing phases of their business. This information is routinely filed in the memories of the corporate mainframe computers. Governmental agencies, universities, and colleges also produce research and scientific data that are stored in large mainframe computer memory. Data banks buy this information, put it in their own computers, and then resell it to other corporations, large research institutions, colleges, and universities.

Dialog Information Services buys reports, statistics, and doctoral dissertations from 140 different corporations, universities, and governmental agencies. Dialog has been used by librarians for over a decade to conduct on-line searches for information as well as to order documents from the data bases. The large Dialog data base includes the Educational Resources Information Center (ERIC, discussed below) and INSPEC, which is a physics, computers, and electronics data base. The smaller data bases available include the Exceptional Child Education Resource (ECER) for special educators and National Foundations (NF) for funding sources used in research and development.

ERIC (located in Washington, D.C.) is designed to provide access to the findings of educational research. This nationwide information network is composed of clearinghouses across the country that abstract, index, and disseminate information about many different topics in the field of education. Many university and college libraries and large district media centers use this service to provide research data for student use. This information generally comes to the research institution in the form of microfiche copy rather than word-processed hard copy.

Dialog was originally developed to index and store the hundreds of thousands of documents generated by the space program in the 1960s. It now offers an index of billions of citations and abstracts on every imaginable subject and is the largest research-based data file in the world. Although Dialog's services are used primarily by professionals at libraries and universities, it is responding to the home market expansion by bringing on line a low-cost service designed for users of microcomputers.

To use the Dialog service, a subscriber dials a toll-free number and locks on. The sign-up fee, which gives the subscriber the lock-on code, is $100. The on-line service can run as high as $300 an hour, a fee that most businesses and universities can afford but that discourages most microcomputer users. The value of the service, although costly, lies in the great number and high quality of the research reports and citations available. For a person engaged in research, a twenty-minute link-up can produce over a hundred citations on most topics.

The clearinghouses listed in Appendix G can provide valuable data on all aspects of the microcomputer as it applies to public school computer use in libraries, classrooms, and laboratories.

GEnie

GEnie is a fast-growing information service due to competitive pricing in non-prime time. The sign-up fee for the service is only eighteen dollars with no monthly minimum use. Its message board format provides special interest groups with easily accessible categories that are posted permanently in subtopics, which users define.

GEnie, located in Rockville, Maryland, has taken the lead in giving users free time to upload files to its libraries. Growing by some twenty-five files each week, for example, the American Apple Roundtable library now holds more than five thousand files and is especially strong in home productivity, education, and entertainment. GEnie's X Modem file transfer is the fastest among the information services in down-loading files to a school's microcomputer. (Consult Appendix G for information on costs and the address of the service.)

Dow Jones News and Quotes Reporter

The Dow Jones News and Quotes Reporter service is an information utility with a much more limited scope than those mentioned above: it offers stock quotes and news from the *Wall Street Journal* and *Barrons* about particular stocks and business sectors. The service is easy to use and the data base is arranged in a highly simplified manner. A code of six or fewer letters is typed in to access the stock or business sector about which you want quotes or news. The information program running in the microcomputer converts this code into a request for information and relays it to the Dow Jones mainframe computer, which returns pages of information in the form of a monitor display. Some pages are menu pages that give two-letter codes and two-line headlines for specific news stories or stock quotes; other nonmenu pages display quotes and news stories.

The McGraw-Hill Information Exchange

The McGraw-Hill Information Exchange (MIX) is another new service that provides a great resource for students and teachers. Perhaps your students would like a pen pal in Canada or would like to discuss politics with students in Mexico or Puerto Rico. You might even want students in a school in California to edit your students' writing projects, or participate in a network conference headed by a teacher who is thousands of miles away. This service provides an easy way for administrators, teachers, and microcomputer specialists to go on-line and ask experts questions about hardware and software, discuss important issues with other educators, or just have an electronic chat.

MIX is a telecommunications service designed specifically for educators and students. Even though MIX also includes the services of the McGraw-Hill World News, it is primarily a service whereby students and teachers can arrange conferences on various subjects, or exchange information with peers. The center of MIX is the Student Information Exchange (STIX), whereby students can participate in conferences on topics ranging from ecology and weather to local and national politics and even journalism and photography. Each conference is moderated by educators from around the country.

Space does not permit discussion of all the various services that are available. The utilities described above provide a cross section of the types of on-line services available. For a complete listing, please consult Appendix G.

Getting Started

There are several ways to join a national network. You can call a network directly on its toll-free number. When you buy a modem or communications software, some networks provide trial kits—available at many microcomputer stores—which give you free hours on the system. You can also purchase a national network's comprehensive manual detailing all services offered, including menus, commands, and log-on procedures, by calling the network's customer service number. Study this manual and the guide book that comes with the kit carefully and map out procedures on paper before attempting to log on to the system. Remember that the national networks can cost from six to fifty dollars per hour, depending on the type of service and time of day; thus your free hours could be used up wandering through menus and never reaching the data you desire to access.

If you live in a major city, you can often access a national network through a local telephone number, thus cutting down the monthly charges. If you live in a smaller city, the phone bill can be kept down by dialing a local packet-switching number. A packet-switching service, such as Telenet or Tymnet (see Appendix G for address and phone numbers), receives computer information, then transmits it directly, via satellite communications, to and from the national network's headquarters. Neither Delphi nor The Source charge extra for the use of Telenet or Tymnet, but CompuServe adds a two-dollar-per-hour surcharge; the additional charge, however, will probably still be much less than the cost of a long-distance phone call.

One of the most difficult features of using a national network may be ending the telecommunication session. Be sure you learn the sign-off methods precisely before starting, or you could be trapped on the network with the phone bill continuing to climb. Simply hanging up the phone is often not sufficient: it could take a network ten to fifteen minutes to realize that the line is disconnected and not in use. Unfortunately, a charge will be made for all this time, so be sure that you know how to log off the network.

An important command to study thoroughly before you log on to the network is the help function, because it may differ from one network to another. All help commands provide essentially the same assistance—a menu that can lead you to much more specific directions for getting around the system. If you get hopelessly lost, you should sign off properly, then redial the network and start over again. Remember—human help can be obtained by dialing the network's customer service number.

COMPUTERIZED BULLETIN BOARDS

The discussion thus far has revolved around commercial, pay-for-access information utilities. But there are actually over fifteen hundred computerized bulletin board systems (BBS) available for home and school that provide free access. Virtually all the bulletin boards systems run on single-user microcomputers. They have been set up by individuals, computer clubs, and commercial outlets (computer stores and centers). Ward Christensen and Randy Suess, two members of the Chicago Area Computer Hobbyist Exchange (CACHE), started the first bulletin board in Chicago in 1978. Their board, BBS #1, is still in operation today and can be reached via modem at (312) 545-8086.

The BBSs do not offer the same broad range of data bases and services provided by the commercial utilities. For most systems the only data base is the current bulletin board of messages, posted by other callers. You can generally get a summary of the current messages as well as read and write messages of your own. Most messages are available to anyone, but some systems let you protect a message with a special password: this approach permits you to leave a private message for someone, provided both parties have agreed upon a password.

Because the BBSs are run on a microcomputer using floppy disk drives, they have limited disk storage for messages. The average capacity is about two hundred active messages, each limited to sixteen or fewer lines (roughly a maximum of one thousand characters per message).

Each BBS establishes its own audience after a short time in operation. The TRS 80–based systems attract TRS 80 enthusiasts and carry the latest news reports, messages, and information about TRS 80 hardware and software. Similarly, the Apple BBSs attract Apple users, IBM systems attract IBM users, and so on. Other BBSs focus on particular topics, clubs, products, or even functions; there is a genealogy BBS in Virginia, a BBS for engineers in Kansas, and one for car buffs in Michigan. There are even BBSs that cover very specialized areas: a number of elderly people were growing Japanese bonsai and discovered a BBS that dealt only with these miniature trees. Several BBSs operated by television stations offer a wide range of topics as well as news and message centers.

Some Handy Tips

When trying your first BBS, it is best to select one close to your home, simply because of the initial trial-and-error period necessary to get to know how to make use of the service. When dialing a board that operates twenty-four hours a day, call during the late evening or on weekends when the phone rates are lowest. Remember that BBSs operate from one individual microcomputer and are connected to a single telephone line, which limits them to receiving one call at a time. This can be both a pleasure and a frustration: when connected you have exclusive use of the line, but you might also experience a long wait when trying to log on.

When dialing a computerized bulletin board the following steps, cautions, and suggestions can help.

1. Be sure that the phone is correctly connected to the modem and the modem to the computer (double-check the connections). Make certain that everything is turned on and set correctly and that the terminal software is ready to operate.
2. Carefully dial the number of the BBS you have selected. After two rings, a continuous, high-pitched tone should be heard. This is normal—the sound of telecomputing.
3. If the modem permits you to dial directly from the computer keyboard, proceed to step 4; if, however, you have used the telephone dial, perform one of

two functions, depending on the make and model of the modem: (a) flip the switch on the modem to either "data" or "terminal" and then hang up the telephone handset, or (b) unplug the cord from the back of the telephone and plug it directly into the modem.

4. The microcomputer will now be connected to the other computer and the word "connect" will usually appear on the monitor screen. It is now up to you to initiate the conversation by holding down the CONTROL key and pressing the C key or by pressing RETURN, ENTER, or BREAK. In many cases you will need to press the RETURN or ENTER key twice.

5. A message will appear welcoming you to that particular BBS. You will then generally be asked to type in your name (or handle) and a password, for future use.

6. You will now be able to make use of what the board has to offer. Most BBSs have a menu of options from which to select. To do this you will need to know some systems commands. These vary from one BBS to another and will be listed when you log on. It is advisable to write them down. Some of the most common are: S (scan messages); R (retrieve or read messages); E or L (enter or leave messages); O (other BBS numbers); H or ? (help—a useful one to remember); and Q, B, or G (quit, bye, or goodbye).

7. Enter the letter of the desired function and press the ENTER or RETURN key. As you explore using the board commands, you will discover that some boards are a waste of time and money; some, on the other hand, will be useful, interesting, and worthwhile. Saving the menu information from the boards you call regularly on a disk or on paper for future reference will save you time and money in the long run.

8. Know how to sign off and do it properly or it could run up your costs substantially. Remember, just because you hang up on your end of the line does not insure that the connection with the computer at the other end is discontinued.

Computerized bulletin boards operate in nearly every state, requiring only a local telephone call to exchange messages. Many users have found that some national BBSs supply valuable information that supplements the local data.

The value to you of the electronic bulletin board system in terms of cost, time, and effort expended will depend on your interest in exchanging information with other computer users. Apart from being enjoyable, a computerized bulletin board adds a human element to the hardware and software processes of the microcomputer. A BBS can be an electronic pen pal as your students send and receive messages across the country. The thoughts of individuals throughout the United States can be summoned to appear on the screen. Daily communications can come to your classroom from the "real" world outside. Special subjects can be explored with experts in other areas of the land. These capabilities introduce a whole new dimension to the chalkboard world of the school.

LOCAL AREA NETWORKS (LAN)

Your school has installed ten microcomputers in the computer laboratory. They are in use every hour of the day, five days a week, but a few things could be improved—the software situation, for one thing. Not only are there insufficient programs, but dispensing and collecting the available programs is getting to be a huge burden. Additionally, students are not as careful with the software as they might be—some packages have even disappeared. You have previewed some excellent software packages, but the cost of purchasing ten programs of each title is more than the budget can handle and most software producers are not yet willing to provide a very good discount for the purchase of multiple copies.

Another problem is that of peripherals. You need letter-quality printers for the language arts program, but the cost is beyond the budget. A direct-connect modem and its software would also be useful. The list continues. Perhaps a local school network is the answer.

A local network is a collection of wires and electronics that connect a group of microcomputers in one location over distances that may range from as many as several thousand feet to as few as twenty-five feet. Each network is composed of at least three parts: the microcomputer and peripherals (such as disk drives, printers, modems, and graphics tablets), the interface boards or units, and the various communications cables or wires (discussed below) that transform the hardware into a network.

It has been estimated that about 40 percent of the schools in the United States that have been working with microcomputers for three years or longer have installed local network systems.* A typical school network connects a set of classroom microcomputers to a host (the teacher's microcomputer) and to one or more floppy disk drives or a hard (Winchester) disk drive, one or two printers, and other peripheral devices. By local network we mean one that is confined to one or several classrooms in the same building.

Cables

Local area networks differ from the telephone networks we have previously discussed in that data is transmitted digitally over twisted-pair wire or coaxial cable at speeds that can range from one million to ten million bits per second. The new fiber-optic cables may play an important role in local area networks in the future because they have the capability of transmitting hundreds of millions of bits per second.

Twisted-pair wire is the simplest and least expensive medium to use in the local network; however, there is a danger that the wires will pick up extraneous environmental noises that may not be filtered out at the receiving computer. The most widely used transmission medium for local network systems is coaxial cable, such as that used in cable television connections. Coaxial cables are capable of much higher data transmission rates than twisted-pair wires but are more expensive (about twice the cost). However, since the cable consists of a wire surrounded by a flexible metal shielding, it does not pick up extraneous environmental noises. Coaxial cable also reduces the number of connecting wires to each component in the system to only two or three. This configuration does mean that data must be

*Kathryn F. Lamb, "Early Writing Utilizing Computer Networks," unpublished Master of Education thesis, University of Utah, 1985.

transmitted in serial form—one bit after another—rather than the parallel transmission normally used by microcomputers.

Network Software

In addition to the regular CAI software, most networks require special software—commonly referred to as protocol software—to manage the network. Some packages offer the teacher a number of interesting capabilities. They allow flexibility in down-loading (moving the data from the teacher's microcomputer to the memory of the individual microcomputers on the network) curriculum programs to the students' microcomputers: teachers can send one program to the whole class or a different program to each student. Some protocol software enables the teacher to communicate with individual students by sending to their monitors on-line messages typed from the central microcomputer keyboard. Some systems even permit the teacher to broadcast what she or any particular student is doing to all the students' microcomputers without disturbing their current work. And some software programs provide a peek function, which enables the teacher to view, on her host screen, what individual students are doing on their screens.

One of the current limitations of all local networks used for CAI, CMI, programming in languages other than BASIC, and word processing lies in the area of applications software. No copy-protected programs can be used on a shared basis; as this category includes most of the popular applications packages, new network users are very often unpleasantly surprised when they cannot boot their favorite software package and send it around the network. Some packages that can be used on a network have posed problems because they were not designed for multiuser environments. Another limitation of some networks is the inability of the host computer to access files or save files from another computer in the network. This problem makes any disk-interactive program useless in networked situations.

It is important once again to emphasize that copyright laws prohibit the copying of diskettes as well as using software intended for single microcomputer use in a multicomputer environment. Some microcomputer software producers allow their programs to be used on multicomputer or hard disk networks but assess the software's list price for each of the computers in the network (that is, if there are ten machines networked to a hard disk drive, they charge for ten copies of the program).

Most network users have had to choose from the limited number of usable package programs or to develop their own customized software. Many network hardware manufacturers, however, are also providing software packages for use on their networks (consult Appendix F for a listing of some of these companies). Many educators believe that as networking becomes more popular, software developers will produce more and more applications packages specifically designed for multiuser environments.

NETWORK CONFIGURATIONS

An aspect that must be considered when installing the network is the path or route the data takes when being transmitted from the teacher's central microcomputer to the other computers in the network. This routing is referred to as networking configuration or topology. Several different network topologies can be utilized, each with its own benefits and limitations. We will discuss the *star, hierarchical,* and *bus networks.* The two most popular configurations used in today's microcomputer networks, star and bus, will be discussed in detail.

Star Network

In the star configuration, a number of microcomputers radiate out from a common center. At the center, a microcomputer (or a minicomputer) acts as the network *controller.* This network controller can manage and direct the functions performed within the network, one or more floppy or hard disk drives, print spoolers (which queue and feed requests for use of printers), modems, graphic boards, music synthesizers, and other peripherals. Each station attached to the central controller is a complete microcomputer that has high-speed access, via the controller, to mass storage, common printers, and all other computers on the network. Individual computers on the network can also have additional peripheral devices added to them as needed. Star networks can handle from ten to thirty microcomputers, but several complete networks can be linked, greatly increasing the total number of stations of the system (see Figure 7.5).

One major advantage of utilizing a star network is that all protocol (procedure or operations) software for network access is centralized in the controller computer. With this arrangement, each component on the network does not require its own interface. The reliability of the central controller becomes the main drawback in star networks, for when it malfunctions, the entire network malfunctions. Many schools using this configuration have a backup computer handy so that the system can be brought back on-line quickly, with little or no inconvenience to the students using the network.

Bus Configuration

As stated earlier, the other most common configuration used by schools in local networks is the *bus* network. Components in a bus network (microcomputers, disk drives, printers, modems, and graphic tablets) tap into a single cable that can run around the classroom or from classroom to classroom as needed. The cable can be either a single coaxial cable or a twisted-pair wire. Each component connects into the bus cable via a line connected to an interface board that is plugged into one of the peripheral slots in the microcomputer. This interface board, which is one of the major costs in a bus configuration, contains both the hardware and

FIGURE 7.5   Star Network
Configuration

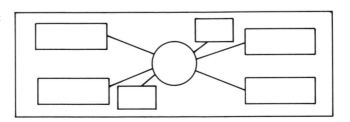

the protocol software needed to allow access to the network while preventing the chance of data loss. The prevention of loss of data is critical because with a bus network, each microcomputer in the network has equal rank and can communicate with any other device on the network (see Figure 7.6).

The circuitry on the interface board, directed by the protocol software program, monitors the network and begins to transmit only if no other station is already transmitting. Once transmitting begins, which can be received at all the microcomputers along the line, the device that prevents data loss listens in to ensure that no other station has begun transmitting at the same time. In simple terms, it prevents two microcomputers from sending data along the bus network at the same time.

One of the major advantages of the bus network is that it is not dependent on any central microcomputer nor any computer on the line. If any one computer fails, the rest of the bus line can continue to function without interruption.

Hierarchical Network

Hierarchical systems, sometimes called tree-shaped networks, consist of a central computer to which several other computers or *nodes* (as this cluster of secondary computers is called) are connected. Within the node, one computer becomes the main computer and the other computers in the node are connected to it. In concept, each node in a hierarchical network forms a star shaped network (see Figure 7.7).

Nationwide organizations with divisional and regional offices, such as Sears Roebuck and American Express, use hierarchical networks. The central computer is generally a mainframe computer, the main computer in the node is a minicomputer, and the other computers in the node are microcomputers or terminals. In a sales application, for example, order entry information is collected at the lowest levels and passed along to the regional offices. There regional customer and order data bases are updated, accounts receivable are processed, and salespersons' performance data are collected. Regional sales information is passed to divisional offices for summary and analysis. Finally, summarized sales information is passed to the corporate office for inclusion in the corporate management information, financial modeling, or decision making processes. Large school districts can link schools together with a hierarchical network. Such tasks as inventory, student attendance records, budgetary matters, school plant planning, and curriculum planning and implementation can be started at the individ-

FIGURE 7.6 Bus Network Configuration

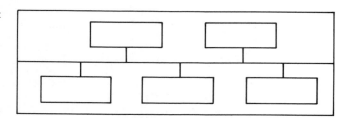

FIGURE 7.7 Hierarchical
Network Configuration

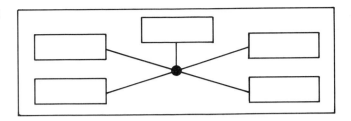

ual school level, collected at strategic levels, such as the high schools that are the intermediate collection points for the feeder elementary and junior high schools, and then finally collected at the district office for analysis, report generation, and decision making.

The Networking Decision

Should your school invest in a local network for a particular curricular situation? If added computer capabilities are needed immediately to carry on the microcomputer literacy program, for example, the question becomes a vital one. Should you purchase additional microcomputers, printers, and disk drives, or should you network? Among the factors that will affect your decision are the concern of multiple copies of software packages (more readily available than multiuser packages), the fact that a printer can be utilized more effectively in a network than having two or three that stand idle a good part of the day, and the problems of student handling and care of the diskettes.

The answer is most likely to be found in a careful analysis of the total costs and benefits involved. If time and money can be saved by sharing resources, you should go ahead with plans for networking; if networking costs for a given situation outweigh the benefits, however, networking should be postponed. As your applications increase in complexity and the number of microcomputers and peripherals in the school grows, you may find networking an option worth considering for next year's budget planning. Whatever you do, plan wisely, know what options are available, and know which networking system is the best (not what you can afford) for your curricular needs.

CLASSROOM APPLICATIONS

Because all areas of this country have access to telephone lines, telecomputing is possible in every classroom in America. Once you have obtained a modem and the necessary software and have arranged for a budget to cover the monthly telephone charges and initial hookup to utilities information networks, you are ready to hook your classroom microcomputers to the world.

One of the major problems associated with classroom or school use of the computer in telecomputing is the monthly cost associated with the use of the phone lines. If you use the phone lines for several hours per week, the fee can be substantial. It is wise to secure as many funds as possible if you plan even a modest telecommunication program in your school. If you find that the school's budget does not provide funds for telecomputing, ask the PTA president for some help; if you are enthusiastic about the value of the programs, you can generally secure help from this organization. You might also try a civic club or business in your community. Detail the value to the program that can come from networking and telecomputing; you may be pleasantly surprised at the amount of support that can be garnered from local sources.

One way to start is to send your students to the library to research the local and national electronic bulletin boards. The students should locate telephone numbers and find out as much about the BBSs as possible from current periodicals, monographs, bulletins, newsletters, and textbooks. Sources and bibliography included in this chapter and Appendix F provide valuable information.

An interesting and useful classroom project is to construct a traditional bulletin board using a map of the United States as a background. As BBSs are located, they can be pinpointed on the bulletin board, thereby providing students with a national map that shows the extent of the availability of BBSs. As the phone numbers of local BBSs are discovered, set aside a period of the school day to place a call, having as many students as possible present when the call is made. If networking capabilities are available in your classroom, connect all microcomputers to the BBS. (If a BBS is not available in your city, select one within a one or two-hundred-mile radius for the first try.)

If the BBS provides a good message service, have students write some messages, staying within the limits suggested in this chapter; then have several students send their messages. A microcomputer pen pal network can be established—students can request that users of the BBS reply to the messages they send. Each day will provide a new and exciting exchange of information with other microcomputer users.

At some point you will locate specialized BBSs that will provide information on specific subjects, such as microcomputer use, health habits, areas of the United States, how to grow bonsai trees, old cars, ecology, and genealogical research. There are bulletin board systems for use in discussing and researching virtually all classroom subjects. With a modem you are also ready to make use of a utility such as CompuServe, MIX, GEnie, or the National Geographic Kid's Network. Although more expensive to access than the BBSs, these services can provide excitement and specific information that will make the microcomputer literacy program the highlight of the students' school day. Establish a regular after school routine of accessing one of the utilities. Couple the modem to the classroom printer so students will have messages and information waiting for them when they come to school each morning. The data supplied will be used in all study areas of the curriculum.

As students make use of a BBS or utility, have them keep a log of the messages, times they used the service, difficulties they might have encountered, unusual occurrences, and so on. After a month or two, these logged anecdotes can be compiled into a newsletter or newspaper to be circulated throughout the school.

This will call attention to the microcomputer program and provide some interesting experiences to write about, adding realism and excitement to the language arts or writing program in the school. Be sure to send a copy of the newsletter or paper to the PTA or any local business that helped sponsor the telecomputing; keeping them informed of the program will encourage these individuals and organizations to continue their support. Invite them also to see the telecomputing in action, and, as part of the demonstration, let your benefactors enjoy sending a message or two.

Another idea that you might try is to set up your own BBS. Dedicate one of your computers and a telephone line for this purpose. Then make the BBS available to students and adults in your community and thus expand the school's sphere of influence. You could have mom and dad log on and see what's on the school program next week—from lunch menus to basketball, football, baseball schedules, when the next math exam will be, the next social event held at the school, and the next PTA meeting. You might even use the BBS to set up a business resource center, inviting local business people to make contributions to the support and information base of the BBS. A local pen pal network or information exchange could also be a part of the BBS.

Your school science or ecology program could be expanded to include the use of telecomputing. Grow corn, track geese, measure acid rain, or monitor weather patterns and compare these findings with those of students across the United States. Measure the outside temperature at 9:00 A.M. local time each day and share this information on CompuServe's Student Forum or Academic American Encyclopedia. Join the National Geographic Kid's Network and conduct a local experiment—up-load the data to the central computer and then read, interpret, and analyze the maps and charts that are down-loaded to your school's microcomputer. The use of telecomputing in these programs will make each day a new highlight for students.

Many elementary programs include a "News and Views" session at the start of the school day during which students report to the class interesting items clipped from the newspaper. A way to vary this program is to hook your microcomputer to a PC projector placed on an overhead projector; connect, via modem, to a local BBS, and project the incoming information so the whole class can participate. Also, have your printer hooked up and make a hard copy so it can be used in your reading program or placed on a classroom bulletin board. The bulletin board can be used as the focal point of your classroom displays by putting up the new information gleaned each day. This hard copy can become a part of the reading program and could even supply spelling words for next week's spelling list. Interesting items taken from these news programs could be incorporated into the weekly or monthly newsletter you prepare for sharing with the rest of the school and the students' parents.

Many students in your class have pets at home and would be very interested in securing specific information about feeding, housing, and health care for their pets. They would also be interested in finding news from national and international animal welfare organizations. Your students can tap into The Advocate, a free BBS that provides special information about pets. This information could be shared with other students and even become a part of the school paper.

Do you have a Radio Shack, Apple, or Commodore 64 computer in your school? Would you like to secure some teacher-created public domain software, some hardware and software tips and even have a place to share some of your own ideas with teachers? The Electronic Bulletin Board System is a free, 24-hour-a-day service devoted exclusively to these activities. A great number of public-domain programs are offered and the sharing of tips and ideas is an exciting part of the service provided.

These classroom activities are but a few of the many possibilities offered by telecomputing. Use your imagination and creativity to come up with other uses of your school's microcomputer, modem, and the telephone lines, and open the world to your students.

SUMMARY

Telecomputing is one of the fastest growing segments of the microcomputer field. Every month new BBSs are added to those already available. The utilities continue to add new services and capabilities to their data bases. Prices for these services have stabilized and in some cases have been reduced as the number of users has increased.

Many schools and school districts are using networks rather than expanding individual microcomputer systems. They are finding that the total costs involved in establishing a network and linking their microcomputers together are less and the system is more functional and easier to manage than are several individual microcomputers in a classroom or school.

In this chapter we discussed the components and services needed for your school to take advantage of the telecomputing capabilities of the utilities and BBSs, plus some suggestions for set-

ting up a network for the school. We discussed the differences between an acoustic coupler and a direct-connect modem, along with the strengths and weaknesses of each.

We provided an in-depth discussion of several of the most popular utilities—the services they provide, their costs, and how to access the data bases—as well as of the BBSs, including the use of the modem for access.

Before you begin telecommunication activities, you should make a careful analysis of the needs of your microcomputer CAI and computer literacy programs so your school will reap maximum benefits. The material in this chapter should provide you with the information needed to conduct the necessary analysis and to make intelligent decisions regarding a telecommunications program.

SELF-TEST

1. Define the two distinct areas that make up the definition for telecommunication.
2. Discuss the main differences between an acoustic and a direct-connect modem; include in your discussion the advantages and disadvantages of each.
3. What is the difference between modulation and demodulation?

4. Discuss the difference between a digital and an analog signal and the role of the modem in the changing of these signals as used in telecommunications.
5. Discuss what baud rate is and how it effects telecommunication. Include in your discussion the significance of 300 and 1200 baud rates.

6. Discuss in detail what terminal software is and what it actually does to the microcomputer when booted up.
7. Detail some of the services offered by CompuServe.
8. Detail some of the services offered by Dialog.
9. What information utility offers stock quotes and news from the *Wall Street Journal* and *Barron's Financial Weekly*? Why is this utility utilized by business people?
10. What is a BBS?
11. Discuss some handy tips you might consider when dialing and using a BBS or information utility.
12. What are some reasons a school might use a LAN?
13. Discuss in detail the basic differences between a bus, star, and a hierarchical network configuration. Include the advantages and disadvantages of each.
14. How might you use telecommunication in your classroom? List as many applications as you can think of.

REFERENCES

Alessi, S., and S. Trollip. *Computer-based Instruction: Methods and Development.* Englewood Cliffs, N.J.: Prentice-Hall, 1985.

Balajthy, E. *Computers and Reading.* Englewood Cliffs, N.J.: Prentice-Hall, 1989.

Beckham, B. "Networking Brown University." *Technological Horizons in Education Journal.* (April 1989): 62–68.

Bitter, G. *Computers in Today's World.* New York: John Wiley & Sons, 1984.

Bitter, G., and R. Camuse. *Using a Microcomputer in the Classroom.* Englewood Cliffs, N.J.: Prentice-Hall, 1988.

Brienne, D., and S. Goldman. "Networking: How It Has Enhanced Science Classes in a New York School . . . And How It Can Enhance Classes in Your School." *Classroom Computer Learning* (April 1989): 44–53.

Bright, G. "Using a Local Network in a College of Education." *Technological Horizons in Education Journal* (April 1988): 90–93.

Chapman, D. "Campus-Wide Networks: Three State-of-the-Art Demonstration Projects." *Technological Horizons in Education Journal* (May 1986): 66–70.

Charp, S. "The Basic Principle of Telecommunication." *Technological Horizons in Education Journal* (April 1988): 94–98.

Coburn, E. *Microcomputers: Hardware, Software, and Programming.* Indianapolis: Bobbs-Merrill, 1984.

Fersko-Weiss, H. "Who Manages the Network?" *Personal Computing* (March 1987): 107–115.

Field, C. "Telecommunication." *inCider* (November 1987): 48–55.

Green, J. "Straight Talk about Local Networks." *Classroom Computer Learning* (September 1984): 72–77.

Lathroum, R. "Queen Anne's QACIN: A Successful Experiment in Educational Networking." *Technological Horizons in Education Journal* (Special Issue, 1988): 55–61.

Lavelle, P. "Now It's Easier to Manage and Train Teachers to Use a Network." *Electronic Learning* (January 1988): 44–47.

Lehrer, A. "A Network Primer: Full-Fledged Educational Networks." *Classroom Computer Learning* (March 1988): 37–44.

Lehrer, A. "A Network Primer: How They're Used and How They Could Be Used." *Classroom Computer Learning* (April 1988): 41–47.

Lehrer, A. "A Networking Primer: When Is a Network Not a Network." *Classroom Computer Learning* (February 1988): 39–46.

Levinson, C. "Education by Telecommunication at the Elementary and Secondary Level: Practices and Problems." *Technological Horizons in Education Journal* (April 1985): 71–73.

Lockwood, R. "What's New in On-line Services." *Personal Computing* (June 1987): 151–161.

Low, L. "BBS and Education: Reaching Beyond the Classroom." *InCider* (June 1986): 56–58.

Maleki, A. "The Automatic Dialer." *inCider* (February 1987): 62 and 108–111.

McCarthy, R. "The Networking Story—What's Available/How They're Used." *Electronic Learning* (January 1988): 24–30 and 62.

McKibbin, W. "BBS and Business: A Profitable Pair." *inCider* (June 1986): 50–56.

McKibbin, W. "What's OnLine." *inCider* (May 1986): 44–48.

O'Brien, B. "More Baud for the Buck." *inCider* (May 1986): 70–74.

Powers, M., et al. *Computer Information Systems Development: Analysis and Design*. West Chicago: South-Western Publishing Co., 1984.

Reinhold, F., and D. Vermot. "Online Information Services: You've Come a Long Way Baby." *Electronic Learning* (November–December 1987): 36–38.

Ritacco, M. "Developing a Telecommunication System." *Technological Horizons in Education Journal* (May 1988): 67–68.

Roth, P. "Let's Talk Telecommunication." *MacUser* (November 1986): 96–98.

Scrogan, L. "The OnLine Underworld." *Class-room Computer Learning* (February 1988): 58–60.

Sherman, T. "Telecommunications: The Software Connection." *inCider* (February 1987): 53–62.

Spencer, C. "RS232 LANs: Inexpensive Office Connections." *Popular Computing* (June 1987): 139–149.

Spencer, D. *The Illustrated Computer Dictionary, 3d ed.* Columbus, Ohio: Merrill Publishing Co., 1986.

Sullivan, D., et al. *Computing Today: Microcomputer Concepts and Applications,* 2d ed. Boston: Houghton Mifflin, Co., 1988.

Wesley, M. "The Modem Is the Message." *MacUser* (February 1986): 74–78.

Zellner, R. *Technology in Education: Implications and Applications*. College Station, Texas: Instructional Research Laboratory, 1987.

CHAPTER 8

Programming and Authoring

CHAPTER TOPICS
- [ ] The nature of programming languages
- [ ] An introduction to the BASIC language
- [ ] Programming in BASIC
- [ ] Classroom activities using BASIC
- [ ] An introduction to the Logo language
- [ ] Classroom activities using Logo
- [ ] Authoring languages and authoring systems

In this chapter we will examine different methods for creating original programs. One common approach is to use one of the many programming languages (such as BASIC or Pascal) to write a program tailor-made for a certain task; another is to use an authoring language (such as PILOT or SuperPILOT), while a third approach is to use an authoring system (such as Course of Action) to write a lesson for instructional purposes.

There are hundreds of different programming languages, each designed with a different capability in mind; but none is as tightly specified as an authoring language. FORTRAN, for example, was designed to solve a broad range of complex scientific and mathematical problems on mainframe computers. This useful language had been adapted to run on many of today's microcomputers, as have other languages not originally designed to do so.

BASIC was developed as a tool to teach programming to students, but it has been expanded in capability and has become the most common language for microcomputers. Logo was created as an open-ended, problem-solving tool simple enough for a small child to use yet possessing features sophisticated enough to challenge secondary students. BASIC and Logo are the most common languages in use in the schools and therefore will be stressed here.

Programming languages are highly versatile. For each unique task the programmer designs a unique program, using a limited set of instructions and a tightly defined syntax to create a tool dedicated to the performance of a specific task. On the other hand, an authoring system is limited to the creation of lessons and requires no programming skills.

Authoring languages were designed to be an easy to use alternative to programming languages. They were developed to enable teachers to create their own computer-based lessons, but they are made up of symbolic commands and rigid syntactical rules that, in the minds of many teachers, are not too far removed from those of a programming language. Indeed, many educators elected to forego authoring activities for the same reason they avoided writing lessons with a programming language: they could not afford to spend the time required to master the craft.

This is where the simpler authoring systems come in handy. While not as versatile as either of the other approaches, they provide a straightforward way to create lessons and tests without the need for extended study and experimentation. It should be added that the more sophisticated authoring systems, while less symbolic than the languages, are still quite demanding to use. As with programming, they require that an algorithm be carefully designed before the actual lesson is created. Although no actual code as such is involved, authoring the lesson can still be complex. However, numerous tools in the form of icons, menus, and other such devices provide help in assembling the instructional sequences. For more on authoring languages and systems, refer to the section on this subject toward the end of this chapter.

PROGRAMMING

Programmers have not always had access to the convenient languages now available. In the early days of computing, programming was a much more demanding task than it is currently. Programmers had to instruct the computer using only binary code. Since the computer could deal directly with the early programs, this served to speed up the processing of information, but there were disadvantages: the binary approach not only required great skill but also was a tedious process that was prone to error. A primitive programming method was with toggle switches: pushing the switch in one direction fed a binary 1 into the machine, pressing it in the other resulted in a 0; various combinations of 0s and 1s made up the instructions in the program. It is easy to see how such a system would lead to operator fatigue.

High-level languages were developed so the programmer could communicate with the machine at a more human level. In this kind of language English words are used, many of which are self-explanatory. A single high-level command or statement might accomplish the same results as an entire series of machine language "words," and the process is much simpler (Figure 8.1). The high-level commands must still be broken down into the binary machine code for the computer to understand them, but this is accomplished automatically through the use of special built-in programs called compilers or interpreters. The development of such high-level languages as BASIC has made learning how to program much easier than before, and many people, including teachers, have developed this skill to some degree.

How important is it that teachers be able to write programs? Obviously, it is not necessary to be a programmer in order to operate a microcomputer. We have already seen that a commercial program on a disk is easy to use—anyone can take advantage of the professional programmer's skills by simply purchasing one of the hundreds of widely available software selections and running it. The teacher's role is such, however, that some familiarity with programming can be useful if she is to function effectively in the computer-age classroom. The degree to

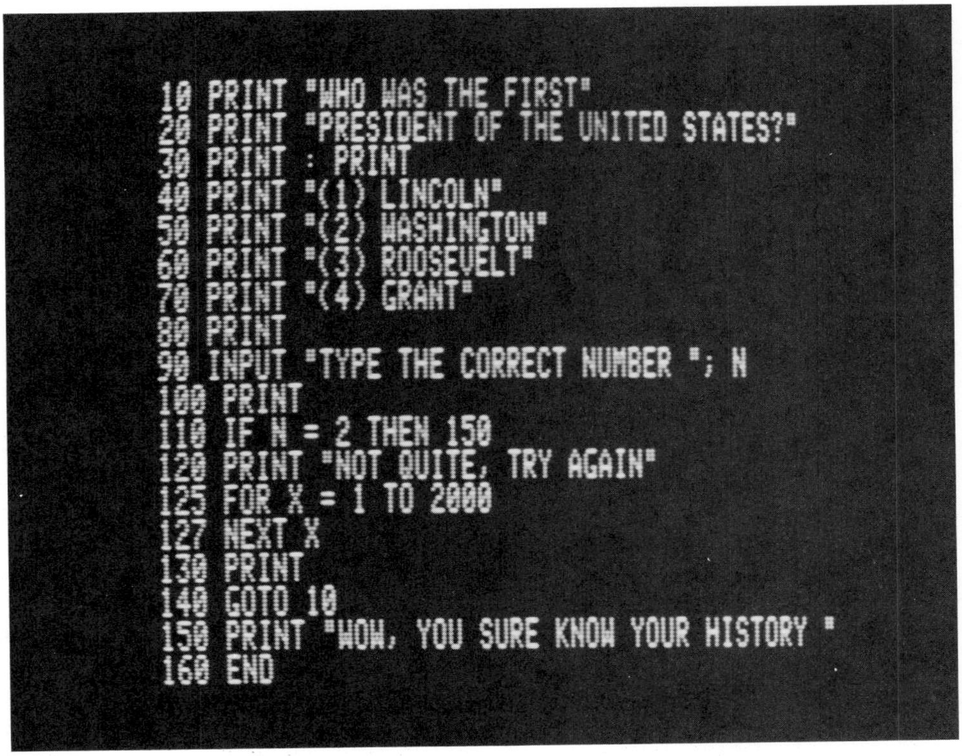

```
10 PRINT "WHO WAS THE FIRST"
20 PRINT "PRESIDENT OF THE UNITED STATES?"
30 PRINT : PRINT
40 PRINT "(1) LINCOLN"
50 PRINT "(2) WASHINGTON"
60 PRINT "(3) ROOSEVELT"
70 PRINT "(4) GRANT"
80 PRINT
90 INPUT "TYPE THE CORRECT NUMBER "; N
100 PRINT
110 IF N = 2 THEN 150
120 PRINT "NOT QUITE, TRY AGAIN"
125 FOR X = 1 TO 2000
127 NEXT X
130 PRINT
140 GOTO 10
150 PRINT "WOW, YOU SURE KNOW YOUR HISTORY "
160 END
```

FIGURE 8.1   The Computer is Programmed by Typing a Sequence of Instructions Made up of Special Words

which a teacher may or may not become involved in programming or related activities depends upon various factors. In some schools the curriculum includes the teaching of programming and computer awareness. To manage the first of these a knowledge of programming is essential; for the second, this skill might also be useful if programming is seen as an important component. Additionally, to succeed in integrating programming into traditional subject matter activities, the teacher must possess some knowledge of programming.

Admittedly, not many teachers develop the skills required to write topflight instructional programs, and those who possess the expertise are often hard-pressed to find the time for such an undertaking. Consequently, few teacher-authored programs approach the quality of the better commercial selections. Generally, unless the objective is to teach programming as a subject to those interested in computer science, it is not necessary for the teacher to be a professional-level programmer to work effectively with the overall school population.

Many teachers see programming not as an end in itself but as just another way to communicate with the computer, to appreciate its capabilities, and to understand better how it works. Thus, some programming is practiced as one of a number of strategies for introducing students to computers. Those who criticize this approach suggest that no programming at all is better than learning bad habits from an inexpert teacher. It is likely that any such bad habits will be readily modified, however, when and if the student moves on to a specialized programming class.

Innovative teachers with programming skills are combining some programming with more traditional activities to lend a new dimension to their classes. For example, one junior high school art teacher has developed an exercise as part of a unit on commercial art in which students create simple computer-generated graphics using the school's Ataris. This approach has proved to be much more successful than the traditional one, in which examples of computer graphics were displayed and the process for creating them discussed. In another school a fourth grade teacher has students create artistic covers for their essays using nothing more than the PRINT statement (PRINT and other special instruction words that direct the computer are discussed later in this chapter). A graph on paper, arranged in the manner of the computer display, is used for the initial planning. The successive lines of computer instructions are then developed from the drawn design and typed on the keyboard in the form of PRINT statements followed by the necessary spaces and asterisks (or other symbols). When printed as hard copy and enlarged the result is a personalized cover (see Figure 8.2).

One teacher developed a simple spelling program using the computer's IF-THEN capabilities. The program was designed so students could update the vocabulary list as desired by substituting new words. For the program to work properly the words had to be spelled correctly; thus the activity of inserting each new word involved considerable vocabulary learning in itself. As a further example, an article by Nancy Kuechle describes how she and her students use a

FIGURE 8.2 A Simple BASIC Program Was Used to Create This Cover Design

```
PETSPETSPETSPETSPETSP
E                   E
T                   T
S  *** *** *** ***  S
P  * * *    *  *    P
E  *** **   *  ***  E
T  *   *    *    *  T
S  *   ***  *  ***  S
P                   P
E                   E
TSPETSPETSPETSPETSPET
```

few selected BASIC commands (PRINT, INPUT, GOTO, and IF-THEN) to create interactive adventure stories. As a story unfolds a situation arises in which the student must make a decision; on the basis of the decision one or another path is taken, which can lead to another decision, and so on. And finally, for an excellent activity involving programming and math, you may wish to refer to an article by Gerald Elgarten entitled "Programming Perimeters"; it includes a handy worksheet that can be most useful for translating the concept of finding perimeters into a finished program in BASIC.

Despite the successes enjoyed by many teachers, the controversy over whether or not to involve the general student population in programming activities continues. One of the more common arguments against requiring programming is that most students won't need it as a vocational tool once they are out of school, so in-school time should be used in more productive ways—becoming more skilled in math and language areas, for example. As computers become more user friendly, so the argument goes, programming skills will be necessary only for those who make computers their profession. (The term *user friendly* is used to describe the extent to which a computer and its programs adapt to the way people do things; conversely, an unfriendly system is one in which the user is forced to adapt to the idiosyncrasies of the machine.) Although a large number of jobs require employees to work with computers, the nature of these machines is such that few people even think of them as computers. The clerk who passes the groceries over the bar code reader is not really concerned about the technology, nor is the teller in the bank who types in the details of a deposit and gives out the deposit slip.

The rationale for the inclusion of programming in computer literacy courses is that it enables students to find out for themselves if they have an interest in this activity. Those who advocate this approach would use a parallel argument for including just about any subject, with the possible exception of the basics, in the curriculum. Others who support the teaching of programming maintain that the main benefit of the exercises involved is the enhancement of the ability to think and reason logically.

Seymour Papert, who was instrumental in developing Logo, defends the teaching of programming throughout his book *Mindstorms*. He states:

> In many schools today, the phrase "computer-aided instruction" means making the computer teach the child. One might say the *computer is being used to program the child*. In my vision, the *child programs the computer* and, in doing so, both acquires a sense of mastery over a piece of the most modern and powerful technology and establishes an intimate contact with some of the deepest ideas from science, from mathematics and from the art of intellectual model building.*

The arguments both for and against teaching programming are most convincing; to date, however, there is little evidence either to support the contention that programming enhances intellectual skills or to indicate that the converse is true.

---

*From *Mindstorms* by Seymour Papert. © 1980 by Basic Books, Inc., Publishers. Reprinted by permission of the publisher.

In any case, teachers who involve their students in programming activities soon discover that they love the challenge of writing programs and relish the sense of control over the computer that programming provides. Obviously, few teachers would involve their students in programming activities without first understanding the essentials themselves. There are various approaches to gaining familiarity or competence in this area.

One way to learn about programming is to obtain a text on the subject (see this chapter's references), sit down at the keyboard, and work carefully through the various exercises. This approach takes considerable dedication and determination, but many teachers have learned the elements in this way. Some excellent tutorials, available on disk, will teach the concepts in a very direct fashion.

A popular program for young beginners is Turtle Tracks from Scholastic. A screen shot of a graphic created with the programming and graphics features is shown in Figure 8.3. The language used in this program is a combination of Logo and BASIC, both of which are described in the following pages. Like the graphic feature in Logo, commands are used to direct the turtle (cursor) to create colored pictures of various kinds; melodies are composed by teaching the turtle to "sing" different combinations of notes.

If you prefer a more formal approach, on the other hand, you might wish to enroll in one of the many classes offered by school districts, universities, and community schools. Learning to program often involves a combination of several of the various methods. Becoming adept at this skill requires a considerable expenditure of time and effort, and many educators do not find the payoff commensurate with the requirements.

Regardless of your approach, you will find that programming is much more involved than simply sitting down at the keyboard and writing a program. Possibly 90 percent of the work is actually done away from the computer in the form of conceptualizing, developing algorithms, formatting, and so on. The following

FIGURE 8.3 A Graphic Created with the Turtle Tracks Program

(Courtesy of Scholastic Software)

information should prove enlightening, whether or not you elect to pursue the topic further.

BASIC

BASIC was the "native language" of many early microcomputers; it was often built into the ROM at the factory, and was available for use by simply turning the computer on. Today, most languages come on a disk (some are still ROM-based on a few computers). These include Pascal, the language used for the advanced placement exam in computer science; Logo, which is popular for problem-solving activities; updated versions of BASIC such as True BASIC and Quick-BASIC; and various other languages.

Commands

Described below are some of the more important commands that are used to control and direct the computer. These commands are fairly straightforward; typing them on the keyboard causes the computer to react in a specific manner. Among the commands are those that enable the disk drives and the computer to work together as a system. Whether or not you write your own programs, it is useful to know at least some of the more common commands: with them you can do such things as save a program onto a disk, delete or change lines in a program that you or someone else has written, or see all the programs stored on a particular disk. Some of the common commands follow.

CATALOG.   Typing CATALOG will signal the computer to display all the programs stored on a disk (the term **FILES** is used with some computers). From these you may select the specific program you wish to run.

DELETE.   DELETE followed by the name of the program deletes that program from the disk (the term **KILL** is used on some systems). Be careful with this command: it completely removes the information, and there is no way to get it back. If the name of your file was "myprog" the command would look like this: DELETE MYPROG.

LOAD.   Typing LOAD and the name of a program will load the program from the disk into the memory of the computer. It can then be listed so you can add to it or delete unwanted segments. An example is LOAD PROG1.

RUN.   Typing the RUN command followed by the name of a program on the disk will load and run that program. An example is RUN PROG1. Typing RUN alone will cause the program currently in memory (if any) to run.

SAVE.   Typing SAVE followed by a program name will save it onto the disk. An example is SAVE EPIC (you can use just about any name you choose).

BASIC Statements

The following exercises and examples are based on the Apple version of BASIC called *Applesoft*.

To begin writing a program you type a line number, which is typically expressed as an increment of 10 (e.g., 10, 20, 30) to permit the insertion of additional lines of instructions between successive line numbers if needed. You then enter one of the special words that make up the BASIC vocabulary, such as FOR-NEXT, GOTO, IF-THEN, LET, or PRINT. Some of these words are described in the following pages. Many others are available, but this selected sample will serve to illustrate how the language works. Next, an expression is generally used, either a numerical one or a word or words (called a string). The following is a complete BASIC statement:

10   PRINT   2 + 4

the line number   the keyword   the expression

This statement, which includes a line number (10), a keyword (PRINT), and an expression (2 + 4), is a fairly typical example of a program line. However, the structure tends to change somewhat, depending upon what the instructions are supposed to do. In the example above, the word PRINT tells the computer to display the results of the computation; in this case, the printout will be 6. If PRINT is followed by words or numbers within quotation marks (such as 10 PRINT "ADDITIONAL EXERCISES"), however, a literal printout of that material will take place. After the statement has been typed in and the RETURN or ENTER key pressed, the line will be sent to the computer's internal memory (RAM), where it is stored temporarily. Each line of the program is stored in like fashion, and the program only executes when the command RUN is entered.

Incidentally, if you want to see what the program you are writing looks like line by line, use the LIST command. If the program is a large one that scrolls up the screen, it can be stopped with CONTROL-S (Apple), CONTROL-BREAK (IBM), or the BREAK key on other machines. LIST followed by a number causes that line only to be displayed; LIST 20, for example, results in a listing of line 20 from the program. This same command followed by two numbers causes the numbers indicated and all those between to be displayed: LIST 30,200, for example, displays all lines from 30 to 200 inclusive.

So far we have considered but one of the special words with which the computer works (PRINT). Following are additional words and a description of what each of them accomplishes.

FOR-NEXT. When a FOR-NEXT loop runs it begins at FOR and ends at NEXT, where it loops back to FOR and continues until the specified condition, set following the FOR statement, is met. The typical way to specify the number of loops is illustrated below:

```
10 FOR N = 1 TO 10
```

This indicates that the loop should be executed ten times, but there is no loop as yet, so we will create one:

```
10 FOR N = 1 TO 10
20 PRINT N
30 NEXT N
```

When the command RUN is given, the number at line 10 is 1; this is printed at line 20. Then line 30 instructs the computer to loop back up to line 10. Because the condition at line 10 instructs the computer to repeat this process until the number 10 is reached, the printout at line 20 will represent first the number 1, then 2, 3, and so on up to 10.

LET. The computer's memory is made up of a large number of spaces, each of which is identified by an address. Values, such as numbers or strings, can be assigned to (or placed into) these spaces. A useful analogy is that of many empty boxes such as those in a post office. Things can be placed in these boxes, each of which has a unique address. When the stored items are needed, they can be found rapidly and with little difficulty. A standard system is commonly used for numbering the boxes, such as letters in various combinations, with numbers appended as needed to provide additional combinations. These labeled boxes are called variables; their contents are values.

Placing a specific item into one of the storage boxes is called assigning a value to a variable. Using the post office analogy, we might say LET the box labeled PC contain a postcard. An important distinction between the memory spaces within the computer and the boxes in the post office should be noted: unlike the boxes in the post office, computer boxes can accommodate only *one* item at a time; thus, if another postcard is pushed into box PC, the one that was there previously is forced out. In actual practice, if memory space PC contained 10, for example, and 15 was then assigned to variable PC, the 10 would be destroyed and the 15 would be installed. Thus

```
20 LET PC = 10
```

means that space PC holds a 10, but the following line changes that:

```
30 LET PC = 15
```

Now variable PC holds 15; the 10 has been replaced.

To hold a word, variables must be modified by adding a dollar sign ($) to a standard variable: A$, D$, or X$, for example. The correct way to write a LET statement using a string variable is

```
10 LET B$ = "BOB"
```

The symbol B$ is called "B string." Now, let's consider how the contents in all these boxes are moved about. Here is a short program using the statements we know:

```
10 LET R$ = "RICHARD"
20 PRINT R$
```

The output is RICHARD (the contents of variable R$)—not R$, as one might expect. With nothing more than the LET and the PRINT statements, it is possible to write some programs that actually do things. As an example, let's try some math.

```
10 LET X = 4
20 PRINT X
30 LET X = X + 1
40 PRINT X
50 LET Z = X
60 LET Y = X * Z
70 PRINT Y
```

Run through the program in your mind to see if you can come up with the quantities that will be printed at lines 20, 40, and 70 before you read the following explanation.

In line 10 the value 4 is assigned to variable X. Line 20 prints out 4. In line 30, 4 is incremented by one, becoming 5; this value is printed out in line 40. Line 50 introduces a new variable, Z. The value in X, which is 5, remains unaltered, but variable Z now contains 5 also. In line 60 another variable, Y, is introduced; it will hold the results of the calculation X * Z (note that * means multiplication in BASIC). Finally, in line 70 the contents of variable Y are displayed. The printout looks like this:

```
4
5
25
```

GOTO.   The GOTO statement directs the computer to go to the line number that follows this statement and then to continue with the execution of the instructions in sequential line number order. The correct line number must follow the GOTO if the branch is to be completed properly. Here is a sample of the use of GOTO:

```
10 LET R$ = "REBECCA"
20 PRINT R$
30 GOTO 10
```

When this program is run, the string REBECCA will be printed out at line 20, then line 30 will direct the computer to return to line 10; it then moves to line 20, where REBECCA is again printed, and so on forever. This is an example of an infinite loop—stop it by pressing CONTROL-C, BREAK, CTRL/BREAK, or RUN/STOP (depending upon the kind of computer being used).

It is very easy to overuse GOTO, which makes the written program both cumbersome and difficult to interpret. A much better approach where possible is to use subroutines, which are described later, in place of GOTO statements.

IF-THEN.   IF-THEN is used in conjunction with conditions that enable the computer to make decisions. For example, we can inform our machine that if some condition prevails, then it should perform a specified task. To do this, we must use standard symbols to indicate such conditions:

<	less than
< =	less than or equal to
>	greater than
> =	greater than or equal to
=	equal to
<>	not equal to

By using the **IF-THEN** statement we now have a way to get out of an infinite loop without having to resort to the use of **CONTROL** or **BREAK** keys:

```
10 LET R$ = "REBECCA"
20 LET C = 0
30 IF  C = 6 THEN 70
40 PRINT R$
50 LET  C = C + 1
60 GOTO 30
70 END
```

When this program is run the name REBECCA will be displayed six times, then the program stops.

INPUT.   The INPUT statement is useful because it permits the user to interact with a running program, inputting information as the computer asks for it. As you will recall, two kinds of input are used—numeric and string—which vary in the way they are written:

```
       numeric       10 INPUT A
       string        20 INPUT A$
```

When waiting for input, the computer stops executing the program until it receives a response from the user. Generally a question will be displayed on the screen. Here is an example of a typical INPUT statement:

```
100 INPUT "WHAT IS YOUR GUESS? ";G
```

There is a unique characteristic about this statement that is worth mentioning. Note that the input statement works very much like a **PRINT** statement; that is, the message **WHAT IS YOUR GUESS?** will be displayed on the screen. When you type your guess and press the return or enter key, it is stored in memory space G.

You can also use the INPUT statement to give control of the pacing of the program to the user. An INPUT statement followed by a message such as **PRESS RETURN TO CONTINUE** will hold the display on the screen until the student presses the return key. The line looks like this:

```
50 INPUT "PRESS RETURN TO CONTINUE";P$
```

Here is an example of a string input:

```
10 PRINT "HI, I'M THE COMPUTER."
20 PRINT "WHAT'S YOUR NAME?"
30 INPUT N$
40 PRINT "PLEASED TO MEET YOU "N$
50 END
```

When this program is run, HI, I'M THE COMPUTER. WHAT'S YOUR NAME? is displayed on the screen, then the computer stops and waits for your response. When you type your name, it is stored in the memory space labeled N$. Whenever N$ appears in the program, its contents (your name) will be printed out. When the program above is run, here's how it looks:

This shows on the screen:

```
HI: I'M THE COMPUTER.
WHAT'S YOUR NAME?
```

You type your name:

```
PATRICIA
```

The computer responds with:

```
PLEASED TO MEET YOU PATRICIA
```

(Note that it prints the contents of memory space N$ which is "Patricia".)

GOSUB-RETURN. A subroutine is a self-contained module in a program. Using this statement permits you to branch to the subroutine from almost anywhere in the program. Here is an example:

```
10 REM GOSUB EXAMPLE
20 HOME
30 GOSUB 1000
40 PRINT "  AUTUMN COLORS"
50 GOSUB 1000
60 PRINT "   ORANGE,GOLD"
70 GOSUB 1000
80 PRINT "   WARMER THAN"
90 GOSUB 1000
100 PRINT "BLUE WINTER'S COLD"
110 GOSUB 1000
120 END
1000 PRINT
1010 PRINT " ! ! ! ! ! ! ! ! ! !  "
1020 PRINT
1030 RETURN
```

When you run the program the result should be:

```
          ! ! ! ! ! ! ! ! ! !

          AUTUMN COLORS

          ! ! ! ! ! ! ! ! ! !

          ORANGE,GOLD

          ! ! ! ! ! ! ! ! ! !

          WARMER THAN

          ! ! ! ! ! ! ! ! ! !

          BLUE WINTER'S COLD

          ! ! ! ! ! ! ! ! ! !
```

The GOSUB statements cause the subroutine, which begins on line 1000, to be executed. A blank line is inserted, then a line of exclamation points, and then another blank line. The RETURN statement on line 1030 causes the program to pick up where it left off—that is, immediately following the last executed GOSUB statement. Thus, following the execution of the first GOSUB at line 30, the program continues with line 40, and the words AUTUMN COLORS are displayed, then the next GOSUB is encountered. This sequence continues until the program ends. Subroutines are generally placed after the main program, which is often very short when several subroutines are included.

GOSUB statements are generally more involved than the sample shown here. For example, you might wish to work out grades for each of your students based on a number of test scores. A subroutine could be designed to add together each student's scores, divide the sum by the number of exams, and match this number with a predetermined scale to produce a letter grade for each student.

Note that there are two new statements in this program. Line 10 introduces the REM (remark) statement, which is used frequently as a prompt or reminder of what the various statements are supposed to do. REMs make the program easier to read and understand and are a common form of documentation. The HOME statement in line 20 is an Apple term that automatically clears everything off the screen in preparation for the run of the program; you would use CLS for the TRS 80 and IBM, and PRINT "CLR/HOME" for the Commodore (these differences are explained in more detail in the sample programming exercise in Appendix H).

Here is an example of a short program that uses many of the statements discussed above:

```
10 REM KITTEN PROGRAM
20 REM K = TOTAL KITTENS
30 REM G = KITTENS GIVEN AWAY
40 REM R = KITTENS LEFT
50 HOME
60 INPUT "HOW MANY KITTENS DO YOU HAVE? ";K
70 GOSUB 1000
80 INPUT "HOW MANY DO YOU WANT TO GIVE AWAY? ";G
90 LET R = K - G
100 IF R < = 0 THEN 150
110 GOSUB 1000
120 PRINT "YOU NOW HAVE "R" KITTENS LEFT."
130 PRINT
140 GOTO 60
150 PRINT "YOU'RE OUT OF KITTENS."
160 END
1000 PRINT:PRINT
1010 RETURN
```

When you run the program it will ask the number of kittens you have and wait for you to answer (line 60). You will then be asked to type in the number you want to give away (line 80). This amount will be subtracted from the current number of kittens (line 90), and the number remaining will be printed (line 120). This loop is repeated until the condition at line 100 is met (all the kittens are gone); then line 150 "you're out of kittens," will be printed. Note the REMs on lines 10 through 40. These have nothing to do with the way the program runs, but they give useful information about it. The subroutine on line 1000 simply inserts two blank lines between the lines of text. Note that a colon (:) can be used to separate two or more statements so they can be placed on a single line.

If you are intrigued with BASIC programming at this point and would like some more extensive hands-on experience, turn to Appendix H, where a BASIC exercise is found. Merely type it into the computer just as it is written to see how the various instructions work. Incidentally, this can be a useful way to get acquainted with programming. Books are available that provide complete line-by-line listings of a variety of programs. Also, many journals include listings that can be typed into the computer and run.

BASIC IN THE CLASSROOM

BASIC programming is typically undertaken in math classes, but it can be used elsewhere as well. Special graphics statements in AppleSoft BASIC such as HLIN (horizontal line) and VLIN (vertical line) can help create colorful graphics and can present art and design students with a new challenge. Programming might also be introduced in conjunction with a careers unit in which positions in the computer industry are being discussed. Various aspects of programming can be most useful in the study of physics: many equations can be included in functional programs to be run on the microcomputer. Programs can also be written to control a programmable robot; the results are much more dramatic than are those displayed on the monitor screen. BASIC can be used to generate sounds in addition to visual displays. Music students will enjoy creating high-tech compositions on the micro—some machines provide a highly capable sound synthesizer as part of the standard equipment.

A number of approaches are used in teaching programming. One is simply to concentrate on one statement at a time, then to tie them together. The opposite extreme involves seating the students at the computers and letting them find their own way. Somewhere between these two is the most common approach: the student works through a series of exercises that proceed from the simpler concepts to the more complex ones. The instructor must be certain that the exercises are bug-free (if they're typed in properly, they will work), but the rest is up to the student. As mentioned, an exercise of this type is found in Appendix H. Note that the lesson should be undertaken only after some discussion and after the student has learned the various system commands and has run several disk-based programs. Any number of exercises of this nature can be constructed.

Also useful are debugging exercises in which intentional mistakes are built into the program to prevent it from executing properly. The students correct the bugs and make the program work—this is an excellent project. The actual writing of programs is an enjoyable activity. A specific outcome is described, and the students use their own selection of statements to produce the desired results. They also enjoy creating their own programs from scratch, with no specific prior instructions from the teacher as to what the programs must do. The results of such exercises are often surprisingly sophisticated.

In another exercise the teacher or capable students type short programs that are displayed on a large monitor or on a wall screen using a projection panel on an overhead projector, so the class can see the programs as they evolve. The class is divided into teams, which try to figure out what the results of a given program will be when it runs. After all the guesses are in, the teacher or student types RUN to display the results on the screen; a discussion period follows, during which correct answers are acknowledged and incorrect ones analyzed.

A similar exercise can be conducted without a computer. The short programs are printed on sheets of paper that contain a "blank screen" with each program (see Figure 8.4). The student writes the output, including correct spacing, formatting, and so on, on the "screen." During the class discussion that follows each program is analyzed and the correct results displayed or written on the chalkboard.

Many of the BASIC statements and commands presented in this chapter can be taught through the use of analogies. A few examples are offered in the following discussion.

Using the analogy of computer memory spaces as mailboxes in a post office makes the LET statement easier to comprehend. The statement LET P = 10, for example, is interpreted as "let the mailbox labeled P contain a 10." The concept that, unlike mailboxes, a memory space can hold only one quantity at a time can be explained by saying that inserting a new letter (a value) into an occupied mailbox (a memory space) pushes the old contents out.

The PRINT statement is easily understood using the analogy of a typewriter. The importance of the quotation marks in relation to literal printout should be noted. A literal printout occurs only if quotation marks enclose the information. To emphasize their use you can play a game of "Simon Says" giving the directions "quotes" and "no quotes."

The GOTO statement is so straightforward that it requires little explanation. However, you can devise a treasure hunt in which this keyword is used to direct students to various places on a map. This statement can also be related to many of the common dice and spinner games in which players go to a particular space on the basis of the number from the spin or die toss.

The IF-THEN statement can be explained using everyday occurrences. For example, if it is cold outside, then I'll wear my coat. It should be stressed that an

```
10 print "how"
20 print
30 print
40 print
50 print "are ";
60 print "you?"
```

FIGURE 8.4   An Example of a Programming Exercise and a "Blank Screen"

alternative *must* follow an IF-THEN statement. In other words, if it is cold out-side, then I'll wear my coat; but if it is not cold, then I'll merely go to school (move to the next line) without donning my coat.

With a bit of imagination, the concept of BASIC keywords, statements, and commands can be made more concrete and therefore easier for the students to comprehend, remember, and use.

LOGO

Logo, unlike PILOT and BASIC, is not an acronym. The name is taken from the Greek word *logos,* which means a word or a thought. The philosophy underlying this language was greatly influenced by the ideas of Piaget, who maintained that children learn by being actively involved. Logo, like most other languages, must be loaded into the computer's memory from a disk. Rather extensive documen-tation accompanies the program, but it is not necessary to spend much time with it; indeed, it's possible to control the turtle (a triangular cursor) the first time the language is used. However, Logo is not just turtle graphics; to realize its full potential takes quite a bit of effort and study. One of the nice things about Logo, though, is that a child can have fun and learn with it from the first press of a key while a high school student can be challenged by its powerful mathematical fea-tures that have applications in geometry, trigonometry, algebra, and calculus: it is a friendly, interactive, extensible tool.

The most common application in the schools is that of creating various geo-metric figures with the turtle (Figure 8.5). Directions are given using a set of words called primitives—everyday, descriptive words such as *forward, right*, and *repeat*—that the turtle understands. One way to teach Logo to children is to have them walk through the commands; by following the moves themselves they are better able to comprehend what the turtle will do.

Incidentally, early versions of Logo used a robot turtle similar to the one shown in Figure 8.6 rather than a screen turtle as the object to direct with Logo com-mands. This approach became inconvenient when more than one computer was used, since the robot required considerable room in which to maneuver. In the following exercises the version of Logo for the Apple (AppleLogo) is used.

To direct a friend using the language of Logo, you might say "go forward 10 steps; then turn right 90 degrees." If you give this same set of directions four times, your friend will walk in a square and end up where she started—this is just what the turtle does when it is given the same set of directions. Here is how the program looks:

```
FORWARD 10
RIGHT 90
FORWARD 10
RIGHT 90
FORWARD 10
RIGHT 90
FORWARD 10
RIGHT 90
```

FIGURE 8.5 A Design Created with Logo

Later, you will learn a shorter way to accomplish such repetitive tasks; but for now, we have just written our first Logo program. The words used (forward, right) are primitives—they are part of the turtle's original vocabulary. Here are some additional primitives:

SHOWTURTLE	Causes the turtle to appear on the screen.
HIDETURTLE	Causes the turtle to disappear.
PENDOWN	Causes the turtle to draw a line as it moves.
PENUP	Allows the turtle to move about but leaving no line.
PENCOLOR	(SETPC, followed by a number from 0 to 5) Determines the colors of the lines that are drawn (SETPC 5, for example, results in a blue line).
PRINT	Prints whatever follows, as long as it is encased in brackets (PRINT [I LIKE YOU]).
LEFT	Causes the turtle to turn left the number of degrees specified (LEFT 90).
RIGHT	Causes the turtle to turn right (see LEFT, above).

FIGURE 8.6   A Robot Turtle for Use with Logo
(Courtesy of Harvard Associates, Inc.)

FORWARD	Causes the turtle to move ahead a specified distance (FORWARD 6).
BACK	Causes the turtle to move backward (see **FORWARD**, above).
REPEAT	Repeats a procedure a specified number of times.
TO	Precedes a new word (not a primitive) that you will invent.
CLEARSCREEN	Clears the screen; the turtle remains in the center, ready to go to work.
END	Used after a procedure has been defined.

Combinations of primitive instructions can be used to create an endless array of geometric designs and graphic displays. Children, and even adults, get caught up in the process and develop a sense of control as they learn to manipulate the turtle. The deeper power of Logo is not realized, however, until its extensibility is brought into play: beginning with the primitives, students can create a whole new vocabulary that the turtle understands. The new words, called procedures, are made up initially from elements of the original language; however, once introduced, they work just as if they had always been there.

In the following exercise a short program is used to create a geometric shape. Once the precise set of instructions had been established, the set, in toto, is given a name; it is then a procedure and becomes a part of the turtle's vocabulary. Whenever the procedure name is used, the product of the total instruction set that made up the procedure will be displayed. It is possible to create some striking effects by combining a number of procedures.

To begin, insert the disk in the drive and boot it. A few simple instructions will appear on the screen; following them causes a blinking cursor to appear, which indicates that the computer is waiting for some input. Typing SHOWTURTLE produces the turtle in the center of the screen. A program can now be typed; here is a simple one:

```
FORWARD 80
RIGHT 90
FORWARD 10
RIGHT 90
FORWARD 80
RIGHT 90
FORWARD 10
```

The product of this little program is an elongated rectangle, as shown in Figure 8.7. We are now ready to create a procedure. First we must select a name—LONGREC, for instance, for long rectangle. To define a procedure, follow these steps:

```
TO LONGREC      (TO followed by the name is the first line of a
                   procedure)
FORWARD 80      (these are the same lines used in the original
RIGHT 90           program)
FORWARD 10
RIGHT 90
FORWARD 80
RIGHT 90
FORWARD 10
END             (END is the last line in a procedure)
```

The computer will respond with the words "LONGREC defined."

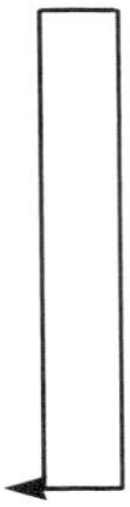

FIGURE 8.7   A Basic Rectangular Shape Drawn by the Logo Turtle

You should normally finish a procedure with the turtle facing in the same direction as it began. In this case, however, we want to continue to enlarge upon the initial procedure and have thus left the turtle pointing in the direction of its next movement.

Now we can simply type the word LONGREC to have the rectangle displayed on the screen. In other words, a new command has been created that gives a predictable output whenever it is used. The magic of Logo begins to emerge when we realize that our new procedures can themselves be used to create additional procedures. To illustrate, LONGREC will be used as the main component in a new procedure we'll call WINDMILL:

```
TO WINDMILL
REPEAT 4 [LONGREC]
END
```

Once again, Logo will respond with "WINDMILL defined," to indicate that this procedure is now a part of its vocabulary. To see what WINDMILL looks like, we simply type that word; the turtle, obeying the instructions to repeat four longrecs, will draw the graphic shown in Figure 8.8 on the screen.

This short exposure to Logo scarcely seems adequate for a language with so much potential, but if it has been of interest, you may want to learn more. One of Logo's most valuable features was alluded to but not demonstrated, due to lack of space: it is highly capable of manipulating words and sentences through the use of a built-in tool called a list. Using lists effectively is reserved for those willing to spend the time and effort to learn the additional commands and the more complex syntax involved; those who have done so speak enthusiastically of Logo's capabilities. For more on Logo turn to Appendix H, where a practical exercise is found.

FIGURE 8.8 The "WINDMILL" Graphic

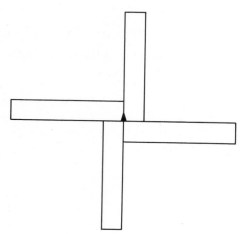

LogoWriter is an expanded version of Logo that maintains the familiar programming features while adding such capabilities as a 40-column word processor and enhanced graphics.

There are now four turtles instead of one, and these can be multiplied many times over using a new command called STAMP; you can literally fill the entire screen with turtles if you wish. Turtles need no longer conform to the traditional triangular configuration either; now you can redesign them to suit your fancy.

The word processor lets you position words any place on the screen, not just in lines. They can even be incorporated into a graphic display as labels or part of the design. With a bit of imagination, teachers in any subject area can incorporate LogoWriter into their classroom activities. Given the many capabilities of the new Logo, you might be forgiven if you should forget that all the programming capabilities of the older version are still there. It is the Logo language that provides the cement for tying all the activities together.

Students might work separately on a project, say an illustrated story, each of them being responsible for a specified segment of the total production. Once all of the "pages" have been completed, they can then integrate the separate parts by writing a program to do this. Since LogoWriter provides the means for controlling presentation rates, certain parts of the project, such as passages of text, might be assigned a longer viewing time. Graphics, on the other hand, might benefit from a shorter viewing period. The program might even be written to make a particular illustration appear and disappear in quick succession for an animated effect.

Many additional ideas for introducing and using Logo can be found in the references listed at the end of this chapter.

LOGO IN THE CLASSROOM

Logo is a sophisticated and powerful language that is said to have "no floor and no ceiling": its potential is nearly unlimited. It is probably the most interactive of the computing languages used in education, lending itself readily to experimentation. It encourages exploration and is friendly toward mistakes. Ideas can be worked through virtually at the point of inception; results are immediate and often dramatic.

Much of what the student learns is unintentional: the Logo experience should be based on the idea of discovery, avoiding the notion of structure in the sense of prescribed goals or objectives. Thus, interacting with the language itself is the primary activity when students use Logo. They conquer the computer and come to control it. They learn about the logic of programming, and they think about thinking.

There are, however, serious problems involved with discovery learning. Quite a bit of time can be spent in "discovering" anew concepts that are commonly known. The demands for accountability often preclude extended use of strategies that lack clear-cut objectives and outcomes. Perhaps the most satisfactory approach could be termed guided discovery, in which the teacher intervenes as needed; the student is not simply turned loose with the language. Rather than being used in isolation, Logo is typically part of a wide range of learning experiences.

The fact that the turtle spends much of its time making turns indicates that students should know about angles if they are to be successful in their programming efforts. Of course, since Logo is discovery-based you might just turn them loose to experiment, but it is more effective for some students (though not all) to give them some help. A useful concept is the relationship of the turtle's turns to the 360 degrees of a full circle.

Most children have little difficulty understanding that the four 90-degree turns the turtle makes when drawing a square add up to 360 degrees. In essence, the turtle completes a circle even as it draws a square. This same idea applies to the construction of many other closed figures besides the square, but it is easiest to see with regular polygons. Equilateral triangles, pentagons, hexagons, and other polygons are simple to construct using a formula to figure the angle of the turns the turtle must make. An equilateral triangle has three sides and a turtle trip is 360 degrees, so the turtle must make three turns of 120 degrees to draw the triangle and come back to rest in its starting position. To figure the number of degrees for each turn (angle) of a pentagon, you simply divide 360 by 5 to arrive at five turtle turns of 72 degrees. A hexagon requires six turns of 60 degrees, and an octagon has eight 45-degree turns. It is easy to construct a useful tool for teaching the concept of degrees (see Figure 8.9). Begin by drawing two circles on

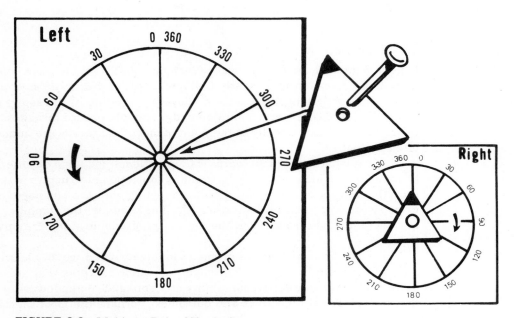

FIGURE 8.9   Making a Pair of Turtle Compasses

pieces of cardboard. Using a protractor, mark off the degrees at various intervals around the edges of the circles (in a clockwise direction for one circle and counterclockwise for the other) and draw lines radiating from the centers to the degree marks, thus dividing the circles into segments. Cut out two triangular "turtles" and fasten them to the centers to act as spinners. Students can use these devices in conjunction with the computer to move the turtle in predefined ways.

Teachers employ a variety of techniques for introducing Logo to their students; we'll mention but a few. Giving turtle commands to children to act out, which we discussed earlier, can become gamelike if teams compete to see who can execute a secret figure, or reach a spot in the room or on the playground, on the basis of directions given by the team leader. A similar game offers a greater challenge by having the players execute the program blindfolded. By placing masking tape in a pattern on a tile floor it is possible to delineate a turtle program, with each tile representing a turtle step. You can construct progressively more complex mazes with additional strips of tape. Students must write the program from the "tracks" the turtle has left on the floor.

A treasure hunt can be conducted using the screen turtle to move from point to point on a terrain map drawn on transparent plastic and taped over the screen. A second map (the pirate's map) or a set of instructions is drawn or written on paper; as the directions are interpreted, the turtle is directed from one point to the next on the plastic screen map. This procedure gives students practice in estimating angles and distances.

Logo can also be used in conjunction with a unit on astronomy. After studying the constellations, students recreate them on the computer screen. Procedures can be developed and named after the constellations they represent or to generate geometric shapes (squares, triangles, and circles, for example) to be used as components in the construction of more complex figures. The basic shapes can be combined in numerous ways to form objects such as houses, animals, and people. This idea is useful for illustrating the concept of modular programming.

AUTHORING LANGUAGES AND SYSTEMS

Authoring languages are designed to assist you in creating your own tailor-made lessons. Several years ago PILOT was a popular program of this kind; it was replaced by an improved version called SuperPILOT with even more features. Other authoring languages might be mentioned, but the fact is that none are widely used these days—authoring systems are much more common.

PILOT uses menus and submenus that appear throughout the program permitting you to select from options such as composing text, creating graphics, or generating music. Help screens can be called up when needed to display information such as cursor moves (for creating graphics), special key functions, or the code for the colors.

The instruction set consists of about forty-five short commands—typically designated with a letter—that are used in various arrangements to construct the lesson. For example, the command for the computer to display information on the screen is T: (for Type); others are A: (Accept), M: (Match), and J: (Jump). A segment of a program written in PILOT is shown below.

```
*PEAKS                    (this is a section label)
T:  How many peaks over   (text on the screen)
 :  13,000 feet are found
 :  in the Uinta Mountains?
A:                        (accept the answer the student types)
M:  9, nine               (check to see if the input matches either
                             of these)
TY:  Good!                (if there is a match, display this text on
                             the screen)
JY:  Lakes                (if there is a match, jump to the section
                             labeled lakes)
```

Rather than commands of this sort, an authoring system provides English language prompts to which the author responds, and a matrix within which the lesson is designed. Here is a short segment of a lesson to show you how a simple kind of authoring system works.

THE SCREEN DISPLAYS THIS	TEACHER TYPES THIS
Name of lesson?	Utah geography
Desired Text?	Let's explore the Uinta Mountains today.
First Question?	Name the highest peak in the Uinta Mountains.
. . . and so on.	

Having typed in the information in response to the preset prompts, you can now sit back and relax as the computer assembles the lesson. There is also a test generation feature in software of this kind that lets you create tests in several formats using an approach much like that used for authoring the lesson.

More sophisticated authoring systems provide menus and icons to assist you. For instance, Course of Action (Authorware) displays all the tools needed to create interactive lessons in an icon palette located along the side of the screen display. As the authoring session evolves, icons are selected and dragged to the "course flow line" which, when complete, represents the lesson from beginning to end. Each icon has a special function. For example, the icon that looks like a computer screen is selected when text and graphics are to be displayed. An icon with arrows indicates an animation sequence, and a stop sign signals a pause in the program's flow. This planning phase for a lesson on art is shown in Figure 8.10.

Clicking on an icon causes it to open into a screen-sized window in which you design whatever content is required, be it text, graphics, animation, or a combination of these. It is a straightforward matter to determine response, reenforcement, and other features of the lesson using a program such as this.

Another similar powerful authoring tool is Course Builder from TeleRobotics. A feature of such programs is extended graphics capabilities. Illustrations, once created, can be moved about the screen and combined to form new arrangements

FIGURE 8.10 Planing a Lesson with Course of Action, an Authoring System from Authorware

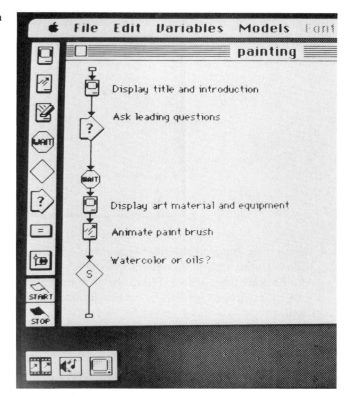

(Figures 8.11 and 8.12). This feature lends itself to some interesting tutorial and testing applications. Other features typically found in sophisticated authoring systems include a text editor that is much like a word processor, sound capabilities, and animation.

In addition to the other applications it provides, HyperCard, the versatile program for the Macintosh, can also be used as an authoring tool. Numerous applications are available as illustrated by the icons on the HOME CARD shown in Figure 8.13. Screen displays and other output are designed as "index cards," each of which has its own identifying code so it can be accessed when required. Multiple cards are combined into "stacks" just as actual paper cards might be.

In order to move around in a stack or perform some other kind of function, "buttons," which are sensitive areas on a card, are provided. These can be identified by whatever name seems appropriate (Figure 8.14). Authoring a lesson involves creating the needed cards using graphics, text, sound, and other features as desired, and then designing buttons so that all the cards are linked together in a manner consistent with the planned flow of the lesson. The manner in which cards can be linked is virtually without limit. You can see that lessons of this kind would afford considerable potential for individualization and branching.

An interesting math lesson for elementary students designed by Professor Donald Peck of the University of Utah teaches various concepts with which children

FIGURE 8.11 An Anatomy Test Using Movable Graphics Designed with Course Builder from TeleRobotics International, Inc.

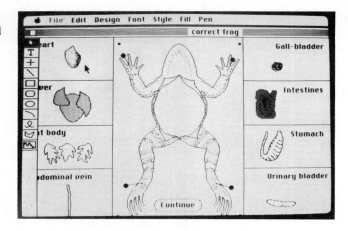

frequently have problems. An example is the concept of the volume of three-dimensional figures. In one part of the lesson students are encouraged to type the dimensions they desire (Figure 8.15) from which the computer generates the figure in its proper size showing the number of units contained within it (Figure 8.16).

Although HyperCard works only with the Macintosh, a similar program for the Apple IIe and IIc called TutorTech (Techware) is available. A minimum of 128K in RAM is necessary for this program to operate, so some upgrading of memory will be necessary in many cases. HyperStudio, a program very much like HyperCard, is a product for the Apple IIGS from Roger Wagner Publishing. Termed an "interactive authoring system," HyperStudio allows you to integrate music, video, text, and other kinds of products into a single "hyperpresentation" using the concepts of cards and stacks just as Hypercard does. The graphics and

FIGURE 8.12 Students can Move the Various Organs to Test Their Knowledge of Anatomy

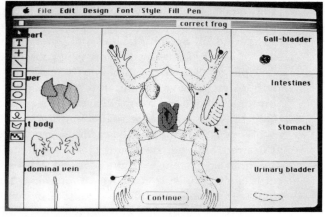

(Courtesy of TeleRobotics International, Inc.)

FIGURE 8.13 The HyperCard Home Card

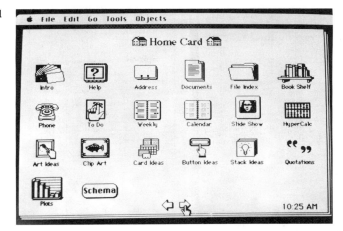

FIGURE 8.14 A HyperCard Display Showing Options for Use with Buttons

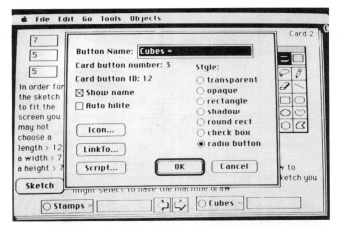

FIGURE 8.15 A Screen Shot of a Program Created with HyperCard Showing the Arrangement for Student Input

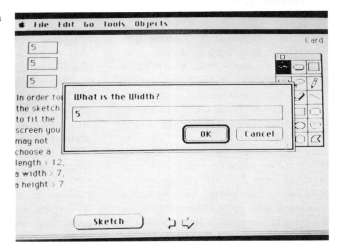

FIGURE 8.16 HyperCard
Generates a Cube from the
Dimensions Typed by the Student

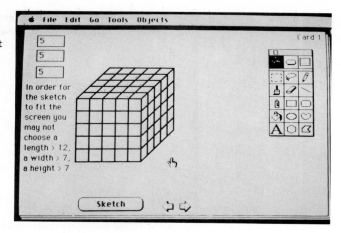

sound capabilities of the IIGS put the presentations created with HyperStudio in a class by themselves. The program is surprisingly inexpensive—as little as $35—and will undoubtedly be acquired and used by an increasing number of schools as time goes on.

Due to the popularity of hypermedia, several other programs of this type have been created for a variety of computers. It is safe to say that hypermedia represents the direction of future educational software development.

The more capable authoring tools such as those mentioned have features that enable them to access information stored on videodiscs and in CD-ROMs. To take advantage of the massive amounts of data these devices can store, the computer is connected to a videodisc player or CD-ROM drive and an authoring system is used to call up information at points in the lesson where it is required. Lessons of incredible richness and variety are possible using this approach.

SUMMARY

Arguments both for and against learning programming have been presented in this chapter. Basically, proponents maintain that this activity enhances the students' ability to think logically and analytically. Opponents maintain that few students will become professional programmers so students can better spend their in-school time mastering the basics.

The nature of computer literacy courses is changing. While these classes continue to be popular, programming activities are giving way to such things as word processing. On the other hand, a strong trend appears to be developing toward offering programming as an elective class to serve the needs of science-oriented students. At the same time, teachers with programming skills are integrating this activity into the traditional curriculum in various ways.

Two programming languages were described in this chapter: BASIC and Logo. BASIC was emphasized because most classroom computers have this language on board. A selection of essential statements and commands was provided to enable the creation of simple programs. A discussion of authoring language systems was provided and the differences between authoring and general purpose programming languages were discussed. Those who wish to try writing more complex programs will find the references at the end of this chapter useful.

SELF-TEST

1. In what way(s) is a programming language different from an authoring language?
2. State the major difference(s) between an authoring language and an authoring system.
3. What is a "high level" programming language?
4. Take a position either for or against requiring teachers to know how to program; defend your position.
5. Refer to question four; substitute "students" for "teachers."
6. Write a short program in BASIC that prints your name three times in succession in this fashion:

    Name
    Name
    Name

    Note that there is more than one way to accomplish this.
7. What will be the output from this program:

```
20 LET D = 10
30 LET G = 20
40 PRINT "D + G ="
50 END
```

8. What will be the result when this program is run?

```
10 PRINT "BILL"
20 GOTO 10
30 PRINT "BETTY"
40 GOTO 30
50 END
```

9. What will be the output from this program?

```
10 LET A$ = "CHARLES "
20 LET B$ = "BABBAGE"
30 PRINT A$, B$
40 END
```

10. What will this program do?

```
10 FOR Z = 1 TO 10
20 PRINT "COUNTING"
30 GOTO 50
40 NEXT Z
50 END
```

11. In the Logo language what are the new words that are taught to the computer called?
12. The words in Logo's original vocabulary are called what?
13. Assume you are programming in Logo. What will be on the screen as a result of the following routine?

```
FORWARD 100
RIGHT 90
FORWARD 50
BACK 100
```

14. Name the Swiss psychologist whose ideas helped influence the development of Logo.
15. List three ways that BASIC might be used in the classroom.
16. List three ways that Logo might be used in the classroom.

REFERENCES

Abelson, H. *Apple Logo.* Peterborough, N.H.: BYTE/McGraw-Hill, 1982.

Apple Computer Company. *Apple PILOT Editor's Manual.* Cupertino, Calif.: Apple Computer Company, 1980.

Babbie, E. *Apple Logo for Teachers.* Belmont, Calif.: Wadsworth, 1984.

Bateson, R., and R. Raygor. *BASIC Programming for the Apple Computer.* St. Paul, Minn.: West, 1985.

Bearden, S., K. Martin, and J. Muller. *The Turtle's Source-Book.* Reston, Va.: Reston Publishing Co., 1983.

Bitter, G., and N. Watson. *Apple Logo Primer.* Reston, Va.: Reston Publishing Co., 1983.

Bitter, G., and R. Camuse. *Using a Computer in the Classroom,* 2d ed. Englewood Cliffs, N.J.: Prentice Hall, 1988.

Bramble, W., and E. Mason. *Computers in Schools.* New York: McGraw-Hill, 1985.

Brownell, G. *Computers and Teaching.* St. Paul, Minn.: West Publishing Co., 1987.

Camp, J., and M. Cogan. "HyperCard: A Milestone in Educational Computing." *Electronic Learning* (March 1988): 46–51.

Camp, J., M. Cogan, and M. Gordon. "Authoring Systems for Developing Courseware." *Electronic Learning* (January/February 1989): 61–64.

Culp, G., and H. Nickles. *Instructional Computing Fundamentals for IBM Microcomputers*. Pacific Grove, Calif.: Brooks/Cole, 1985.

Elgarten, G. "Programming Perimeters." *Classroom Computer News* (March 1983): 68–69.

Harper, D. *LOGO Theory and Practice*. Pacific Grove, Calif.: Brooks/Cole, 1989.

Heller, R., C. Martin, and J. Wright. *Logoworlds*. Rockville, Md.: Computer Science Press, 1985.

Jones, J. *The Applesoft BASIC Primer*. Rockville, Md.: Computer Science Press, 1985.

Kuechle, N. "BASIC Adventures." *Classroom Computer Learning* (January 1984): 66–67.

Linn, M. "The Cognitive Consequences of Programming Instruction in Classrooms." *Educational Researcher* (May 1985): 14–16; 25–29.

Lockard, J., P. Abrams, and W. Many. *Microcomputers for Educators*. Boston: Little, Brown, 1987.

Mandrell, S. *Introduction to BASIC Programming*, 2d ed. St. Paul, Minn.: West Publishing Co., 1985.

Milone, M., Jr. "Hypercard: Sizzle or Substance." *Classroom Computer Learning* (January 1988): 52–54.

Nickles, H. and G. Culp. *The Practical Apple*. Pacific Grove, Calif.: Brooks/Cole, 1988.

Olson, J., and S. Eaton. "Curriculum Change and the Classroom Order." In *Exploring Teacher's Thinking,* Calderhead, J., ed. London: Cassell Educational Limited, 1987.

Papert, S. *Mindstorms*. New York: Basic Books, 1980.

Papert, S. "New Views on Logo." *Electronic Learning* (April 1986): 33–36, 63.

Phillipo, J. "An Educator's Guide to Interfaces and Authoring Systems." *Electronic Learning* (January/February 1989): 42–45.

Radin, S., F. Lee, and M. Marrapodi. *Computers in the Classroom, Logo Edition*. Chicago: SRA, 1985.

Riedesel, C., and D. Clements. *Coping With Computers in the Elementary and Middle Schools*. Englewood Cliffs, N.J.: Prentice-Hall, 1985.

Roberts, N., R. Carter, S. Friel, and M. Miller. *Integrating the Computer into the Elementary and Middle School*. Englewood Cliffs, N.J.: Prentice-Hall, 1988.

Shane, J. *Apple II BASIC*. Boston: Houghton Mifflin, 1983.

Thompson, J. *Practical BASIC for Teachers*. Columbus, Ohio: Merrill, 1985.

Tipps, S., T. Riordon, and G. Bull. *Nudges-IBM Logo Projects*. New York: Holt, Rinehart and Winston, 1984.

Troutman, A., J. White, and F. Breit. *The Micro Goes to School*. Pacific Grove, Calif.: Brooks/Cole, 1988.

Watt, D. *Learning with Logo*. New York: McGraw-Hill, 1983.

CHAPTER 9

Planning and Implementation

CHAPTER TOPICS
☐ Acquiring a microcomputer system
☐ Funding for microcomputer systems and software
☐ An in-service program
☐ Location and layout of the microcomputer facility
☐ Administration of the microcomputer facility
☐ Basic information needed to manage the microcomputer facility
☐ Staffing the microcomputer program

Many schools have no systematic plan for acquiring and using microcomputers. They might purchase a basic system with money from a variety of sources and then turn it over to an interested teacher to use as she sees fit. Little planning and practically no staff involvement are necessary with this approach. But when a school makes a serious decision to develop a functional microcomputer program, the situation changes dramatically—a host of issues most be dealt with.

A number of questions concern support. For a program to be successful the majority of teachers and administrators must be convinced of its usefulness. How can this be achieved? How will teachers, administrators, and students acquire the necessary training to enable them to work and learn most effectively with the computers? The question of funding is a critical one. Where will the money to purchase the hardware and software come from? Who will be responsible for acquiring the needed equipment and programs? After these have been purchased, where will they be housed? The location of the systems, who has access to them, and when access will be provided are factors that will determine the amount of use by the students and staff. Provisions for maintenance, safety, security, and service may well determine how available computers will be to the teachers, students, and administrators. The arrangement and location of the microcomputer center (if the computers are housed in a central location) will also determine the extent of use.

Solutions to these crucial concerns are needed if the program is to reach its full potential as a viable methodology for changing students' behavior. This chapter will provide information about developing and implementing a microcomputer program and will offer suggestions for coping with the various problems that arise.

HOW TO ACQUIRE A MICROCOMPUTER SYSTEM

The exact procedures followed to acquire a microcomputer system are unique to each school; however, the decision-making process can be either centralized or on an individual school basis.

Centralized Approach

Many school districts acquire their equipment and supplies in a centralized administrative fashion, moving from the superintendent down to the individual school principals. The process of selecting machines, funding them, and placing them in the school is thus directed by the central administration—generally the district educational media director. An emerging role in some school districts is that of a specialist whose only responsibility is the direct administration of a microcomputing, computer literacy, or district computer program.

The logic of a centralized approach is clear and understandable. The expenses involved and the large numbers of people and equipment needed to establish and maintain a microcomputer program require the coordination, expertise, and accountability available in a centralized administrative structure. The rationale for centralized administration of the microcomputer program after it has become operational is not so logical, however. The program is best administered on an individual school basis, with the coordination and cooperation of the central administration.

Several advantages can accrue from the purchase and installation of a microcomputer system on a district basis:

1. There is a possible financial advantage when a school system bids to purchase a large number of microcomputers and peripherals, compared with each individual school purchasing a smaller number of microcomputers (especially of several different makes or brands).
2. Specialists may be available to train teachers and administrators in the use of the microcomputer systems, to answer technical questions about their equipment, and to set up workshops on how to install, use, and maintain the equipment.
3. Service centers can provide maintenance and repair to districts and individual schools at reasonable repair rates.
4. With the advantage of large-volume purchase of software programs, some districts are able to realize substantial savings on the purchase of multiple sets of programs, just as they are able to get books, filmstrips, slides, or transparencies at reduced rates.

There are also coordination and cooperation advantages when microcomputer programs are handled centrally:

1. There is improved coordination of curricular uses of the microcomputer program so students are not taught the same things about or with microcomputers in more than one grade—a coordinated computer literacy program.
2. A trained staff is available for in-service programs for individual school teachers and administrators, under the direction of the central administration.
3. There are procedures for obtaining preview software on a district basis, including the creation of locally produced software and the production of teacher guides for software packages.

4. The establishment of a hardware maintenance facility for repair of monitors and other peripheral devices may be feasible.
5. A districtwide evaluation process of microcomputers and peripherals for durability and reliability can also be used to evaluate the CAI program and to recommend appropriate modifications, revisions, and updates.

Individual School Approach

Many microcomputer programs were started by individual teachers or parents (especially at the elementary level), sometimes acting alone, sometimes in conjunction with their colleagues, and always in cooperation with the school principal. These programs generally occur in small school systems, rural areas, or suburban areas where parents are anxious to have their children use microcomputers and the principals have considerable autonomy over their budget and curricula.

Among the advantages of the individual school approach over the centralized approach are the following:

1. The teachers have more control of the curriculum, and the district has less say about the software to be used.
2. Individual teachers are less dependent on the judgment and decisions of others and more involved in the selection process.
3. Teachers and schools have more influence concerning the equipment that is acquired (when a district determines that a certain brand of computer will serve all needs, many compromises must necessarily be made).
4. Teachers and schools have greater access to microcomputers and district assistance if they are free to determine which programs should have priority— when the central administration establishes priorities, resources may be allocated in an inequitable manner (the high school business classes, for example, may get most of the microcomputers).

The individual school microcomputer acquisitions program must be a combined effort. Because funds are generally insufficient to implement all new programs desired, a school must establish priorities, set goals, and undertake a logical course of action. The effort must be a coordinated one: microcomputer programs that depend on the energies, enthusiasm, expertise, and presence of only one or two persons are unlikely to survive. A joint fund-raising effort involving the school PTA, local civic clubs, business owners, heads of departments, and the school administrators, students, and teachers will most likely succeed.

It may be necessary to begin modestly, with only one or two microcomputers with double disk drives for them, a printer (a good quality dot matrix—24-pin if possible), and some software the first year. Long-range plans, however, should provide for the acquisition of the total system within two to five years. Because all microcomputers do not have the same capabilities or available software, be sure that the brand of microcomputer system purchased will handle as many needs of the emerging program as possible and that it is not so limited that after the newness wears off it will sit idle.

FUNDING FOR MICROCOMPUTER SYSTEMS AND SOFTWARE

Computers—and news about them—abound. Tiny microprocessors found in modern automobiles, kitchen appliances, high-fidelity and video equipment, and children's toys are increasing our awareness of the current computer revolution. Personal computers are now found in thousands of American homes. More and more school board members and other officials in positions that critically affect education are showing a great deal of interest in computers, thus making computers and their various applications timely, school-related issues. As a result, funding for school microcomputer projects is generally less difficult to obtain than funding for other educational projects.

The prices of most microcomputers, peripherals, and many good software packages have declined dramatically, making it possible to acquire a computer system for hundreds rather than thousands of dollars. Consequently, many schools and districts are now able to integrate the purchase of computers into their budgets under tax-levy funding—a regular part of the operating budget of the school or district. Because, in most cases, outside funding is needed to set up a microcomputer system, we will identify several sources: public funds, private foundations, local support, and the individual school. It will be advantageous to tap as many sources as possible, because funding for education is still under par. The following sources and ideas can be helpful in obtaining funding for microcomputer projects.

Public Funding

The enactment of the Educational Consolidation and Improvement Act of 1981 brought about significant changes in sources for public funding of educational projects. This legislation substantially reduces the federal fiscal role and also limits its regulatory role, giving states and local districts much greater autonomy in planning, maintaining, and monitoring educational programs. The Elementary Secondary Education Act, Title 1 (now defunct), was reworked as Chapter 1 of the new act. Although funding was reduced, local educational agencies are much less restricted in how they can utilize the funds they receive. Monies forthcoming under the new Chapter 1 of the Educational Consolidation and Improvement Act can be earmarked for a variety of microcomputer programs.

Chapter 2 of the act sets up the block grant concept, whereby federal money comes to the states in one large block rather than being allocated in several specific categories. These block grants now filter down to the districts and schools, where they are used at the discretion of local authorities. The specified categories of activities that may be funded through block grants—special projects, basic skills, support services, and educational improvement—provide adequate leeway to permit the use of funds for microcomputer projects. Federal funds are also available under the Special Education Act, Public Law 94-142, for use in mainstreaming and special programs for the handicapped student; here, again, implementation of the law is flexible enough to provide financial assistance for microcomputer programs.

To tap into these funds you will need the most up-to-date list available of major public funding sources. You can obtain such a list by writing to or visiting the appropriate person at your state education department; you should then request the following information from the organizations on that list:

1. Titles of federal and state programs that provide public monies to local schools.
2. Authorizing legislation (Public Law 94-142, for example).
3. Name of the contact person, with address and phone number.
4. Total amount of funding available during previous and present fiscal years (to give you an idea of emphasis in any particular fiscal year).
5. Total amount of funding allocated to computer projects during the previous fiscal year (again, to identify areas of emphasis).
6. A brief description of the particular funding program's mandate (how to secure the funds, what is the intent of the program, and such).

In some cases a proposal must be written to obtain public funds, so some skill in grantsmanship will help. Many school systems have a specialist to assist in writing and securing grants: be sure to see if this help is available, either at the district office or in your own school. If not—and if you do not have the necessary experience yourself—solicit the aid of a colleague who has prepared a grant proposal or two.

Private Sources

A number of foundations (such as Ford and Carnegie) provide schools, school districts, universities, and colleges with financial support for educational activities. The larger foundations are well known; however, hundreds of smaller agencies also welcome worthy proposals, and although they have fewer dollars to share, they also receive fewer applications. The smaller foundations are more apt to support microcomputer projects because they tend to fund a wider variety of activities.

An easy way to identify private funding sources is to examine a current foundation directory—available in most public and university libraries (it is updated annually)—which lists the name of virtually every private foundation in America. The directory provides the information needed—address, contact person, restrictions, types of projects funded, extent of written proposals needed—to decide whether to contact a particular foundation regarding a microcomputer project.

Along with the private funding sources and foundations already mentioned, the microcomputer corporations (including Apple, IBM, and Tandy/Radio Shack) have funding programs for instructional applications of computers. These companies furnish hardware, software, and funding for instructional applications of their products.

If your district's central administration has a grant specialist, be sure to contact her for assistance, coordination, and cooperation regarding obtaining funding through a foundation (in some districts, you must get initial permission from this person before you begin to apply for outside funding).

Another way of locating active funding organizations is to talk with local schools, districts, and educational agencies that have already succeeded in securing funds for their projects. The following suggestions may help identify these sources.

1. Read relevant magazines, journals, and newsletters. Many publications contain articles that provide the names of schools or districts that have implemented successful microcomputer projects.
2. Attend relevant lectures, workshops, and conferences with the idea of contacting people who have been successful in funding their projects. Do not be reluctant to ask these people how, who, when, and where in relation to their successes.
3. Join one or more appropriate microcomputer organizations. If you have a state organization, you can make valuable contacts attending conventions, meetings, or workshops. It is also a worthwhile investment to join a national organization—if you become active the district will often fund your trip to a national convention, workshop, or special meeting. The contacts made at these meetings are a great source of ideas of all kinds—not just funding.
4. Obtain a copy, from your local university or college, of the *Microcomputer Directory: Applications in Educational Settings*. In it are listed, by states, brief descriptions of hundreds of educationally relevant computer projects, along with the names, addresses, and phone numbers of contact people.
5. Solicit advice from faculty members at your state or local college or university who may be eager to share their knowledge, experience, and advice. They may be interested in helping you write the grant proposal or even in submitting a proposal whereby the college or university will work jointly with your school or district on a microcomputer project.

Local Support

The financial support that parents and civic groups can provide is generally insufficient to underwrite a major microcomputer project. These groups can, however, provide seed money for acquiring some basic equipment and getting the program started. When appealing for assistance to either a PTA or civic group, the following suggestions may help:

1. Make the proposal brief, to the point, and specific. Avoid technical jargon—you need to communicate with your potential benefactors, so don't try to impress them with esoteric computer terms.
2. Organize a workshop and invite a vendor to demonstrate, using an actual microcomputer, at least one of the machine's more dramatic uses.
3. Seek out parents or civic group members who use or own microcomputers and invite them to take an active role in the planning and presentation stages of your proposal.
4. Include your students who are already involved in microcomputing. They will be the best spokespersons of all. An interested student can influence a parent who may be the civic club president.

5. Include your principal and colleagues in the proposal and presentation. If you have the support of the administration, many teachers will also fall in line and offer their support.

After you have made the proposal to the PTA and one or more civic groups, present it to the school board. The school board members may be business people from the community who are currently using computers and who therefore realize their importance in education.

Business contributions to schools enhance public relations and can be good advertising. Many schools have been successful in funding medium-to-large microcomputer projects through business contacts. As you contact a local business regarding funding, point out some of the ways the school can reciprocate that will benefit the business.

1. Thank the contributors for their support at public gatherings such as a PTA meeting, a back-to-school night, intermission during a school play, or during halftime at a basketball game.
2. Invite a representative from the business to formally present and dedicate the microcomputer system (or whatever they purchased) at a public meeting or a special assembly held for that specific purpose.
3. Print an announcement or article in the school's newsletter. Special mention, including pictures, could be made in the yearbook, activities book, or any other school publications.
4. Have students make posters or other artwork based upon the contribution to the school; these can be displayed in the school or even at the place of business.
5. Send a press release about the contribution to the local newspapers, accompanied by a photograph of the key persons involved. You could also arrange with the local TV station to have a human interest spot on their local news broadcast or public forum program.
6. Provide the community with monthly, bimonthly, or quarterly reports, using the above-mentioned sources, detailing such things as how the equipment is being used, the success of the program, how many hours the program is being used, and students' anecdotes.

Individual School Support

As we have mentioned, district funds can be used for the purchase of microcomputers and software—your school principal will be aware of these. Additionally, several departments or teachers may be persuaded to allocate some portion of their budgets for microcomputer hardware or software purchases. The discretionary funds controlled by the school principal may also be available for the microcomputer program (in some large schools this could represent a considerable sum).

To be successful in obtaining funding, develop a well-defined plan of action and be aggressive in promoting your plan. Once the program begins to gain momentum, the funds available within the district may be sufficient to support the continuation and expansion of the ongoing microcomputer curriculum and facility.

IN-SERVICE PROGRAM—PREPARATION OF FACULTY AND ADMINISTRATORS

As the program expands, an in-service training program to provide all interested persons with the skills needed to use the microcomputer system will become necessary. Some faculty members will not look forward to having the microcomputers introduced into the school—they may still view microcomputers with suspicion. A well-planned, meaningful in-service program may therefore help allay some of these fears.

Following are some points that are worth considering in the preparation and administration of an in-service program.

1. What are the objectives? You will not find a ready-made course or program that will exactly suit your needs. Portions of a course or program prepared by some other school or district may be useful, but they will have to be modified. It is wise to set your own in-service objectives by asking the following questions.

   a. What is the topmost priority? You will be operating within limits set by the school's schedules of classes, budgets, and available resources. You must therefore establish priorities for the role the microcomputers will play in the school curriculum. It may be better to concentrate on specific areas rather than to try to cover an entire literacy program—CAI for fourth, fifth, and sixth grades, for instance, Logo in grades kindergarten through three, and a special program for the ninth grade only.

   b. How much computer literacy should be provided for the faculty? Knowledge of the workings of the microcomputer system? the computer's impact on society? programming skills? software selection and evaluation skills? As you plan your training program, you and your colleagues will need to decide exactly what to include in the in-service program.

   c. Where should the program be in five years? Plan a long-term program that reflects the ideal; then work backward, year by year. What you have for the first year is the starting point; the long-term plan will guide the development of the total program.

2. Who should receive the in-service training? You must be realistic here. It would be nice to include everyone in the first training session, but that is not always practical. Concentrate on those members of the faculty and administration who are most interested and could be most beneficial to the continuation of the program—teachers, school and district-level administrators, and decision makers. It might be wise to divide the in-service program into two elements: introductory sessions for both teachers and administrators, and intense hands-on work that focuses on the applications specific to each group (CAI for teachers and CMI for administrators, for example). Decisions about which teachers in which grades or departments are to receive the in-service training will depend largely on priorities and resource limitations. Selectively limiting computer use to specific departments and individuals may make better use of scarce resources, but care must be taken that the computers are not regarded as the domain or property of any one department. The first in-service

program may be most successful if it is limited to those who display a sincere interest in the school CAI program.

3. Who should do the instructing? There are several sources for instructors. A teacher who has taken a class and has a basic understanding of the microcomputer and its use in a CAI program could be an effective instructor. The media specialist or coordinator in your school may be qualified, but if this person is not interested, a teacher who could attend seminars, classes at the university, or conferences might become qualified to conduct the training.

The best source may be an outside consultant, perhaps someone from the state department of public instruction, a state college or university, or even a local organization. Select wisely and be sure of the person's qualifications, both in subject matter and in methods of conducting the in-service program. Nothing will be more deadly to your in-service program than someone who simply lectures rather than providing hands-on experience and other interesting and exciting methods for learning about concepts and applications.

One problem with outside consultants is that they are not members of the school staff and therefore lack a sense of commitment—they may conduct a session and then hurry away. Before leaving, however, these consultants should have trained one or two members of the staff well enough to carry on for them after each session and after the conclusion of the workshop.

4. Should participants learn to program the microcomputer? This critical question always arises in an in-service program. Its answer should be determined by the school's software policy: is the plan to purchase most of the needed software from commercial sources, or will teachers help develop and program materials in-house? It is critical that the in-service program teach software evaluation and selection skills; the amount of time devoted to programming skills, however, will depend on the overall objectives. Keep in mind, though, that most students will want to learn to program; some basic programming skills instruction may therefore be necessary so teachers will be able to assist their students at a basic level.

5. Should parents and other lay people be involved? If the PTA, civic groups, or business people have contributed financially to the microcomputer program, they must be included in the in-service training, if they are interested. Their interest and support can be long-term if they are involved from the beginning of the program. They may only attend one or two sessions, but the public relations value will be well worth the effort of inviting them.

6. What about the future? Even the best workshops will fail to answer everyone's needs or to take them as far as they want to go. At the onset of the program, plans should be made for the participants' future growth. They can follow up be reading current periodicals in the field and new textbooks and monographs; access one of the commercial data bases; arrange methods and procedures for additional in-service training by the state university or college (even district-paid, if possible); or attend a local or national convention.

The ultimate proof of the in-service program's success will be whether the teachers use the microcomputers in their classrooms. The value and effectiveness of microcomputers as tools to help change student behavior are in the hands of the teachers: if they are not willing to use microcomputers to educate students, the machines will sit in a corner and draw dust. Teachers must also use them themselves—for keeping grades, recording student data, preparing lesson plans, and so on. Often the use of a microcomputer as a tool to ease the classroom management load is the first step toward eventual classroom use.

FACILITY—LOCATION AND LAYOUT

For the great majority of our schools, the placement of the micros has evolved in haphazard fashion similar to the microcomputers' acquisition. In many cases the proposal for obtaining the microcomputers is presented in a bare-bones fashion so they can be purchased with funds from a parent-teacher organization, a civic club, a business establishment, or a local school administrator. Then the search begins for an old physics lab, a little-used classroom, a space in the media center or library, or any place secure enough to house the new microcomputer systems. The number of peripheral devices adds to the concern: plotters, joysticks, printers, larger monitors, and modems must be housed with, or at least near, the microcomputer, so room must also be found for these items. As the program grows and more equipment and software are acquired, the need for better facilities becomes apparent. Possible placement of the micros will differ widely from school to school, but a common set of factors will influence decisions about placement. Among these are the type and amount of equipment available; current long- and short-term instructional goals; the physical layout of the school; and constraints imposed by networking, available personnel, various uses of the micros (after-school hours, in-service, or community use, for example), and security or maintenance considerations.

The microcomputer program's long- and short-term instructional goals are so important in determining location that we will discuss three possible configurations for the placement and utilization of the micros. As we have discussed earlier, the main academic uses of microcomputers fall into three categories: CAI, the computer as a tool, and computer literacy training. Each one places its own requirements upon the placement and physical arrangement of the microcomputer facility.

Central Location

The common thread in most CAI programs in schools is the self-paced approach. As a result, students need cubicles where they can spend undisturbed time working with the microcomputers and appropriate software programs to master the subject being presented. These cubicles can be as small as four by four feet and have a shelf and counter space to hold the microcomputer system (microcomputer, monitor, disk drive) plus a work area to allow for leaving books open and doing pencil-and-paper exercises. The traditional student study carrel, with some slight modifications, such as a larger upper shelf and removal of the rear-project apparatus, works nicely. The single power switch module built into the student study carrel reduces wear and tear on the microcomputer power switch. The student should have a comfortable swivel chair, which facilitates movement from the work area to the microcomputer and back. The cubicles might be located in the school media center or library because it is a secure area and the mechanism for checking in and out has long since been established. Several possible arrangements of study carrels are illustrated in Figure 9.1.

The microcomputer system can also be set up on tables within the media center, although the individual study areas are more conducive to quiet, independent study. When two or three students need to work together at one station, the cubicle is, again, the most desirable arrangement. Figure 9.2 shows a possible placement of the microcomputers within the confines of the media center.

If there is not enough space within the media center or library to accommodate the cubicles, a classroom next to the media center or library should be converted into a microcomputer laboratory. If the wall between the media center and this new laboratory can be removed, enlarging the original space, management of the microcomputer laboratory will be possible with only one additional media center staff member—a microcomputer specialist. This arrangement will retain the management/storage/retrieval capabilities and availability of instructional materials common to the media center and will couple these functions with the new microcomputer capability. This administrative arrangement adds a totally new dimension to the capabilities of the media center. Figure 9.3 shows how a classroom might be incorporated into the media center or library.

Since each cubicle within the laboratory or media center will be drawing two to three amps of electricity, it is advisable to place them on an independent thirty-amp line. This will avoid spikes (changes in the electrical current coming to the cubicle), that can freeze up a microcomputer when any other piece of equipment or machinery starts up, often even in a location remote from the lab.

Teaching programming and conducting computer literacy instruction can be accommodated in the microcomputer laboratory with the addition of a dry marker board (used in preference to a chalkboard to eliminate the chalk dust), a wall screen at least seventy inches square in size (perhaps an overhead projector), and

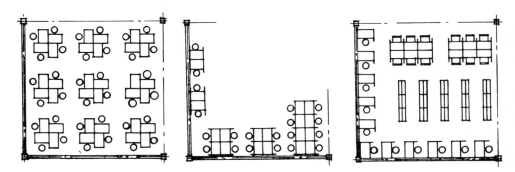

FIGURE 9.1 Arrangement for Study Carrels

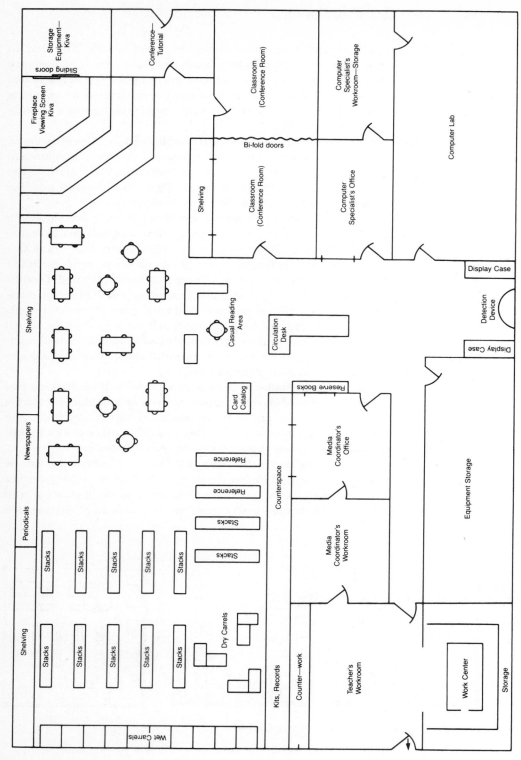

FIGURE 9.2 Placement of Microcomputers in Media Center or Library

296

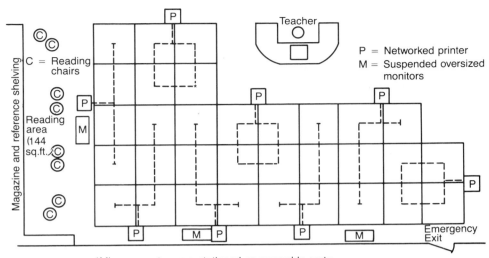

*Microcomputers are stationed on moveable carts
Dotted lines show networked printers (4 computers to 1 printer)
Microcomputer stations—32 stations ×16 sq. ft. per station (512 sq. ft.)

FIGURE 9.3 Incorporation of a Classroom Into a Media Center to Create a Microcomputer Laboratory

a teacher's instruction station—including a microcomputer, at least two twenty-five-inch color monitors, and a double disk drive. By scheduling the laboratory to avoid conflicts, this program can be maintained along with the independent study needs of the CAI program. It is advisable to have the teacher's station at the rear of the classroom so the students can swivel around for instruction and then turn back to the microcomputer in the cubicle for the hands-on portion of the class. It is extremely difficult to carry on instruction with the students looking over the tops of the cubicles.

If you can afford both the laboratory and an instructional classroom, this is even better. In this situation students are instructed in the classroom with the teacher's microcomputer system only; they then go to the laboratory for hands-on practice.

Location within the Classroom

For microcomputer use in a self-contained elementary classroom, the ideal situation would be one microcomputer, monitor, and disk drive for every one to three students. An effective program can, however, be carried on with a minimum of five microcomputer systems per classroom. In the self-contained classroom, scheduling can be controlled so students can do seat work between their scheduled times at the microcomputers.

The microcomputers should be located at the back or sides of the classroom so that those working on them will not disturb their classmates doing seat work, small group work, or individual reading. The computer literacy training can be carried on with the entire group; then students, on a scheduled basis, can go to the microcomputers for hands-on use. The CAI work can also be scheduled into specific time slots during the school day.

In the junior and senior high schools, where microcomputer use is totally integrated into the science, social studies, English, or mathematics curriculum, there will be a great demand for the computers. In such cases, five microcomputers located permanently in each classroom or department laboratory is an absolute minimum. The program should be designed to allow a maximum of three students per computer station at any one time.

The software that supports the microcomputer program should also be located within the classroom. It is not efficient use of resources, especially teacher time, to keep this specialized software in a central location such as the media center or library. Just as with textbooks, the program is best facilitated when the instructional materials that support the curriculum are right in the classroom. However, classroom storage and use will place a heavy burden on the teacher, who must see that care and caution in the utilization and storage of the diskettes and accompanying documentation are exercised.

Placement of the microcomputers in the individual classroom creates some special problems, one of which is the dust and dirt that tend to collect not only on the microcomputers but also on the disk drives and diskettes. The microcomputer system should not be located next to the chalkboard, nor should it, or the diskettes, be in direct sunlight. For this reason an overhead projector is recommended in preference to the chalkboard: exclusive use of an overhead projector greatly reduces the dust in the environment. Location in the individual classroom might also create security concerns, because a classroom is not as secure an area as a media center or library, for example. Some special security measures might be employed, such as a locked cabinet for the software and devices to lock the microcomputers, monitors, and disk drives to the carrel or tabletop. A microcomputer table can be purchased with detachable, locking hood that can be fastened in place when you are finished with the computer system but completely removed when the system is in operation. Figure 9.4 details a possible placement of the microcomputer system within a classroom.

In the preceding discussion we have detailed an ideal classroom situation. In many classes in the United States, however, the ratio is one microcomputer to one or two classrooms. In this situation the suggestions concerning group instruction and careful scheduling of student microcomputer time become even more important.

Some teachers use a rotating system wherein students are scheduled twenty-minute blocks of time on the microcomputer and then their names are moved to the end of the list. This system ensures that all students will have time on the microcomputer and that no one person will monopolize the time available. This plan can even assist in scheduling nonclass hours.

Portable Systems

There may be a time when all the microcomputers need to be available at once in one classroom or area. Some elementary school teachers and secondary math

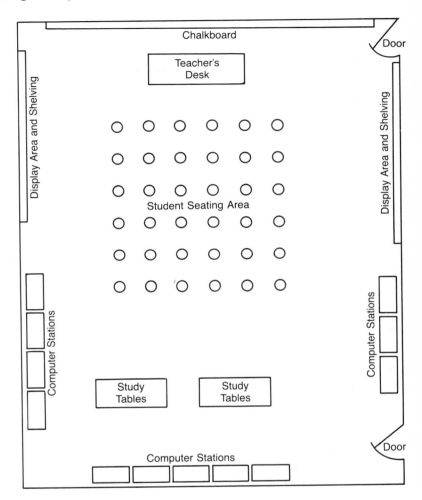

FIGURE 9.4   Classroom Placement of the Microcomputers

or science teachers may want to use the computers in units designed to introduce students to computers or in a CAI remedial or accelerated program; such units may run from one week of intense, daily use to several weeks involving use of the computers for only one period a week. Since several classes might be involved in this endeavor simultaneously, it would be helpful if the microcomputer systems were on portable carts, self-contained, with extension cords and cables to connect all peripheral devices. These carts need to be stable and strongly constructed so there is no danger of their tipping over or collapsing as they are moved from classroom to classroom. It is recommended that the microcomputer systems not be transported up or down flights of stairs—a stumble could result in damage to a complete system.

When microcomputer systems are placed on a portable cart, problems with security, particularly in regard to software, are increased. It is suggested that portable systems be locked up in one central location at the end of a school day and that the software be housed in a locking storage cart that accompanies the portable microcomputers; only those programs that are in use during any one period should be removed from the storage cart. The software programs in the storage cart can be arranged in a logical filing order (perhaps by Dewey decimal classification) so any single program can be located quickly and easily.

The use of portable systems for microcomputers and software will provide considerable flexibility for teachers throughout the building. The various constraints mentioned above are not insurmountable and should not rule out this procedure as a way to accomplish the goals of the program.

FACILITY ADMINISTRATION

Management of the various functions needed for a successful program is an important concern. In this section we will discuss access and time allocations, rules and regulations, and basic hardware and software needs.

Access and Time Allocations

Who will have access to the microcomputers? Students only, teachers only, both teachers and students, students in the computer literacy program only, students in the CAI program only, or anyone who has the time? The management pattern in American schools seems to be divided between allowing anyone to use the microcomputers—open access (except for scheduled periods)—and having an established procedure that limits access in some way (controlled access). Generally, schools new to computing and inner-city schools (with their special security concerns) have the most restrictions on access. As the faculty and students become more knowledgeable and comfortable with the computer facility and microcomputers, access is handled as it is in most media centers: availability is provided for the total school population, with an imposition of only those rules needed to maintain order and equipment and software security.

There is growing concern that the microcomputer facility is male territory exclusively. Many schools are experiencing a high percentage of female drop-out in computer literacy programs beyond the very basic introductory level. The problem is not so acute in the area of CAI, because both male and female students achieve success with drill-and-practice programs, tutorials, and such. A concerted effort should be made to include female students in the literacy program in programming classes and in management as student aides to help run the microcomputer laboratory. Many schools are succeeding in breaking down this male-territory image by developing a combined male-female orientation to the management and utilization of the microcomputers.

As the need for full-time use of the microcomputers for classroom activities eases, administrators may desire to make use of the computers to perform CMI functions such as managing pupil and personal records, keeping inventory, scheduling, and processing and managing the budget. Schools will need to develop clear, precise guidelines regarding student and teacher rights to their own files and limits on access to these files by others. Students are adept at breaking codes, so a different and uniquely protected computer system should be considered for records that require any degree of confidentiality. Teachers who use software packages and maintain their daily classroom rolls and records on diskettes must take precautions to protect these diskettes from student access.

Access to the microcomputers depends on the total number available, where they are located, the intent of the program, and the scheduling procedure followed in the school. In some schools computer access is allowed only during class, regardless of the kind of program involved; others allow computer use at times other than during the regular school day—perhaps one-half to one hour before and after school, and during all lunch periods. In other situations, schools provide free access only after school, since the microcomputers are used for classes during the day, including the lunch hour.

Some considerations that have proved helpful in developing access rules in school microcomputer programs follow.

1. Doing intense work on a microcomputer often requires much greater blocks of time than do most other educational tasks. Many students will desire to spend thirty minutes to two hours on CAI programs, especially drill-and-practice, tutorials, and simulation exercises. Programming activities may take up to three hours of sustained effort. If students are allowed to do instructional gaming, they can spend one to four hours at this activity, and word processing activities are notorious for the time they take.

2. If teachers are developing curriculum-related software, they will need to have one- to four-hour time blocks on the microcomputers. It is not uncommon for teachers to stay after school and even work on Saturday to keyboard their curricular material.

3. If the goals of the program dictate extended hours, who will staff the microcomputer facility? In the case of teacher use, those using the facility can be responsible when they are working alone; however, when students use the microcomputers, supervision will probably need to be provided. Many schools have been successful in supplementing the regular staff and teachers with community volunteers such as parents and retired citizens. In almost all schools with extended hours, reliance on students as computer room aides has been necessary. These students can be trained during the regular program and can not only provide supervision and assistance but also gain valuable work experience that may help them secure full-time employment after they graduate from high school. This experience also helps many students as they enter colleges and universities, especially in institutions of higher learning where there is a strong emphasis on computer utilization.

Rules and Regulations

Consideration must be given to some specific rules and regulations that will make the utilization of the microcomputer facility both fair to users and efficient in operation. These guidelines should provide procedures for administering the facility by addressing the following concerns:

1. Priority of usage. The question of who has first priority in using the microcomputers must be considered. This decision will depend on the goals of the program. All persons involved (students, teachers, administrators, parents, and lay citizens) must know exactly what the priorities are and why they were established. These should be discussed, formulated, and finally presented in written form so all patrons of the facility know what to expect. If the program was established for CAI only, for example, or strictly for student programming use, or for teacher and student use under certain conditions and at certain times, this needs to be detailed and a written policy issued so all users are treated as the policy dictates.

2. Length of time allowed at a station. The length of time allowed at the microcomputer is task-dependent; that is, it depends on the activity being conducted. Some tasks take more time at the computer than others, and it may take some experimentation to determine just how much time should be allowed for each type of activity. Once some idea of the needed time has been obtained, specific time limits should be assigned for specific tasks. Most schools do not have enough machines to allow students unlimited time on the micros. Many have completely eliminated game playing during regular school hours, relegating this activity to special after-school hours or very low demand time (if there are such times). In some schools the time allocation is controlled by the use of a pass from the teacher detailing what the student is to work on, how much time is allowed, what she must accomplish, and so on. In others the students must come to the microcomputer facility as a group. The pattern varies from school to school and is generally dictated by the overall goals and needs of the program. It is important, however, that a policy is established, that all patrons know the details of the policy, and that enforcement of the policy is uniform—no special favors should be granted.

3. Number of students per station. As part of the policy statement governing the use of the facility, there should be a statement concerning how many persons are allowed at any one station, since this can affect the noise level in the facility and the general atmosphere of the room. The noise level is difficult to control because the very nature of some microcomputer activity calls for high levels of student interaction and discussion, sharing ideas, or asking for help. This is especially true when students are learning to program using either BASIC or Logo. The quality of the exercises can deteriorate when a group of five or six students crowd around a station and all want to get in on the activity. It is recommended that no more than three students be permitted at a station at any one time. This number allows for interaction, idea sharing, and problem solving without the noise and confusion that a larger number of students can generate.

4. Maintenance of order. Established rules of order and conduct for the microcomputer facility are critical to its operation. These rules should be formulated in consultation with students, teachers, and administrators. An excellent

source would be a committee of representatives from these three groups plus a parent from the school's parent-teacher organization. Once the rules have been articulated and approved by the student council, the teachers, and the administrators, they should be written up, distributed to the student body and teachers, and prominently displayed in the microcomputer facility. This may seem like a lot of work; however, if all students, teachers, and administrators, plus the PTA, are involved in the formulation of the rules, enforcement is generally simplified because all feel responsible for the policy and thus tend to adhere to their own rules and regulations. Some items that could be included in this policy statement follow.

a. No food or drink allowed in the facility.
b. No loitering—microcomputers may be limited in number, so unnecessary time at the keyboard should be minimized.
c. No loud talking, shouting, pushing, or shoving—all of which disturb others and might result in damaged computers and peripherals or injured students.
d. Each student must have a legitimate reason for being in a facility, such as a pass from a teacher, counselor, or administrator (conduct could be controlled by asking the student to surrender his ID card, with misconduct resulting in the card being kept and disciplinary action instigated).
e. A statement of the policy governing payment of fees for such items as word processing paper, data diskettes, and networking costs.
f. A statement of the policy governing the copying of software. No pirating of software should be allowed, and anyone violating this policy should be permanently excluded from the use of the microcomputers and laboratory facilities and possibly subject to disciplinary or legal action.

Basic Information Needed in the Facility

Within the microcomputer facility there needs to be a detailed set of instructions on how to use the microcomputer systems and the facilities. This can be presented either as data sheets in a loose-leaf notebook or as posters displayed on bulletin boards. Although this information will be presented in the in-service or literacy training program, the reminder in the notebook or on a poster will help reduce the amount of individualized instruction the staff will need to provide within the microcomputer facility. Some suggested items to include in the instructions follow.

Microcomputer

1. How to turn on and off; proper use of either study carrel or microcomputer switch.
2. How to handle diskettes or cassettes properly.
3. How to boot up the disk operating system.
4. How to initialize a data diskette.
5. How to access a particular program.
6. What to do when the microcomputer malfunctions.
7. Log-on procedures for time-sharing or networking.

8. How to secure the microcomputer when finished: lid or cover over the computer to protect it from dust and dirt, security process, unplugging power cords, and so on.
9. Any idiosyncrasies.

Monitors

1. How to turn on and off (it should be noted if microcomputer is attached to carrel plug or surge control device and left in the "on" position, so students won't use the monitor on/off switch).
2. How to adjust the color, contrast, vertical and horizontal functions.
3. How to plug into the microcomputer in case the plug is inadvertently loosened or unplugged.
4. Procedure for changing from a color to a black-and-white monitor if the student is doing work that is better facilitated without color (word processing or programming, for example).

Peripheral Devices

1. Printer
   a. How to turn on and off.
   b. How to load paper into the printer.
   c. How to activate the printer—getting data from the microcomputer to the printer.
   d. How to secure the printer when finished—covering, handling paper, security concerns, and so forth.
   e. Any idiosyncrasies.
2. Modems
   a. How to activate the modem.
   b. How to activate the microcomputer.
   c. How to perform the log-on procedure
   d. How to conduct proper log-off procedure, including how to hang up properly.
   e. Accounting procedures (if needed).
   f. Any idiosyncrasies.
3. Other peripherals (e.g., joysticks, graphic tablets, mouse, light pen, optical mark reader, CD-ROM, laser disk drive, PC projector)
   a. How to attach these items to the microcomputer.
   b. How to utilize these devices (e.g., use of mouse to pick up menu items).
   c. Special handling procedures (e.g., how to move the arm on the graphics tablet, move the joystick handle and fire button, maneuver the mouse and use the buttons, how to activate the CD-ROM).
   d. Any idiosyncrasies.

In addition to instructions on how to use the microcomputer system, the facility should contain several additional items to assist users.

All the manuals that accompanied the microcomputer system—those for the microcomputer, the disk drive, the monitor, and any peripheral devices—should be catalogued, provided with a catalog card and pocket, and placed in a book rack within the facility, to be checked out just as any library book. It is critical that the check-out procedure be followed because manuals have a way of disappearing—especially when they are most needed. In most microcomputer facilities, manuals are restricted to use *only* within the facility.

The facility's software should also be catalogued, and a card catalog, accession file, or some other system of listing the materials must be provided for the patrons. If a card file system is used, the software programs could also be listed in the media center or library card catalog. In filing the software programs, it is important to file the diskette or cassette and its accompanying documentation together as a set: with many programs the diskette cannot be used, or is difficult to use, without the documentation.

Information about new software or hardware purchases, or any changes in either, should be provided for all students, teachers, and administrators. Among the several avenues for disseminating the information are a bulletin board within the facility, newsletters to teachers and administrators, or an announcement over the school's public address system along with the daily news. The microcomputer center can provide a special service to students, teachers, and administrators by having available a selection of current periodicals, newsletters, and books. There is considerable debate as to whether these materials should be placed in the microcomputer facility or in the media center or library. If the microcomputer facility is a part of the media center, the debate, of course, is moot. If, however, there is a separate microcomputer lab, the materials are most often housed in the lab. The location may not really matter, however; what is important is that a good selection is provided for the patrons' use.

One final matter, which will help the management and general atmosphere of the facility, concerns the procedures for cleaning up and putting items in their proper place when a patron has finished. Most staff members and volunteer aides in the facility do not have the time (nor should they) to tidy up the desks and study carrels, push chairs back in place, replace diskettes in file drawers, match diskettes with correct documentation, replace specialized peripheral devices, or perform a variety of other housekeeping tasks. These necessary responsibilities must be stressed during the in-service or initial training program and should be enumerated on a poster and displayed in the facility.

AMORTIZATION SCHEDULE

In developing the microcomputer program and securing and expending monies to purchase equipment and software and to maintain the program, a budget package must be prepared that covers system and software replacement and equipment repair costs. These maintenance costs must be included as a regular line item in the yearly school budget.

Maintenance costs, equipment repair, and the costs for cleaning, spare parts, extra cables, and expendable items should be budgeted at 8 to 10 percent per year of the original equipment costs. For example, a microcomputer system that

cost $3,000 initially should be budgeted at $240 to $300 annually for mainte-
nance. If funds are left at the end of the school year, these can either be carried
over to the next fiscal year or used to purchase supplies. Most service contracts
provided by microcomputer stores or service centers are based on this 8 to 10
percent per year figure.

When a service agreement is written, it generally covers all maintenance and
repair costs. The major problem with a service contract is that usually the microcomputer system must be delivered to the service center. Maintenance and repair
service can keep the system from your school for two to ten days.

An amortization schedule should be a major part of any school maintenance
budget. The microcomputer systems will eventually wear out or become obsolete
because of new technologies, so a schedule of replacement, based on a four- to
six-year cycle, must be prepared. Because most systems have not been in operation for four years, there are no studies or cost procedures to substantiate this
schedule. However, most microcomputer specialists feel that a system will need
to be replaced during the sixth year (maximum) of its use.

A maintenance budget is extremely important for the microcomputer program;
otherwise several machines could be out of service at the same time during the
school year. For most microcomputer programs, the loss of even one microcomputer system severely hampers the program's overall effectiveness.

SECURITY

One final area of administration and management of microcomputer systems in a
laboratory, media center, or classroom environment is the issue of security—of
both the hardware and software and the information stored on the microcomputer.

It is mandatory that the computer facility be locked when it is not in operation,
and when it is open it should never be left unattended. Software programs, peripheral devices, manuals, data diskettes, and the computers, disk drives, and
monitors are all highly valued and desired items. Unattended areas provide temp-
tations for people to help themselves to these items. As we have suggested earlier
in this chapter, machines can be bolted to the desk, diskettes and manuals stored
in lockable cabinets, and books, periodicals, and newsletters checked out using a
proven system. In general, security problems are eliminated by providing supervision (by adults or reliable students) and procedures and practices to be followed
by a security conscious staff, student body, and administration.

Data security is a different issue because it may involve different motives than
acquisition of equipment or software for personal use or financial gain. Breaking
through a data security system to steal or change information or to steal computer
time is seen by some computer users as an intellectual challenge. Procedures
must be developed to protect student records, log-on procedures, and access to
sensitive materials. Security can be improved by being conscious of the problem
and not leaving diskettes in unlocked drawers, disk drives, or other places where
they can be accessed by unauthorized persons.

STAFFING THE MICROCOMPUTER PROGRAM

Staffing patterns for a school's microcomputer program will depend on the program goals and objectives. If the program is a beginning one, the microcomputers may be housed in individual classrooms and controlled by the individual teacher. If the program is departmentalized and the microcomputers are housed in various departments, a department chairperson will be responsible for the program. And if the equipment is housed in the media center or a special microcomputer facility, responsibility will be assumed by a microcomputer specialist. In some circumstances, however, a combination of the above situations might exist. Regardless of the arrangement, the supervisory personnel must possess some basic competencies and provide some basic services for the program to succeed. We will discuss these services and competencies at three levels: the individual classroom, the department, and the microcomputer laboratory.

Individual Classroom

A teacher who will be using a microcomputer system in his classroom must possess some minimum competencies, including basic knowledge of:

1. procedures for the selection and evaluation of software programs;
2. sources of software programs in various subject areas;
3. how to incorporate CAI into the classroom environment and curriculum;
4. how to set up and provide basic maintenance for the microcomputer system, including the microcomputer, disk drive(s), monitor, interface boards, and any peripheral devices used;
5. standards for the selection and purchase of the microcomputer system;
6. how to initialize a diskette;
7. how to boot up the disk operating system;
8. how the microcomputer handles data;
9. programming skills (if basic programming is part of the curriculum)—perhaps Logo for kindergarten through fourth grade, introductory BASIC programming for fifth through ninth grade, and Pascal for ninth through twelfth grade;
10. how peripheral devices (e.g., graphics tablet, touch screen, mouse, joystick) work and how to make use of them in the curriculum;
11. sources of networks and bulletin boards and how to use a modem to access these data bases;
12. how to utilize CMI for roll keeping, test score maintenance, and use of the microcomputer system for generating reports to be used by students, parents, and administrators;
13. how to do word processing and use a printer (if the curriculum involves creative writing, theme paper production, and the generation of reports);
14. the latest sources of information in the field—titles of periodicals, newsletters, and text materials in the microcomputer area and an active reading program to keep abreast of the latest developments;

15. the various sources of funding for the procurement of the microcomputer system, software, and furniture; and
16. how to set up and manage classroom facilities for microcomputer use, including access and time allocations, rules and regulations, and security.

Department

When the microcomputers are housed in a department, the person in charge will need to have the same competencies listed above for classroom teachers; she might also have to assume the following duties:

1. Be responsible for maintaining and administering the program at the department level.
2. Be the microcomputer literacy teacher for the program, responsible for teaching the various courses in the curriculum.
3. Be responsible for some of the in-service training of the school's teachers and administrators.
4. Produce a newsletter, weekly bulletin board, or other vehicle for keeping faculty members apprised of new software titles, changes in scheduling, and so forth.
5. Develop procedures for securing, previewing, evaluating, and purchasing software.

Media Center or Library—Microcomputer Laboratory

A fully integrated microcomputer program that is part of the media center provides students and teachers with a rich environment composed of not only the microcomputer hardware and software but also the total resources of the center, including research and study materials in all instructional formats—printed materials, filmstrips, pictures, slides, audio and video tapes, and microcomputer software. The fully integrated program will necessitate the addition of a microcomputer specialist, a technician (if the budget can accommodate this person), and some aides to the media center or library staff.

Within a fully integrated program, the pattern of staff organization and responsibilities will result in assignments that provide services to teachers, students, and administrators. The media coordinator and microcomputer specialist will work with teachers by:

1. Assisting in the selection and planning of educational experiences for students.
2. Keeping teachers informed about the latest instructional materials and media equipment (including microcomputer systems) available.
3. Participating as a team on curriculum committees, study groups, seminars, and panels at various grade levels, subject areas, and departmental levels.
4. Providing in-service programs in proper selection and use of all instructional materials, with special emphasis on microcomputer and other new technologies.

5. Providing interested teachers and administrators with information about the instructional technology field, especially microcomputer and new technologies, gleaned from reading current literature.
6. Identifying and applying suitable criteria for the evaluation of all types of instructional materials, including microcomputer software and media and microcomputer hardware.
7. Assisting in application for research projects conducted by teachers and administrators, analysis of data collected during the project, and final evaluation of results and findings.

Technicians and aides, under the direction of the media coordinator and the microcomputer specialist, will provide the following services:

1. Produce instructional materials and microcomputer programs, doing the production and keyboarding (the program components and design will be produced by the specialist).
2. Assist where needed in arranging classroom, media center, or microcomputer laboratory displays, exhibits, and bulletin boards.
3. Assist in designing and illustrating promotional items and publications for the school, a grade, a department, or a subject area.
4. Provide bibliographic searches and assistance in locating instructional materials, including microcomputer software and all aspects of information and materials processing needed to supplement the curriculum.
5. Do minor repairs and maintenance (under the guidance of the specialist) on all equipment used by teachers and students.
6. Prepare instructional materials (under the guidance of the specialist) used by teachers and students, including producing backup copies of software programs, initializing diskettes, and making copies of documentation (and possibly also recording audiotapes, doing photographic and darkroom work, and producing transparencies).
7. Assist in the operation of microcomputer systems and audio and video equipment for classroom or individualized purposes, as requested by teachers and students.
8. Secure and schedule the use of microcomputers, peripheral devices, instructional materials in all formats, and media equipment requested by teachers for both classroom and individualized purposes.
9. Prepare and distribute to teachers and administrators, for their ordering or information purposes, catalogs, brochures, newsletters, and announcements of microcomputer software, hardware, and peripherals, and inform them about other instructional materials, equipment, and services available in the media center or microcomputer laboratory.
10. Assist in the maintenance of the facility's physical environment in a manner that encourages and facilitates its use, including proper shelving and storing of instructional materials; cleanliness and order of study carrels, microcomputer areas, and word processing areas; and the arrangement of all other study areas.

TECHNOLOGY SPECIALIST LICENSE
MEDIA/MICROCOMPUTER CENTER

has completed the required course of training,
has demonstrated proficiency in operation of initial equipment, and shows
a satisfactory understanding of classroom learning conditions.

CALUTE HIGH SCHOOL DISTRICT

FIGURE 9.5   Certificate & ID Card

When students, parents, and lay citizens are used as volunteer aides, the in-service program must be comprehensive and thorough. These volunteers will perform a valuable service in direct proportion to the degree and quality of their training. It is recommended that they be carefully and precisely trained in all aspects of the functions they are to perform and the tasks for which they will be responsible. This training may take several weeks; however, once there is a cadre of trained people, they in turn can assist in training new volunteers entering the program.

Many media coordinators and microcomputer specialists present their volunteer aides with a certificate and identification card upon completion of the in-service training (see Figure 9.5), which identify the person as a special individual who is performing an extremely valuable service for the school. Most aides hold these items in high regard and are proud to be a part of the microcomputer team.

SUMMARY

A report on the availability of computers in schools throughout America indicates that purchases have skyrocketed over the past several years. Not only are large urban schools purchasing computer systems, but others such as small rural or medium-sized inner-city schools are also. This increase in acquisition necessitates the development of an orderly, systematic approach to planning if the schools are to realize the maximum benefit from each dollar spent. Once the resources have been acquired, a further effort is necessary to develop efficient procedures for maintaining and utilizing both hardware and software.

In this chapter we outline systematic methods for obtaining funds and support for a microcomputer program, for acquiring hardware and software, and for establishing and operating a microcomputer facility. Specifically, funding sources are identified, including those from internal sources such as schools and districts, and from

external sources including businesses and others. Federal money is also available, but grant proposals must be written to obtain these funds. Suggestions for writing a proposal are included in this chapter.

An in-service program is described that will not only provide teachers and administrators with computer-related skills but will also recruit advocates and supporters for the larger computer-based instructional program.

The necessity of managing microcomputers so they are maximally available to those who wish to use them is emphasized. The availability of equipment and software for use by teachers, students, and administrators will directly determine whether the resources are used or are left to collect dust.

Three trends in microcomputer assignment are identified. Commonly, they are assigned to a specified classroom, which tends to diminish access to some extent. Often a department is given responsibility for the microcomputers (many times the math department). Finally, a special room is sometimes set aside as the computer center; this room might serve as a general resource center in which print and nonprint materials are housed along with the computers.

The problem of who should have access to the computers is also addressed. A routine should be established to ensure that girls have equal access with boys. Also, patrons, teachers, and others who have an interest in the program should be accommodated. In conjunction with the access issue, we emphasize the importance of establishing and publicizing appropriate rules and regulations. Security concerns are also identified.

In the final section of this chapter job descriptions for those who will be involved in running the program—the specialist, technician, and aide—are developed.

SELF-TEST

1. Discuss the logic behind a centralized approach to acquiring a microcomputer system.
2. Discuss the advantages of the individual school approach over the centralized approach when acquiring a microcomputer system.
3. Detail how the enactment of the Educational Consolidation and Improvement Act of 1981 brought about changes in sources for public funding of educational projects.
4. Discuss how you might secure public funds to build a microcomputer system.
5. Detail ways you might secure private funds to build a microcomputer system.
6. Parents and civic groups can provide some funding for building a microcomputer system or securing software. Discuss ways you might secure this funding.
7. Discuss ways you might enhance public relations and secure positive advertising when thanking groups for their financial support of your microcomputer program.
8. Discuss in detail some points that are worth considering in the preparation and administration of a microcomputer in-service program.
9. Discuss in detail the reasons for and components that constitute a centrally located microcomputer facility.
10. Discuss the advantages and disadvantages of the microcomputer facility as part of the library/media center or as a separate facility.
11. Discuss some reasons why and how microcomputers can be effectively used in an individualized classroom.
12. Where should the microcomputers be placed in an individual classroom? Include in your discussion the reasons for such a placement.
13. What are some considerations that have proved helpful in developing access rules for the school microcomputer program?
14. Consideration must be given to some specific rules and regulations to make use of the microcomputer facility efficient and fair in operation; detail some of these rules and regulations.
15. Within the microcomputer facility there must be detailed sets of instructions on how to use the facilities. Discuss the needed instructions for the following:
    a. microcomputers
    b. monitors
    c. peripheral devices.
16. Discuss the minimum competencies needed by a classroom teacher to effectively utilize a microcomputer system.
17. Detail the additional competencies needed by the person in charge of a department microcomputer program.
18. Discuss how the media coordinator and microcomputer specialist will work with teachers.
19. Discuss the services that might be provided to faculty, staff, and students by technicians and aides.

REFERENCES

Balajthy, E. *Computers and Reading: Lessons from the Past and the Technologies of the Future.* Englewood Cliffs, N.J.: Prentice-Hall, 1989.

Barbour, A. "Computer Coordinator Survey." *Electronic Learning* (February 1986): 35–38.

Barbour, A. "Office Romance—Why Administrators Are Hooked on Technology." *Electronic Learning* (April 1987): 18–23.

Beatty, L. *Instructional Media Centers.* Englewood Cliffs, N.J.: Education Technology Publications, 1981.

Bitter, G. and R. Camuse. *Using a Microcomputer in the Classroom,* 2d ed. Englewood Cliffs, N.J.: Prentice-Hall, 1988.

Clements, D. *Computers in Elementary Mathematics Education.* Englewood Cliffs, N.J.: Prentice-Hall, 1989.

Collis, B. *Computers, Curriculum, and Whole-Class Instruction: Issues and Ideas.* Belmont, Calif.: Wadsworth Publishing Co., 1988.

Conkle, B. "An Innovative Funding Scheme Has Schools Going Dutch in Kentucky." *Electronic Learning* (January/February 1989): 19.

Dixon, S. "How to Organize an Efficient, Smooth-running Computer Room." *Electronic Learning* (December 1983): 64–65, 83.

Edwards, M. "Business-School Partnership." *Electronic Learning* (March 1986): 28–32.

Holloway, M. "Automating the Media Center." *Technology Horizons in Education Journal* (September 1988): 95–99.

Long, C. "Four Ways to Increase Your Community's Financial Support." *Electronic Learning* (March 1985): 39–41.

Lucas, H., Jr. *Managing Information Services.* New York: Macmillan Publishing Co., 1989.

McGinty, T. "Growing Pains: A Portrait of Our Emerging Profession." *Electronic Learning* (February 1987): 18–23.

Nickles, H., and G. Culp. *The Practical Apple: A Guide for Educators.* Pacific Grove, Calif.: Brooks/Cole Publishing Company, 1988.

Olds, H., Jr. "Teacher vs. Students: In Whose Hands Should We Put the Computers?" *Classroom Computer Learning* (April 1989): 33–42.

Olivas, J. "Yes, You Can Run the Front Office on a Microcomputer." *Classroom Computer Learning* (March 1988): 46–49.

Overfield, K. "Training for the Trainer." *Technological Horizons in Education Journal* (June 1989): 50–56.

Pelfrey, R. "How To Sell a School Board by Really Trying." *Electronic Learning* (February 1988): 16.

Prostano, E., and J. Prostano. *The School Library Media Center,* 3d ed. Littleton, Colo: Libraries Unlimited, Inc., 1983.

Roberts, N., et al. *Integrating Computers into the Elementary and Middle School.* Englewood Cliffs, N.J.: Prentice-Hall, 1988.

Salpeter, J. "Inservice Training: Help From Publishers?" *Classroom Computer Learning* (February 1989): 20–24.

Soloman, G. "The Role of the Federal Government in Educational Technology." *Electronic Learning* (October 1988): 46–49.

Swartz, T. "Finding Funding for Your Computer Project." *Classroom Computer Learning* (March 1984): 36–41.

Taffee, S., ed. *Computers in Education,* 3d ed. Guilford, Conn: Dushkin Publishing Group, Inc., 1988.

Troutman, A., and J. White. *The Micro Goes to School: Instructional Applications of Micro Computer Technology.* Belmont, Calif: Brooks/Cole Publishing Co., 1988.

White, C., and G. Hubbard. *Computers and Education.* New York: Macmillan Publishing Co., 1988.

Zellner, R., et al. *Technology in Education: Implications and Applications.* College Station, Tex.: Instructional Research Laboratory, 1987.

CHAPTER 10

Problems and Promises

CHAPTER TOPICS

☐ Some beneficial contributions of computers to society
☐ The varieties of computer crime:
    The theft of money and goods
    The theft of information
    The piracy of software
☐ Ways to combat computer crime
☐ The issues of privacy in the electronic age
☐ Computer viruses
☐ Computer equity problems
☐ Steps to ensure equitable access to computer technology
☐ Computers in the workplace
☐ The future: software and hardware, applications, and educational computing
☐ Teaching about issues

A unique array of ethical problems has appeared with the introduction of computers and related technology into the society. Merely teaching about the mechanics of computers is not enough; the moral implications involved must also be addressed.

Because of the complexity and uniqueness of the problems spawned by new technologies, people are experiencing considerable difficulty as they try to cope with them. The apparently benign nature of many of the issues has caused a number of lawmakers to underestimate the seriousness of the situation. Typically, computer crimes involve no violence. Privacy issues have always been difficult to address, and computer viruses are unlike anything we have experienced before. But increasingly, steps are being taken to solve these and other computer-related problems.

Virtually every child will attend public or private schools, and it is here that the informed teacher can begin to make an impact. But in order to teach students about issues of ethics in a world of computers, educators themselves must understand what these are. Many issues affect students directly; others will have their impact as young people graduate and move into the work force. At the school level students are confronted with the ethical issue of software piracy, and those who are proficient with telecomputing routines must deal with the concern of privacy. There is also the problem of equity—who benefits from the technology and who is cut out. Later, students as workers might lose their jobs to computer-controlled robots, have their private records searched, or read that a confidential government data base has been penetrated by foreign agents. Students may themselves get caught up in various aspects of computer crime. Though most would never commit a robbery at gunpoint, the impersonal quality of computer crime makes an equivalent electronic holdup seem much less immoral. To gain a sense of the extent and variety of computer-related issues it is only necessary to browse through the daily paper. Figure 10.1 shows a representative selection of articles that were published in an urban newspaper over a short period of time. Although some experts would argue the point, many see the implications as being so serious and far-reaching that, unless they are addressed at all levels, the future of our open society could be in jeopardy.

As bleak as all this seems, it represents but one side of the picture. Every innovation brings with it promises along with problems, and the computer is no exception. The positive contributions of the computer revolution, like those of the industrial revolution before it, greatly outweigh the negative ones and promise a better life for all. The transition from an agrarian to an industrialized society was not very smooth, however. Because many of the problems were not dealt with directly and systematically, havoc often resulted as people tried to find solutions as best they could.

The industrial revolution came about as society found ways to supplement and replace muscle power with machines. Vast smokestack industries evolved, and with them came a dramatic change in the way people lived and worked. Christopher Evans, in *The Micro Millennium,* describes the power of the movement as follows: "once the process of the Revolution was fully underway, its dynamic growth was remorseless, and no power, no man nor combination of men, could set it back against its course."

FIGURE 10.1 Newspaper Articles on Computer-Related Issues

The transition to a high-technology information society has been made inevitable by the development of highly capable computers. Whereas the industrial society was characterized by the amplification of muscle power by machines, the high-technology information society will see computers amplifying the powers of the brain.

As with the industrial revolution, this new revolution will radically alter society. It will, in Christopher Evans' words, "have an overwhelming and comprehensive impact affecting every human being on earth in every aspect of his or her life." And, again as with the industrial revolution, there will be no way to stop or reverse its course. However, there is a significant difference between the earlier revolution and the present one: having survived one hectic transition, we are in a unique position to control and direct the current one.

Past experience dictates that we make an effort to identify and deal with problems as they evolve, rather than hoping they will resolve themselves. The problems associated with the transition to a high-technology information society are not really new—they consist of moral and ethical issues of a perennial nature made unique by the new context. As a society we should begin to develop an awareness and sensitivity to these problems, and the schools can play a major part in this. By familiarizing themselves with what is taking place, teachers will be better able to encourage the open discussion of issues in their classes. Open dialogue is a traditional and effective technique for dealing with philosophical and moral issues, and it is appropriate for computer-related concerns. The following information is presented in the hope that it will serve as the catalyst to encourage issue-related classroom activities.

OVERVIEW

Before moving on to the discussion of issues, let us review a few of the many benefits that have resulted from the introduction of the computer and related technologies.

Computers are routinely used by hospitals as monitoring and diagnostic devices. Many more victims would have died from accidentally ingested poisons were it not for the Computerized Clinical Information System now in place in many hospitals. With this system, toxicologists are able to match poisons and antidotes in less than five seconds. The recent advances in genetic engineering would have been impossible without computers, which recently enabled scientists to create a "photograph" of a DNA molecule, enlarging it one million times. While some computers permit microscopic worlds to be enlarged, others encourage miniaturization. An example is a tiny pacemaker, small enough to fit within a spoon yet as powerful as a microcomputer, which is now keeping troubled hearts beating at a normal pace.

A computer database designed by the Veterans of the Vietnam War enables veterans to locate comrades with whom they have lost contact even if no information other than a nickname or military unit is available. In Argentina a database is being compiled that will enable young victims of the repressive regime of the late 1960s and early 1970s to determine their true identities. During this period, many children were kidnapped or lost their parents; they were subsequently adopted by others, often illegally. The database contains genetic information obtained from relatives, which has proved to be highly effective in matching children to families. Thanks to the computer, many lost children are finding their way home.

Dairy farmers can improve their herds using a computer program designed to determine the best match between available cows and bulls. For example, the computer will pair a cow having a specific defect with a bull who possesses characteristics that offset the unwanted feature. Farmers as a group use computers to balance their improved production capabilities with such market variables as demand and operating costs.

Law enforcement agencies use computers to match an unidentified fingerprint with those on file in a massive, electronic repository. Formerly, agents were forced to search laboriously through the stored prints in an effort to come up with a match, a task that might take months to carry out. In contrast, the computer-based system works so rapidly and efficiently that identification is generally made within minutes.

The striking artistic effects we enjoy on television and in the movies are products of the computer artist's electronic palette. Another approach involves the production of actual oil paintings on canvas using a computer that scans the original illustration and directs a movable jet printer to spray dots of the proper color onto the canvas. In a different kind of studio, the electronic-age musician creates music and special sound effects using the computer.

Computers are now able to translate English from Japanese, a boon to tourists who are not bilingual. Modern automobiles would not run without their on-board computers, and their improved gas mileage is a byproduct of electronics that balance the air and fuel mixture with such factors as engine speed and temperature. And the space program would be nothing more than science fiction had the computer not been available.

Examples such as these point to the marvels that are possible in the computer age. All is not entirely rosy, however; along with the good comes the bad—promises and problems. Thus, while the ubiquitous computer presents society with a promise of Utopia, it simultaneously introduces the threat of Big Brother.

Commissions have been appointed, laws have been framed, and dialogue is ongoing, but solutions to the concerns spawned by the wholesale integration of computers into society are difficult to come by. No one seems to know exactly what to do about the theft of information, for example. Although the commodity is stolen, it hasn't been physically removed—it remains in the data bank where it was initially. And what should be done about *hackers*? Although this term formerly was used to describe someone who was hooked on computers, it now has a negative connotation and refers to those electronic interlopers who enter data bases illegally. When a burglar enters a home and wanders about, the statutes are quite clear concerning his punishment. What is the difference between this kind of trespass and a hacker breaking into a large data base filled with private records? Again, what steps should be taken to ensure that equal access to computers is enjoyed by all? Is the answer to be found in the allocation of equal blocks of time to every individual? Could such a cumbersome system actually work, and is it really necessary?

The complexion of the work force and the nature of the workplace will never again be the same thanks to the introduction of computer-controlled robots. What will be the short- and long-term impact of such technology from a humanistic perspective? What steps can be taken to make the transition less painful?

Finally, what of the fifth generation "thinking"computers? Not only do they promise to alter the manner in which humans perceive themselves, but they threaten to alter the way people actually think and to change the definition of intelligence itself. This may seem a bit farfetched, but before deciding whether any credence should be given to it, let us examine the evidence in greater detail.

COMPUTER CRIME

Computer-related crimes range from acts that might be construed as pranks to international espionage in which the security of nations is put at risk. In San Diego a group of high school students gained access to the school's computer system via their home computers and, once inside, raised havoc with everything from grades to student records. Some records were destroyed, others altered. Grades were changed and some were simply obliterated. What should be done under such circumstances? The school viewed the act as the equivalent of a physical break-in and suspended those involved until the case could be examined in depth.

At the other end of the spectrum is the case of Soviet scientists who apparently succeeded in breaking into two large computer systems in the West from their base in Central Europe. This incident and other related ones have led to the fear that the U.S. Defense Department computers, with their massive store of top secret data, are vulnerable to such penetrations.

Theft of Money and Goods

Most crimes committed with the aid of computers are not detected immediately. The various reasons for this state of affairs are all based on the uniqueness of the technology. When a gang of thieves tunnels into a bank and empties the vault over the weekend, the crime is discovered on Monday morning when the employees open the vault. When computer thieves rob a bank, however, the crime may not be detected for months or even years. The fact that data—which can represent personal files, defense secrets, or even money—is stored in a relatively inaccessible fashion makes it possible for individuals to effect modifications in the information that are quite difficult to detect. An auditor is able to thumb through the corporation's books or count the cash and checks, but accessing the data in computer storage is a more formidable task.

Most people who operate computers know little about the inner workings of the machines and accept the output on faith, but experts are able to manipulate programs with relative ease and are therefore able to commit a variety of dishonest acts if they are inclined to do so. Such individuals are able to survive audit after audit because most auditors simply rely on a printout for their information, and the printout is merely a product of the manipulated program.

The amount of money stolen each year by "keyboard bandits" is highly speculative, but the figures range somewhere between $3 billion and $5 billion, depending on which reports are being quoted. One reason for this discrepancy is that many computer crimes go undetected for varying periods of time, and some are never discovered. Also, victims of such crimes are often reluctant to report them for one reason or another. Indeed, it is not uncommon for the victim to hire the perpetrator in order to profit from his expertise—a person who is clever enough to execute a complex computer crime is most likely knowledgeable enough to assist in devising safeguards that will protect the system from similar crimes in the future (Figure 10.2).

Numerous cases of fraud against the federal government are uncovered each month. Reports indicate that fully one-half of the fraud cases are found accidentally, whereas only about one-fourth are discovered through the use of built-in system controls. Such findings lead to the conclusion that innumerable computer crimes simply go undetected. Most of the reported thefts were committed by people who were less than affluent but had the necessary expertise to use the computer in an illegal fashion. In most cases nonqualifying parties obtained some type of federal benefit through the manipulation of records.

The list of computer crimes is virtually without end and includes all kinds of clever and ingenious schemes. An attempted domestic crime that would have come close to setting a record involved a bank employee and several others in a scheme to steal millions of dollars from the First National Bank of Chicago using a complex series of computerized cash transfers. The final repository for the

FIGURE 10.2

money was to have been a bank in Vienna, where accounts had been prepared in advance by those involved. The crime was made possible by the manner in which money is transferred from one account to another by computer. By obtaining the essential computer codes and establishing a network of bank accounts, unscrupulous individuals would be able to transfer money into an international bank where it would be available for their personal use. Fortunately, efficient operating procedures and controls enabled the bank to discover the plot in time and thwart what would have been one of the all-time largest computer thefts.

Crimes of this type, while having a serious impact on large companies, are particularly difficult for small businesses to survive. The Small Business Computer Security Education and Advisory Council of the Small Business Administration recently issued a report dealing with the potential effects of computer crime on such companies. The report predicted that computer crime would become by far the most common variety in the future because " . . . the use of computers for business applications in small business will be so pervasive that it will be impossible to commit a non-violent crime except in the presence of computers." To make matters worse, the switch to computer crime brings with it a significant increase in the amounts involved. According to the FBI, a fraudulent transaction carried out in the traditional fashion nets the perpetrator about $23,000 whereas one using computers averages about $600,000.

Theft of Information

The most critical secrets of nations around the world reside in computerized databases. Now and then an announcement is made indicating that the cat and mouse game continues to go on between foreign agents trying to tap into the information and governments trying to stop them from doing so. A brash plan to steal military and research secrets from the United States, Japan, and Western Europe was recently defeated by a patient Harvard computer expert and astronomer who, for several months, single-handedly tracked the activities of the hackers breaking into restricted databases. He devised a network and database which he filled with phoney information. The hackers eagerly took the bait, breaking into the system and spending enough time online to enable the professor to track them to their lair, which turned out to be in Hamburg, West Germany.

Before the ring was broken up, however, the members had succeeded in gaining access to several data banks of critical importance to the west. These included computers used by the Los Alamos National Laboratory and the Fermi National Accelerator Laboratory; a computer used for Star Wars research; and the Optimus system used by the U.S. Defense Department. Although over fifty different computers were entered, the hackers apparently did not obtain the classified information they might have because many essential passwords were not available to them. (What happened to the information that was obtained? Apparently it was sold to communist agents, ending up in the hands of the Russians, who undoubtedly put it to good use.)

A considerable amount of domestic hacking is also taking place. Recently, an 18-year-old hacker was sentenced under the Computer Fraud and Abuse Act of

1986 to two-and-a-half years probation and ordered to pay a fine of $10,000 for breaking into Defense Department computers and stealing software. The young computerphile also penetrated computers at AT&T and NATO. The programs that he pilfered were valued at over 1 million dollars, and the damage done to AT&T equipment was set at $174,000, altogether a costly episode for those involved.

There are also ways to obtain data from stand-alone computers (those that are not hooked up to a network). Because signals are generated when a computer runs, it is possible to pick these up using sensitive but relatively inexpensive equipment stationed away from the computer itself. Various schemes are routinely used to prevent the escape of signals that can be collected by agents and decoded. One effective approach is to use cables that bleed leaking signals harmlessly into the ground; a more costly system involves the use of special electronic traps arranged in patterns around the computer area. Ideally, the most sensitive computer facilities would be protected by one or a combination of protective devices; in reality, many are not because of the costs involved.

Various ways of combating the theft of information are available, some of which have been mentioned. These include setting up dummy networks to lure intruders, protecting systems using electronic shields, maintaining constant vigilance, and encrypting data (a process described in a later section). A common practice nowadays, once it has been determined that a hacker has gained access to a system, is to deliberately leave some computers in the network relatively unprotected to encourage the intruder to continue using them. Once the hacker is connected to a computer, scientists attempt to track him down using the familiar approach used in a telephone tap.

Piracy of Software

Multimillion-dollar taps into international banks and the clandestine acquisition of computer technology by foreign governments are highly publicized events. But a much less dramatic and often overlooked problem is the illegal copying of disk-based programs. Although this activity is not as spectacular as the crimes already described, its critical nature becomes apparent when the extent to which it is being practiced is considered. Estimates are that for every program sold legally in the United States, one is pirated. The ratio changes dramatically in Asia, Latin America, and certain other foreign countries, with ten unauthorized copies being distributed for each legal version sold (Figure 10.3). In addition to its illegality, copying provides unintended ethical models for students who observe it being practiced openly. Duplicating an entire book is both too costly and too time-consuming to make it viable, but pirating the equivalent of a complete book from a disk is both quick and inexpensive. The simplicity with which a program can be transferred from one disk to another causes many people to overlook the fact that the programmer spends as much time and effort creating his material as does the author of a traditional hard-copy textbook.

Recent reports conclude that close to 100 percent of the nation's schools now contain at least one microcomputer; thus the potential for copyright abuse is virtually universal. Though some teachers make a point of addressing the issue of software piracy, others actually assign the task of making copies to students—a practice that tends to legitimize the activity. Through condoning and even encouraging software piracy, educators may be teaching values that will transfer to other situations. If it is all right to steal people's creative works, is it therefore acceptable to steal other things from them?

The long-term implications of mass copying are not pleasant to contemplate. Creative people must be compensated for what they do. If they are not, their tendency will be to stop turning out quality products. When this happens consumers, including the schools, will be the ones to suffer.

Indeed, some companies have actually gone bankrupt as a result of widespread copying of their products. These have generally been small operations charging a modest price for their software, which has frequently been excellent in quality despite the small cost. To compensate for lost sales, many companies routinely increase their prices; thus, honest users end up paying for the "free" copies made by pirates.

Just how much of a profit does a software publisher make on a product? Bodie Marx, vice president of Mindscape Software, indicates that it is a rather modest amount when all costs are figured in. He cites a sample case in which a package has a suggested retail price of forty dollars but brings only $9.80 in net revenue. The expenses deducted from the original forty dollars include a 45 percent dealer discount, a 10 to 15 percent royalty to the author, the costs of packaging, and a 10 percent promotional expense. All these add up to a whopping $30.20, leaving the publisher with much less than might be expected. You can see how widespread pirating could cut the profit margin of a smaller company to the point where staying in business might be difficult and even impossible.

1 purchased   10 pirated

FIGURE 10.3 The Ratio of Legally Acquired to Pirated Software (Estimated)

In an attempt to cut down on illegal copying, publishers have resorted to many schemes, the most common of which is the traditional copy protecting of their disks. Most software publishers continue to use this scheme, but this makes installing the program on a hard disk difficult to do. With such storage becoming increasingly popular, publishers are under pressure to make their products compatible with hard disk technology, but to do so makes widespread pirating a possibility. Because of the various problems involved, some companies have elected to do away with copy protection altogether on certain programs, trusting their clients to obey the copyright law.

Explicit in the copyright law is the right of the purchaser to have a backup disk at his or her disposal in case something goes wrong with the primary copy. Backup disks are to be used for archival purposes only; they cannot be used routinely to run a second computer but must be stored away to be put into service only if the first disk malfunctions. Also, their use must cease as soon as a replacement is received.

Backups are provided through a number of approaches. The most common, particularly with copy protected software, is to furnish a second disk in the package. Or, a single disk is sent along with instructions on making your own backup. Generally, the program will allow you to make but one copy, then a locking scheme comes into play. Another approach, which is more cumbersome since it usually involves filling out a card and a check, is to send back to the publisher for the backup. Interestingly, the passage in the copyright law giving the purchaser the right to a backup has led to the creation of programs that override the electronic locks on protected software, thus permitting the contents of the disk to be copied. It is perfectly legal to use programs such as Unlock, Copy II Plus, Copy II Mac, or LockSmith as long as they are used only to make backup copies for the personal use of the legal purchaser.

Provisions are also included in the copyright law for the purchaser to make whatever changes are needed so that the program conforms to his or her needs; this includes adding features to customize the program if need be. However, it is against the law to sell or otherwise dispose of the altered software without the express permission of the original author.

The most common way of pirating software is to copy a disk-based program onto another disk. But it is also possible to make a memory-resident copy that works in much the same way as the illegal disk even though no tangible copy is involved. A program that is capable of being stored in the RAM so that it works even after the disk has been removed from the drive is termed memory-resident. A program of this kind can be multiple-loaded into several computers from a single disk and used by many students simultaneously. The copyright law is a bit vague concerning the legality of this practice, but a large percentage of software producers feel that it is illegal. In 1987 the ICCE (International Council for Computers in Education) issued their updated Policy Statement on Software Copyright in which the suggestion is made that, unless specifically spelled out, multiple loading should be avoided. Some software companies state their policy in the program's documentation, so it would be well to read through this material to see if multiple loading is permitted. Finally, a letter or call to the publisher might be useful if you wish to explore all avenues before giving up.

School districts and software publishers are currently engaged in efforts to deal with the problem of piracy, and some positive results are being seen. Publishers have devised several plans to make their programs more widely available, one of which involves selling a site licensing plan to a school for each program purchased; the school may then either duplicate the program for each of its computers or load each machine in turn from the disk. An increasing number of publishers are making software available for use on networks; a central disk drive can then be used to load a program into all the machines on the network. Still other publishers offer a discount on multiple copies of the same program. And, though not the most common approach, several companies sell programs that can be copied freely.

Schools and districts are trying to do their part also. Some districts have negotiated contracts that permit them to duplicate programs centrally for distribution to the schools in an effort to discourage illegal copying on the part of teachers by providing them with the software they need. Other districts stress the serious consequences associated with pirating software. Some have adopted the International Council for Computers in Education Guidelines, which prohibit copying software beyond the initial backup copy. The fact that they can be held liable for the illegal activities of teachers has caused some districts to enforce the rules strictly. Teachers have been reprimanded, and it is conceivable that the time will come when one or more might actually be dismissed because of noncompliance. In addition, some schools emphasize the moral issues involved. Students who are permitted to copy software, or who see the teacher involved in this activity, are getting the wrong message: it is acceptable to steal from another. Greater progress toward the solution of the piracy problem can be expected as consumers and producers work even more closely together to come up with an equitable and workable plan.

PRIVACY ISSUES

Concerns for individual privacy have brought about the formation of various organizations and the enactment of legislation to safeguard the rights of citizens. Despite the ongoing effort to ensure that the privacy of the individual is not compromised, the rise of our high-tech society has introduced problems that were not anticipated when many of the initial safeguards were put into place.

When records were kept in folders in filing cabinets the very nature of this cumbersome system made it impractical to access extensive data files efficiently and quickly; the computer has changed all that. Little time and effort are required to conduct a search on virtually any subject or person. Massive personal files are maintained by a wide range of organizations. For example, a gigantic database containing medical information on the 32 million Medicare recipients has been created by the U.S. government. The information is being used to determine which treatments tend to be most effective for particular ailments, an exemplary goal. As always, however, the potential infringement on the privacy of those included in a database is always present and, in this case, exists on a massive scale (Figure 10.4).

The Medicare data bank is but one example of the large number currently in use. Virtually all organizations of any size, and many that are small, find this method of storing data to be convenient, efficient, and often indispensable. Governments, both national and local, support large electronic repositories of information of various kinds. For instance, the National Crime Information Center maintains an extensive database containing information on convicted criminals as well as other crime-related data. The driver's license bureau is an example of a state-level entity making wide use of computer storage. Commercial businesses would find it very difficult to operate if they were forced to move back to the laborious process of maintaining records by hand. Most everyone is aware of the degree to which large corporations rely on computers, but small businesses have come to depend on them as well.

While their contributions to society are mainly of a positive nature, computerized data banks are not without problems. As an illustration let us consider an operation carried out thousands of times each day by people interested in movies: renting a video. Depending upon whether or not the vendor uses a computer (most do) this minor event can add your name, address, and other personal information—including the videos you rented—to a database. Once the video is returned, the transaction is concluded, but all the information remains to be accessed at some future time if desired. Multiply this personal file by the many others (such as the one in the driver's license bureau computer) and you can see how easily a very complete personal profile might be compiled without your knowledge.

Obviously, uses for the information in the various databases are well-intentioned, but there continues to be a certain amount of abuse. Businesses routinely sell customer records to others who then use the information to identify prospec-

FIGURE 10.4

tive customers. This is not the only way in which private information becomes available however: it might also be stolen.

How is it possible that information, tucked away in a seemingly secure data bank, can be pirated by someone unseen and unknown? The answer lies in the nature of electronic data transmission. Sending information from one computer to another is done over the telephone lines, as you know from reading the chapter on telecommunication. If an individual could somehow gain access to a remote database, he or she would be able to roam through the files without ever leaving the security of home. It would be necessary to know the telephone number, passwords, and other key details to gain access to the database. This information is acquired in various ways, including programming a home computer to generate random passwords until one is found that "unlocks" a remote computer system so that it can be entered illegally.

Other less exotic methods are also used to acquire such information. In some cases you can obtain information merely by asking for it; much data is not confidential and, if you show reasonable cause to have access, will be supplied free for the asking. Even when a database is confidential, an employee might provide a critical password either intentionally or inadvertently. Details might be obtained about an inaccessible database from one which is accessible. A snooper might find written information lying about an office; a little bit here and a little bit there and soon all the parts fall into place.

Often, hackers break into databases just for the fun of it. Harboring no malicious intentions, they desire only to outwit the system. The challenge of hacking was summed up by a young member of a computer group in Milwaukee when he stated "It was like climbing a mountain: you have the goal of reaching the top or accessing a computer, and once you reach the peak, you make a map of the way and give it to everybody else." Indeed, some hackers do share with their fellows; as you would guess, they do this electronically also. Using an online bulletin board such as that mentioned in Chapter Seven, hackers are able to provide particulars for use by others in the fraternity to gain access to closed systems.

Once inside the system unscrupulous individuals might steal data, including personal records. Most generally, hackers would do something of a prankish nature, but this frequently infringes on someone's privacy as the following cases illustrate.

Recently, a hacker broke into the computer message system of the Community Action Program in Salt Lake City and erased a message designed to provide information to the needy on food distribution. In its place the hacker left the following: "Listen you bums, if you want cheese, go out and get a job and buy your own cheese. Who do you think you are, leeching on the taxpayers like this? Stop sleeping on park benches and go out and get a job." Needless to say, callers were insulted and embarrassed by this message. The complaints were numerous, and officials were hard pressed to explain what had happened.

In England, two individuals illegally entered the electronic mail system reserved for royalty and left various messages addressed to Prince Phillip. They also entered other divisions in the British information service system where they modified personal records in various ways. When apprehended, the culprits claimed that this was done to alert the public to problems in the system. Because no specific law seemed to apply, prosecutors used existing forgery and counterfeit laws to charge the defendants, who were found guilty. Interestingly, the judicial panel of the House of Lords, which is the British equivalent of our Supreme Court, overturned the decision, stating that trickery had been used to enter the system and trickery is not a crime in England.

There are various ways to protect a system from break-in, the simplest of which is observing care and caution with passwords and other critical information that provide access to the database. However, this alone is not sufficient to keep determined and knowledgeable hackers at bay. An effective device for protecting data is an encryption system that scrambles information, making it unintelligible until it is unscrambled once again, using secret codes available only to privileged individuals. Theoretically, however, hackers might randomly generate an infinite number of codes in an attempt to come up with the one to unscramble the data, just as they do when searching for ways to enter a database.

In addition to developing mechanical safeguards, society is addressing the problems at the social and philosophical levels. An interesting innovation is the insurance plan being offered by a handful of companies to counter hackers and thieves. Traditionally, insurance policies have protected such things as automobiles, houses, and lives. But the age of technology has brought about a situation in which electronically stored information is of greater value than the storage mediums themselves. Thus, the data on a hard disk could easily be priceless, whereas the disk and drive could be replaced for a relatively small amount. The new insurance policies protect against both the person with criminal intent (our electronic bank robber) and the hackers or pranksters whose damage might be inadvertent.

Computer Viruses

In addition to break-ins such as those mentioned, there are now intrusions from small segments of computer code that act so much like organisms they have been given the label of viruses. Viruses must be planted by a knowledgeable individual; they cannot simply appear all by themselves. But once implanted in a program, they propagate themselves in an ongoing frenzy until an entire network is infected by them. The computer virus, like its namesake, cannot exist without a host to feed on. Also, like an actual virus, the electronic variety can lie dormant for long periods of time before it makes its presence felt. Computer worms, on the other hand, are able to exist independently; they do not destroy data as do viruses; however, worms are able to proliferate to the extent that they fill the memory space with so much data that computers slow down or even stop functioning. They might also cause a printer to turn out never ending masses of hard copy, thus wasting both time and materials.

You will recall that an essential component in the functioning of a computer is the operating system. The operating system has many commands of its own that enable the user to write programs to direct it to perform specific tasks. It is this characteristic that allows a knowledgeable user to insert commands to call up the block of code that constitutes the virus. When an infected program is run, it automatically infects another program in a process that is repeated over and over again. Viruses destroy information to varying degrees, and can even completely wipe out the contents of a floppy or hard disk. Worse than this is their potential to infect thousands of computers in a network, a situation that would result in a national emergency of grave consequences (Figure 10.5).

Military experts are concerned that this could be the ultimate offensive weapon of the future. Viruses contrived as part of a complex battle plan would be planted not only in military computers, but in any of several essential civilian systems such as those used for electronic banking, air traffic control, and like applications, to disrupt the normal day-to-day operations so critical to a functioning society. The viruses might be implanted over a period of time, remaining hidden within their hosts until such a time as a specific condition existed to trigger them and make them active.

Those who create viruses do so for various reasons. Vengeance is one incentive for this activity. A.K. Dewdney, in *Scientific American,* describes the case of a hypothetical programmer who is unhappy with his company's management. To get even, he plants a virus that becomes active the day he leaves the company. The trigger to activate the program is the removal from the computer of his payroll file. The result is the destruction of information and programs or the introduction of faulty data into the system. While his former colleagues are struggling to overcome the problems he has left them, our programmer is far away enjoying his strange brand of vengeance.

The crime is not without penalty, however. In an actual case a programmer was convicted of introducing a virus into the computers of his former employer

FIGURE 10.5

which deleted over 100,000 important records. This was in retaliation for being released from his job with the insurance firm. The perpetrator was tracked down and found guilty of "harmful access to a computer," a crime carrying a maximum sentence of ten years in jail and a fine of $5,000.

A case of widespread infection from commercial software made news recently when it was found that a program titled FreeHand from the Aldus Corporation contained a virus or worm. Spread from both the GEnie and CompuServe tele-communication services through some public domain software, the infection soon struck thousands of Macintosh computers in the United States and several other countries. The problem forced Aldus to recall the programs and debug them, a costly and time-consuming task. The writer of the virus turned out to be a computer user who claimed to have designed the program to impress those using pirated versions of Macintosh software with the dangers of making unauthorized copies.

An incident that was highly publicized because of its massive scale involved a young graduate student who wrote a worm program that spread like wildfire through the Advanced Research Projects Agency Network (ARPAnet), a system containing 50,000 scientific computer stations.

Although data were not destroyed, the slowdown of the system caused valuable time to be lost. The speed with which the worm spread is illustrated by the fact that over 6,000 computers were affected in a single day.

The culprit made it clear that he had no intention of causing as much grief as he did, indicating that he inserted the worm as a prank, and it got away from him. FBI director William Sessions, whose agency investigated the episode, stated that intent was an important consideration when making the determination as to whether or not a criminal act has been carried out. Individuals found guilty of such acts have a bleak future to look forward to: under the Computer Fraud and Abuse Act the maximum fine is $250,000 along with a prison term of 20 years.

The common way in which viruses get started is through activities of insiders who have access to the computers involved. Once a program on a disk is infected it becomes "contagious"; viruses and worms can be spread by passing disks around or sharing them on a network. This method has the greatest potential for dissemination, as you would suspect. Electronic bulletin boards hooked together electronically through a telecommunications system permit individuals to provide shareware to all others having access to the bulletin board. The numbers of potential users can easily run into the thousands.

Because the information posted on bulletin boards is generally in the public domain, and therefore copyable and free, it has great appeal for educators who see this as a good way to expand their software libraries. When a program that appears to be useful is located, it is downloaded off of the system and a disk copy made. The problem with infected programs is that they can erase other programs on the floppy disk or wipe out the entire contents of a hard disk. Some, however, are a bit slower to do their work. These contain counting routines which keep track of the number of times you use the program; once the number has been

reached the virus takes over, doing its damage and sometimes displaying a taunt-
ing message of some kind on the screen.

Some operating systems have proved to be more susceptible to virus attacks
than others. For instance, a network using Unix, a popular standard, was the
target of a recent widespread invasion that made nationwide headlines. Due to
its openness, which is a feature that has made it popular, this operating system
has proved an easy mark for trouble makers. Having been burned in this fashion,
the makers of Unix immediately took the necessary steps to insulate the system
from future attacks of this kind. If anything positive can be said about such activities as virus attacks, it is that they alert designers to problems inherent in
their software, enabling them to respond with changes that tend to strengthen
their product.

Society is gearing up to meet the challenge of viruses and their kin. For instance, the National Computer Security Center at Fort Meade has been established to defend against such threats. A high-level effort such as this is needed in
light of the many large networks that have been affected. Among the systems
involved have been the National Oceanic and Atmospheric Administration,
NASA, IBM's electronic mail system, and numerous universities. Other organizations, such as the Computer Virus Industry Association, have also been developed to contend with the problem.

Networks have notoriously been "open" and security has been lax. While tight-
ening security is a partial answer to virus invasions, it can also be a problem
because it diminishes the convenience of a network, making legitimate uses more
difficult to carry out.

Virus killer programs, called "vaccines," are available to enable users to check
software before using it. Several programs of this kind have been designed to
check for the more common and universal viruses such as CyberAIDS and Fes-
tering Hate which are found in some public domain software titles. Also available
are universal virus checkers. These search through a program looking for the
clandestine codes of the virus and worm programs. One program of this kind,
designed for the Macintosh, is called Virus Rx. It is available from authorized
Apple dealers.

Several basic safeguards should be employed if you suspect that a virus might
be lurking on a disk or network you plan to use. To begin, you should be careful
when selecting bulletin boards from which software is to be downloaded. Those
having tight controls are the best bet. Bulletin board operators who require identification from you are likely to offer a safer product than those who do not. The
problem as it relates to public domain software is a growing one, with at least fifty
viruses being reported by those who obtain programs of this kind from bulletin
boards. As partial protection, you should never download a program to a hard
disk; always use a floppy.

If you use an external hard disk drive, it should be turned off as new software
is tested. This will prevent computer diseases from finding their way into the
programs stored there, thus creating the possibility that the contents will be com-

pletely lost or ruined. Also, you and your students should avoid copying software illegally; this is a common way in which viruses are proliferated.

COMPUTER EQUITY

The problem of providing all segments of society with equal access to computer technology was formerly an issue that received considerable attention. The greatest concern was shown during the computer literacy era, when it was argued that knowing about computers (and particularly about programming them) was critical to survival in an electronic society; today, less is said about computer equity.

This change is due in part to the realization that knowing how computers work is not as essential to the average person's well-being as people were led to believe. The idea that students would need to be computer literate to land a good job has not been borne out in actual practice. Although many prospective employers perceive some familiarity with computers to be useful, they tend to rank such qualities as leadership ability and personality well above knowledge about computers. Obviously, this does not hold true for those being recruited for employment in the computer industry; rather, it reflects a general trend in other areas.

While most employers do not place a great deal of weight on how much a prospective employee knows about computers in general, many consider the ability to use one for practical applications such as word processing and spreadsheet manipulation to be useful, and often decide in favor of those having such skills when choosing between applicants who are otherwise more or less equal in other respects. Although equal access to traditional computer literacy courses is no longer considered to be as important as it once was, and interest in this aspect of schooling has waned to some extent, perhaps the time has come to redefine equity so that it comes to mean that all students have the opportunity to experiment with computers and explore their productive potential to whatever extent they desire (Figure 10.6).

A second reason that the stress on computer equity is not as great as formerly is that the situation has improved for females (and others who lack equal access to the technology) until today it is much closer to being on a par with that of the traditional middle-class male computer user. In 1982, for instance, fewer than 15 percent of poor schools provided computers for their students as compared with over 30 percent of the wealthier schools. Today, the figure is much higher for both the poor and wealthy schools. Additionally, efforts have been made to involve females in computer-related activities that they have tended to shy away from. Also, several software producers have redesigned their products to negate aspects girls found uninteresting and to emphasize features either more neutral in nature or more attractive to girls.

For instance, a series of simulations featuring girls in different settings, such as the South Seas, a cave culture, and so on, is available; another program on math has an animated female figure carry out the various computational activities. Many instructional games have been changed to downplay the violence common to the game format (particularly the arcade format). This is in response

FIGURE 10.6 No Student Should be Excluded from Having the Opportunity to Work with Computers to Whatever Extent They Desire

to the fact that most girls do not find destroying an "enemy" to be a very appealing thing to do.

While these various trends are positive, there still remains much to be done before the problems of equity are resolved. Having stressed the importance of using the computer as a general-purpose tool we must recognize that, in middle schools and high schools, programming continues to be a major activity. The trend for males to dominate in such classes is still in evidence despite some effort to make them more accessible to females. Computer use in math is greater at all grade levels than in any other curriculum area, and this tends to favor males since working with mathematics generally is perceived to be a male activity. As Hess and Miura (1985) point out "The public stereotype of computers projects images of science, mathematics, engineering, and other male-dominated professions." The phenomenon is not a recent one. The mathematics prodigy Ada, the Countess of Lovelace, was discouraged from pursuing a career in this field by her tutor, who said that a mathematician must be capable of a "fierce concentration" and must have an "unremitting strength of intellect" in order to succeed. Both characteristics were held to be beyond the capability of a female. Ada persisted and, in the early 1800s, devised programs for the mechanical computers conceived by Charles Babbage—the first programmer was thus a woman.

Perhaps the tendency to associate programming with math is due in large part to the fact that math courses are typically prerequisites for programming classes.

Again, this reenforces the idea in both sexes that programming belongs in the male domain.

According to Sanders and Stone (1986) this perception is basic to the problem of restricted computer use on the part of female students. The authors point out that peer acceptance has much to do with the extent to which teenagers form behaviors seen as appropriate for this particular sex. Because competence in both math and computers is seen as characteristically male, girls typically tend to shy away from manifesting too much interest in either subject for fear that their status with peer groups might be damaged.

Additional reasons for the phenomenon of gender differences in using computers have been proposed by various researchers. Hess and Miura (1985) list various explanations extracted from the literature, including the tendency of educational software and games to "portray male-oriented themes." Also mentioned is the inclination of parents to "encourage computer use by boys rather than girls," along with the possibility that "symbolic and visual-spatial features of programming appeal more to boys than to girls."

In spite of attempts to overcome discrimination against females, subtle and not-so-subtle forms of stereotyping continue to appear regularly in media related to computers. In studying the sex-role messages conveyed by pictures in computer magazines, Ware and Stuck (1985) found significant evidence of discrimination and bias against females. Despite the fact that women outnumber men in the population, men were portrayed twice as often in the magazine illustrations. When women were shown they tended to occupy lesser positions than the men, and were frequently "shown as sex objects, while men were never shown as such." Also, women were seldom portrayed in active roles; they were most often unengaged or passive. Finally, the authors found that if a person in an illustration was shown "avoiding the computer" this person was a woman.

Such pictorial stereotyping is unfortunate, for it reenforces established attitudes that many educators and others are trying to overcome. There is considerable evidence to indicate that such stereotypes have little if any basis in fact. Linn (1985) cites various studies which suggest that there is no significant difference in the way male and female students perform in programming courses. Additionally, studies show that both sexes display equivalent interest once they are engaged in computer learning.

Although a step in the right direction, providing sufficient equipment and lab time for computer activities will not automatically lead to greater female participation and acceptance. Rather, a course of action must be devised that appeals to the needs and interests of girls. Schools should begin early on to attend to the problem of stereotyping. While evidence indicates that girls are as capable as boys when it comes to understanding and using the computer, they must be convinced that this is so. One way to address this problem is to begin at the elementary level to familiarize students with women's contributions to the fields of math and computer science. Many outstanding programmers are women; some have their own companies. Women have made some noteworthy contributions to computer science: in addition to Ada, the world's first programmer, Admiral Grace

Hopper developed the programming language COBOL, which is widely used for business applications. Visits by female computer science majors and women from industry would add a new dimension to a unit on technology.

At the secondary level it would be useful to identify computer-related careers that girls perceive as being attractive. Many traditional jobs are gradually becoming computerized, and it takes little effort to find a link between a girl's career choice and the computer. Once girls are aware of the importance of understanding technology regardless of career choice, it is much easier to encourage them to get involved in courses they might otherwise shun.

When it comes time for hands-on activities, either in a classroom setting or in the computer lab, girls with little or no background often feel intimidated. One way to make the experience a positive one is to have girls with expertise help those who are inexperienced. Both tutors and their tutees learn from this kind of arrangement and typically find the social interaction an enjoyable bonus. As a rule, only girls should be included in these learning groups, because boys generally end up taking things over. After the girls gain confidence, they typically hold their own, and it is not uncommon, particularly in the higher grades and in college, to see both sexes working together at a computer.

That strategies designed specifically to encourage girls to use computers can work has been clearly demonstrated by The Women's Action Alliance, a nonprofit organization devoted to enhancing computer equity for females. A set of guidelines has been designed by the Alliance to help teachers overcome their female students' reluctance to engage in computer activities. This and other useful information is found in the brochure *Do Your Female Students Say "No, Thanks" to the Computer?*, available from the Women's Action Alliance (see Appendix D for the address). Also available is a six-page brochure from Apple Computer devoted to this subject.

Although the many factors contributing to gender differences present a formidable barrier to the achievement of complete equity, Hess and Miura (1985) conclude that "none offers an obstacle that cannot be removed or changed." Among the more promising indications that such differences are not inevitable is the increasing participation of female teachers in computer activities. Becker (1985) points out that their involvement is not a recent phenomenon, but can be traced back to the early stages of instructional computing. In his words "In elementary schools, in particular, as primary computer using teachers, women have been leaders in innovating and creatively using microcomputers in their classroom—in some respects, more than their male counterparts in other schools." Such teachers, serving as role models for girls, "may be an important factor in any future decline of the association between gender and computer skills."

COMPUTERS IN THE WORKPLACE

The transition to the computerized workplace has not been entirely without problems, but initial predictions of a wholesale displacement and alienation of workers have failed to materialize. This is not to say that some workers have not suffered from the introduction of computerized robots or from computerized monitoring systems that keep track of their activities second by second (Figure 10.7). On the whole, however, the widespread adoption of computer technology in the workplace has proved to be more beneficial than otherwise. For one thing, the United States would be hard pressed to compete with other industrialized nations who rely heavily on computerized tools if the status quo had been maintained.

The robot represents one such tool, which was introduced over the objections of many workers and their unions (Figure 10.8). Predictions were rampant that these devices would usurp the bulk of the jobs in labor-intensive industries and would create a pool of unemployed and unemployable workers. Although some jobs were lost, many of them were repetitive, boring, and even dangerous. Often, the humans who performed these tasks were retrained to do more interesting things, such as controlling and maintaining the robots themselves.

With high-technology occupations increasing at a rapid pace, jobs for computer operators, repair personnel, and systems analysts have become more plentiful. But there is a dark side to the technology picture: when examined closely, the fact that the high-tech job segment is quite narrow becomes apparent. According to some estimates only 6 percent of the newly created jobs over the next ten years will be in the high-tech area. Although respectable numbers of people will be employed by high-tech firms, only about 20 percent will actually be directly involved in technologically oriented activities. The great majority will do such tasks as assemble components, work in the stock room, and do clerical work. Many experts predict that most jobs will actually require less training and a lower skill level than is currently the case.

The modern office is a good illustration of this phenomenon. Activities that once required a broad knowledge of office routines can now be broken down into small, repetitive segments, each of which is assigned to a particular worker. One

FIGURE 10.7

FIGURE 10.8 An Industrial
Robot

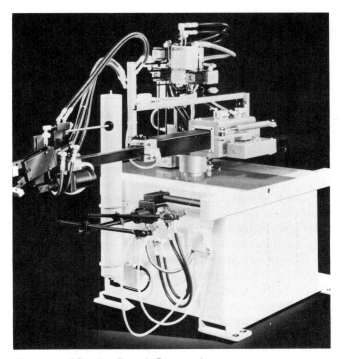

(Courtesy of Sterling-Detroit Company)

individual performs the same fragmented task over and over; the next worker in
the production line performs the next one, and so on until the larger task is
finished. This approach seems as if it should result in greater efficiency, but this
tends not to be the case. It is little different than any kind of production line in
which boredom and fatigue cause actual output to be much less than theory suggests it should be. The result of this sweatshop mentality is that the turnover of
clerical workers is higher than ever before, and those who stay on the job exhibit
high levels of stress.

The analogy between computerized offices and sweatshops becomes even more
appropriate when it is realized that computers make possible the precise measurement of an employee's productivity. Thus, production times for various tasks
can be established, and workers held to these; or, they can be paid a certain
amount for each piece of work completed, a common practice in the sweatshops
of the past.

Although less than sufficient attention has been paid to conditions such as
these, there is some evidence that awareness is growing. For instance, the first
law of its kind, one aimed at protecting clerical workers who use computers for
long stretches at a time, was recently passed in Suffolk County, New York. For
some time workers across the country have complained of a syndrome of aches
and pains that is consistent from one setting to another, but little attention has
been paid to them; fortunately, things are changing. Under the new law employers

must provide certain considerations to anyone who spends over 26 hours each week at the computer terminal. Equipment must be furnished with nonglare screens and must be adjustable so that the employee can modify it to fit his or her individual physical requirements. After spending three consecutive hours at the terminal, the user must be given a 15-minute break, or a different task to do. Also, provisions are included for employers to pay a significant percentage of the cost of glasses and eye exams for employees. Laws such as this should become more common as legislatures, labor groups, and others come to recognize the problems confronting those who spend concentrated periods of time working with the electronic technologies.

There are many success stories involving computers in the workplace. Rather than adding to the routineness of doing a job, computers frequently do just the opposite. In many cases, they have relieved workers of laborious, time consuming operations, thus permitting them to spend their time more productively. Teachers who have successfully integrated CAI into their curriculums find that assigning the computer to the task of drilling students can give them more time to interact with those needing individual attention. And electronic gradebooks make maintaining records and calculating grades much more efficient than when traditional methods are used. In most cases the results of computer operations are more accurate and complete than those carried out by humans. For instance, evidence shows that computers do a better job of diagnosing illnesses than do many physicians, and mechanics would be hard pressed to identify many of the persistent mechanical problems of the new generation of automobiles if they lacked computerized diagnostic devices.

In addition to serving as tools that assist workers to do their jobs more efficiently, computers are now being used as the primary trainers for new employees, as well as for those who are established but wish to upgrade their skills. The most commonly used kind of instructional program is the simulation. You will recall from the discussion of the varieties of CAI software in Chapter Three that simulations are designed so as to provide the user with an experience as close as possible to that he or she would encounter in the real world.

Companies design simulations based on the unique way that they conduct business; each program is tailor-made to meet the needs of a specific company. Simulations are used in every conceivable occupation. Airline pilots practice flying different kinds of aircraft using computer simulations that are so realistic you can even hear the tires crossing the seams in the tarmac. Airports appear in the distance, each having the distinct look of the real-life facility. Controls respond exactly as do those in the actual airliner, and results are just as immediate. Valuable experience is gained from using such a simulation, which provides a realistic environment without the potential dangers related to an actual training flight.

Back on the ground, those learning first aid can respond to a simulated emergency and then find out whether their diagnosis and treatment were the proper ones. Many business simulations are currently in use, some of which merely simulate the clerk-customer relationship. Others are much more complex than this, involving operations at all levels within the company. Fully 75 percent of the organizations that use computers for training purposes use them to teach personnel how to use computers, an indication of the extent to which the technology has become an important and even indispensable part of doing business.

THE FUTURE

So far in this chapter we have dealt with the present and a bit of the past; the future has only been alluded to. Let us now consider in greater detail what might possibly lie ahead, using the best information futurists can provide as the basis for our predictions.

A peek at the future is available today in the form of the artificial intelligence (AI) research and complex simulations made possible by extremely fast and powerful computers like the one shown in Figure 10.9. As even more powerful machines are developed, scientists believe they will have the potential to create programs that move ever closer to working like the human intellect. In the meantime, the development of programs has given the microcomputer some AI capabilities, which means that teachers and their students can begin to enjoy the benefits of this exciting new application.

FIGURE 10.9 The Cray Y-MP/ 832 Computer System, a Powerful Supercomputer for Use in Artificial Intelligence Research, Simulation, and other High-level Applications

(Photo by Paul Shambroom. Courtesy of Cray Research, Inc.)

Not only will the technology of the future be different, but society will also evolve in reaction to the technological changes. Since the beginning of the computer revolution, we have seen institutions discard standard ways of doing things in favor of digital methods that promise greater efficiency and effectiveness. In some areas, however, the anticipated changes have not been as dramatic as many predicted. While the electronic cottage as envisaged by Toffler and others has materialized to some extent, most workers continue to earn a living away from their homes.

The predictions that telecommuting (doing your work at home and using the computer to send the product to a remote office) would become the norm were made without adequate thought to certain human traits, including the social nature of people. Most workers would jump at the chance of being freed from the structure imposed by a traditional job, and few would miss the daily commute. But benefits such as these frequently are not sufficient to offset the loss of personal contacts and the stimulation gained from working with others on a common task.

Only certain types of people are able to work productively at home. Those who require stimuli from the outside have difficulty performing well on their own. Some establish regular work hours which they follow religiously; others have been known to make trips to the office on a regular basis even though they are not required to do so. Employees having skills that enable them to do their jobs in isolation from others generally adapt well to working at home. Programmers, writers, graphic artists, accountants, and engineers, among others, find telecommuting to be an excellent arrangement; they are used to working alone and often find the relative turmoil of the office to be distracting (Figure 10.10).

FIGURE 10.10 Some Employees have the Skills to Enable Them to Work at Home (courtesy of Apple Computer, Inc.)

Many telecommuters are clerical workers who are paid low salaries, often based on the amount of work they produce. They might also receive reduced benefits. On the other hand, this arrangement is convenient for parents who have young children or who wish to work only part-time to supplement a second salary.

To date, the numbers of people who work at home using the computer as the tie to a central office is significant, but not nearly as large as was once predicted. The numbers are large enough, however, that Scholastic, Inc. recently changed the name as well as the content of one of its popular journals from *Family Computing* to *Home Office Computing* in response to this trend.

Predicting the extent to which telecommuting will grow in the next several years is difficult to do. Some believe that, given the small pool of individuals who are able to be maximally productive on their own, the trend has reached its peak. Others suggest that as home computers become more common and as individuals become more capable with them, an increase in telecommuting will be seen. Indeed, a recent survey by Fuji Photo Film USA indicated that the use of computers in home offices is increasing at a greater rate than any other application.

Toffler's (1980) idea of the electronic cottage not only involves working at home, but also learning at home (Figure 10.11). He predicted that the classroom would shift to the home for an increasing number of students as long-distance learning systems become more generally available and lessons more adequate. This trend has not developed to the extent anticipated, although many students do obtain their formal learning in their homes. Most, however, prefer the traditional school environment. This tendency is most likely directly related to the

FIGURE 10.11   The Computer Will Bring the Classroom into Many Students' Homes (courtesy of Apple Computer, Inc.)

need for interpersonal relationships with friends. When questioned, a significant percentage of students identify interaction with peers as the primary reason for going to school.

Some experts also predicted that offices of the future would be operated without paper—data would all be on computers. In actuality, more paper is used today than when the predictions were made. This is in part due to the fact that the quantity of information is growing daily, and there must be ways to store it; more computer space is also filled with data than formerly.

But more than this, computer-based materials are not as convenient to read as a book or magazine, at least not yet. Turning back to check a page is easier to do with a journal than with a computer. Some readers like the familiar printed page better than a screen display, and an illustration on paper has a familiarity and feel lacking in the electronic medium.

Because many hypothetical scenarios did not materialize, futurists tend to be a bit more cautious about making broad predictions these days. Technological developments, however, make possible rather safe guesses about some aspects of computing. There is little doubt as to characteristics of the new generations of hardware. Based upon what we see happening today, it is safe to say that the computer's memory and capacity to do work will continue to expand. The power of the newer equipment is illustrated by the Evans and Sutherland supercomputer, which has the capability of sixty IBM 3090 computers all working at once. An enhanced version of the Cray-2 supercomputer is capable of performing almost 2 billion operations per second, which is about twelve times faster than the Cray-1. It is calculated that the Cray-3 will perform 16 billion calculations per second!

Is there a limit to how fast computers can operate? Using the traditional silicon technology, the limit has about been reached. But newer materials such as gallium arsenide are being used to overcome these limitations. This substance transmits electrical current with less resistance than silicon and holds the charge longer. These characteristics enable scientists to design chips that require less power and take up less space in addition to operating faster. Superconducting materials will also be used to increase the processing speed of future computers.

Such refinements should lead to some startling applications. Supercomputers have been steadily coming down in size using traditional technologies. They will become still smaller and more powerful as the newer materials and processes become available; a supercomputer on a single chip is even a possibility.

The quest for intelligent computers will undoubtedly continue, but no one can predict with any measure of confidence that the goal will ever be reached. Innovations such as parallel processing should bring this goal closer than ever. Traditional computers process data in serial order, taking the bits of information one after another and then performing operations one at a time. Computers structured around the parallel processing concept are more like the human brain in the way they work. Like the brain, many paths are used simultaneously to transmit information for processing and storage. Not only does this arrangement make the whole operation go faster but the potential for branching within the networks is considerably enhanced.

Research on neural networks is involving an increasing number of scientists in many countries. The Japanese for example, have set a high priority on such research, hoping to be the first to market devices based on this technology. If successful, neural networks will be able to function much as the human brain does. They will enable computers to recognize patterns, generalize from one situation to another, work with concepts, and even learn from their "experiences."

A hint of the direction in which research is moving is provided by two examples of software now available for use on microcomputers. The first is HyperCard, a program for the Macintosh that enables the user to access and arrange data using associations rather than traditional indexing techniques. Assume, for instance, that you are browsing through information on impressionist painters and you encounter a description of the colors they used. You can quickly select color as the keyword and jump to this subject. From color it is a short move to light, and perhaps from light back to Impressionism, for it was the vital effects of light that these artists attempted to portray. Note how different from using an alphabetical index this approach is—it is more like the process humans use as they think, often relying on serendipity, hunches, guesses, and curiosity to come up with solutions. Other programs based on the hypermedia idea are HyperStudio for the Apple IIgs and SuperCard for the Macintosh.

A second product of interest is the program from Scholastic called A.I.: An Experience with Artificial Intelligence. Available for most models of school computers, this program is fascinating for students because it enables the computer to exhibit certain human traits such as progressive "learning" and "foresight."

In the first of two modes the computer learns how to play a new game from scratch. At first it loses to the human player consistently, but as the games progress, it "remembers" the winning moves and soon becomes an expert player. In the second mode, the student can teach the computer the rules. By using this approach he or she comes to understand the process by which the computer learns and remembers.

Programs of this kind provide insights into how artificial intelligence works and how it can be used in actual applications. They also help students to think about their own learning, and they provide exciting problem-solving environments that challenge young scientists.

While future computers will themselves become"smarter," smaller components designed with the aid of micromechanics will perform dedicated tasks in a number of different settings. Micromechanics is a new discipline in which engineers actually form silicon into three-dimensional mechanical devices of microscopic proportions. Because of the great promise shown by devices of this kind, the effort to perfect and manufacture them will expand dramatically in the future.

The amazing strength and flexibility of silicon make micromechanics possible. Stronger than stainless steel, this material can be flexed over and over again without breaking; thus scientists are able to construct miniature structures of all kinds that respond to slight changes in input, sending signals to indicate the magnitude of the changes. For instance, a microsensor containing projections like tiny tuning forks picks up the vibrations in machines, sending signals to indicate the relative smoothness of operation.

Today's cars use microsensors capable of sensing the smallest variation in air pressure. Through constant monitoring and adjusting, these devices control air intake to maximize combustion, thus improving both mileage and emissions.

Many medical applications have been found for microsensors. Blood pressure readings can be taken with great accuracy using a microsensor attached to a catheter that is inserted directly inside a blood vessel. Another application is in devices to improve impaired hearing. Components made in this way are small enough to be implanted inside the ear. Work is also progressing on microsensors capable of responding to signals from the brain to activate artificial limbs.

Microsensors, when coupled with technological innovations such as parallel processing and neural networks, will aid scientists in their quest for intelligent computers. Extremely small and inexpensive, they will be the answer to the problem of coordinating the constantly changing input from a variety of sources and using this to control the output from computerized devices such as robots.

Innovations appearing today indicate that the world of the future will be more dependent on computer technology than ever before. As educators, we might well ask what impact such changes will have on the schools. Again, making prognostications on the basis of what is happening at the cutting edge of research is a fairly safe, though not foolproof approach. A breakthrough in a single area might throw all of our projections into disarray. Just one example of such an instance is the virtual replacement of 16mm instructional films by videotapes.

One scenario projected for education depicts students obtaining most of their formal schooling at home in the electronic cottage. It is doubtful that this will ever become a popular trend, though, given our social nature. Schools will most likely be around for a long time to come, but they are certain to change. There will always be students who are taught at home, because their parents prefer this arrangement, because they are disabled, or for other reasons. Through technology such students will receive a rich and varied experience, fully as stimulating in content as that provided for children in regular settings.

While distance learning using the telephone lines and cable hookups will continue to be the common ways instruction is delivered to homes, other techniques, requiring no wires, will become increasingly important. Satellites provide one means for accomplishing long distance delivery; although fraught with problems, using radio signals to link home computers to a central teaching computer might also become practical.

Distance learning also has important implications for those in remote schools where personnel trained in subjects such as math and science are in critically short supply. Many rural schools also have difficulty providing a full curriculum, and they frequently lack adequate resources for use in the courses they do offer. All signs indicate that distance learning will become an increasingly important segment of the total educational picture as people search for options to the established educational model.

Mention was made previously of the likelihood that advances in technology will make instructional computers of the future smaller, lighter, and less expensive than they are today. Miniaturization efforts have led to the production of a tiny computer screen smaller than a book of matches and capable of displaying the same amount of information as a standard sized monitor. Numeric keypads small enough to be coupled with wrist calculators are available from many sources; keyboards containing the alphabet and other symbols can be made just as small or even smaller. Clearly, the technology is available to make a pocket-sized computer, but would it be very useful to educators? Perhaps not, given the trouble that students have with standard-sized keyboards, let alone ones having keys too small to press with the fingers. The small size of a pocket screen would be a problem also, but voice input and output could be the answer to problems such as these. Talking word processors represent a step toward solving the problems of input and output on computers of any size. Speech-based software of this kind adds the dimension of sound to the written language by pronouncing words typed by the student. Most use synthesized speech in which phonemes are generated and joined together for audio output. Synthesized speech sounds rather robotic, but this shortcoming is certain to improve as the technology advances.

The next step is to develop systems capable of responding to common words spoken by the user. Called voice recognition or interfacing, this approach poses an array of problems for developers. Although various voice interfacers are currently in use, they are cumbersome to use and also somewhat unpredictable. You must speak slowly, and you cannot change voice pitch once the computer has created a template to match distinct voice characteristics. Vocabularies are restricted in the number of words the computer can understand, so a regular dialogue is not possible. You can, however, direct the computer to perform a set of defined operations just by speaking the commands. The main problem confronting the developers of speech systems is that everyone speaks a bit differently. Thus, the computer, like a well-trained pet, performs for but one master—that is, unless it is programmed to react to each and every individual user, a task of considerable proportions.

Things are changing rapidly however. Voice interfaces now being developed not only have great tolerance for voices of different qualities, they also provide much larger word banks (up to 20,000 words in some instances). Predictions are that in the future computers will not only obey words spoken in several different voices; they will be able to respond to sentences and even to distinguish between homophones on the basis of the context in which the words are used.

Systems of this kind will be useful to traditional learners, of course, but they will be a special boon to those who can benefit from alternative approaches to learning. In addition to speech interfacing, other ways are being devised to allow such learners to interact with computers. A system called Ultrasonic Mouse Typing, which was developed at the University of Utah, enables disabled users to access the various keys on a keyboard displayed on the computer screen by moving their heads in various directions. A headset containing receivers sensitive to slight changes in position is worn by the user. Signals are transmitted to the computer, where they are interpreted just as movements of a mouse would be, guiding the cursor around on the screen and enabling the user to activate keys on the keyboard display. Another approach now in the experimental stage is to use brain waves for activating computer functions. This system has great potential for individuals with a high level of disability. Although the approach has proved to be practical, much additional work needs to be done before such a system will be widely available.

The storage capability of computers continues to expand by leaps and bounds, making the maintenance of large databases and the operation of extensive, complex programs much less of a problem than before. One of the most promising of the new generation of storage mediums (discussed in Chapter 4) is CD-ROM. Capable of storing massive amounts of data, this technology is destined to become an important ingredient in instructional computing in the future. Although CD-ROM is thought of mainly as a repository for data, the newer CD-I (compact disk–interactive) provides interactive capabilities similar to those possessed by interactive computer-controlled videodisc systems.

Until recently, data on optical disks could only be read; you could not write (add information) to the disk. But now erasable disks are available, making the system an even more versatile storage medium than it was before. Continued development will enable optical disks to hold ever greater amounts of data, and costs are certain to plummet, making them easier for schools to afford. With CD-ROM and hard disks widely available, the relatively inefficient and bulky five-inch floppies will become much less common in the future, and will eventually be phased out entirely.

The essential programs, or software, that run the instructional computer will also be much improved. With greater available memory, sharper displays, and other improvements, the hardware will be able to accommodate much more capable programs. The computer will be able to deal effectively with virtually any response, gently taking appropriate steps to get the students back on track if they stray too far afield. Intelligent computer-assisted instruction (ICAI) programs will be able to maintain an ever-expanding pool of knowledge which, like human knowledge, can be accessed as needed and when appropriate. In other words, future instructional programs will be more responsive and sensitive and will teach much as a human teacher does if the promises of ICAI research are realized. Programs will be able to identify those areas in which students need additional help, and to diagnose the problems in detail. They will then proceed to prescribe the needed remediation and present appropriate learning sequences to bring the student up to the desired performance level. Many of the newer tutorials display characteristics of this nature, although most are not as highly developed as they promise to be in the future.

Simulations are becoming more realistic: the Science Toolkit and Microcomputer Based Laboratory described in Chapter 4 are just two examples of this trend. Tool software such as graphics generators, word processors, and page layout programs are getting more capable all the time. Based on what is happening today, it is certain that future instructional software will come much closer to making the computer the effective teaching tool educators had hoped it would be.

As a result of the expanded capabilities of technology, teachers will have different functions than they do today: they will spend more time attending to the needs of individual students and less time worrying about class norms; they will be relieved of tedious nonteaching tasks such as maintaining attendance and performance records; and they will become the skilled managers of complex instructional systems that bear little resemblance to today's classrooms.

Like the weather, the future is very difficult to predict. Given the phenomenal development of computer technology over the past several years, it is probably safe to say that any prediction we might make will have to take into account the potential for equally unanticipated developments in coming years. Thirty-five years ago who could possibly have guessed that a classroom in 1990 would contain the equivalent of all the computer power available in the United States at that time. And who could have believed a mere fifteen years ago that millions of homes would contain computers that were purchased for little more than the cost of most standard household appliances. Ten years ago having students interact with a microcomputer as readily as they use a textbook was little more than a dream held by a few visionaries. In light of these developments, the futures we have projected do not seem so farfetched after all.

TEACHING ABOUT ISSUES

Most educators agree that computer ethics is not a subject that lends itself to ready conclusions—right and wrong are often hard to distinguish. What is more important than firm conclusions, however, is the process involved as classes get caught up in dilemmas. The idea is to present short scenarios whose outcomes vary according to specific actions taken; as a result of these actions, legal and moral ramifications arise that lead to additional discussion and research, and the pattern continues to widen. Those who are most successful at teaching about issues do few of the traditional things. Instead, they stir things up a bit and then let the students take over. In essence, they identify issues, discuss typical instances of questionable computer-related activities, and describe some dilemmas; then they become moderators.

This is an excellent time to acquaint students with various laws that impact on computer-related activities. For example, the amended copyright law deals directly with such activities as the copying of commercial programs. As the discussion evolves, it may be constrained and focused somewhat by the framework created by the set of appropriate laws. However, the fact that certain laws exist should not discourage students from proposing a different, possibly more desirable, alternative. Also, the discussion need not always center around what is; it might evolve around the best and worst possible technological futures.

Many discussion topics are offered in this chapter, but other sources, such as newspaper articles and actual experiences, should be considered also. The students themselves are often a good source of topics. Many are able to offer a variety of suggestions that can be enlarged upon in the classroom, such as the following actual examples. One girl talked about the fact that her mother, a stenographer, was attending a seminar to learn word processing in order to keep her job. A second girl wondered how it is that so much personalized mail reaches her home from companies her family has never heard of. A boy brought up the fact that his parents are angry with the computer at the natural gas company because it cannot seem to provide accurate bills. Another boy has heard his father, who works for a computer firm, express concern that some of the high-tech developments may have been stolen by a former employee. Still another student mentioned a newspaper article in which a hacker admitted to breaking into private data bases on over one hundred occasions. Student-generated concerns such as these provide a point of departure for class discussions.

Discussions can take the form of dilemmas—short scenarios involving imaginary individuals confronted with a computer-related problem. Various courses of action are provided, with different consequences accruing from each. The dilemmas are typically conceived by the teacher, but students are perfectly capable of generating their own. For more information on this approach, together with sample dilemmas, refer to the article "Teaching Ethics in the Computer Classroom," by Hannah and Matus. As the discussions progress, students frequently take sides, and things begin to heat up. On the other hand, activities can also slow down considerably as interest in a given topic wanes. In any case, the teacher must be actively involved in guiding and encouraging the discussion, at the same time avoiding the imposition of personal values or conclusions on the students. This takes practice, but the results can definitely be worth the effort.

SUMMARY

Emphasis has been placed on the technological aspects of computer use to the near exclusion of related social and ethical issues. However, a growing awareness of the importance of these latter issues has caused many scholars and leaders to suggest that the schools assume a major part of the responsibility for addressing them. In order to involve students in meaningful discussions, teachers must be aware of the various issues involved. In this chapter we outlined several topics that can serve as the basis for class activities. A concern that is particularly pertinent to educators is how the computer will influence both how and what students learn. Computer crime, which continues to make headlines as money and goods are stolen through ingenious schemes involving individuals knowledgeable about computers, is another important subject to consider.

Technology is a big commodity for computer thieves, with both foreign and domestic organizations paying premium prices for stolen secrets.

Less skillful thieves simply fill their pockets with chips, then turn around and sell them to the highest bidder. Hackers unlock protected data bases with their electronic keys and sometimes create havoc by altering information; at other times they silently slip away, leaving no trace of their unauthorized entry. Issues of privacy arise when masses of personal information—often of a sensitive nature—are accessed by strangers who sometimes use the information for unethical purposes.

Viruses and worms are segments of computer code placed in legitimate programs with malicious intent by knowledgeable individuals. Computer "diseases" are highly contagious, spreading from one program to another through the computer's operating system until entire networks are infected. They can destroy masses of valuable data, or slow down equipment and even cause it to malfunction.

As society changes from an industrial to a high-technology orientation, the displacement of certain segments of the work force is bound to take place. The situation is akin to the transition from an agrarian to an industrialized society that took place over a century ago. The question is, will society be better equipped to cope with the current phenomenon than it was the earlier one?

The problem of computer equity continues to persist, despite efforts to make opportunities more widely available to those who are being excluded. Females have traditionally not had the degree of access to computer-related training and jobs that males have enjoyed. Several reasons for this state of affairs have been identified, but the major factor appears to be sexual stereotyping.

Predictions for the future include everything from electronic cottages to biochips that supplement human organs. The implementation of futuristic technologies will surely lead to radical changes in society as it currently exists. This, in turn, will generate unique social, moral, and ethical problems.

Teaching about issues typically takes the form of a class discussion. A dilemma can be devised by the teacher or students to pose a hypothetical problem with several alternative ways to proceed, each with its own consequences. The teacher serves as a moderator during class activities, offering suggestions, providing information and support, and maintaining control over the discussion as it progresses. Involving students in issue-related activities is a most important function of the schools—although great emphasis has been placed on the acquisition of cognitive knowledge, the area relating to moral issues has been ignored to a large extent. By including activities of this kind in the curriculum a better balance will be obtained, and students will be better able to cope with the technological future, whatever form it may take.

SELF-TEST

1. The current computer revolution has been likened to which of the following:
   a. French Revolution
   b. Industrial Revolution
   c. the change from a hunting and gathering society to one based on agriculture
   d. the development of atomic power
2. For every program legally sold in Asia and Latin America how many unauthorized copies are distributed?
   a. 1
   b. 5
   c. 10
   d. 15
3. Copyright law states that the purchaser of a program may make how many copies of that program?
   a. as many copies as desired
   b. no copies
   c. no more than three copies
   d. only one archival copy
4. Which of the following is the main purpose for using an encryption system?
   a. sending data through a network
   b. copy protecting a disk
   c. scrambling data so it cannot be read
   d. killing a virus

5. For which reason do hackers generally break into restricted databases?
   a. to steal information
   b. to outsmart the system
   c. to alter data
   d. to pilfer money and goods
6. How are viruses introduced into the programs they infect?
   a. through the operating system
   b. from a utility program
   c. from the ROM
   d. by careless programming practices
7. The most prevalent reason for girls to shy away from computers is that they
   a. see computers as having no practical value.
   b. lack talent for using computers.
   c. fear that status in their peer group might suffer.
   d. find computers to be boring.
8. When discussing computer equity, which of the following women would be your first choice as a role model for girls?
   a. Mary Cassatt
   b. Bertha, Duchess of Bavaria
   c. Ada, Countess of Lovelace
   d. Mary, Queen of Scots

9. In the future traditional students will likely communicate with their computers using
   a. simple programming languages.
   b. Ultrasonic Mouse Typing.
   c. voice interfacing and speech synthesis.
   d. infrared keyboards.
10. List three common contemporary activities that would not be possible were it not for computers.
11. Describe why an electronic bank robbery is generally more difficult to deal with than one committed the old-fashioned way.
12. The theft of information is a growing computer crime. What kind of information is most commonly stolen?
13. List three precautions that might be taken if you suspect that a virus might be lurking in some software.
14. Define the word "telecommuting."
15. Why does parallel processing hold greater promise than serial processing for developing "intelligent" computers?
16. True or false: Software producers typically make a 75 percent profit on their products.
17. True or false: Smaller software companies have been known to go bankrupt due to uncontrolled piracy.
18. True or false: It is alright for a teacher to copy software because it is done to benefit the students.
19. True or false: If a program is not copy protected it is permissible to make multiple copies of it.
20. True or false: The copyright law states that you may use both the original and backup copies of a disk to run two computers simultaneously.

REFERENCES

Becker, H. "Men and Women as Computer-Using Teachers." *Sex Roles: A Journal of Research* (August 1985): 137–148.

Bitter, G., and R. Camuse. *Using a Computer in the Classroom* 2d ed. Englewood Cliffs, N.J.: Prentice Hall, 1988.

Bracey, G. "Computing at Risk: Students Get Bad Grades on First Report Card." *Electronic Learning* (September 1988): 36–37.

Brady, H. "Artificial Intelligence: What's in It for Educators?" *Classroom Computer Learning* (January 1986): 26–29.

Brandt, R. "Micromechanics: the Eyes and Ears of Tomorrow's Computers." *Business Week* (March 17, 1988): 88–89.

Brawer, J. "A + Teacher's Toolbox: Computer Equity Project Seeks To Close the Computer-use Gender Gap." *A + Magazine* (September 1988): 61, 63.

Chaffin, E. "Computer Viruses: An Epidemic Real or Imagined?" *Electronic Learning* (April 1989): 36–37.

Dewdney, A. "Computer Recreations: Of Worms, Viruses, and Core War." *Scientific American* (March 1989): 110–113.

Evans, C. *The Micro Millennium.* New York: Washington Square Press, 1979.

Fennema, E. "Girls, Women and Mathematics." In E. Fennema and M. Ayer, ed., *Women and Education.* Berkeley: McCutchen, 1984.

Fischer, M. "Telecommunications: Ways To Battle Computer Viruses." *A + Magazine* (August 1988): 81–82.

Hannah, L., and C. Matus. "Teaching Ethics in the Computer Classroom." *Classroom Computer Learning* (April/May 1984): 32–36.

Hawkins, J. "Computers and Girls: Rethinking the Issues." *Sex Roles: A Journal of Research* (August 1985): 165–180.

Hertzberg, L. "Down with Software Copy Protection! Let's Hear It for Mutual Trust!" *Electronic Learning* (March 1989): 8–9.

Hess, R., and I. Miura. "Gender Differences in Enrollment in Computer Camps and Classes." *Sex Roles: A Journal of Research* (August 1985): 193–203.

Kreidler, W. "Teaching Computer Ethics." *Electronic Learning* (January 1984): 54–57.

Lillie, D., W. Hannum, and G. Stuck. *Computers and Effective Instruction.* New York: Longman, 1989.

Linn, M. "Fostering Equitable Consequences from Computer Learning Environments." *Sex Roles: A Journal of Research* (August 1985): 229–240.

Marx, B. "What the Publisher Pockets." *Electronic Learning* (May/June 1989): 15.

McGinty, T. "Three Trailblazing Technologies for Schools." *Electronic Learning* (September 1987): 26–30.

NYS Division of Women. *Computer Equity: Proceedings of a Conference.* Albany, NY: New York State Division for Women, 1989.

Raghavan, K., and A. Katz. "Smithtown: An Intelligent Tutoring System." *T.H.E. Journal* (August 1989): 50–53.

Reed, S., and R. Sautter. "Visions of the 1990s." *Electronic Learning* (May/June 1987): 18–23.

Reinhold, F. "Sorting Out the Equity Issues." *Electronic Learning* (February 1985): 33–37.

Salpeter, J. "Have It Your Way." *Classroom Computer Learning* (January 1988): 34–43.

Sanders, J., and A. Stone. *The Neuter Computer: Computers for Girls and Boys.* New York: Neal-Schuman, 1986.

Toffler, A. *Future Shock.* New York: Random House, 1970.

Toffler, A. *The Third Wave.* New York: William Morrow, 1980.

Ware, M., and M. Stuck. "Sex-Role Messages vis-a-vis Microcomputer Use: A Look at the Pictures." *Sex Roles: A Journal of Research* (August 1985): 205–214.

GLOSSARY

Acoustic coupler: A type of modem that uses the handset of a standard telephone through which signals are sent to and received from remote computers.

Address: A location within the computer's random access memory (RAM) into which data and instructions can be "written" and from which they can be "read."

Analog: Continuous electrical or physical currents that flow smoothly as opposed to distinct on/off signals (see *Digital*).

Application program: A program written for a specific application, such as word processing.

Arithmetic logic unit (ALU): That part of the central processing unit that performs arithmetic operations and carries out logic operations.

ASCII Code: The American Standard Code for Information Interchange. Composed of binary 0s and 1s in various combinations; this code is used to represent the standard alphanumeric characters (the letters, numbers, and symbols on the keyboard).

Assembly language: A low-level language that uses short, mnemonic "words" instead of the common words used for higher-level languages.

Authoring language: A language whose structure lends itself to the in-house development of educational software such as tutorials and drill-and-practice lessons.

Authoring system: A program for use in creating computer-based materials such as lessons and tests. Using an authoring system requires no knowledge of programming; typically, material is entered in response to prompts and the software organizes this into the lesson. Sophisticated systems include a text editor, graphics and sound generation, and animation features, as well as branching and tracking capabilities.

Backup: A duplicate of a program. A backup disk contains a second copy of a particular program or document.

Bandwidth: The width, or total range, of the frequencies available for transmission of data on a specific channel (the total up-and-down movement of the wave length as it is being transmitted).

BASIC: Beginner's All-purpose Symbolic Instruction Code—the most commonly used language for microcomputers, generally programmed into the ROM of the microcomputer.

Baud: A unit of speed equal to the number of discrete signals per second, that is, the speed at which bits are transmitted (e.g., 300 baud equals 300 bits per second).

Binary: The number system that computers use that uses the digits 0 and 1 and has a base of 2.

Bit: Stands for binary digit: the smallest unit of information, a 1 or a 0; combined in units of eight to represent characters (see *Byte*).

Boot: Loading the operating system from the disk so large programs can be run; getting the disk operating system (DOS) up and running.

Bug: A problem in the program which keeps it from working properly (see *Debug*).

Bus: The electronic circuitry that connects all the parts of the computer together and over which the data and instructions flow.

Byte: Eight bits combined in a code to represent a character (e.g., *A, 8, @*).

Chip: The small section of silicon that contains the etched-in integrated circuit.

Compact disk read only memory (CD ROM): Information is stored in digital rather than analog form and a laser beam is used to read the information. Very large amounts of data can be stored in this manner.

Computer-assisted instruction (CAI): The use of computers in education for such exercises as drill-and-practice, tutorials, instructional games, and simulations.

Computer-managed instruction (CMI): The use of the computer for management functions such as diagnostic testing, record keeping, study, prescription generation, and scheduling.

Control program for microcomputers (CP/M): A common type of disk operating system.

Courseware: The program on a disk or tape and the printed material that supports it.

Cursor: The block of flashing light or other configuration that indicates where the next character will occur on the screen.

Daisy wheel printer: A printing device that uses a matrix with multiple spokes (or petals) upon whose tips the characters are located; these are transferred when the spoke is hit by a small impact device.

Data base: A collection of information in a central location that is accessible to remote computers, generally through telephone lines and a modem.

Data base management system (DBMS): A program that provides an efficient way to access and manipulate information in a data base. This type of system, while similar to the file management system used in schools, is more versatile, being capable of managing several files at the same time.

Debug: To find and fix the errors in a program.

Demodulation: The process of receiving tones from a transmitted sequence and converting them into electrical pulses that can be interpreted by the microcomputer; changing analog to digital signals (see *Modulation*).

Demonstration: Using the microcomputer to show how to make or do something, or how something operates or performs.

Desktop publishing: Using a computer and publishing programs to create materials such as newsletters and brochures that formerly required the services of a professional printing shop to produce.

Digital: The electronic system utilized by microcomputers that consists of distinct on/off pulses rather than continuous electrical currents (see *Analog*).

Digitizer: A device that translates the light and dark tones of a picture or object into digital signals the computer uses to restructure the picture as a screen display.

Direct-connect modem: The device used to access remote data bases over phone lines, but bypassing the telephone handset; it is attached directly to the computer and plugs into the phone jack (see also *Acoustic coupler*).

Diskette: A flat, magnetically sensitive storage device used for the mass storage of data outside of the computer. The most common format is currently the five-inch variety (see also *Hard disk*).

Disk operating system (DOS): The program that enables the computer and disk drives to work together in the storage and retrieval of data.

Display: The visual representation of data or graphics on the monitor or television screen.

Documentation: The printed (as well as the software-based) materials that serve as instructions for the proper use of the software and hardware.

Dot matrix printer: An impact printer having a matrix of wires that can be selectively activated to form a character.

Down-load: The process of sending information from a large computer to a smaller one; to capture the information sent to your computer by another computer as hard copy or on a data disk, as opposed to letting it disappear as it scrolls off the screen.

Drill and practice: A type of computer-based instruction that allows students to practice or study information with which they are familiar but not proficient.

Execute: The cycle the computer goes through as it carries out a particular instruction.

External memory: Memory that resides outside of the computer; common external storage devices are disks and tapes.

File: Related collections of data that are stored together under a common name in a mass storage medium such as a disk.

File management system: A simplified database management program useful for classroom applications, limited to the use of one file at a time. (see also *Database management system*).

Firmware: Programs wired into read only memory (ROM) when the computer is manufactured. An example is the BASIC interpreter.

Floppy disk: See "Diskette."

Foundation: An institution, corporation, or legal entity that endows funds for special research projects of an educational nature.

Frame: A self-contained visual display seen as a unit on the monitor; a screen.

Function key: A key that instructs the computer to perform a specified task rather than printing out a character; some computers have numerous function keys, others very few.

Grant application or proposal: The written request submitted to a foundation for the purpose of securing funding for educational research programs or projects.

Graphics: A computer-generated pictorial display that may also be printed as hard copy; there are two kinds: high-resolution (fine dots and lines) and low-resolution (blocks).

Hacker: Formerly used to describe one who was hooked on computers; now has the negative connotation of one who enters restricted computer data bases and does mischief.

Hard copy: Computer output on paper created through the use of a printer or plotter.

Hard disk: A finely machined aluminum disk coated with a magnetic material capable of holding millions of bytes of data; much faster and more efficient than the floppy disks. (see *Disk*).

Hardware: The mechanical components of the computer system, including the computer, disk drives, monitors, and printers.

High-level language: A programming language that uses common words in its vocabulary; must be translated into binary code that the computer can work with by a program such as an interpreter or compiler.

Initialize: To format the surface of and place DOS commands on a new disk so it can store information.

Inkjet printer: A nonimpact printer that forms characters by forcing tiny droplets of ink through orifices.

Input: The activity of introducing information into the computer; the most common input device on microcomputers is the keyboard.

Instruction: A statement that informs the computer of the operation it is to perform with a specified piece of data.

Instructional games: A motivational strategy used to achieve specific learning objectives using the unique capabilities of the microcomputer; requires a student to follow prescribed rules and includes some form of competition with herself, another student, or the computer.

Integrated application program: A program containing several applications such as a spreadsheet, word processor, and data base management system; data can be transferred among modules for modification and integration.

Integrated circuit chip (IC chip): The complete electronic system, consisting of the transistors, diodes, and other elements formed together on a single silicon chip.

Integrated learning system (ILS): A central microcomputer or minicomputer with a hard disk or CD ROM and software consisting of planned sequential lessons in various subject areas.

Interactive: A characteristic of some CAI materials in which the user and the computer interact.

Interactive video: A system composed of a computer, a videotape or videodisc player, and software from which students receive immediate and varied feedback; provides branching based on student performance or preference and generally includes authoring features so lessons can be tailored to specific needs.

Interface: The go-between—such as between a printer and the computer or between two computers—that permits two parts of the system to work together.

Kilobyte (K): When used to indicate computer capacity, K means 1024 bytes or characters; (K normally means 1000).

Laser printer: Patterned after the electrostatic copier, this type of printer has a light-sensitive drum upon which images are formed with a laser; a toner adheres to the image area and is transferred to paper to create very high quality text and graphics.

List: A display of the actual program as it was written by the programmer.

Local area network (LAN): A system of interconnected data processing equipment, generally several computers with the support of peripherals such as printers and hard disk storage in a limited physical area.

Logo: A programming language that uses a graphics mode (turtle graphics) for the introduction of geometric concepts; also incorporates a powerful text mode.

Low-level language: A symbolic programming language using coded commands rather than common words.

Machine language: A code that is directly understood by the computer; instructions and data composed of the 0s and 1s that the computer deals with directly.

Mainframe computer: A large, powerful computer.

Media center: A learning environment that provides a systematically collected source of all forms of information, cataloged, classified, and stored to be available upon request.

Megabyte: A measure of storage roughly equal to one million bytes (actually 1,048,576 bytes); abbreviated M, MB, or meg.

Memory: The storage area in which instructions and data are stored; also holds the results of processing (see *Random access memory* and *Read only memory*).

Microcomputer-based laboratory (MBL): Provides probeware for students to use in conducting real-time experiments; the computer collects data as it is generated by the on-going experiment using probes and interfaces and the data are interpreted and displayed on the screen in the form of dynamic charts and graphs.

Microcomputer system: A system that consists of at least a microcomputer, a monitor, and an external storage device and may include additional peripheral devices.

Microprocessor: The part of the microcomputer that actually does the computing; a processor on a single chip.

Microsecond: One millionth of a second.

Millisecond: One thousandth of a second.

Modem: Stands for modulator-demodulator: this device converts binary code into audio signals that can be transmitted over telephone lines; it also does the converse for input to the computer.

Modulation: Process whereby signals are made compatible with telephone communication facilities; changing digital to analog signals (see *Demodulation*).

Monitor: A program in read only memory that controls basic computer functions; also a video display device based on a cathode ray tube.

Mouse: An input device used in place of the keyboard for certain functions such as making selections from a menu.

Nanosecond: One billionth of a second.

Network: Several computers and their peripherals that work together over lesser or greater distances, through a common set of connections.

Nonvolatile: Used to describe memory that is not erased when power is removed (see *Read only memory*).

Operating system: A program that permits the computer to operate effectively with its peripherals; the disk operating system (DOS) is the most familiar variety.

Output: The information that is sent from the computer to any kind of peripheral (such as a monitor or printer).

Parallel: A way of managing the transmission and storage of a byte so that all bits are handled together as a unit; (see also "serial").

Pascal: A high-level block-structured programming language consisting of two parts: a heading, which names the program and specifies the variables it will use, and the body of the program, subdivided into six sections.

PC projector: A device hooked to a microcomputer's output port that allows a computer program to be outputted directly to a transparent LCD screen; this screen is placed on an overhead projector and the program is projected onto a classroom screen.

Peripheral: An electronic device, such as a printer or monitor, that is part of the total system but separate from the microcomputer.

PILOT: Programmed Inquiry Learning or Teaching—an interactive computer language that employs a text editor, graphics editor, and music editor capability, thereby enabling teachers without prior computer experience to develop and test dialog programs for classroom application.

Pixel: Stands for picture element: an illuminated dot on the monitor screen.

Port: The electronic circuitry through which data enters and leaves the computer.

Printer: The peripheral device connected to the computer to produce output on paper (hard copy).

Probeware: See *Microcomputer-based laboratory*.

Program: The sequence of instructions designed to make the computer carry out a given task.

Random access memory (RAM): The internal storage area of the computer in which instructions and data are stored temporarily; volatile memory that can be accessed directly and altered by the user; the computer's working memory.

Read: To obtain information from a storage medium; memory is read from and written into.

Read only memory (ROM): The internal storage area in which programs are placed at the time the computer is manufactured; nonvolatile memory that usually can't be changed.

Register: An electronic storage space inside the central processing unit in which information is stored temporarily while the computer is working on it.

Scrolling: The movement of a program either horizontally or vertically on the display screen.

Sector: A storage area on a floppy disk.

Semiconductor: A material, such as silicon, that can behave either as an insulator or as a conductor of electrical current.

Serial: The method of transmitting data one bit after the other (see "parallel").

Simulation: A kind of computer-based instruction that allows students to interact with models of reality that may otherwise be impossible, dangerous, or impractical.

Site licensing: An arrangement between a software producer and a school or district in which software is provided to the purchaser for use only at a specified site.

Software: The programs that provide instructions to the computer.

Spelling checker: A program used in conjunction with a word processor to examine the document for misspellings, double words, and perhaps other mistakes.

Station: An area, such as a study carrel, where a microcomputer system is housed for student use.

Study carrel: A study center usually consisting of three partitions attached to a desk area and equipped with electrical power needed to run a microcomputer system.

Style checker: A program used in conjunction with the word processor: allows the user to examine the document for problems such as wordiness, redundancy, and overuse of passive voice.

Telecommunications: Communication across distances via telephone lines or reserved lines.

Template: A predesigned file stored on a disk that defines the form of a spreadsheet; the format and formulas are in place and data are entered by the user.

Terminal: A keyboard and monitor used to communicate with a remote computer.

Thermal printer: A printer that uses heated wires in a matrix to form characters on sensitized paper.

Thesaurus: A program used with a word processor to provide a list of synonyms for selected words; may also provide antonyms, homonyms, and homophones.

Tutorial: Uses the computer to present a concept that a learner does not yet know, presenting the lesson in segmental individualized steps.

Up-load: To send information via a modem to another computer directly from a floppy disk (see *Download*).

User friendly: A computer or program that operates in human terms rather than forcing the user to operate on the machine's terms; also the tolerance of the system for user mistakes.

Videodisc: A disk that has been encoded using lands and pits to represent the 0s and 1s used by a computer. The disk is capable of storing both words and graphics. The data stored on the disk are read by a laser beam.

Virus: Computer viruses are clandestine commands or program segments inserted into a system to reproduce themselves and do damage to legitimate data.

Volatile: Describes random access and other memories that lose their contents when power is removed.

Whole class instruction: The teacher uses a single computer as a presentation device for the entire class; usually with multiple monitors, a large monitor, a PC projection panel, or an overhead projector and a wall screen.

Word: The unit of data with which the computer works; a specified number of parallel bits (8, 16, or more depending on the size of the computer) that are always handled as a unit.

Word processing: Using a computer and special software to write and edit various kinds of text materials.

APPENDIX A
Software Publishers and Suppliers

Academic Hallmarks, Inc.
P.O. Box 998
Durango, CO 81302
(800)321-9218

Academic Software
1415 Queen Anne Road
Teaneck, NJ 07666
(800)227-5816

Accolade, Inc.
20813 Stevens Creek Blvd.
Cupertino, CA 95014
(408)446-5757

Action Research
11442 Marine View Dr., S.W.
Seattle, WA 98146
(206)241-1645

Active Learning Systems, Inc.
5365 Avenida Encinas, Suite J
Carlsbad, CA 92008
(800)423-0818

Activision
(see Mediagenic)

Addison-Wesley Publishing Co.
2725 Sand Hill Road
Menlo Park, CA 94025
(415)854-0300

AdLib, Inc.,
50 Staniford St.
Suite 800
Boston, MA 02114
(418)529-9676

Advanced Ideas
2902 San Pablo Ave.
Berkeley, CA 94702
(415)526-9100

Aeius Corporation
P.O. Box 700457
San Jose, CA 95170
(408)257-0658

Aldus Corporation
411 First Ave.
Suite 200
Seattle, WA 98104
(206)622-5500

American Educational Computer, Inc.
7506 N. Broadway, Suite 505
Oklahoma City, OK 73116
(405)840-6031

Apple Computer, Inc.
20525 Mariani Ave.
Cupertino, CA 95014
(408)995-1010

Aquarius Instructional
P.O. Box 128
Indian Rocks Beach, FL 34635
(800)338-2644

Aspen Publishers, Inc.
P.O. Box 6018
Gaithersburg, MD 20877
(800)638-8437

Authorware, Inc.
8400 Normandale Lake Blvd.
Suite 430
Minneapolis, MN 55437

Awareness Software
P.O. Box 18134
Portland, OR 97213
(503)278-3530

Baudville
5380 52nd St. SE
Grand Rapids, MI 49508
(616)698-0888

Beagle Bros.
3990 Old Town Ave.
Suite 102C
San Diego, CA 92110
(619)296-6400

Berkeley Softworks
2150 Shattuck Ave.
Berkeley, CA 94704
(415)644-0883

Berta-Max, Inc.
3420 Stone Way N
P.O. Box 31849
Seattle, WA 98103
(206)547-4056

Blue Chip Software
(see Britannica Software)

Blue Lion Software
90 Sherman St.
Cambridge, MA 02140
(617)876-2500

Bobbing Software
67 Country Oaks Dr.
Buda, TX 78610
(512)295-5045

Boring Software Co.
P.O. Box 568
Boring, OR 97009
(503)663-4464

Brewster Software Systems
Route 1
Markville, MN 55048
(612)242-3236

Britannica Software
345 Fourth St.
San Francisco, CA 94107
(800)572-2272

Broderbund Software Inc.
17 Paul Dr.
San Rafael, CA 94903
(415)492-3200

Burrows Software
807 College Ave.
Wooster, OH 44691

Bytes of Learning, Inc.
150 Consumers Rd.
Suite 202
Willowdale, Ont. M2J 1P9
Canada
(416)495-9913

CAE Software
P.O. Box 6227
Washington, DC 20015
(202)966-3686

C&C Software
5713 Kentford Cir.
Wichita, KS 67220
(316)683-6056

Cambridge Development Laboratory, Inc.
P.O. Box 605
Newton Lower Falls, MA 02162
(800)637-0047

Chancery Software Ltd.
#500 1168 Hamilton St.
Vancouver, B.C. V6B 2S2
(800)663-8831

Chariot Software Group
3659 India St.
Suite 100C
San Diego, CA 92103
(800)CHARIOT

Chatterbox Voice Learning Systems
2265 Westwood Blvd.
Suite 9
Los Angeles, CA 90064
(800)531-5314

Claris
440 Clyde Ave.
Mountain View, CA 94043
(408)987-7000

Class1 Systems
17909 Maple
Lansing, IL 60438

Classroom Consortia Media, Inc.
#1 Edgewater Plaza
Suite 209
Staten Island, NY 10305
(800)237-1113

Collamore/D.C.Heath and Co.
2700 No. Richart
Indianapolis, IN 46219
(800)428-8071

College Board Publications
P.O. Box 886
New York, NY 10101
(212)713-8000

Columbia Computing Services
1380 Burrard St.
Suite 600
Vancouver, B.C. V6Z 2H3
Canada
(800)663-0544

CompTech Systems Design
P.O. Box 516
Hastings, MN 55033
(612)437-1350

Compu-Teach
78 Olive St.
New Haven, CT 06511
(800)44-Teach

Computer Curriculum Corporation
P.O. Box 10080
Palo Alto, CA 94303
(800)227-8324

CONDUIT
University of Iowa,
Oakdale Campus
Iowa City, IA 52242
(319)335-4100

The Continental Press, Inc.
520 E. Bainbridge St.
Elizabethtown, PA 17022
(800)233-0759
In PA: (800)847-0656

CPI Software
145 East 49th St.
New York, NY 10017
(212)753-3800

Cricket Software
30 Valley Stream Pkwy.
Great Valley Corporate Center
Malvern, PA 19355
(215)251-9890

Cross Cultural Software
5385 Elrose Ave.
San Jose, CA 95124
(408)267-1044

Cross Educational Services
P.O. Box 1536
Ruston, LA 71270
(318)255-8921

CUE SoftSwap
P.O. Box 271704
Concord, CA 94527-1704
(415)685-7289

Dataflo Computer Services, Inc.
HC 32, P.O. Box 1,
Enfield, NH 03748
(603)448-2223

Datapak
14011 Ventura Blvd.
Suite 507
Sherman Oaks, CA 91423
(818)905-6419

Davidson and Associates, Inc.
3135 Kashiwa Street
Torrance, CA 90505
(800)556-6141

D.C. Heath (see Collamore/D.C. Heath)

Decision Development Corp.
2680 Bishop Dr.
Site 122
San Ramon, CA 94583
(415)830-8896

DesignWare, Inc.
(see Britannica Software)

Didatech Software Ltd.
3812 William St.
Burnaby, B.C. V5C 3H9
Canada
(604)299-4435

Digital Learning Systems
4 Century Dr.
Parsippany, NJ 07054
(201)538-6640

Digital Research, Inc.
60 Garden Ct.
Monterey, CA 93942
(408)649-4343

Digital Vision, Inc.
66 Eastern Ave.
Dedham, MA 02026
(800)346-0090

Walt Disney Personal Computer Software
4563 Colorado Blvd.
Los Angeles, CA 90039
(818)956-3005

DLM
1 DLM Park
P.O. Box 4000
Allen, TX 75002
(800)527-4747

E. David & Associates
22 Russett Ln.
Storrs, CT 06268
(203)429-1785

Education Systems Corp.
6170 Cornerstone Ct. East
Suite 300
San Diego, CA 92121
(619)587-0087

Educational Activities, Inc.
P.O. Box 392
Freeport, NY 11520
(800)645-3739

Educational Publishing Concepts
P.O. Box 715
St. Charles, IL 60174
(800)323-9459

Educational Technology
6150 N. 16th St.
Phoenix, AZ 85016
(800)422-4339

Educational Technology Center (ETC)
Harvard Graduate School of Education
337 Gutman Library
Appian Way
Cambridge, MA 02138
(617)495-9373

Educational Testing Service
Rosedale Rd.
Princeton, NJ 08541
(609)734-5732

Educomp
2431 Oxford Ave.
Cardiff, CA 92007
(800)843-9497

Educulture, Inc.
1 Dubuque Plaza
Dubuque, IA 52001
(800)553-4858

EduSoft
P.O. Box 2560
Berkeley, CA 94702
(800)EDUSOFT

EduWare
(See *Britannica Software*)

Electronic Arts Inc.
1820 Gateway Dr.
San Mateo, CA 94404
(415)571-7171

Electronic Learning Systems, Inc.
2630 NW 39th Ave.
Gainesville, FL 32605
(800)443-7971

E.M.A. Inc.
P.O. Box 339
Los Altos, CA 94023
(415)969-4679

E.M.E. Corp.
P.O. Box 2805
Danbury, CT 06813-2805
(203)798-2050

Epyx Inc.
600 Galveston Dr.
P.O. Box 8020
Redwood City, CA 94063
(415)366-0606

Estes Industries
1295 H St.
Penrose, CO 81240
(303)372-6565

First Byte
2845 Temple Ave.
Long Beach, CA 90806
(800)523-8070

Focus Media
P.O. Box 865
839 Stewart Ave.
Garden City, NY 11530
(800)645-8989

FutureComp Technology Co.
358 Grantwood Ave.
Staten Island, NY 10312
(800)255-6553

Gamco Industries, Inc.
P.O. Box 1911
Big Spring, TX 79721
(800)351-1404

Gessler Educational Software
900 Broadway
New York, NY 10003
(212)673-3113

Great Wave Software
5353 Scotts Valley Dr.
Scotts Valley, CA 95066
(408)438-1990

Grolier Electronic Publishing
95 Madison Ave.
New York, NY 10016
(212)696-9750

Harcourt Brace Jovanovich
1250 Sixth Ave.
San Diego, CA 92101
(619)699-6213

Hartley Courseware, Inc.
P.O. Box 419
133 Bridge St.
Dimondale, MI 48821
(800)247-1380

High Technology Software Products Inc.
8200 N. Classen Blvd.
Suite 104
Oklahoma City, OK 73114
(405)848-0480

Holt, Rinehart & Winston
1627 Woodland Ave.
Austin, TX 78741
(512)440-5700

Houghton Mifflin Co.
Educational Software Division
Mount Support Rd.
Lebanon, NH 03766
(800)258-9773

HRM Software, A Division of Queue, Inc.
562 Boston Ave.
Bridgeport, CT 06610
(800)232-2224
(203)335-0906

Humanities Software
2210 Wilshire Blvd.
Suite 365
Santa Monica, CA 90403
(213)396-1868

IBM
PC Software Department
One Culver Road
Dayton, NJ 08810
(800)IBM-2468

ICR Future Soft
P.O. Box 1446-DE
Orange Park, FL 32073
(800)221-3333

Ideal Learning, Inc.
5005 Royal Ln.
Irving, TX 75063
(214)929-4201

Impetus, Inc.
458-41st St.
Richmond, CA 94805-2224
(415)231-0199

Inductel, Inc.
18661 McCoy Ave.
Saratoga, CA 95070
(800)367-4497

Intelligent Software, Inc.
9609 Cypress
Munster, IN 46321
(800)521-4518

Interlearn
Box 342
Cardiff by the Sea, CA 92007
(619)481-4676

ISI Publishing
3501 Market St.
Philadelphia, PA 19104-9981

J&S Software
140 Reid Ave.
Port Washington, NY 11050
(516)944-9304

Jefferson Software
2 Players Club Dr.
Charleston, WV 25311
(800)468-4227

K-12 MicroMedia
6 Arrow Rd.
Ramsey, NJ 07446
(800)922-0401

Krell Software
Flowerfield #7
St. James, NY 11780
(800)245-7355

Laureate Learning Systems
110 East Spring St.
Winooski, VT 05404
(802)655-4755

LCSI
1000 Roche Blvd.
Vaudreuil, Quebec J7V 6B3
Canada
(800)321-5646

The Learning Company
6493 Kaiser Dr.
Fremont, CA 94555
(800)852-2255

Learning Odyssey
CAD/CAM Publishing, Inc.
841-Turquoise St.
Suite E
San Diego, CA 92109
(619)488-0533

Learning Research, Inc.
1065 Park Ave.
Suite 8D
New York, NY 10128
(212)534-5402

Learning Technologies
13633 Gamma Rd.
Dallas TX 75244
(214)385-2351

LINC Resources, Inc.
Publications Division
91 Vine St.
Pawtucket, RI 02861
(401)725-3973

Logo Computer Systems, Inc., Massachusetts
121 Mt. Vernon St.
Boston, MA 02108
(800)321-5646

Logo Computer Systems, Inc., Quebec
9960 Cote de Liesse Rd.
Lachine, P Q Quebec H8T 1A1
Canada
(514)631-7081

Macadamia Software
2503 Essex Place
Nashville, TN 37212
(615)383-2413

Macmillan Publishing Co.
866 Third Ave.
New York, NY 10022
(212)702-2000

MCE Inc.
157 S. Kalamazoo Mall
Suite 250
Kalamazoo, MI 49007
(800)421-4157

CTB/McGraw-Hill
2500 Garden Rd.
Monterey, CA 93940
(408)649-8400

MECC (Minnesota Educational Computing Corp.)
3490 Lexington Ave. N.
St. Paul, MN 55126
(800)228-3504

Media Materials Inc.
2936 Remington Ave.
Baltimore, MD 21211
(800)638-1010

Mediagenic (Activision)
3885 Bohannon Dr.
Menlo Park, CA 94025
(415)329-0800

Merit Audio Visual
157 Chambers St.
New York, NY 10007
(212)267-7437

Merrill Publishing Co.
P.O. Box 508
Columbus, OH 43216
(800)848-1567

Micro Power & Light Co.
12810 Hillcrest Rd. #120
Dallas, TX 75230
(214)239-6620

MicroIllusions
17408 Chatsworth St.
Granada Hills, CA 91344
(818)360-3715

Micromatics, Inc.
P.O. Box 28211
Baltimore, MD 21234
(301)529-0541

Microsoft Corporation
16011 N.E. 36th Way
Redmond, WA 98073
(206)882-8080

Microsystems Software Ltd.
P.O. Box 3123
Tempe, AZ 85281
(602)966-8615

Midwest Software
Box 214
Farmington, MI 48332
(313)477-0897

Milliken Publishing Co.
1100 Research Blvd.
St. Louis, MO 63132
(800)643-0008

Mindplay
100 Conifer Hill Dr.
Building 3, Suite 301
Danvers, MA 01923
(800)221-7911

Mindscape, Inc.
3444 Dundee Rd.
Northbrook, IL 60062
(800)221-9884

Mindwork Software
100 Pacific St.
Suite 555C,
Monterey, CA 93940
(408)375-1531

Morning Star Software
P.O. Box 5364
Madison, WI 53705
(800)533-0445

Mount Castor Industries, Inc.
P.O. Box 488
East Orleans, MA 02643
(800)942-9008

Music Systems For Learning, Inc.
311 East 38th St.
Suite 20C
New York, NY 10016

National Educational Software Services
1879 Locust Dr.
Verona, WI 53593
(608)845-8410

National Geographic Society Educational Services
Dept. 88
Washington, DC 20036
(800)368-2728

Opportunities for Learning, Inc.,
20417 Nordhoff St.
Dept. W2X
Chatsworth, CA 91311
(818)341-2535

Optical Data Corporation
30 Technology Dr.
Warren, NJ 07060
(800)524-2481

Optimum Resource, Inc.
Weekly Reader Software
10 Station Pl.
Norfolk, CT 06058
(800)327-1473

Oryx Press
2214 North Central at Encanto
Phoenix, AZ 85004
(602)254-6156

P11 Enterprises
P.O. Box 5185
Bridgeport, CT 06610
(203)366-0258

Pelican Software Inc.
8833 Reseda
Northridge, CA 91324
(800)247-4641

Periscope Press
P.O. Box 6926
Santa Barbara, CA 93160
(805)564-2518

PLATO Educational Services
Box 1305
Minneapolis, MN 55440
(800)328-1109

Polarware
1055 Paramount Pkwy.
Suite A
Batavia, IL 60510
(800)323-0884

Power Up!
2929 Campus Drive
P.O. Box 7600
San Mateo, CA 94403
(800)851-2917

Prentice Hall School Division
Sylvan Ave.
Englewood Cliffs, NJ 07632
(800)848-9500

Quark, Inc.
300 S. Jackson
Suite 100
Denver, CO 80209

Queue Inc.
562 Boston Ave.
Bridgeport, CT 06610
(800)232-2224
(203)335-0908

Random House Media
400 Hahn Rd.
Westminster, MD 21157
(800)638-6460

RDA/Mind Builders
P.O. Box 848
Stony Brook, NY 11790
(800)654-8715

Reality Technologies, Inc.
3624 Market St.
Philadelphia, PA 19104
(215)387-6055

Roger Wagner Publishing
1050 Pioneer Way
Suite P
El Cajon, CA 92020
(619)442-0524

Scholastic Software
P.O. Box 7502
2931 East McCarty St.
Jefferson City, MO 65102
(800)541-5513

Scott, Foresman and Company
1900 E. Lake Ave.
Glenview, IL 60025
(312)729-3000

Scribner-Laidlaw Educational Publishers
Front and Brown Streets
Riverside, NJ 08075
(800)257-5755

Sensible Software, Inc.
335 East Big Beaver
Suite 207
Troy, MI 48083
(313)528-1950

Seven Hills Software
2310 Oxford Rd.
Tallahassee, FL 32304
(904)576-9415

Shenandoah Software
P.O. Box 776
Harrisonburg, VA 22801
(703)433-9485

Sierra On-Line Inc.
40033 Sierra Way
Oakhurst, CA 93644
(800)344-7448

Simon and Schuster Software
One Gulf and Western Plaza
New York, NY 10023
(212)373-8862

Sir-Tech Software, Inc.
P.O. Box 245, Charleston
Ogdensburg Mall
Ogdensburg, NY 13669
(315)393-6633

Society for Visual Education Inc. (SVE)
1345 W. Diversey Parkway
Chicago, IL 60614
(800)621-1900

Software Discoveries, Inc.
137 Krawski Dr.
South Windsor, CT 06074
(203)872-1024

Software Toolworks
One Toolworks Plaza
13557 Ventura Blvd.
Sherman Oaks, CA 91423
(818)907-6789

Softwriters Development Corp.
4718 Hartford Rd.
Baltimore, MD 21214
(800)451-5726

Southeastern Software
7743 Briarwood Dr.
New Orleans, LA 70128
(504)246-8438

South-Western Publishing Co.
5105 Madison Rd.
Cincinnati, OH 45227
(800)543-0487

Spinnaker Software
One Kendall Sq.
Cambridge, MA 02139
(800)826-0706

Springboard Software
7808 Creekridge Cir.
Minneapolis, MN 55435
(800)654-6301

Stone Edge Technologies, Inc.
  P.O. Box 200
  Maple Glen, PA 19002
  (215)641-1825

Student Awareness Software
  P.O. Box 18134
  Portland, OR 97213
  (503)287-3530

Styleware, Inc.
  5250 Gulfton, No. 2E
  Houston, TX 77081
  (713)668-1360

Sunburst Communications
  39 Washington Ave.
  Pleasantville, NY 10570
  (800)431-1934

SVE (see Society for Visual Education)

Teacher Support Software
  P.O. Box 7130
  Gainsesville, FL 32605
  (800)228-2871]

Techware, Inc.
  P.O. Box 1085
  Altamonte Springs, FL 32715
  (305)834-3431

TeleRobotics International, Inc.
  8410 Oak Ridge Hwy.
  Knoxville, TN 37931
  (615)690-5600

Terrapin, Inc.
  376 Washington St.
  Malden, MA 02148
  (617)322-4800

Timeworks
  444 Lake Cook Rd.
  Deerfield, IL 60015
  (800)535-9497

Tom Snyder Productions
  90 Sherman St.
  Cambridge, MA 02140
  (800)342-0236

True Basic, Inc.
  39 South Main St.
  Hanover, NH 03755
  (800)TRBASIC

Unicorn Software Co.
  2950 East Flamingo Rd.
  Suite B
  Las Vegas, NV 89121
  (702)737-8862

Vernier Software
  2920 S.W. 89th St.
  Portland, OR 97225
  (503)297-5317

Videodiscovery
  (206)285-5400

Visible Software
  22 The Western Way
  Princeton, NJ 08540
  (609)683-4386

Weekly Reader Software
  (see Optimum Resources)

Wescott Software
  2316 Park Pl.
  Evanston, IL 60201
  (312)328-1367

J. Weston Walch, Publisher
  Box 658
  Portland, ME 04104
  (800)341-6094

Whitney Educational Services
  415 S. Eldorado St.
  San Mateo, CA 94402
  (415)341-5818

Wicat
  1875 S. State St.
  Orem, UT 84058
  (800)328-1145

Wiley Professional Software
  603 Third Ave.
  New York, NY 10158
  (212)850-6009

WordPerfect Corp.
  288 W. Center St.
  Orem, UT 84057

World Book, Inc.
  Merchandise Mart Plaza
  Fifth Floor
  Chicago, IL 60654
  (800)323-6366

Xerox Corporation
  PO Box 24
  Rochester, NY 14692
  (800)TEAM-XRX

Ztec Co.
  P.O. Box 1968
  Lexington, KY 40593
  (800)247-1603

APPENDIX B
Sources of Free or Inexpensive Software

American Software Publishing Company
1010 16th Street, N.W.
Washington, DC 20037

A.P.P.L.E. Co-op
290 Southwest 43rd St.
Renton, WA 98055

Boston Computer Society
Three Central Plaza
Boston, MA 02108

Center for Math Literacy
San Francisco State University
1600 Holloway Ave.
San Francisco, CA 94132

Chicago Public Library
North Pulaski Branch
4041 West North Ave.
Chicago, IL 60639

Commodore International Ltd.
(Consult local dealers for public domain software)

CONDUIT
P.O. Box 388
Iowa City, IA 52244

COSMIC
112 Barrow Hall
University of Georgia
Athens, GA 30602

Davis, Jack
c/o The Learning Center
College of Education
Gabel 8, Northern Illinois University
De Kalb, IL 60115

Educational Computing Network
12680 Hollyglen
Riverside, CA 92503

"Educational Programs for Children"
Report FPO1
P.O. Box 611
Palmyra, NJ 08065

Enrich/Ohaus
2325 Paragon Dr.
San Jose, CA 95131
Catalogs of free software for Apple, Atari, Commodore, and TI99/4A are $8.95 each)

First Osborne Users Group (FOG)
P.O. Box 11683-A
Palo Alto, CA 94306

FOLLK, Friends of LISP/Logo & Kids
436 Arballo Dr.
San Francisco, CA 94132

FreeSoft Co.
10828 Lacklink
St. Louis, MO 63117
(314)423-2190

Free Ware
P.O. Box 862
Tiburon, CA 94920

Georgia Micro Swap
Department of Math Education
University of Georgia
Athens, GA 30601
(Users must donate programs in order to receive programs)

International Apple Corps
P.O. Box 2227
Seattle, WA 98111
(Contact local Apple computer clubs for additional information)

International Home Computer Users Association (ICA)
P.O. Box 371
Rancho Santa Fe, CA 92067

Lawrence Hall of Science
MCEP, University of California
Berkeley, CA 94720
(414)642-5133

Micro-Ed
P.O. Box 24156
Minneapolis, MN 55424

Micro X Change
Suite 101
222 East Carrillo Street
Santa Barbara, CA 93101

National LOGO Exchange
P.O. Box 5341
Charlottesville, VA 22905
(Send stamped, self-addressed envelope)

National Public Domain Software
1533 Avohill Drive
Vista, CA 92083
(619) 727-1015 or (619) 941-0925

National Technical Information Service
Springfield, VA 22161

New York Amateur Computer Club
P.O. Box 106, Church Street Station
New York, NY 10008
(Catalog of public domain software for IBM personal computer and compatibles)

Nibble Magazine
P.O. Box 325
Lincoln, MA 01773

North Central Regional Library
Software Library Mail-Order Department
238 Olds Station Rd.
Wenatchee, WA 98801

Northwest Kaypro Users Group
c/o Charles Hornisher Communications
4700 Southwest MacAdam Avenue
Portland, OR 97201

Oklahoma Educational Computer Users Program (OECUP)
University of Oklahoma
601 Elm St.
Norman, OK 73019

Palos Computer Concepts
P.O. Box 560
Palos Park, IL 60464

PC Software Interest Group
1556 Halform Ave.
Suite 130 B
Santa Clara, CA 95051

People's Computer Company
Computertown, USA!
P.O. Box E.
Menlo Park, CA 91025
(Consult your local area telephone directory for additional addresses of Computertown, USA!)

Public Domain Software (for Atari)
297 Missouri Street
San Francisco, CA 94107
(Consult your local dealers for additional addresses)

Queue, Inc.
Five Chapel Hill Dr.
Fairfield, CT 06432

SOFTSWAP
c/o Ann Lathrop, Library Coordinator
San Mateo County Office of Education
333 Main St.
Redwood City, CA 94063

San Francisco Apple Core
1515 Sloat Blvd. #2
San Francisco, CA 94132

Technology Communications Group
38 Melrose Place
Montclair, NJ 07042

3A Computer Products
Apple Avocation Alliance
1803 Warren Avenue
Cheyenne, WY 82001
(307) 632-8561

Some valuable books that detail sources are listed below:

Apple Software for Pennies
by Bertram Gader
Warren Books
New York, NY

How to Get Free Software
by Alfred Glossbrenner
St. Martin's Press
New York, NY

APPENDIX C
Software Guides, Directories, Catalogs, and Reviews

Addison-Wesley Book of Apple Computer Software
16720 Hawthorne Blvd.
Lawndale, CA 90260

Allenbach Industries *(Software Reports)*
2101 Las Palmas
Carlsbad, CA 92008

American Peripherals
122 Bangor St.
Lindenhurst, NY 11757

Apple Software Directory,
Vol. 3—Education
WIDL Video
5245 West Diversey
Chicago, IL 60639

Atari Program Exchange
Atari, Inc.
P.O. Box 427
Sunnyvale, CA 94086

California Library Media Consortium Reviews
San Mateo County, Office of Education
333 Main St.
Redwood City, CA 94063

Commodore Software Encyclopedia
Commodore Business Machines, Software Group
681 Moore Rd.
300 Valley Forge Square
King of Prussia, PA 19406

Computer Information Exchange
P.O. Box 159
San Luis Rey, CA 92068

The Computing Teacher
Department of Computer and Information Science
University of Oregon
Eugene, OR 97403

Courseware Report Card
Elementary and Secondary Editions
Educational Insights
150 West Carob St.
Compton, CA 90220

Curriculum Products Review
530 University Avenue
Palo Alto, CA 94301

Data Text Company
Dresden Associates
P.O. Box 246
Dresden, ME 04342

Digest of Software Reviews
1341 Bulldog Lane, Suite C
Fresno, CA 93710

DISC Project
IICD Oakland Schools
2100 Pontiac Lake Rd.
Pontiac, MI 48054

Dvorak's Software Review
704 Solano Ave.
Albany, CA 94706

Educational Insights
150 West Carob St.
Compton, CA 90220

Educational Software Directory
Sterling Swift Publishing Company
P.O. 188
Machaca, TX 78652

Educational Software Selector (TESS)
EPIE Institute
P.O. Box 620
Stony Brook, NY 11790

Educational Software Sourcebook
Catalog No.26-2756
Radio Shack Educational Division
400 Atrium, One Tandy Center
Fort Worth, TX 76102

Educator's Handbook and Software Directory
Vital Information, Inc.
350 Union Station
Kansas City, MO 64108

EduSoft
Department EE, Box 2560
Berkeley, CA 94702

Edu-Soft
4639 Spruce Street
Philadelphia, PA 19139

Elsevier
Science Publishing Company, Inc.
New York, NY 10017

EPIE Evaluations
Educational Products Information Exchange
P.O. Box 839
Water Mill, NY 11976

Follett Library Book Company
Microcomputer Division
4506 Northwest Hwy.
Crystal Lake, IL 60014

Huntington Computing Catalog
Box 1297
Corcoran, CA 93212

ICP Software Directory
International Computer Programs Inc.,
9000 Keystone Crossing, P.O. Box 40946
Indianapolis, IN 46240

Instant Software
80 Pine St.
Peterborough, NH 03458

International Microcomputer Software Directory
420 South Howes St.
Fort Collins, CO 80521

J. M. Hammett Company
Microcomputer Division
P.O. Box 545
Braintree, MA 02184

Journal of Courseware Review
The Foundation for the Advancement of
Computer-aided Education
(FACE)
20525 Mariana Ave.
Cupertino, CA 95014

K–12 Micro Media
P.O. Box 17, Dept. G
Valley Cottage, NY 10989

Linc Associates
1875 Morse Rd.
Suite 215
Columbus, OH 43229

Marck
280 Linden Avenue
Brandon, CT 06405

Microcomputer Corporation Catalog
34 Maple Ave., Box 8
Armonk, NY 10504

Microcomputer Research Clinic
College of Education
Arizona State Univerisity
Tempe, AZ 85287

Microcomputers in Education Newsletter
Queue, Inc.
Five Chapel Hill Drive
Fairfield, CT 06432

MicroSift
N.W. Regional Educational Library
500 Lindsay Blvd.
710 S.W. Second Ave.
Portland, OR 97204

MicroWorld
Microcomputer Vendor Directory
Auerbach Publishers Inc.,
6560 North Park Dr.,
Pennsauken, NJ 08109

MISCO, Inc
Box 399
Holmdel, NJ 07733

Online Micro-Software Guide & Directory
Online Inc.
11 Tannery Lane
Weston, CT 06883

Opportunities for Learning, Inc.
8950 Lurline Ave.
Dept. 6 FM
Chatsworth, CA 91311

PC: The Buyer's Guide
Ziff-Davis
One Park Avenue
New York, NY 10016

PC Clearinghouse—Software Directory
PC Clearinghouse
Middleburg, VA 22117

PC Telemart Software Directory
PC Telemart
11781 Lee Jackson Highway
Fairfax, VA 22033

PC Telemart/Vanlove's Apple Software Directory
PC Telemart/Vanloves
Suite 108
8575 West 110th St.
Overland Park, KS 66210

Personal Software
Hajgden Publishing Company, Inc.
50 Essex St.
Rochelle Park, NJ 07662

Pipeline—Conduit
University of Iowa
P.O. Box 388
Iowa City, IA 52244

Queue
Five Chapel Hill Drive
Fairfield, CT 06432

Scholastic Inc.
904 Sylvan Avenue
Englewood Cliffs, NJ 07632

School Microware Reviews
Dresden Associates
Box 246
Dresden, ME 04342

Series Eighty Software Catalog
Reston Publishing Company, Inc.
11480 Sunset Hills Road
Reston, VA 22090

Society for Visual Education (SVE) Catalog
35 East Wacker Drive
Chicago, IL 60601

Sofsearch
Route 20, Box 3572
Gladiolus Dr.
Fort Myers, FL 33908

Softtalk Publishers, Inc.
7250 Laurel Canyon Blvd.
Hollywood, CA 91603

The Software Catalog
Elsevier Science Publishing Company
52 Vanderbilt Ave.
New York, NY 10017

The Software Directory
Software Central
P.O. Box 30424
Lincoln, NE 68503

Software Reports
Trade Service Publications
10996 Torreyena Road
P.O. Box 85007
San Diego, CA 92138

Software Reports
Allenbach Industries
2101 Las Palmas
Carlsbad, CA 92008

Special Education Technical Online Resources
Exceptional Child Center
Utah State University
Logan, UT 84322

The Specialware Directory
Oryx Press
2214 North Central at Encanto
Phoenix, AZ 85004

Sterling Swift Publishing Company
P.O. Box 188
Manchaca, TX 78652

Swift's Educational Software Directory
Sterling Swift Publishing Company
7901 South IH-35
Austin, TX 78744

Texas Instruments Program Directory
Texas Instruments
P.O. Box 53
Lubbock, TX 79408

TRS-80 Agricultural Software Sourcebook
TRS-80 Educational Software Sourcebook
(Available at Radio Shack Computer
Centers—consult your local stores)

TRS-80 Users Journal
Box 7112
Tacoma, WA 98407

User's
2520 Broadway Dr.
St. Paul, MN 55113

APPENDIX D
Computer Magazines and Newsletters

A+
Ziff-Davis Publishing Co.
One Park Ave.
New York, NY 10016

Apple Education News
P.O. Box 20485
San Jose, CA 95160

Apple Educator's Newsletter
9525 Lucerne
Ventura, CA 93003

Arithmetic Teacher Magazine
1906 Association Dr.
Reston, VA 22091

Byte
70 Main Street
Peterborough, NH 03458

Classroom Computer Learning
19 Davis Dr.
Belmont, CA 94002

Classroom Computer News
International Education
51 Spring St.
Watertown, MA 02172

Closing the Gap
Box 68
Henderson, MN 56044

Commodore Magazine
681 Moore Rd.
King of Prussia, PA 19406

Compute! Magazine
P.O.Box 5406
Greensboro, NC 27403

Computer-Using Educators
Mountain View High School
Mountain View, CA 94041

Computer-Using Educators Newsletter
Computer-Using Educators
Independence High School
1776 Education Park Dr.
San Jose, CA 95133

The Computing Teacher
Department of Computer & Information Science
University of Oregon
Eugene, OR 97850

Creative Computing
Box 789-M
Morristown, NJ 97690

CUE Newsletter
c/o Don McKell
Computer-Using Educators
Box 18547
San Jose, CA 95158

Digit Magazine
P.O. Box 29996
San Francisco, CA 94129

Education Computer News
1300 North 17th St.
Suite 1600
Arlington, VA 22209

Educational Computer Magazine
P.O. Box 535
Cupertino, CA 95015

Educational Resources & Techniques Magazine
Texas Association for Educational Technology
Eastfield College
3737 Motley Dr.
Mesquite, TX 75150

Educational Technology
140 Sylvan Ave.
Englewood Cliffs, NJ 07632

80 Computing
Pine St.
Peterborough, NH 03458

Electronic Education
Electronic Communications, Inc.
1311 Executive Center Dr.
Suite 200
Tallahassee, FL 32301

Electronic Learning
Scholastic, Inc.
902 Sylvan Ave.
Englewood Cliffs, NJ 07632

Enter
Children's Television Workshop
One Lincoln Plaza
New York, NY 10003

Family Computing
730 Broadway
New York, NY 10003

Hands On!
Technical Education Research Center
8 Eliot St.
Cambridge, MA 02138

inCider
CS Communications
80 Elm St.
Peterborough, NH 03458

InfoWorld
375 Cochituate Rd.
Box 800
Farmington, MA 01701

Journal of Computer-Based Instruction (ADCIS)
Computer Center
Western Washington University
Bellingham, WA 98225

Journal of Computers in Mathematics and Science Teaching (ACMST)
P.O. Box 60730
Phoenix, AZ 85082

Journal of Computers, Reading and Language Arts (CRLA)
NAVA
Box 13247
Oakland, CA 94661

Journal of Educational Computing Research
Baywood Publishing Company, Inc.
120 Marine St.
Box D
Farmington, NY 11735

Journal of Research on Computing in Education (IACE)
1230 Seventeenth St. N.W.
Washington, DC 20036

Logo and Educational Computing Journal
Suite 219
1320 Stony Brook Rd.
Stony Brook, NY 11790

Macazine
Icon Concepts Corporation
P.O. Box 1936
Athens, TX 75751

MACUL Journal
Michigan Association for Computer Users in Learning
Wayne County, ISD
33500 Van Born Rd.
Wayne, MI 48184

Mathematics Teacher
National Council of Teachers of Mathematics
1906 Association Dr.
Reston, VA 22091

Microcomputers in Education Queue
Five Chapel Hill Drive
Fairfield, CT 06432

Nibble
45 Winthrop St.
Concord, MA 01742

PC Magazine
1528 Irvine St.
San Francisco, CA 94122

PC World
P.O. Box 6700
Bergenfield, NJ 07621

Personal Computing
P.O. Box 2941
Boulder, CO 90321

Pipeline
P.O. Box 388
Iowa City, IA 52244

Popular Computing
70 Main St.
Peterborough, NH 03458

Rainbow
5803 Timber Ridge Dr.
Prospect, KY 40059

School Microcomputer Bulletin
Learning Publications, Inc.
P.O. Box 1326
Holmes Beach, FL 33509

School Science and Math Journal
 FMC-College of Education
 Arizona State University
 Tempe, AZ 85287

Science Teacher (NSTA)
 1742 Connecticut Ave. N.W.
 Washington, DC 20009

Social Science Microcomputer Review
 6697 College Station
 Durham, NC 27650

Teaching and Computers
 902 Sylvan Ave.
 Box 2001
 Englewood Cliffs, NJ 07632

T.H.E. Magazine
 Information Synergy, Inc.
 2626 South Pulman
 Santa Ana, CA 92705

Turtle News
 Young People's Logo Association (YPLA)
 P.O. Box 855067
 Richardson, TX 75085

Woman's Action Alliance
 370 Lexington Ave.
 New York, NY 10017

APPENDIX E

User Groups and Associations

Interested individuals should contact their local dealers for information about user groups involved with specific kinds of computers. (International Applecore for example, specializes in the Apple Computer.) The following list of state educational user groups is not complete, but it represents a cross section of active organizations that should be helpful. For additional information contact the various state departments of education. We have included in this appendix a listing of various associations. These groups can provide valuable information about sources, utilization, ideas, software, and special programs.

ACES, Computer Center
205 Skiff St.
Hamden, CT 06514

American Council on the Teaching of Foreign Languages
579 Broadway
Hastings-on-Hudson, NY 10706

American Vocational Association (AVA)
2020 North Fourteenth St.
Arlington, VA 22201

Association for Computers in Mathematics and Science Teaching
P.O. Box 4
Austin, TX 78765

Associations for Computing Machinery, Inc.
1133 Avenue of the Americas
New York, NY 10036

Association for the Development of Computer-based Instructional Systems (ADCIS)
Computer Center
Western Washington University
Bellingham, WA 98225

Association for Educational Communications and Technology (AECT)
1126 Sixteenth St. N.W.
Washington, DC 20036

Board of Cooperative Educational Services (BOCES)
Statewide Instructional Computing Network
Mexico, NY 13114

Computer Assisted Language Learning and Instruction Consortium (CALICO)
233 SFLC
Brigham Young University
Provo, UT 84602

Computer Information Exchange
P.O. Box 159
San Luis Rey, CA 92068

Computer Learners, Users, Educators Association (CLUES)
50 Nellis Dr.
Wayne, NJ 07047

Computer Resources, Inc.
Route 4
Barrington, NH 03825

Computer Software Committee
American Home Economics Association
2010 Massachusetts Ave. N.W.
Washington, DC 20036

Computer Technology and Reading Committee
International Reading Association
800 Barksdale Rd.
P.O. Box 8139
Newark, DE 19714

Computer Users in Education
Box 27561
Phoenix, AZ 85061

Computer Using Educators (CUE)
Box 18547
San Jose, CA 95133

Computers, Reading and Language Arts (CRLA)
P.O. Box 13039
Oakland, CA 94661

Council for Exceptional Children
1920 Association Dr.
Reston, VA 22091

DC AEDS
2216 Rand Place, N.E.
Washington, DC 20002

Educational Computing Consortium of Ohio (ECCO)
4777 Farnhurst Rd.
Cleveland, OH 44124

Florida Center for Instructional Computing
College of Education
University of Florida
Tampa, FL 33620

Harvard Graduate School of Education
Monroe C. Gutman Library
Appian Way
Cambridge, MA 02138

HumRRO
300 North Washington St.
Alexandria, VA 22314

I E R Institute for Educational Research
739 North Main Street
Glen Ellyn, IL 60137

Illinois AEDS
Box 128
DeKalb, IL 60115

Indiana Computer Educators
1230 South Clinton
Fort Wayne, IN 46825

International Association for Computing in Education (IACE)
1230 Seventeenth St. N.W.
Washington, DC 20036

International Council for Computers in Education (ICCE)
Department of Computer and Information Science
University of Oregon
Eugene, OR 97403

International Institute of Applied Technology, Inc.
2121 Wisconsin Ave. N.W.
Suite 400
Washington, DC 20007

Iowa AEDS
Educational Computer Center
500 College Dr.
Mason City, IA 50401

Maryland Association for the Educational Uses of the Computer (MAEUC)
c/o Catonville Community College
800 S. Rolling Rd.
Baltimore, MD 21228

Michigan Association for Computer Users in Learning
Wayne County ISD
33500 Van Born Rd.
Wayne, MI 48184

Michigan Educational Resources Information Center
Microcomputer Resource Center
Library of Michigan, Department of Education
P.O. Box 30007
Lansing, MI 48909

Mid-South AEDS
EBAS, COE, Memphis State University
Memphis, TN 38152

Minnesota Educational Computing Consortium (MECC)
2520 Broadway Dr.
St. Paul, MN 55113

National Council for the Social Studies (NCSS)
Instructional Media and Technology Advisory Committee
3501 Newark St. N.W.
Washington, DC 20016

National Council of Teachers of Mathematics
1906 Association Dr.
Reston, VA 22091

National Science Teachers Association (NSTA)
1742 Connecticut Ave. N.W.
Washington, DC 20009

Nebraska AEDS
Educational Service Unit #3
4224 South 133rd St.
Omaha, NE 68137

New Hampshire Association for Computer Education Statewide (NH ACES)
Computer Service, Stoke Hall
University of New Hampshire
Durham, NH 03824

New York State AEDS
c/o Ardsley High School
500 Farm Rd.
Ardsley, NY 10502

North Carolina AEDS
c/o Department of Education
116 West Edenton St.
Raleigh, NC 27611

North Dakota Association of School Administrators
Divide County School District #1
Box G
Crosby, ND 58730

Northwest Council for Computer Education
Computer Center, Eastern Oregon State College
LeGrande, OR 97850

Ohio AEDS
6391 Maxtown Rd.
Westerville, OH 43801

Oklahoma Educational Users Program (OECUP)
University of Oklahoma
601 Elm St.
Norman, OK 73019

PIE, Corporation for Public Information In Education
1714 Illinois
Lawrence, KS 66044

Project Direct
100 Hillside Rd.
Greenville, DE 19807

Special Interest Group-Computers and Social Education (SIG-CASE)
National Council for the Social Studies
3501 Newark St. N.W.
Washington, DC 20016

So. Micro Systems for Educators
P.O. Box 1981
Burlington, NC 27215

Technical Education Resources Center (TERC)
Computing Resource Center
8 Eliot St.
Cambridge, MA 02138

Texas AEDS
Box 632
Austin, TX 78767

Texas Computer Educators Association
Box 2573
Austin, TX 78768

UNICOM
297 Elmwood Ave.
Providence, RI 02907

Utah Council for Computers in Education (UCCE)
1295 North 1200
West Mapleton, UT 84663

Visual Arts Association
National Art Education Association (NAEA)
1916 Association Dr.
Reston, VA 22091

Wisconsin AEDS
Racine Public Schools
Racine, WI 53404

Wyoming Educational Computing Council
Laramie County School District #1
2810 House St.
Cheyenne, WY 82001

Young People's Logo Association (YPLA)
P.O. Box 855067
Richardson, TX 75085

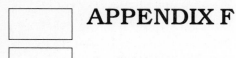

APPENDIX F

Telecommunications

CompuServe is located at 5000 Arlington Centre Boulevard, Columbus, Ohio 43222 (800) 848-8199. It costs $39.95 for the initial sign-up, with no monthly minimum charge for use of the service. The hourly rates run from $6.00 per hour (300 baud) to $12.50 per hour (1200 baud). Both MicroNet and CompuServe are accessed through the (800) 848-8199 number.

Delphi is located at 3 Blackstone Street in Cambridge, Massachusetts, 02139 (800) 544-4005. Their sign-up fee is $49.95 with no monthly minimum, and hourly rates of $6.00 (6:00 P.M. until 8:00 A.M.) and $16.00 during peak daytime hours. These rates apply for both 300 and 1200 baud.

Dialog Information Services, Inc. has headquarters at 3460 Hillview Avenue, Palo Alto, California, (800) 3-DIALOG. To use Dialog service, a subscriber dials a toll-free 800 number (listed above) and locks-on. The sign-up fee is $100.00, which gives the subscriber the lock-on code.

The ERIC Clearinghouses are listed below:

ERIC Clearinghouse of Elementary and Early Childhood Education
University of Illinois
College of Education
Urbana, IL 61801
(217) 333-1386

ERIC Clearinghouse on Information Resources
Syracuse University, School of Education
130 Huntington Hall
Syracuse, NY 13210
(315) 423-3640

ERIC Processing and Referencing Facility
4833 Rugby Avenue, 303
Bethesda, MD 20814
(301) 656-9723

GTE Telenet
8229 Boone Blvd.
Vienna, VA 22180
(703) 442-1000, Customer Service (800) 336-0437

Tymnet
2070 Chainbridge Rd.
Vienna, VA 22180
(703) 827-9110
Customer service (800) 336-0149

UniNet
10951 Lakeview Ave.
Lenexa, KS 66219
(800) 821-5340

The following are suppliers of online information services:

BRS Information Technologies
1200 Route 7
Lathan, NY 12110
(800) 227-5277

Dialog Classroom Instruction Program
Contact: Anne Caputo, CIP Administration, Dialog
1901 No. Moore St., Suite 500
Arlington, VA 22209
(800) 334-2564

Dow Jones News/Retrieval
P.O. Box 300
Princeton, NJ 08540
(800) 257-5114

EasyLink/InfoMaster
Western Union
1 Lake St.
Upper Saddle River, NJ 07458
(201) 825-5000

Educational Products Information Exchange Institute (EPIE)
P.O. Box 839
Water Mill, NY 11976
(516) 283-4922

Einstein
Addison-Wesley Publishing Co.
Information Services Division
2725 Sand Hill Rd.
Menlo Park, CA 94025
(800) 227-1936

Electronic Networking Association (ENA)
2744 Washington St.
Allentown, PA 18104
(215) 821-7777

Electronic University Network
Telelearning Systems
1150 Sansome St.
San Francisco, CA 94111
(800) 22-LEARN

GEnie Online Services
401 N. Washington St.
Rockville, MD 20850
(800) 638-9636

Interactive Communication Simulations
(Role Playing games)
ICS Staff,
University of Michigan,
School of Education,
Ann Arbor, MI 48109-1259
(313) 763-6717

Long Distance Learning Network
Contact: Margaret Riel
AT&T Long Distance Learning Network
PO Box 716,
Basking Ridge, NJ 07920-0716
(619) 943-1314

McGraw-Hill Information Exchange
Contact: Lynne Schrum (503) 345-8527
Griff Wigley (507) 645-9347
MIX
PO Box 382
Northfield, MN 55057

National Geographic Kids Network
Contact: Dorothy Perraca, Project Manager,
National Geographic Kid's Network,
National Geographic
Washington, DC 20036
(202) 775-6580

Newsnet
NewsNet Inc.
945 Haverford Road
Bryn Mawr, PA 19010
(800) 345-1301 or (215) 527-8030

Online Journal of Distance Education and
Communications
Contact: Jason Ohler
University of Alaska Southeast
11120 Glacer Hy.
Juneau, AK 99801
(907) 789-4417

Pals Across the World
Contact: Jim Irwin
4974 SW Galen
Lake Oswego, OR 97035
(503) 697-4080 or (503) 635-0338

The School Board
Department of Computer Education
National College of Education
2840 Sheridan Rd.
Evanston, IL 60201
(312) 474-1100, extension 2256

Service:FrEdMail (Free Educational Mail)
(A low-cost, teacher-created, grassroots network
of 90 bulletin boards across the United States)
Contact: Al Rogers
4021 Allen School Road,
Bonita, CA 92002

SpecialNet
National Association of State Directors of Special
Education
2021 K St., N.W.
Suite 315
Washington, DC 20006
(202) 296-1800

You can use a bulletin board service to obtain free programs, to leave and read messages, to play games, to order products (books for example, by calling via modem: PMS, McGraw-Hill, New York 212-512-2488), to gather information on movie reviews (Dickenson's Movie Guide, Mission, Kansas 913-432-5544).

For the latest listing of BBSs, you can call (213) 881-6880, 24 hours a day. This service is provided by Novation, Inc., of Tarzana, California, a manufacturing firm that produces modems. Another good first source for information about BBSs is the Peoples' Message System, Santee, California (619) 561-7277. This system provides an extensive listing of BBSs around the U.S.

The following books and newsletters will provide you with a great place to start in your utilization of electronic bulletin boards:

■ *The Computer Phone Book* by Mike Crane. Plume Books, New York (212) 697-8000. A listing of over 400 on-line BBSs with hours, fees, and general descriptions of services offered.

■ *OMNI Online Database Directory* by Mike Edhart and Owen Davies. Macmillan: New York (212) 702-2000. Descriptions of more than 1,000 data bases, with information including telephone numbers and addresses.

■ *Computer Shopper,* Jim Cambron, publisher. P.O. Box 1000005, Kansas City, Missouri, 64111 (913) 383-2229. $9.95 for one year, $15.95 for 2 years. A directory of new bulletin boards, with news of interest to BBS users.

■ *PLUMB,* Rec Manning, editor. P.O. Box 300, Harrods Creek, Kentucky 40027, (502) 228-3820. $26.50 per year (8 issues). The newsletter prints relevant news, lists new bulletin boards with phone numbers, addresses and services and listing and reviews of telecommunications software.

There are also some specialized national BBSs:

■ *UFONET,* Golden, Colorado, (303) 278-4244, is an exciting system that covers a wide variety of subjects, among them high technology news with the specialty on space items, and programming tips on Apple, Atari, and Radio Shack microcomputers.

■ *HEX,* Silver Spring, Maryland, (301) 593-7033, is a clearinghouse for information on using technology to aid the handicapped, also serving as a message center for deaf microcomputer users. This BBS devotes the entire system to the exchange of information for handicapped individuals. It is a great source of information for students in university and college departments of special education who need contacts and specialized information.

■ *Energy Tree,* Sausalito, California, (415) 332-8115, presents an open forum for anyone interested in the use of alternative energy sources. Users of this BBS exchange data and even documents on various topics relating to alternative energy sources.

■ *The Kid's Message System,* San Diego, California, (619) 578-2646, is a BBS that was set up to encourage children to exchange messages and jokes, and learn about microcomputers. This BBS is used by children in school districts all across the country in the exchange of all kinds of messages; it's a center for funny kids' jokes and a valuable source of information on how to utilize your microcomputer.

■ *Connection-80,* Petersborough, New Hampshire, (603) 924-7920, specializes in literature criticism. Users can read or contribute poetry, short stories, book reviews, and children's fiction. This BBS has become a valuable source of literary works with many users willing to critique and referee works for authors.

Additional bulletin board services are:

inCider BBS
80 Elm St.
Peterborough, NH 03458
(603) 924-9471

National Geographic Society BBS
Educational Media Division
17th and M St. N.W.
Washington, D.C. 20036
(202) 857-7378 or (202) 775-6738 (300 and 1200 baud)

A.P.P.L.E. Crate BBS
Apaple PugetSound Program
Library Exchange
290 S.W. 43rd St.
Renton, WA 98055
(206) 251-0543

The Advocate
(303) 223-1297
(Pet information)

The Electronic Bulletin Board System
(602) 783-0484
(For Radio Shack, Apple, or Commodore 64 Users)

NETWORKING INFORMATION

A good networking management software program is *The Classroom Monitor* manufactured by Software Connections of Santa Clara, California.

A notable manufacturer of both hardware and software for networking is WICAT Systems, Inc., Orem, Utah (801) 224-6400. They have some excellent software programs.

APPENDIX G

Word Processing Exercises

EDITING WITH THE APPLEWORKS WORD PROCESSOR

For this exercise you will need the AppleWorks Startup and Program Diskettes and a data disk for storing your work. AppleWorks is designed for use on the Apple II series of computers, including the IIe, IIc, and IIGS.

We have chosen a passage from Melville's classic *Moby Dick* to be edited. Several common errors have been included, each of which is identified by referring to its line number. Following the passage below, a line-by-line description of the approach to correcting each error is provided.

(1)   And thus, through the the serene tranquilities of the tropical sea

(2)   among waves whose hand-clappings were supended by exceeding

(3)   rapture, moby dick moved on, still withholding from sight

(4)   the full terrors of his sumberged trunk, entirely hiding the

(5)   wrenchedhideousness of his jaw. But soon the fore part of him

(6)   slowly rose from the water; for an instant his whole marbleized
(7)   body formed a high arch, like Virginia's Natural Bridge, and

(8)   warningly waving his bannered flukes in the sea, the grand god

(9)   revealed himself, soundded, and went out of sight. Hoveringly

(10)   halting, and dipping on the wing, the white sea fowls longingly

(11)   lingered over the pool agitated he had left.

(12)   With oars apeak, and paddles down, the sheets of their sails

(13)   adrift, the three boats now stilly floated, awaiting Moby Dick's

(14)   reappearance.

When you are ready to begin, place the startup diskette in Drive 1 and turn the computer on. When the screen prompt appears telling you to do so, replace the startup disk with the program disk and press the RETURN key. Enter the current date and again press RETURN.

You will now see a diagram on the screen that looks like a file folder with the words "Main Menu" printed on the tab (Figure G.1). The available options are listed so you can make a choice and then go immediately to work. At the top of the screen are the same words as those on the first

FIGURE G.1

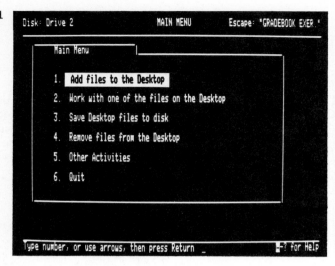

```
Disk: Drive 2                    MAIN MENU        Escape: "GRADEBOOK EXER."

     ┌─ Main Menu ───────────┐
     │                       │
     │  1. │Add files to the Desktop│
     │                       │
     │  2. Work with one of the files on the Desktop
     │                       │
     │  3. Save Desktop files to disk
     │                       │
     │  4. Remove files from the Desktop
     │                       │
     │  5. Other Activities
     │                       │
     │  6. Quit
     │                       │
     └───────────────────────┘

Type number, or use arrows, then press Return _        ⌖-? for Help
```

folder: Main Menu. These captions at the top of the screen indicate your location in the stack of folders. As you move through the folders, the caption will change to reflect your new position; you can never get lost with this system. Also helpful are the short instructions at the bottom of the screen, which tell you how to move or make selections. Note that the instructions now on screen tell you to type the number of the selection or use the arrow keys to move to that selection.

Making a selection from the main menu causes a new folder to appear on top of the current one, thus giving you a new set of options to choose from. At this point select the option "Add Files to the Desktop" and press RETURN to place the Add Files folder on top of the Main Menu folder (Figure G.2). The selections on the Add Files menu let you get a file from a disk or create a new one. You can choose to work on the word processor, the database, or the spreadsheet, all of which are listed as options on the folder.

If the Moby Dick exercise has been stored on a lesson disk by your instructor you should place the disk in Drive 2 (if you have two drives) and select option 1, "The Current Disk: Drive 2" from the menu. If Drive 1 is shown as the current drive you should change this by selecting option 2, "A Different Disk." Follow this by pressing the RETURN key, and then select the option "Drive 2" and press RETURN. If you have only one drive you will naturally select Drive 1. The computer

will display the name of the Moby Dick exercise and those of any other files currently on the disk. Use the arrow keys to select this file and press RETURN. You should now have the Moby Dick exercise displayed on the screen.

If the lesson is not available on a disk you will have to type it yourself. Select option 1, "Add Files to the Desktop," from the Main Menu and press RETURN. Select option 3, "Word Processor," from the Add Files menu and press RETURN. Select option 1, "From scratch," from the Word Processor menu and press RETURN, then give the document that you are about to create a name, perhaps your own, so you can save it onto a data disk when it is finished. If you must type the exercise yourself, be sure to type it *exactly* as it appears in the text. Do not make any corrections until after the entire document has been typed. If you should make an error as you type, it can be corrected by moving the cursor (blinking line) to the space immediately following the error and deleting with the DELETE key and then typing the correct letter. You should press the RETURN key twice at the end of each line (except line 6) to double-space the document.

Let us now proceed to correct the errors in the document.

Line 1. To correct this line you must remove the extra *the*. Use the arrow keys to move the cursor to the space following one or the other *the*, then

FIGURE G.2

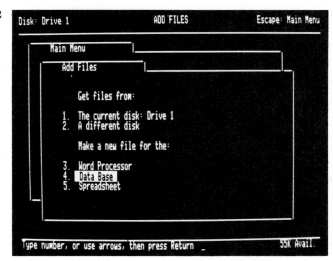

press the DELETE key four times to remove the unwanted word and space.

Line 2. This line contains a misspelled word: *supended* should be *suspended*. To make the correction, move the cursor to the *p*, type an *s*, and the spelling will be correct.

Line 3. The whale's name, Moby Dick, must be capitalized. Move the cursor until it is to the right of the *m* in *moby*, press the delete key to remove this letter, and type a capital *M*. Use the same procedure for *dick*, then move on to line 4.

Line 4. Use the same approach as in the previous lines to correct the spelling in *sumberged*.

Line 5. A space is needed between the words *wrenched* and *hideousness*. Move the cursor to the *h* in *hideousness* and press the space bar to insert the space.

Lines 6 and 7. A space must be inserted between lines 6 and 7 so they conform to the double-spaced format. Place the cursor after *marbleized* on line 6; press RETURN and the blank line will be inserted between the two lines.

Line 8. The word *sea* should be *air* in this line. Move the cursor to the *s* in *sea*, type the word *air*. With the cursor under the *s* in *sea* press the Open-Apple key and the letter D key to move into the DELETE MODE. The cursor will be replaced by

a nonblinking highlight that will be positioned over the *s*. The REVIEW/ADD/CHANGE caption at the top of the screen is replaced by the caption DELETE TEXT and instructions appear at the bottom of the screen. Each time you press the right arrow key, an additional letter in the word *sea* is highlighted. When all the letters are highlighted, press RETURN to remove the unwanted word. If you change your mind about deleting a word, simply press the ESCAPE key.

Line 9. There is an extra *d* in *soundded*. Because you have had practice in deleting you should know how to correct the error in this line without assistance.

Line 10. There are two spaces between *wing* and *the:* one must be removed. Use the same procedure as you would to delete a letter.

Line 11. We will use the MOVE function to correct the problem of the transposed words *pool* and *agitated*. With the cursor on the *p* in *pool*, press the Open-Apple-M combination to get into the Move mode; the prompt line at the bottom of the screen will ask if you want to move the text "Within document," which means the document you are currently working on, or "To clipboard" meaning a different document. Select the Within document option and press RETURN. The letter *p* will be highlighted. Use the arrow keys to highlight the rest of the letters. When all four are highlighted, press RETURN. The prompt line at the bottom of the screen will tell you to move the cursor to the location where you want the highlighted word to be inserted. In response, move the cursor to a point following *agitated* and press RETURN; the word *pool* will reappear in the correct position. Change the spacing as needed and move on to the next line.

Line 12. This line should be indented to begin a new paragraph. Position the cursor under the first letter, *W;* press the space bar five times to indent the line.

The document should now be error free. To double check it, hold down the Open-Apple key and press the up arrow to move to the top of the screen. Do this once more to get to the beginning of the document. Read through your work, making certain that all corrections have been made; you are now ready to save the document on a disk or print it as hard copy (or both).

To save the corrected lesson on a disk, use the Open-Apple-S command. The drive will turn on and a message will tell you to place the data disk in Drive 1 if you are using only one drive. Press RETURN to begin saving; a screen message will appear that tells you the document is being saved. You will recall that a name was given to the document before actual typing began. The computer will save your work as a file with this name.

To make certain the lesson has been saved, press the ESCAPE key to return to the Main Menu; select option 5, "Other Activities," and press RETURN. From the Other Activities menu that appears select option 2, "List all files on current disk drive"; press RETURN. If there are many files on the disk, and you don't see your file on the list, use the arrow keys to move through the list until you find the name you gave the Moby Dick lesson.

To print the document, press Open-Apple-P (RETURN), then select the printer you will be using from the print menu that appears; press RETURN once again and the printer will begin printing.

If you have difficulty remembering the various commands used in AppleWorks you can call up the Help Screen whenever needed. To do this simply hold down the Open-Apple and press the

question mark *(?)*. A list of commands will immediately be displayed for you to examine.

EDITING WITH MACWRITE

This exercise, like the preceding one, is based on the Moby Dick document found on the first page of this section. Although the mistakes to be corrected are the same for all three exercises, the approach to correcting them differs considerably from one program to the next.

The word processor used in this exercise was designed for the Apple Macintosh computer. This machine offers an operating environment based on various menus and icons from which different functions are selected. The mouse is used to move the cursor to an icon or an option in a menu, which is then activated (selected) by clicking the mouse button. Text is typed at the keyboard in the traditional fashion.

To begin, insert the MacWrite program disk into the drive and start the computer. Soon the MacWrite icon will appear on the right side of the screen. Move the cursor to this icon with the mouse and click the mouse button twice in rapid succession to load the program; the screen will then look like the illustration in Figure G.3, with words, numbers, and bars along the top. You should type the lesson exactly as it is printed, mistakes and all. The lines are double-spaced throughout the document with the exception of lines 6 and 7; for double-spacing press the return key twice at the end of each line.

If you have a lesson disk containing the Moby Dick document it should be in the second drive; the MacWrite disk should be in drive one. An icon representing the lesson disk and one for MacWrite will be displayed on the screen. Click twice on the lesson disk to see a display of files available. To retrieve the lesson so you can work on it, select "Moby Dick" (or other lesson file name) and double click as before.

With the lesson on the screen, position the cursor at the beginning of the first line (if it is not already there) by using the mouse, then proceed as follows.

Let us begin by giving the document a title. Press the RETURN key two or three times to move the text down so you have room to work.

FIGURE G.3

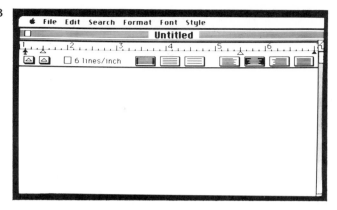

Move the cursor to the FONT menu at the top of the screen; click the mouse button and hold it down. From the list of type styles select New York by pulling the cursor down to this style and releasing the mouse button (Figure G.4).

Next, move the cursor to the line of boxes just below the ruler; select the third box from the right (the center-justify box) and click on it; this will cause the title to be centered (Figure G.5).

We will now change the size and boldness of the letters by making selections from the STYLE menu. Move to this menu and click; hold the button down as you move the cursor to 18 Point and release the button. Repeat the process, stopping on Bold this time.

Type *MOBY DICK EXERCISE,* then press RETURN.

The body of the text should not be centered, so you will have to change to the normal left-jus-

tified format. To do this you must insert a RULER. Move the cursor to the FORMAT menu, press the mouse button, move down to the Insert ruler option, and release the button. You should now see a new ruler just under your title (Figure G.6). Now, move to the left-alignment box and click on it; all text from here on out will be aligned on the left-hand side of the document.

Go back to the FONT and STYLE menus and undo the changes you made earlier for the title. The letters should be changed to 12 point; select plain text (rather than bold); and change the font style to Geneva. Now, click on the FORMAT menu once again, select Hide Rulers, and release the mouse button; the rulers will disappear. Let us now proceed to make the necessary corrections in the lesson.

Line 1. There is an extra *the* in this line. Position the cursor after the *e* in the extra *the.* Hold

FIGURE G.4

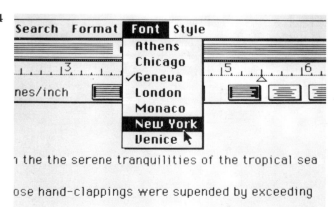

FIGURE G.5

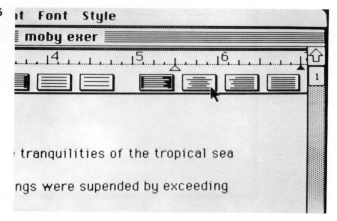

down the BACK SPACE (delete) key until the extra word has been deleted. Move the cursor to line 2.

Line 2. There is a misspelled word (suspended) that must be corrected. Move the cursor until it is in front of the *p* in *supended*. Type an *s* and the word will be fixed. Move to line 3.

Line 3. The whale's name, Moby Dick, needs to be capitalized. Move the cursor in front of the *o* in *moby*. Press the backspace key to erase the *m;* now press the shift key and the *m* to form a capital *M* and *moby* is fixed. Do the same thing with *dick*. Move to line 4.

Line 4. The position of the letters *m* and *b* are reversed in *submerged*. Move the cursor in front of the *b* and press the backspace key to remove

the *m*. Move the cursor in front of the *e* and type an *m* to fix the word. Move on to line 5.

Line 5. There is a space missing between *wrenched* and *hideousness*. To insert the space move the cursor between the *d* in *wrenched* and the *h* in *hideousness* and press the space bar to insert the space. Move to line 6.

Line 6. A space must be inserted between this line (6) and the following one (7). First move the cursor to the end of line 6 by dragging it with the mouse. When the cursor is at the end of the line, press the RETURN key and there is the space. At this point you are getting close to the bottom of the screen. To move up or down through the document, select the small square (called the Scroll Box) located in the Scroll Bar that extends

FIGURE G.6

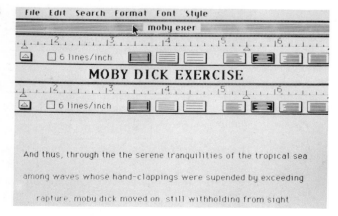

vertically along the extreme right side of the screen and drag it up or down to expose succeeding lines of text.

Line 7. This line is okay, so move on to line 8.

Line 8. The word *sea* should be *air.* Position the cursor in front of the *s* in *sea*, then press the mouse button and hold it down as you drag the cursor over the word to highlight it. The letters will now be white on a black bar (Figure G.7). Press the backspace key once to remove that word; now type the word *air.* When the correction has been made, move to line 9.

Line 9. The word *sounded* has an extra *d* in it. By now you know how to delete words and letters, so delete the extra *d* and move on to line 10.

Line 10. There are two spaces between *wing* and *the;* one must be deleted. You delete a space exactly as you do a character. After this is done, move to the next line.

Line 11. In this line the words *pool* and *agitated* are reversed. Click the mouse button and drag the cursor over the word "pool" to highlight the letters. Now pull down the EDIT menu and select the CUT option to activate it (Figure G.8). When you release the mouse button "pool" will be gone. The word is not lost, however, but is stored in temporary memory until you call it back. Next, move the cursor to a position following "agitated" and press the space bar to provide a space. Now select

PASTE from the menu to place *pool* in its new location. Sentences, paragraphs, and larger blocks of text can all be manipulated in this fashion. Check to make sure the spacing around the relocated words is okay, then move to line 12.

Line 12. This line should be indented to form a paragraph. Move to the FORMAT menu and select INSERT RULER. If the tab marker (small triangle) on the ruler is not in the desired position, drag it either way using the mouse. If a tab marker is not found on the ruler, select one from the tab well (farthest left box directly under the ruler) and drag it to the ruler; place it where you want an indented line to begin. Position the cursor in front of the first letter (W) on line 12. Press the TAB key on the keyboard; hide the ruler when finished.

Lines 13 and 14. These two lines are okay so you can leave them alone. Finally, move back up through the document and double check your corrections. To save your corrected lesson choose SAVE AS from the FILE menu. A dialog box will appear on the screen asking for a name for your document. Type your name or other identifying label (but not mobydick or whatever the original, uncorrected lesson was named); click on the SAVE option in the dialog box or press RETURN to save your document. Note: before saving you should check the box at the top of the display to make sure you are saving onto the lesson or data disk and not onto the MacWrite (program) disk.

FIGURE G.7

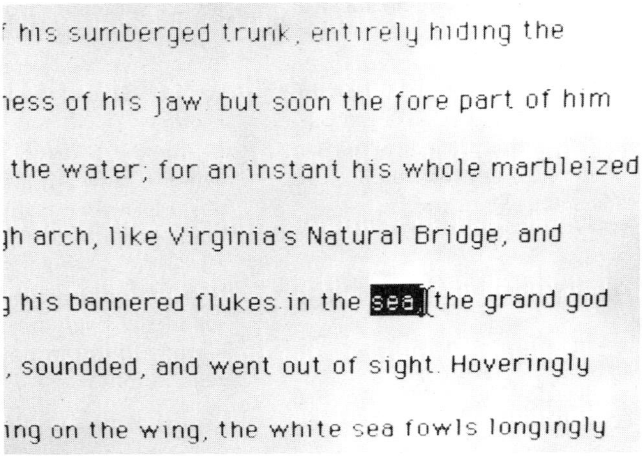

FIGURE G.8

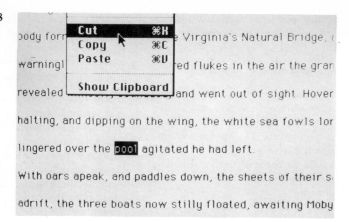

To change from one to the other place the cursor in the box named DRIVE and press the mouse button.

If you wish to print your document, choose PRINT from the FILE menu. A box showing the printing specifications will appear on the screen. For the best quality letters click on High; for faster printing but less refined letters select Standard. Set the other specifications (Page Range, Copies, Paper Feed) if need be, and then click on OK to tell the printer to start printing.

To exit the program, move the cursor to the FILE menu. Press the mouse button and hold it down; move to the QUIT option and release. If you have not previously saved the lesson a prompt will ask if you want to save the changes. Select No if it has been saved or if you do not wish to save it. The menu titles will disappear momentarily; when they reappear, move once again to the file menu, click the button, and hold it down. Move to the EJECT option, and release the button to eject the disk. Follow this procedure to eject the second disk if you are using two of them; turn the computer off to conclude the exercise.

EDITING WITH WORDPERFECT (MS DOS VERSION)

This exercise is based on the same Moby Dick document as used with AppleWorks (see the first page of Appendix G). Although the mistakes to be corrected are the same for the three word pro-

cessing exercises, the approach to correcting them differs considerably among programs.

You will note that the keyboard on the computer you will be using looks somewhat different from the Apple used for the AppleWorks assignment or the Macintosh used with MacWrite. There is a set of function keys to the left of the keyboard (PC version) or above it (enhanced version). The keys are labelled with the letter *F* followed by a number. Other special keys you will use in the exercise are CTRL, ALT, and SHIFT; you might want to locate these now.

To begin, start WordPerfect and wait until the blinking cursor appears in the upper left corner of the screen. You will also see several numbers in the lower right corner; these give the position of the cursor as well as other information. If you have a lesson disk containing the Moby Dick document, it should be in the second drive (drive B). To retrieve the lesson so you can work on it, press the SHIFT and the F10 keys, then respond to the prompt "Document to be Retrieved" by typing *B:* (for the B drive), and the name of the lesson, which is typically Mobydick. If you do not have the lesson on a disk you should begin by typing the material exactly as it is printed, mistakes and all.

With the lesson on the screen, position the cursor at the beginning of the first line (if it is not already there) by using the arrow keys, then proceed as follows:

Line 1. There is an extra *the* in this line. Using the right arrow key (key 6 on the numeric pad), move the cursor under the *t* in *the*. Hold down the CTRL key and press the BACK SPACE (delete) key; the extra word will be gone. Note that you can use CTRL with the right or left arrow keys to move the cursor a full word rather than just a letter at a time. To move to line 2, press the down arrow key. To move to the beginning of the line press the HOME key (on the numeric pad) and the left arrow key.

Line 2. There is a misspelled word, *supended,* that must be corrected to *suspended*. Move the cursor until it is under the *p* in *supended*. Type an *s* and the word will be fixed. Move to line 3.

Line 3. The proper name Moby Dick needs to be capitalized. Press the right arrow key until the cursor is under the *o* in *moby*. Press the backspace key to erase the *m;* now press the shift key and the *m* to form a capital *M* and "moby" is fixed. Do the same thing with *dick*. Move to line 4.

Line 4. The position of the letters *m* and *b* are reversed in *submerged*. Move the cursor under the *b* and press the backspace to remove the *m*. Press the right arrow key once to move the cursor under the *e*. Type an *m* to fix the word. Move on to line 5.

Line 5. There is a space missing between *wrenched* and *hideousness*. To insert the space, move the cursor under the *h* in *hideousness* and press the space bar to insert the space. Move to line 6.

Line 6. A space must be inserted between this line (6) and the following one (7). First, move the cursor to the end of line 6. A quick way to do this is to press the HOME key and then the right arrow key. The cursor will appear at the end of the line. Now press the return key and there is the space.

Line 7. This line is okay, so move on to line 8.

Line 8. The word *sea* should be *air*. To correct this we will use the typeover function. Position the cursor under the *s* in *sea*, press the INS (insert) key, and type *air*. As you type, the new letters will replace the old ones. Once the correction has been made, press the INS key to move out of typeover mode. Move to line 9.

Line 9. The word *sounded* has an extra *d* in it. By now you know how to delete words and letters, so delete the extra *d* and move on to line 10.

Line 10. There are two spaces between *wing* and *the;* one must be deleted. You delete a space exactly as you do a character. After this is done, move to line 11.

Line 11. In this line the words *pool* and *agitated* are reversed. Move the cursor to the space before the *p* in *pool*. We need to single out this word and move it. Press the ALT key and the F4 key (the BLOCK function). You will notice a blinking prompt at the bottom of the screen that says "Block On." Press the right arrow key five times (once for the space and once for each letter) to highlight the word. Now press the CTRL and the F4 keys (the MOVE combination). A prompt line will appear at the bottom of the screen; select the option 1 Cut Block; that is, press the *1* key on the top row of number keys; the word *pool* will disappear. It is not lost, however, but is stored in temporary memory until you call it back.

Now, move the cursor to the space following *agitated*. Press the shift key and the F10 key (this is the retrieve combination). A prompt line will appear at the bottom of the screen that says "Document to be Retrieved." Press the return key and the word pool will appear in the proper place. Sentences, paragraphs, and larger blocks of text can all be manipulated in this fashion.

Line 12. This line should be indented to form a new paragraph. Position the cursor under the first letter *W,* then press the shift and the F4 combination to indent. Another option is to press the tab key located near the little finger of your left hand.

The last two lines are okay so you can leave them alone. One last thing might be done to complete the exercise: you can give it a title.

1. Move back to the top of the document. Press the HOME key twice then press the up arrow key. The cursor should be under the *1.*
2. Press the return key once or twice to give yourself room to work.
3. Move the cursor to the top of the screen with the up arrow.

4. Press the shift key and the F6 key to activate the center function.
5. Press the F6 key to bold the letters.
6. Press the caps lock key to the right of the space bar.
7. Type *MOBY DICK EXERCISE* and press return.
8. Delete the bold function by pressing F6 again; do the same with the caps function.
9. To save your corrected lesson, press the F10 key. In response to the prompt Document to be Saved type your name (or other identifying label, but not *mobydick* or whatever the original, uncorrected lesson was named); press RETURN to save your document.
10. If you wish to print your document, press the F7 (print) key.
11. In response to the prompt line that appears at the bottom of the screen select "2 Page" (if the document were longer than one page you would select "1 Full Text"), then press the RETURN key.
12. It is important that you exit WordPerfect properly; here are the steps to follow: Press the F7 (exit) key. In response to the prompt "Save Document? (Y/N)Y" type *N* (because you have already saved your document). In response to the next prompt "Exit Word-Perfect? (Y/N)N" type *Y.* The drive will run for a couple of seconds, and then will stop. You are now out of WordPerfect and can remove the disk(s) and turn off the computer.

APPENDIX H

Programming Exercises

A PROGRAMMING EXERCISE IN BASIC

The following exercise is useful in the early stages of a unit on programming. It has been widely used by a number of students and has been well accepted by them. Note that the lesson should be undertaken only after some discussion and after the student has not only learned the various system commands but also run several disk-based programs. This exercise can be carried out on the Apple II+, Apple IIe, Commodore, Franklin, IBM, TRS-80 and several other machines with few modifications. The major change concerns the word HOME, which is an Apple term used to clear the screen. When you come to this word, use instead CLS for the TRS-80 and IBM and PRINT "CLR/HOME" for the Commodore (note: do not type the words *clr/home;* instead, press the key of that name after typing the first quotation mark, then follow up with the second quotation mark).

1. Type the following (you can change the numbers):

   PRINT 4 + 5

   Then press RETURN or ENTER. What did you get?
2. Type the following (use your own name if you wish):

   PRINT MY NAME IS WHATEVER

   Then press RETURN/ENTER. What did you get?
3. Type the following:

   PRINT "MY NAME IS WHATEVER"

   Press RETURN/ENTER. What did you get this time? Note the difference the quotation marks make.
4. Type LIST. What do you get?
5. Now type the following, then press RETURN/ENTER.

   10 PRINT "MY NAME IS WHATEVER"

   What did you get? Can you figure out why?
6. Type:

   20 PRINT "I LIKE COMPUTERS"

   (Note: from now on press RETURN or ENTER whenever you complete a line or enter a command.)
   What happened? Now type LIST. What did you get? Next, type RUN. Now what do you get? Think about all of this—can you explain it?
7. By now the screen is filled with all kinds of things, so let's see if we can clean it off. Type HOME. What does this command do?
8. Type LIST. What did you get? Can you explain what happened?
9. Next type NEW.
10. Now type LIST. What happens? Why is this listing different from the last one? Explain what NEW does.

11. Type the following short program:

```
10 PRINT "HELLO"
20 PRINT
30 PRINT
40 PRINT
50 PRINT "THERE"

RUN
```

What does **PRINT** with nothing following it do?

12. Next, type this program:

```
10 PRINT "20 + 5 = " 20 + 5
20 PRINT
30 PRINT "NOW WE'RE ADDING"
40 PRINT "TWO NUMBERS"
50 PRINT "EASY, ISN'T IT"
60 END
```

(Note: from now on type **HOME** anytime you want to clear the screen.)

13. Now type RUN. How did we get the results on the first line? What do the quotation marks do?

14. Type **NEW**.

15. Type the following:

```
10 PRINT "I LIKE"
20 GOTO 50
30 PRINT "ICE CREAM AND"
40 PRINT "CAKE AND"
50 PRINT "COMPUTERS"
60 END
```

16. Type RUN. What happened to lines 30 and 40, ICE CREAM AND CAKE AND?

17. Now type NEW and then the following:

```
20 PRINT "THIS IS"
30 PRINT "AN INFINITE"
40 GOTO 20
50 PRINT "LOOP"
60 END
```

18. Now type RUN. What is happening? Quickly, do you remember how to stop a runaway program? Do it now (press CTRL-C on the Apple, the stop key on the Commodore, the break key on the TRS 80, or the control and break on the IBM). What happened to line 50 (the word LOOP)?

19. Clear both the screen and the memory (do you remember how?).

20. Let's see what a semicolon does. Type in this program:

```
10 PRINT "YOUR NAME";
20 GOTO 10
```

Then run it. Oops, another runaway—better stop it.

21. Clear the screen and the memory, then type the same program with a comma:

```
10 PRINT "YOUR NAME",
20 GOTO 10

RUN
```

Now you know what a comma does. Stop the program and clear the screen and the memory.

22. Let's try the comma and the semicolon again, but this time we won't let the program run away. Type:

```
5 HOME
10 PRINT "HERE ARE THE FISH I HAVE IN MY TANK"
20 PRINT
30 PRINT "TETRAS", "ZEBRAS", "KOI"
40 PRINT
50 PRINT 12, 4, 6
60 END
```

Now, run it—is it clear what the comma does? Also, did you notice what line 5 did? You can include HOME in a program to clear the screen automatically each time the program is run.

23. Type the fish program again, but this time replace the commas with semicolons (;). What happens when you run this one?

24. Type the following:

```
10 REM ASSIGNING VALUES TO VARIABLES
20 LET X = 5
30 LET Y = 10
40 LET Z = 15
50 PRINT X, Y, Z
60 END
```

Run the program. Notice that the output is not made up of letters (X, Y, Z)—why? See what the commas did? Neat, isn't it? There is a brand new word on line 10 (REM). Did it have any effect on the way the program worked? If you think not, you are correct. It's a remark, and it is included as a reminder; it is useful when programs get very long. Type NEW and move on to item 25.

25. Type the following:

```
7 LET X = 5
11 LET Y = 10
19 LET Z = X + Y
40 PRINT Z
56 END
```

Run this program. Explain what it does. Note that you do not have to use 10, 20, 30, and so on as line numbers, but they are fairly standard. Incidentally, in the program above, X, Y, and Z are called variables; they are like memory boxes. The numbers 5 and 10 are values, which are placed in the boxes. Type NEW and move on to the next item.

26. Let's try some more stored numbers. Remember that X, Y, and Z are the names of storage spaces (like the boxes in the post office) so we can put numbers in them (this is called assigning a value to a variable). Type:

```
10 HOME
20 LET X = 10
30 LET Y = 5
40 PRINT X, Y
50 PRINT X + Y, X - Y
60 PRINT X * Y, X / Y
70 END
```

What happens when you run this one? Type NEW and go to the next item.

27. A variable such as X, Y, or Z can hold a word if it is changed to a string variable. This is easy to do—just add a dollar sign ($) to the letter and this tells the computer that a word can be stored in that memory space.

```
10 LET A$ = "CHARLES"
20 LET B$ = "BABBAGE"
30 PRINT A$, B$
40 END
```

Now run the program. If you don't like the format, substitute a semicolon for the comma. Do this by typing LIST and then the following at the bottom of the list:

```
30 PRINT A$; B$
```

28. Now type RUN to see the new arrangement. If the spacing between the names bothers you, list the program again and then type this:

```
10 LET A$ = "CHARLES "
```
                        ↑
              (leave a space here)

Run the program again. What difference did this change make?

29. Let's try an interactive program. Type this:

```
10 PRINT "HI, WHAT'S YOUR NAME?"
20 PRINT
30 INPUT N$
40 PRINT
50 PRINT "WELL"; N$; "GLAD TO KNOW YOU"
60 END
```

30. Run this program. When the computer stops and asks HI, WHAT'S YOUR NAME? type your name. What happens? How does the computer know your name? Note the crowded spaces next to your name. Retype this line (number 50) and fix it.

31. Here's an IF-THEN statement using relational symbols (>< =). Type the following:

```
5 PRINT
10 PRINT "HOW MANY INCHES IN ONE YARD?"
20 PRINT
30 INPUT I
40 PRINT
50 IF I = 36 THEN 90
60 IF I > 36 THEN PRINT "TOO HIGH, TRY AGAIN"
70 IF I < 36 THEN PRINT "TOO LOW, TRY AGAIN"
80 GOTO 5
90 PRINT "YOU GOT IT"
100 END
```

When you run this one, try putting in wrong answers as well as right ones. Analyze the program to see how it works. Type NEW and go to the next item.

32. Remember our program that ran away? It looked like this:

```
10 PRINT "YOUR NAME"
20 GOTO 10
```

One way to get it to stop is to use a FOR-NEXT loop. Type this:

```
10 FOR X = 1 to 6
20 PRINT "YOUR NAME",
30 NEXT X
40 END
```

How many times did the program print your name? Why? Can you figure out why it stopped at this number?

33. For our last program we'll combine several of the statements we have learned to create a new program that permits only so many guesses before the computer moves on to another question. Type this:

```
10 REM MULTIPLICATION PROGRAM
20 HOME
30 REM THREE TRIES
40 FOR T = 1 TO 3
50 PRINT "WHAT IS 7 × 9?"
60 PRINT
70 INPUT A
80 PRINT
90 REM CHECK THE ANSWERS
100 IF A = 63 THEN 160
110 IF A > 63 THEN PRINT "TOO LARGE"
120 IF A < 63 THEN PRINT "TOO SMALL"
130 PRINT
140 NEXT T
150 GOTO 170
160 PRINT "GOOD, YOU GOT IT"
170 PRINT "LET'S TRY ANOTHER"
```

(Continue adding lines as desired.) When you run this program, you'll get three tries, then you will move on to line 170. But if you get the right answer before the three tries have been used, you will move to line 160, then to line 170 for the next question (which you will need to add). Try tracing this through to see that it all makes sense.

A PROGRAMMING EXERCISE IN LOGO

The following exercise, designed with Apple Logo, can be used in conjunction with class demonstrations and other Logo activities. Type the program lines (shown in capital letters) exactly as you see them, including brackets, quotation marks, and any other symbols. Explanations are given in lower case letters and are generally enclosed in parentheses; do not type this material.

To begin, place the Logo disk in the drive and start the computer; respond to the prompt telling you to press the RETURN key. You will see the words WELCOME TO LOGO at the top of the screen; you can now begin programming. If you should make a typing mistake use the left arrow key to remove the character(s), then type the corrections. When using the EDIT mode, various key combinations let you move about in the program. For example, pressing the CONTROL key and the N key enables you to move to the (N)ext line; pressing the CONTROL key and the E lets you move to the (E)nd of a line, and so on. Examine a book on Apple Logo to see what the other commands are, or check with your instructor for specific commands. Later in this exercise you will be introduced to the EDIT mode. Let us now pro-ceed with the exercise; remember to press RE-TURN after each line has been entered.

1. Type the following:

```
PRINT [HI THERE] (press the RETURN key)
PRINT [WHAT IS YOUR NAME?] (press the RETURN key)
```

2. To remove the words on the screen, type CLEARTEXT. Try typing these words without the brackets. What purpose do the brackets serve?
3. Let us now create a procedure; this is similar to a stored program in BASIC. Type the following:

```
TO WELCOME (press the RETURN key after each line)
PRINT [HI THERE]
PRINT [WHAT IS YOUR NAME?]
END
```

(Logo will respond with "WELCOME DEFINED")
Why do you suppose that the words you typed are not automatically displayed as they were in the first exercise?
4. Type WELCOME (the name of the procedure) to make it run.
5. Try the REPEAT command; type

```
REPEAT 100 [WELCOME]
```

How did Logo know how many times "welcome" was to be repeated?
6. Type CLEARTEXT to clear the screen.
7. Use the turtle to create graphics; type

```
SHOWTURTLE
```

In what location does the turtle appear on the screen?
8. Move to the EDIT mode to create a procedure. Type the following:

```
EDIT "SQUARE (press the RETURN key)
```

(when the words TO SQUARE show at the top of the screen, press RETURN and type the following:)

```
FORWARD 50 RIGHT 90
FORWARD 50 RIGHT 90
FORWARD 50 RIGHT 90
FORWARD 50 RIGHT 90
```

(Now press the CONTROL key and the C key simultaneously to let the computer know that your program is finished; the words SQUARE DEFINED tell you that the program is in memory).
What might you have typed in place of FORWARD and RIGHT? What does 90 mean?
9. Type SQUARE to run the program.
How is it that the turtle knew how to draw a square?
10. To create a design using the SQUARE procedure, type the following command seven times:

```
RT 45 SQUARE
```

This sequence will make an eight-sided star. Why did it not make a seven-sided one?

11. A much easier way to make this figure is to use the **REPEAT** command introduced in item 5. See if you can rewrite the exercise in item 10 using this command. Let us move to the **EDIT** mode and use **REPEAT** to create a new procedure; we will call it SNOWFLAKE.

12. Type the following:

EDIT "SNOWFLAKE (When **TO SNOWFLAKE** appears on the screen press the **RETURN** key and type the words below.)
REPEAT 8 [RT 45 SQUARE]

(Press the **CONTROL** key and the **C** key simultaneously; the words **SNOW-FLAKE DEFINED** will show on the screen.) See if you can determine what the words and numbers within the brackets mean.

13. Type CLEARSCREEN (or CS)

14. Type SNOWFLAKE to run the procedure. Type CS after the graphic is finished.

15. Having made a square, we will now create a triangle. Type the following:

```
EDIT "TRIANGLE
FD 30 RT 120
FD 30 RT 120
FD 30 RT 120
```
Press **CONTROL C**

Note the similarity between this procedure and that for **SQUARE**; what is the major difference between the two?
(Note: a simpler way to create this procedure is to use **REPEAT**; see if you can figure out how to do this).

16. By now you should know how to make the procedure run; do this now. You should also know how to clear the screen; do this also.

17. Let us create a design using **TRIANGLE**:

```
EDIT "PLANET
REPEAT 30 [RT 12 TRIANGLE]
```
Press **CONTROL C**

How many times will the turtle draw the triangle?

18. Run the **PLANET** procedure.

19. Clear the screen.

20. We will now make more planets and move them to various places on the screen.

```
EDIT "MORPLANETS
PLANET (This will create a planet.)
PENUP (This lets the turtle move without drawing.)
FD 70 (This moves the turtle to a new position.)
PENDOWN (The turtle can now draw.)
PLANET (What does this do?)
SETPC 3 (This changes the color of the next planet.)
PENUP (What will this do?)
LEFT 120 (What is the purpose of this command?)
FD 80 (See if you can visualize where the next planet will appear on the screen.)
PENDOWN
PLANET
```

Press CONTROL C

21. Type **MORPLANETS** (What is the consequence of typing this word?)
22. Type **CLEARSCREEN (CS)**
23. Let us change the colors of the night sky; type the following:

```
EDIT "SKY
SETBG 1 WAIT 100
SETBG 2 WAIT 100
SETBG 3 WAIT 100
SETBG 4 WAIT 100
SETBG 5 WAIT 100
SETBG 0 WAIT 100
```
Press CONTROL C

(What do you suppose the WAIT command will do?)
24. Type **MORPLANETS** to get the planets back.
25. When the planets have been drawn on the screen, type **SKY** to change the sky color. Type CS when all the colors have been shown. See if you can write a single procedure using **MORPLANETS** and **SKY** that provides the same effect as above by typing the name of the procedure only once (note that it was necessary to type **MORPLA-NETS** and then **SKY** to run the program as it now stands).
26. Having drawn a square and a triangle, let us now try a circle. Type the following:

```
TO CIRCLE
REPEAT 360 [FD 1 RT 1]
END
```

(See if you can mentally trace the turtle's tiny steps as it makes a circle; how many steps must the turtle take?)
27. Run the procedure; clear the screen.
28. Let us create a design using CIRCLE:

```
FULLSCREEN (This gives a full graphics screen with no text.)
REPEAT 8 [RT 45 CIRCLE]
```

Be patient; it takes quite a while for the turtle to draw this design.
29. Continue working with Logo creating designs of your own. If you are unsure as to how many degrees to turn the turtle for a specific shape, here is a hint: note that in each exercise a complete "turtle trip" around a figure (the square, triangle, and circle) always equals 360 degrees. With this in mind you should have little trouble making your own designs using regular figures.

INDEX

DATE DUE

MAY 2 5 1991			
AUG 5 1991			
JUL 30 1991			
OCT 2 4 1991			
SEP 1 5 1992			
FEB 4 1993			
MAY 2 7 1993			
JUL 0 3 1993			
MAR 2 1 1994			
MAY 0 9 1995			
JAN 2 2 1997			
JUN 1 0 1997			
MAY 0 4 1999